The

PURSUIT *of*

HAPPINESS

How Classical Writers on Virtue

Inspired the Lives of the Founders

and Defined America

JEFFREY ROSEN

President and CEO, National Constitution Center

SIMON & SCHUSTER

New York London Toronto Sydney New Delhi

100 YEARS
SIMON &
SCHUSTER

1230 Avenue of the Americas
New York, NY 10020

First Simon & Schuster hardcover edition February 2024

SIMON & SCHUSTER and colophon are registered trademarks of Simon & Schuster, LLC

Simon & Schuster: Celebrating 100 Years of Publishing in 2024

For information about special discounts for bulk purchases, please contact Simon &
Schuster Special Sales at 1-866-506-1949 or business@simonandschuster.com.

The Simon & Schuster Speakers Bureau can bring authors to your live event. For
more information or to book an event, contact the Simon & Schuster Speakers
Bureau at 1-866-248-3049 or visit our website at www.simonspeakers.com.

Interior design by Ruth Lee-Mui

Manufactured in the United States of America

1   3   5   7   9   10   8   6   4   2

Library of Congress Cataloging-in-Publication Data has been applied for.

ISBN 978-1-6680-0247-6
ISBN 978-1-6680-0249-0 (ebook)

For my beloved father,

Sidney Rosen,
July 14, 1926–May 19, 2022

"Even as man imagines himself to be, such he is,
and he is also that which he imagines."
—PARACELSUS

Contents

The PURSUIT *of* HAPPINESS

Notes on Cicero's *Tusculan Disputations*

This morning haze obscures the firmament
Sunlight and clouds in serried blue alloy
A narrow clearing opens, fortune sent
I glimpse a sparkling sun beam and feel joy

Stoics praise calm joy without elation
Its motion placid and to reason aligned
When it transports with wanton exultation
It fires the perturbations of the mind

The four disordered passions are emotions
That lack the moderation reason brings
Elation, lust, fear, grief are their commotions
Prudence and temperance are their golden rings

The soul that's tranquil, calm, restrained, at rest
The happy soul, the subject of our quest

One

ORDER

Twelve Virtues and the Pursuit of Happiness

I n his early twenties, Benjamin Franklin recalled, "I conceiv'd the bold and arduous project of arriving at moral perfection." He had been reading some of the classical Greek and Roman philosophers— Pythagoras, Xenophon, Plutarch, and Cicero—as well as scanning the popular magazines of the day for self-help advice to print in *The Pennsylvania Gazette*. Based on his reading, he had become convinced that the key to self-improvement was daily self-examination. Accordingly, he devised a spiritual accounting system, drafting a list of twelve virtues: temperance, silence, order, resolution, frugality, industry, sincerity, justice, moderation, cleanliness, tranquility, and—saving the one he found most challenging for last—chastity. Franklin later expanded his list to thirteen by adding another virtue a Quaker friend told him he needed to work on: humility. He resolved each day to run through a checklist of whether or not he had lived up to each virtue, placing a black mark next to the virtue where he had fallen short. Franklin worried that if word got out about his plan for moral perfection, it might be viewed as "a kind of foppery in morals" that "would make me ridiculous." (Perhaps he imagined the reaction to a book called "*Humility*, by Benjamin Franklin.") Daunted by all the black marks, he eventually abandoned the project. But "on the whole," he concluded, "tho' I never arrived at the perfection I had been so ambitious of obtaining, but fell far short of it, yet I was, by the endeavor, a better and a happier man than I otherwise should have been if I had not attempted it."[1]

Franklin's conclusion was that "without Virtue Man can have no Happiness in this World."[2] And as the motto for his project, he chose these lines from one of the most widely read books of Stoic self-help philosophy, Cicero's *Tusculan Disputations:*

> O philosophy, guide of life! O searcher out of virtue and extermina-
> tor of vice! One day spent well and in accordance with thy precepts
> is worth an immortality of sin.[3]

Franklin wrote about his virtue project in his autobiography, and it has been widely imitated ever since. It was admired, for example, by Menachem Mendel Lefin, a Ukrainian rabbi who, in 1808, almost twenty years after Franklin's death, published *Cheshbon HaNefesh*, or a *Book of Accounting of the Soul*, introducing Franklin's thirteen virtues to Hebrew readers as the foundation of the Jewish school of Mussar, or character improvement.[4] I came across Lefin's book a few years ago on the recommendation of a rabbi, which led to a brief attempt to practice the Franklin system of daily self-accounting with a friend. (Like Franklin, we found the exercise daunting and soon gave up.)

At the beginning of the COVID pandemic, however, I noticed an unexpected connection I hadn't seen before: Ben Franklin wasn't the only Founder to cite Cicero's *Tusculan Disputations* as a key source for the connection between virtue and happiness. In 1815 Amos J. Cook, the head of a boarding school in Maine, wrote to Thomas Jefferson asking him for some wisdom in Latin to enlighten his students. Although he had no original Latin verses to add, Jefferson wrote, he wanted to offer some "humble prose" from Cicero's advice manual:

> Therefore the man, whoever he is, whose soul is tranquillized by restraint and consistency and who is at peace with himself, so that he neither pines away in distress, nor is broken down by fear, nor consumed with a thirst of longing in pursuit of some ambition, nor maudlin in the exuberance of meaningless eagerness—he is the wise man of whom we are in quest, he is the happy man.[5]

Praising the passage as "a moral morsel, which our young friends under your tuition should keep ever in their eye," Jefferson emphasized to Cook the ancient wisdom of Cicero's philosophy, in words remarkably similar to Franklin's: "[I]f the Wise, be the happy man, as these sages say, he must be virtuous too; for, without virtue, happiness cannot be."[6]

In another uncanny synchronicity, Jefferson, like Franklin, was inspired by *Tusculan Disputations* to draft his own list of twelve virtues—he called them "a dozen cannons of conduct in life"—that he believed were key to the pursuit of happiness. Jefferson's virtues were almost identical to Franklin's, although he conveniently left chastity off his list, given his children with Sally Hemings, all of whom he held, like her, in bondage. And Jefferson, like Franklin, accompanied his list of virtues with practical maxims about how to follow each one, beginning with industry, which Jefferson reduced to the following: "Never put off to tomorrow what you can do to-day."[7] (Franklin's version was "Lose no time; be always employ'd in something useful; cut off all unnecessary actions.")[8]

Intrigued by the fact that Cicero's now forgotten self-help manual had inspired both Franklin and Jefferson to draft similar lists of twelve virtues for daily living, I decided to read Cicero myself. I then set out to read the other books of ancient wisdom that shaped Jefferson's original understanding of the famous phrase in the Declaration of Independence about "the pursuit of happiness."[9] In 1825, writing to the historian Henry Lee, Jefferson said that the Declaration "was intended to be an

expression of the American mind, resting on the harmonising sentiments of the day," as expressed in conversations, letters, printed essays,
and what he called "the elementary books of public right." He named
four authors in particular: Aristotle, Cicero, John Locke, and Algernon
Sidney.[10] But who were the other philosophers who influenced Jefferson,
and which of their books did he consider most valuable?

A reading list that Jefferson first drafted in 1771, five years before he
wrote the Declaration, provided an answer. Jefferson sent the list to his
friend Robert Skipwith, who had asked for books to include in a private
library, and revised it over the years. Under the category of "religion,"
Jefferson's reading list includes Cicero's *Tusculan Disputations*, as well as
a top ten list of other works of classical and Enlightenment moral philosophy:[11]

1. Locke's *Conduct of the Understanding in the Search of Truth*.
2. Xenophon's memoirs of Socrates, translated by Sarah Fielding.
3. Epictetus, translated by Elizabeth Carter.
4. Marcus Aurelius, translated by Collins.
5. Seneca, translated by Roger L'Estrange.
6. Cicero's Offices, by Guthrie.
7. Cicero's Tusculan questions.
8. Ld. Bolingbroke's Philosophical works.
9. Hume's essays.
10. Ld. Kaim's Natural religion.

During the COVID quarantine, I set out to read these ten books,
as well as others on Jefferson's reading list, nearly all of which I had
somehow missed. I've had the privilege of a wonderful liberal arts education and have studied literature, history, political philosophy, and law
with great teachers at great universities. But despite my elaborate education, I'd never encountered the great works of Greek, Roman, and
Enlightenment *moral philosophy* that offered guidance about how to
live a good life.

In college, I remember yearning for this kind of guidance. The 1980s were the "Greed is good" decade, and I was looking for an alternative to the unchecked hedonism and materialism celebrated by popular culture. Unconvinced by the rigors of Puritan theology, which I had been studying as an English major, I craved an answer to the question of whether spiritual and moral truth could be obtained by reason rather than revelation, by good works and reflection rather than blind faith. What I didn't realize, because classical moral philosophy had fallen out of the core curriculum, was that this was precisely the question the ancient philosophers had set out to answer. These texts were an essential part of the curriculum of American high school, college, and law students in the eighteenth, nineteenth, and early twentieth centuries, but were no longer considered central to what educated Americans should know by the time I graduated from college and law school. It was this gap in my education that led to my quarantine reading project.

Inspired by Jefferson's daily reading schedule, I got up every morning before sunrise, read a selection from his list, and found myself taking notes on the reading in sonnet form, so that I could easily remember the daily lesson. (This practice seemed unusual, to say the least, until I discovered that many readers in the founding era also wrote poems summarizing the wisdom of these classic texts, including Ben Franklin, Mercy Otis Warren, Phillis Wheatley, Alexander Hamilton, and John Quincy Adams.) I've included some of these sonnets as brief introductions to the chapters that follow, along with ten of the most cited books on Jefferson's reading list in the appendix,[12] in the hope that you may be inspired to work your way through the list yourself.

What I learned in my year of daily reading between March 2020 and March 2021 came as a revelation. Scholars have debated for centuries about which books most influenced Jefferson when he wrote the Declaration, but surprisingly few of them focus on the original meaning of "the pursuit of happiness."[13] The best-known books on the Declaration interpret that phrase as a substitute for the right to own property and make little reference to the influence of the classical authors.[14] But when

I read the books of moral philosophy on Jefferson's reading list, I found that the similarities were far more important than the differences. With the help of electronic word searches, I was surprised to discover that many of the books contain the phrase that appears in the Declaration: "the pursuit of happiness." And many cite the same source for their conclusion about the original meaning of the pursuit of happiness: Cicero's *Tusculan Disputations*.

In addition to these surprises, working my way through Jefferson's reading list changed my understanding of the famous phrase. Today we think of happiness as the pursuit of pleasure. But classical and Enlightenment thinkers defined happiness as the pursuit of virtue—as *being* good, rather than *feeling* good. For this reason, the Founders believed that the quest for happiness is a daily practice, requiring mental and spiritual self-discipline, as well as mindfulness and rigorous time management. At its core, the Founders viewed the pursuit of happiness as a lifelong quest for character improvement, where we use our powers of reason to moderate our unproductive emotions so that we can be our best selves and serve others. For the Founders, happiness required the daily cultivation of virtue, which the Scottish philosopher Adam Smith defined as "the temper of mind which constitutes the excellent and praiseworthy character."[15] If you had to sum it up in one sentence, the classical definition of the pursuit of happiness meant being a lifelong learner, with a commitment to practicing the daily habits that lead to character improvement, self-mastery, flourishing, and growth. Understood in these terms, happiness is always something to be pursued rather than obtained—a quest rather than a destination. "The mere search for higher happiness," Cicero wrote, "not merely its actual attainment, is a prize beyond all human wealth or honor or physical pleasure."[16]

Why was Cicero's self-help book such a key text in influencing the Founders' understanding of happiness? Because it offered a popular summary of the core of Stoic philosophy. To achieve freedom, tranquility, and happiness, according to the ancient Stoics, we should stop trying to control external events and instead focus on controlling the only things that we have the power to control: namely, our own thoughts, desires, emotions, and actions. In this sense, Stoic philosophy has many similarities with the Eastern wisdom traditions, including Buddhism and Hinduism. "Our life is shaped by our mind; we become what we think," said the Buddha in the Dhammapada, emphasizing the need to master our selfish impulses—including envy, arrogance, anger, and the pursuit of short-term pleasure—in order to achieve lasting well-being.[17] The Hindu wisdom literature, including the Vedas, Upanishads, and Bhagavad Gita, sums up a similar teaching on happiness in a phrase often quoted by Mahatma Gandhi: "Renounce and enjoy."[18] In other words, only by renouncing selfish attachments to the results of our actions, only by acting selflessly, can we conquer our ego-based emotions—including anger, fear, and jealousy—live in the present, and "live according to nature," as the Stoics put it, in harmony with the natural laws of the universe.

John Adams was excited to learn that Pythagoras, one of the founders of Greek moral philosophy, was said to have studied with the Hindu masters during his travels in the East,[19] and in his correspondence with Thomas Jefferson at the end of their long lives, Adams discussed the Hindu Vedas as a possible source of the ancient wisdom regarding happiness. For the Founders, the pursuit of happiness included reading in the wisdom traditions of the East and West, always anchored by the canonical text of the Bible, in an attempt to distill their common wisdom about the need to achieve self-mastery through emotional and spiritual self-discipline.

The Greek word for happiness is *eudaimonia*, meaning "good daimon," or good spirit, and the Greek word for virtue is *arete*, which also means "excellence." In *The Nicomachean Ethics*, Aristotle famously defined happiness as virtue itself, an "activity of soul in conformity with excellence."[20] These terms are confusing to us, because excellence and virtue aren't self-defining. For this reason, although *eudaimonia* is hard to translate, it might be rendered as "human flourishing," "a purpose-driven life," or, in modern terms, "being your best self." The Latin word for virtue is "virtus," which also means valor, manliness, excellence, and good character. What Cicero and Franklin called "virtue," therefore, might be translated as "good character." Today, modern social psychologists use terms like "emotional intelligence," which they define as "the ability to understand, use, and manage your own emotions in positive ways to relieve stress, communicate effectively, empathize with others, overcome challenges, and defuse conflict."[21]

What I also learned from reading Cicero and the other ancient sources is that the Founders framed their quest for self-regulation and emotional intelligence through a psychological lens: the dramatic struggle between reason and passion. The Greek words for reason and emotion are *logos* and *pathos*, so for the Founders, *passion* was a synonym for emotion. The Founders didn't mean we should lack emotion; only that we should manage our emotions in productive ways. Cicero traces the distinction between reason and passion back to Pythagoras, who divided the soul into two parts: the rational and irrational. Pythagoras further divided the irrational parts of the soul into the passions and the desires, leading his disciples to suggest a three-part division of the soul: reason, passion, and desire. In his dialogue *Phaedrus*, Plato popularized Pythagoras's three-part division with his metaphor of a charioteer, representing reason, driving a chariot pulled by two horses. One horse, representing the passionate part of the soul, careened toward earthly pleasures; the other, representing the noble or intelligent part of the soul, inclined upward toward the divine. The goal of the charioteer was to use reason to align the noble and passionate horses so that both pulled in the same direction.[22]

In his writings on happiness, Plato argued that we should use our faculty of reason, located in the head, to moderate and temper our faculties of passion, located near the heart, and appetite, in the stomach. When all three faculties of the soul were in harmony, Plato maintained, the state that resulted was called "temperance," but, as Adam Smith noted, it might be better translated as "good temper, or sobriety and moderation of mind."[23] (The Latin word "temperentia," or temperance, also means good temper, sobriety, and self-control; therefore, for the classical writers, virtue, or good character, was synonymous with temperance, or self-control.) Plato's theory of the harmony of the soul became the basis for the "faculty psychology" that was developed by Enlightenment philosophers such as Thomas Reid in the eighteenth century and that was at the core of the Founders' education. Faculty psychology held that the mind is separated into different mental powers, or faculties, including the intellect, the emotion, and the will. According to this view, the goal of education was to strengthen the intellect, or reason, so that it could moderate and control the will and the emotions in order to achieve the self-control that was key to happiness. Faculty psychology drew on Cicero's idea that we are born with certain innate faculties, including a moral sense, that could aid our powers of reason in calming our emotions. "[W]e must keep ourselves free from every disturbing emotion," Cicero wrote in his treatise *On Duties*, "not only from desire and fear, but also from excessive pain and pleasure, and from anger, so that we may enjoy that calm of soul and freedom from care."

In their private letters and diaries, public speeches and poems, the Founders talked constantly about their own struggles to control their tempers and to be their best selves by using reason to regulate their selfish passions. "Men are rather reasoning tha[n] reasonable animals, for the most part governed by the impulse of passion," Alexander Hamilton wrote in 1802.[24] John Adams's wife, Abigail, gave similar advice to their son, John Quincy Adams. "The due Government of the passions has been considered in all ages as a most valuable acquisition," she warned,"[25] emphasizing in particular the importance of subduing "the passion of Anger." Her conclusion: "Having once obtained this self government you will find a foundation laid for happiness to yourself and usefullness to Mankind."[26]

Nearer to our time, Justice Ruth Bader Ginsburg told me that her mother gave her precisely the same Stoic advice. "[E]motions like anger, remorse, and jealousy are not productive," she said. "They will not accomplish anything, so you must keep them under control."[27]

Ben Franklin summed up the classical understanding of happiness as a balance between reason and passion in his 1735 essay "On True Happiness." "The desire of happiness in general is so natural to us, that all the world are in pursuit of it," he wrote in *The Pennsylvania Gazette*. "Reason represents things to us not only as they are at present, but as they are in their whole nature and tendency; passion only regards them in the former light." Franklin concluded that we need to use our powers of reason to check our immediate emotions and desires so that we can achieve the harmony of the soul that allows us to flourish, emphasizing that "all true happiness, as all that is truly beautiful, can only result from order."

In his virtues project, Franklin defined *order* in terms of impulse control: "Let all your things have their places; let each part of your business have its time." And, in emphasizing the importance of delaying short-term gratification for long-term character improvement, Franklin was summarizing the essence of the ancient wisdom. The classical authorities viewed the pursuit of happiness as a daily version of the famous marshmallow test, an experiment on delayed gratification conducted at Stanford in 1972. Researchers gave the subjects, who were children, a choice between one immediate reward (such as a marshmallow) or two rewards for those who could wait fifteen minutes to receive them. The study found that children who were able to wait for two marshmallows rather than eating one immediately performed better in school years later and had better life outcomes.

Dr. Samuel Johnson's *Dictionary of the English Language*, published in 1755, is the leading source for how words were understood in the founding era. Johnson notes an older definition of *happiness* as "good luck or fortune," stemming from the Old English word *hap*. But his principal definition of happiness is "Felicity; state in which the desires are satisfied."[28] To illustrate the definition, Johnson cites a text that also appears in Franklin's autobiography and on Jefferson's reading list: namely, John Locke's *Essay Concerning Human Understanding*. Johnson's selection comes from book 2, chapter 21, "Of Power," which repeatedly uses the phrase "pursuit of happiness."[29] And Locke's point, which he takes from Cicero, is that we should control our desires through calm deliberation so that we come to realize that our true and substantial happiness will best be served by long-term self-regulation rather than short-term gratification.

In the course of working my way through Thomas Jefferson's reading list, I discovered that, throughout American history, the meaning of the pursuit of happiness has evolved in unexpected ways. The ancient wisdom that defined happiness as self-mastery, emotional self-regulation, tranquility of mind, and the quest for self-improvement was distilled in the works of Cicero, summed up by Franklin in his thirteen virtues, and used by Adams in his "Thoughts on Government." After Jefferson inscribed the idea in the Declaration of Independence, it showed up in *The Federalist Papers*, the essays Madison and Hamilton wrote in support of the Constitution, focusing on the promotion of public happiness. It was evoked by Presidents John Quincy Adams and Abraham Lincoln, as well as by the abolitionist Frederick Douglass, to defend the ideal of self-reliance and to advocate for the destruction of slavery. It became the basis of Alexis de Tocqueville's idea of "self-interest properly understood" and of Justice Louis Brandeis's idea of freedom of conscience. The ancient wisdom fell out of fashion in the 1960s and in the "Me Decade" that followed, however, when our understanding about the pursuit of happiness was transformed from being good to feeling good. But the classical ideal of happiness was resurrected and confirmed in the 1990s by insights from social psychology and cognitive behavior therapy, which found that we can best achieve emotional intelligence by developing habits of emotional self-regulation—training ourselves to turn negative thoughts and emotions into positive ones—through the power of the imagination.

After reading the books that shaped the Founders' original understanding of the pursuit of happiness, I set out to explore how they applied the ancient wisdom in their own lives. What I learned changed the way I thought about the psychology of the Founders and, in particular, about their use of time. The Founders talked incessantly about their struggles for self-improvement and their efforts to regulate their anxieties, emotions, and perturbations of the mind. They tried to calm their anxieties through the daily practice of the habits of mindfulness and time management. Aristotle said that good character comes from the cultivation of habits, and it's remarkable how much time and energy many of the leading members of the founding generation devoted to their own lifelong quests to practice the habits that would improve their character. They took seriously the Pythagorean injunction to use every hour of the day to cultivate their minds and bodies. They created disciplined schedules for reading, writing, and exercise, and they kept daily accounts of their successes and failures in living up to the ideals they found in the books of ancient wisdom, trying to use each moment productively by living in the present with calm but intense purpose and focus. The Founders may not have meditated, but they practiced the habits of mindfulness.

At times, of course, the Founders shamefully betrayed the moral ideals they set for themselves. Some of them spent their lives as enslavers and notoriously denied the humanity, equality, and inalienable rights of those they enslaved. At least some of the enslaving Founders were aware of their own hypocrisies. Jefferson and other enslavers from Virginia recognized that it was craven greed—following Cicero, they called it avarice—that kept them from freeing those they held in bondage, even as they called for the "total emancipation" of all enslaved people in the future. In other words, they denounced slavery as a violation of the self-evident truth that all men (by which they meant all individuals) are created equal, but in their more self-aware moments acknowledged that they were too dependent on the lifestyle slavery afforded them to consider the consequences of giving it up.

In March 1775, weeks before war broke out at Lexington and Concord, Thomas Jefferson listened as the Virginia delegate Patrick Henry urged the Second Virginia Convention to send troops to support the Revolution. In his famous "Give Me Liberty or Give Me Death" speech,

Henry quoted Joseph Addison's play *Cato: A Tragedy* about the need to choose freedom over slavery. "Is life so dear, or peace so sweet, as to be purchased at the price of chains and slavery?" he asked. "Forbid it, Almighty God! I know not what course others may take; but as for me, give me liberty or give me death!"[30] How could Henry justify urging white Americans to throw off what he called the chains of British slavery while he himself continued to enslave Black Americans? He didn't even try. Henry considered it "amazing" that he and his fellow Americans, who were so "fond of Liberty," also allowed slavery, a practice "as repugnant to humanity as it is inconsistent with the Bible and destructive to liberty." And Henry admitted that it was avarice that made him choose not to follow his moral principles: "Would any one believe that I am Master of Slaves of my own purchase!" Henry asked. "I am drawn along by [the] general inconvenience of living without them. I will not—I cannot justify it."[31]

In addition to changing the way I thought about the Founders, my reading also changed the way I thought about how to be a good citizen. Following the classical and Enlightenment philosophers, the Founders believed that *personal* self-government was necessary for *political* self-government. In their view, the key to a healthy republic begins with how we address our own flaws and commit to becoming better citizens over time. In *The Federalist Papers*, Madison and Hamilton made clear that the Constitution was designed to foster deliberation so that citizens could avoid retreating into the angry mobs and partisan factions that can be inflamed by demagogues. Ancient Athens had fallen because the demagogue Cleon had seduced the Athenian assembly into continuing the war with the Peloponnesian League; Rome had fallen because the people were corrupted by Caesar, who offered them luxury in exchange for liberty. Only by governing their selfish emotions as individuals could citizens avoid degenerating into selfish factions that threatened the common good. The way for citizens to create a more perfect union, the Founders insisted, was to govern themselves in private as well as in public, cultivating the same personal deliberation, moderation, and harmony in our own minds that we strive to maintain in the constitution of the state. Madison would have urged us to think more and tweet less.

In this sense, the Founders believed that the pursuit of happiness regards freedom not as boundless liberty to do whatever feels good in the moment but as bounded liberty to make wise choices that will help us best develop our capacities and talents over the course of our lives. They believed that the pursuit of happiness includes responsibilities as well as rights—the responsibility to limit ourselves, restrain ourselves, and master ourselves, so that we achieve the wisdom and harmony that are necessary for true freedom.

"Obviously freedom must carry with it the meaning of freedom to limit oneself," the composer Leonard Bernstein said of Beethoven's choice of a single note in his *Eroica* Symphony. "Freedom is not infinite, not boundless liberty, as some hippies like to think—do anything you want, anytime, anywhere you want to. No, freedom isn't that. It means being free to make decisions, to determine one's own course." Bernstein went on to connect Beethoven's struggle to balance freedom and harmony in the symphony with the same freedom of citizens to govern themselves in a democracy. "In Beethoven, as in democracy, freedom is a discipline, combining the right to choose freely, with the gift of choosing wisely."[32]

Citing Cicero's famous analogy between "harmony in song" and "concord in the State," John Adams, too, compared the harmony of a well-tempered state constitution to the harmony of a well-tempered orchestra.[33] "As the treble, the tenor, and the bass exist in nature, they will be heard in the concert," Adams wrote in his *Defence of the Constitutions of Government of the United States of America*. "[I]f they are arranged by Handel, in a skilful composition, they produce rapture the most exquisite that harmony can excite; but if they are confused together, without order, they will 'Rend with tremendous sound your ears asunder.'"[34] This was the classical understanding of the pursuit of happiness: the freedom to make daily choices about how to balance emotion and reason that lead to truth, order, harmony, and wisdom, aligned with the divine will or the natural harmonies of the universe. The Founders understood the importance of our spiritual nature, and for many of them, the pursuit of happiness was a spiritual quest.

This book is an attempt to travel into the minds of the Founders, to understand their quest for the good life on their own terms. By reading the books they read and following their own daily attempts at self-accounting, we can better understand the largely forgotten core of their moral and political philosophy: that moderating emotions is the secret of tranquility of mind; that tranquility of mind is the secret of happiness; that daily habits are the secret of self-improvement; and that personal self-government is the secret of political self-government. It's not a surprise that the Founders often fell short of their own ideals of moral perfection. But what is a surprise is the seriousness with which they took the quest, on a daily basis, to become more perfect. In his autobiography, Franklin called the great moral errors of his life "errata," or printers' errors.[35] And he remained hopeful, as he wrote in an epitaph he drafted for himself, that life was like a manuscript whose errors, in a "new & more perfect edition," could always be "Corrected and amended By the Author."[36]

Notes on Plato's *Phaedrus*

Our souls are forged of three-part composite
A charioteer and pair of winged steeds
One horse is noble temper's reposit
The other, seeking pleasure, passion leads

The driver's task: both horses to align
Transporting soul to immortal realm of truth
The noble steed soars up to the divine
The vain and haughty steed careens to earth

Approaching love, the chariot gyrates
The shameless steed propelled by fierce desire
The driver pulls his reins and remonstrates
The lovers meet in reason's sacred fire

When temperance tames passion's base alloys
Two lovers merge in happy equipoise

Two

TEMPERANCE

Ben Franklin's Quest for Moral Perfection

A t the age of seventy-nine, Ben Franklin attributed the "constant felicity of his life" to his daily practice of the classical virtues:

To Temperance he ascribes his long-continued health, and what is still left to him of a good constitution; to Industry and Frugality, the early easiness of his circumstances and acquisition of his fortune, with all that knowledge that enabled him to be a useful citizen, and obtained for him some degree of reputation among the learned; to Sincerity and Justice, the confidence of his country, and the honorable employs it conferred upon him; and to the joint influence of the whole mass of virtues, even in the imperfect state he was able to acquire them, all that evenness of temper, and that cheerfulness in conversation, which makes his company still sought for and agreeable even to his younger acquaintances.[1]

It's remarkable that Franklin attributed the happiness of his long life to his "evenness of temper" rather than his public accomplishments. For at the time, he had become one of the most famous men on the planet. When he met Voltaire in Paris in 1778, the French hailed him as "the illustrious and wise Franklin, the man of all America most to be respected."[2] His electric rod brought lightning from the heavens, his charting of the Gulf Stream changed the course of international travel, and his experiments with fire warmed homes around the world. In his adopted city of Philadelphia, his influence continues to be felt from block to block in the range of institutions he created, all within walking distance of one another: the Library Company, the American Philosophical Society, the University of Pennsylvania, Pennsylvania Hospital, and the Union Fire Company, known as Franklin's "bucket brigade." As if this wasn't enough, he was America's leading diplomat and practical politician, whose conciliating temper proved to be crucial in the drafting of both the Declaration of Independence and the US Constitution.

Franklin conducted his first electricity experiments in 1752, the same year he drafted a plan of union for the colonies to pursue common policies for security and defense. During nearly twenty years in London, as an agent for Pennsylvania and other colonies, he invented the glass armonica and urged the repeal of the Stamp Act, the British tax on American newspapers that helped to spark the Revolution. Returning to America in 1775 after being hauled before Parliament for leaking letters about the agitation in Massachusetts, he was elected postmaster general and then served on the committee of five that drafted the Declaration of Independence. After the British defeat at Yorktown in 1781, he returned to Europe, where he negotiated the peace treaty with England, served as America's first ambassador to France, and invented bifocals. Returning to the United States in 1785, he served as president of the Pennsylvania Supreme Executive Council and as a delegate to the Constitutional Convention and also found time to invent the mechanical "long arm" for removing books from shelves. Before he died in 1790 at the age of eighty-four, he became president of the Pennsylvania Society for Promoting the Abolition of Slavery.

Of course, Franklin's self-accounting at the end of his life is necessarily selective. Although he acknowledges the "imperfect state" in
which he achieved the classical virtues, he doesn't dwell on those that
he famously failed to achieve—in particular, chastity. He fathered an
illegitimate son, William, while he was courting Deborah Read, who
became his common-law wife. He then all but abandoned Deborah, who
remained in Philadelphia during his long diplomatic stints in London
and Paris, where he at least flirted with a succession of young admirers.
Order was another challenge for Franklin: John Adams was shocked by
his colleague's disorganized schedule when they served as peace commissioners in Paris. And Franklin's clashes with Adams, even if they
were provoked mostly by Adams's envy, suggest that Franklin's efforts to
achieve humility remained a work in progress. Still, Franklin's "evenness
of temper" makes him the most relatable Founder: he acknowledged the
limits of his own wisdom and remained until the end of his life willing to
change his mind—most notably about slavery, which he had initially tolerated but came to oppose. In this sense, Franklin deployed his youthful
lessons in self-control, temperance, and emotional intelligence to remain
a lifelong learner, disarming conflicts through humor, not seeking sole
credit, and always acknowledging the legitimacy of other points of view
while recognizing the limits of his own.

Franklin's conciliating temperament came in part from his parents.
His father, Josiah Franklin, an artisan and silk dyer, was a Presbyterian
Whig dissenter who, in 1683, fled political and religious oppression in
England under the Catholic-leaning monarchy of Charles II for America
and liberty. In his memoirs, Franklin described his father as a "mechanical
genius" whose "great excellence lay in a sound understanding and solid
judgment in prudential matters" and who was "frequently chosen an ar-
bitrator between contending parties."[3] His mother, Abiah, was said to
have been a "very sensible woman" who taught him practical habits of
self-control in daily life. For example, when a female relative gave Franklin
unexpected spending money, and he used all of it to buy a whistle from
a street vendor, Abiah explained to her son that he could have bought

twenty for the price and advised him that, whenever he wanted anything
in the future, he should ask himself, "[H]ow much is the whistle worth?"
Franklin told the French physiologist Pierre Jean Georges Cabanis that
he never forgot the lesson and, since then, had never entertained a violent
passion ("violent désir") for anything without repeating it to himself.[4]

But Franklin also attributed his even temper to his attempt in his
twenties to practice the classical virtues. He found the task more difficult
than he had imagined because the classical philosophers disagreed about
how to define the virtues in question. "Temperance, for example, was by
some confined to eating and drinking, while by others it was extended
to mean the moderating every other pleasure, appetite, inclination, or
passion, bodily or mental, even to our avarice and ambition." Franklin
proposed, for the sake of clarity, to list more virtues, with fewer ideas attached to each, and initially came up with his list of twelve:

1. Temperance
    Eat not to dullness; drink not to elevation.
2. Silence
    Speak not but what may benefit others or yourself; avoid
    trifling conversation.
3. Order
    Let all your things have their places; let each part of your
    business have its time.
4. Resolution
    Resolve to perform what you ought; perform without fail what
    you resolve.
5. Frugality
    Make no expense but to do good to others or yourself; i.e.,
    waste nothing.
6. Industry
    Lose no time; be always employ'd in something useful; cut off
    all unnecessary actions.

7. Sincerity
   Use no hurtful deceit; think innocently and justly; and, if you
   speak, speak accordingly.

8. Justice
   Wrong none by doing injuries, or omitting the benefits that
   are your duty.

9. Moderation
   Avoid extreams; forbear resenting injuries so much as you
   think they deserve.

10. Cleanliness
    Tolerate no uncleanliness in body, cloaths, or habitation.

11. Tranquillity
    Be not disturbed at trifles, or at accidents common or
    unavoidable.

12. Chastity
    Rarely use venery but for health or offspring, never to dulness,
    weakness, or the injury of your own or another's peace or
    reputation.[5]

When a Quaker friend informed him that people thought of him as
proud and overbearing, Franklin realized that he had neglected an important virtue. Accordingly, he wrote, "I added *Humility* to my list," along
with the two most inspiring models of perfection he could imagine:

13. Humility
    Imitate Jesus and Socrates.[6]

Always practical, Franklin decided to focus on improving one virtue
a week for thirteen weeks, to avoid distracting himself with multitasking.
He made a little self-accounting book, and on each page, he drew a grid
with seven vertical columns—one for each day of the week. These were
crossed by thirteen horizontal columns—one for each virtue. Each night,

132   MEMOIRS OF   PART II.

FORM OF THE PAGES.

———

TEMPERANCE.

Eat not to dulness : drink not to elevation.

	Sun.	M.	T.	W.	Th.	F.	S.
Tem.							
Sil.	*	*		*		*	
Ord.	*	*			*	*	*
Res.		*				*	
Fru.		*				*	
Ind.			*				
Sinc.							
Jus.							
Mod.							
Clea.							
Tran.							
Chas.							
Hum.							

I determined to give a week's strict attention to each of the virtues successively. Thus, in the first week, my great guard was to avoid every the least offence against *Temperance ;* leaving the other virtues to their ordinary chance, only marking every evening the faults of the day. Thus, if in the first he resolved to put a "little black spot" in the daily box allotted to the virtue he was focusing on, if he decided he had fallen short of it.[7]

Franklin decided to begin with temperance, "as it tends to procure that coolness and clearness of head, which is so necessary where constant vigilance was to be kept up." Then he planned to move on to silence— in order to develop listening skills and to break his habit of "prattling, punning, and joking," which got him into trouble in social conversation. Next came order, which he "expected would allow me more time for attending to my project and my studies." In the spirit of order, he created an hourly schedule for maximum productivity:

> 5:00 to 7:00 a.m., rise, breakfast, and focus on the resolution of the
> day.
> 8:00 to 11:00 a.m., work.
> Noon to 1:00 p.m., read, dine, and review accounts.
> 2:00 to 5:00 p.m., work.
> 6:00 to 9:00 p.m., put things in their place, supper, music, diversion,
> conversation, examination of the day.
> 10:00 p.m. to 5:00 a.m., sleep.[8]

Franklin soon found that his twenty-four-hour plan for maintaining order tripped him up. It might be practical to use every hour productively when he was master of his own time as a journeyman printer, but he could hardly keep up his schedule of work and reflection when he had to report to a boss, mix in the world, and receive business clients on their own schedules. He also found it hard to acquire order "with regard to places for things, papers, etc.," owing to his early habits of being disorganized. He made so little progress in improving his organizational skills that he eventually gave up.[9]

Even after he abandoned his daily self-accounting, Franklin continued in his twenties to devise practical projects to help him and his friends practice the classical virtues. In 1727, he recalled in his *Autobiography*, he formed a "club of mutual improvement which we called the Junto." (The word means "to join.") The rules he drafted "required that every member in his turn should produce one or more queries on any point of Morals, Politics, or Natural Philosophy, to be discuss'd by the company."[10] Franklin's standing queries for the Junto included: "What unhappy effects of intemperance have you lately observed or heard? of imprudence? of passion? or of any other vice or folly?" "What happy effects of temperance? of prudence? of moderation? or of any other virtue?"[11] Franklin took these questions almost word for word from an essay by John Locke (which he neglected to cite) proposing the "Rules of a Society," where members would meet once a week "for their improvement in useful knowledge, and for the promoting of truth and christian charity."[12]

Franklin hoped that the model for the Junto would spread, convincing young men to form local chapters for the practice and promotion of virtue. He proposed that members of the Junto and its spinoffs would eventually be known as "*The Society of the Free and Easy:* free, as being, by the general practice and habit of the virtues free from the dominion of vice; and particularly by the practice of industry and frugality, free from debt."[13] He also conceived of what he called a "*great and extensive project* that required the whole man to execute"—namely, the formation of "a United Party for Virtue" that would bring together the "virtuous and good men of all nations into a regular body, to be govern'd by suitable good and wise rules." Franklin proposed to write a practical self-help book called *The Art of Virtue*, which would have "shown the means and manner of obtaining virtue" through daily practice, demonstrating that it was in "every one's interest to be virtuous who wish'd to be happy even in this world."

What books in particular focused Franklin on the connection between the pursuit of virtue and the pursuit of happiness? The memoir of Franklin's friend George Cabanis provides the most extensive testimony reflecting Franklin's own account of the books he found most influential in his youth. "Before he left his father's home, he happened on a few volumes by Plutarch," an ancient Roman biographer who chronicled the *Lives of the Noble Greeks and Romans*, including Cicero and Caesar. "[H]e read them ravenously," Cabanis wrote. "Nothing ever impressed him more than the simple and grand manner, the wise and generous philosophy of that writer, except perhaps for the exquisite good sense and the, as it were, more familiar virtue of Socrates, who is depicted so vividly by Xenophon in his *Memorabilia*."[14] As young men, most of the Founders were inspired by Plutarch's *Lives*, which compared and contrasted pairs of heroic characters from Greek and Roman history as examples of how to live a good life.

According to Cabanis, Franklin's reading of the classical moral philosophers influenced not only his worldview but also his diet and daily habits. In his autobiography, which he began in 1771, Franklin wrote that he had been converted to vegetarianism around the age of sixteen after reading a combination cookbook and self-help manual written by the Baptist preacher Thomas Tryon. Franklin took some of the aphorisms for his list of virtues from Tryon, who was also the author of *Pythagoras's Mystick Philosophy Revised*.[15] According to Cabanis, however, Franklin said he was actually converted to vegetarianism after reading Plutarch's treatise "On the Eating of Flesh."[16] (Plutarch's treatise explains Pythagoras's objection to eating meat on the grounds that we have a moral obligation "to act justly toward other creatures.")[17] When Franklin's mother learned that some "mad philosopher" had converted him to vegetarianism, she declared, according to Cabanis, "There is little harm done; it teaches him self-control."[18] Franklin said later that he abandoned his strict vegetarianism after smelling fried cod while becalmed off of Block Island during his first trip away from Boston. If fish eat one another, why shouldn't we eat fish? he concluded, joking that men find a reason to justify everything they're inclined to do anyway.[19]

Despite falling short of Pythagoras's vegetarian injunctions, Franklin, in his autobiography, said that Pythagoras's *Golden Verse*s convinced him that daily self-examination was necessary for moral improvement.[20] And a fictional 1758 letter from "Father Abraham, to his beloved son," which some have attributed to Franklin, also recommends Pythagoras's method of daily self-examination. "[F]or the Acquirement of solid, uniform, steady Virtue, nothing contributes more, than a daily strict SELF-EXAMINATION," Father Abraham wrote. "This Method is very antient. 'Twas recommended by Pythagoras, in his truly *Golden Verses*, and practised since in every Age, with Success, by Men of all Religions." The letter then quoted from *The Golden Verses*'s suggestion of a daily practice of self-accounting before bed, recommending the 1707 translation by Nicholas Rowe, the English poet and playwright who is considered the first editor of the works of William Shakespeare:

> *Let not the stealing God of Sleep surprize,*
> *Nor creep in Slumbers on thy weary Eyes,*
> *Ere ev'ry Action of the former Day,*
> Strictly *thou dost, and* righteously *survey.*
> *With Rev'rence at thy own Tribunal stand,*
> *And answer justly to thy own Demand.*
> *Where have I been? In what have I transgrest?*
> *What Good or Ill has this Day's Life exprest?*[21]

To understand the philosophical sources that inspired Franklin's understanding of self-accounting as the secret of happiness, therefore, let's begin with Pythagoras. Known as "the fair-haired Samian," Pythagoras was born, according to tradition, on the Greek Island of Samos around 580 BC. His father, Mnesarchus, was a ring maker; his mother changed her name to Pythais, after Pythia, the Oracle of Delphi, prophesied that she would bear a son who would "exceed all men that ever were in Beauty and Wisdom, and through the whole course of his life bring much benefit to mankind." Some philosophers held that the god Apollo was his real father. Pythagoras was renowned in his youth for his beauty, as well as for his temperance and prudence, and his "sweet inimitable serenity."[22] At the age of eighteen, he left Samos to study astronomy, geometry, and the divine mysteries with the highest spiritual authorities of the East. Tradition holds that he may have studied with the priests of

Egypt at Memphis and Thebes, the magi of Persia, the rabbis of Babylon, the Brahmans of India, and the oracles of Delphi, Sparta, and Crete.

Based on his travels, Pythagoras was said by his biographer Iamblichus to be the first to name the study of philosophy, which he defined as "[a] longing and love of wisdom." The philosophy he developed distilled the universal truths now recognized by the Eastern and Western wisdom traditions: through the daily discipline of mastering our thoughts, we can learn to resemble divinity itself. As Pythagoras taught, "[A] man must be made good, then a God."[23]

After about twenty-two years in Egypt and twelve years in Babylon, he returned to the island of Samos around the age of fifty-six and then set off for the city of Croton in southern Italy. There he established an academy to train his disciples to live like gods by cultivating the virtues of self-discipline, self-mastery, and mindfulness. He taught them by example to live as he did: sleeping and eating little, and abstaining from wine and meat. The Roman poet Ovid, in his famous account of Pythagoras in book 15 of the *Metamorphoses*, relates his speech to his disciples on the importance of vegetarianism: "O Mortals! from your Fellow's Blood abstain, / Nor taint your Bodies with a Food profane."[24] His most peculiar injunction was that his disciples should rather die than eat or touch beans. According to Iamblichus, forty devoted Pythagoreans allowed themselves to be slaughtered in a bean field, because to escape, they would have had to trample on the beans. The enemy commander, a tyrant named Dionysius, offered to spare the life of the pregnant wife of one of the few survivors if she answered one question: "Why [do] your companions cho[o]se rather to die, than to tread on beans?"[25] Instead of disclosing Pythagoras's secret, she bit off her tongue and spit it at him. According to Thomas Stanley's *History of Philosophy*, published in 1687, the consensus among philosophers is that Pythagoras forbade beans because of their resemblance to fetuses. "Pliny says he condemned beans, because the souls of dead are in them"; Porphyry emphasized the fact that they looked like living creatures; and Cicero said, "[I]t was because beans disturb the tranquility of mind."[26]

In addition to rigorous vegetarianism (with a ban on beans), Pythagoras taught by example, with his extraordinary self-discipline of body and mind. He gave speeches to the people of Crotona emphasizing the importance of overcoming unproductive emotions such as anger, jealousy, and fear by the daily practice of temperance and moderation. He told the children of Crotona, in M. Dacier's 1707 translation of the *Life of Pythagoras*, "that Hardships and Difficulties contribute more to Virtue than Ease and Pleasure; that the drowsiness and insensibility of the Soul are near a-kin to Death; that all the Passions of the Soul are more cruel than Tyrants, and the enemies of our Happiness."[27]

Pythagoras's disciples distilled his philosophy into seventy-one easily understood *Golden Verses*, which emphasize the importance of disciplining our thoughts by using reason to modulate our passions. Here is a selection:

> *By use thy stronger Appetites asswage,*
> *Thy Gluttony, thy Sloath, thy Lust, thy Rage:*
> *From each dishonest Act of Shame forbear;*
> *Of others, and thy self, alike beware.*
> *Let Rev'rence of thy self thy Thoughts controul,*
> *And guard the sacred Temple of thy Soul.*[28]

Pythagoras's injunction "Reverence Thyself" was so influential that the Founders quoted it frequently, although sometimes they forgot its source. In 1783 Abigail Adams wrote to a close family friend extolling "the maxim of Epictetus or Pythagoras, I forget which, 'Reverence thyself.'"[29] John Adams left out the source entirely when he wrote to the Massachusetts Founder Rufus King in 1786: "Reverence thyself, is a Prœcept of private Morality, but it is equally applicable And equally necessary to States & Individuals."[30] And in 1760, as we will see, Adams, too, would resolve in his diary to make a mental accounting each evening of his daily vices and virtues, as recommended by Pythagoras's *Golden Verses*.

The way to practice self-reverence, Pythagoras told his disciples, was to exercise physical as well as mental self-discipline. Self-reverence required thinking before you speak and deliberating before you act. It also required cultivating body and mind through exercise, temperance, and, of course, vegetarianism. Pythagoras emphasized the importance of moderation in all things—diet, lifestyle, speech, thought, and action. He summed this up in his axiom of the golden mean: "Seek not in needless Luxury to waste / Thy Wealth and Substance, with a Spendthrift's Haste. . . . / Distant alike from each, to neither lean / But ever keep the happy GOLDEN MEAN."[31] By daily examination and moderation of our thoughts and actions, he concluded, we can realize that we bear within our own minds the keys to our own happiness—or misery.

In addition to *Golden Verses*, Franklin encountered Pythagoras in the works of Plutarch, who discusses Pythagoras in his *Life of Numa*, which Franklin read as a child. Plutarch's most extensive discussion of Pythagorean philosophy is in his *Moralia*, or moral works, which contain the treatise on vegetarianism that Franklin told Cabanis he'd also read. Regardless of exactly where and when Franklin absorbed Pythagorean philosophy, he incorporated its essential elements into the "proposals and queries" he set in 1732 for the Junto, with the Pythagorean injunction "Let all your observations be committed to writing every Night before you go to Sleep." His queries focused on the connection between the pursuit of virtue and happiness. "[O]f the many Schemes of Living which are in our Power to pursue," Franklin asked, "which will be most probably conducive to our Happiness"?[32]

If Pythagoras inspired Franklin to pursue happiness by disciplining his body and his thoughts, Socrates gave him another model for improving his soul. "There was nobody he wanted to resemble more than Socrates," Cabanis said of Franklin. "Xenophon's *Memorabilia* of Socrates had made the strongest impression on him: the simplicity and moderation, the subtlety and the common sense of that philosopher, particularly suited his way of feeling and of seeing things."[33] Xenophon emphasizes Socrates's habits of living and self-control, which inspired others to develop habits of self-mastery. And Xenophon expresses surprise that Socrates could have been condemned for corrupting the youth with his impiety, since "in control of his own passions and appetites, he was the strictest of men."[34] Book 1 of the *Memorabilia* quotes Socrates's discourse to his disciples on the importance of self-control. "Should not every man hold self-control to be the foundation of all virtue, and first lay this foundation firmly in his soul?" he asks.[35]

Franklin took from Socrates a model for how to achieve moral perfection through emotional self-regulation. As Franklin recalled in his autobiography, his early moral essays, written for the Junto and published later, included "a Socratic dialogue, tending to prove that, whatever might be his parts and abilities, a vicious man could not properly be called a man of sense; and a discourse on self-denial, showing that virtue was not secure till its practice became a habitude, and was free from the opposition of contrary inclinations."[36] In trying to imitate Socrates, Franklin also worked to master the art of conversation, emphasizing the importance of dialogue as a way of seeing all sides of a question and winning his points through gentle persuasion rather than slashing debate. He was so fond of speaking and writing in Socratic dialogues that, years later, when the daughter of one of his English friends was reading Xenophon's *Life of Socrates*, she cried out, "Mamma, Socrates talks just like Dr. Franklin!"[37]

After he resolved to imitate Socrates, Franklin decided to avoid direct assertions of his own opinions or to contradict the opinions of others. "I even forbid myself, agreeably to the old laws of our Junto, the use of every word or expression in the language that imported a fix'd opinion, such as *certainly, undoubtedly*, etc., and I adopted, instead of them, *I conceive, I apprehend*, or *I imagine* a thing to be so or so; or it *so appears to me at present*," he recalled. This modest way of proposing his opinions initially required effort, since it went contrary to Franklin's natural inclinations, but it eventually became "so easy, and so habitual to me, that perhaps for these fifty years past no one has ever heard a dogmatical expression escape me." Franklin found that when he offered his opinions gently, they were more likely to be accepted: "And to this habit (after my character of integrity) I think it principally owing that I had early so much weight with my fellow-citizens when I proposed new institutions, or alterations in the old."[38]

In addition to classical authors such as Pythagoras, Socrates, Plutarch, and Cicero, young Franklin was influenced by the *Spectator*, a weekly London magazine that helped popularize those authors for an eighteenth-century audience. George Washington, John Adams, and James Madison were all avid fans. According to Cabanis, John "Locke taught [Franklin] how to think; the *Spectator* taught him how to write."[39] Indeed, Franklin recalled in his autobiography that, after his father indentured him in his teens to serve as an apprentice to his brother James, who had set up a printing shop in Boston, he taught himself to write by reading moral essays from the *Spectator*, setting them aside, and then reconstructing them from memory. Working early in the morning or after his work at the printing house, he would turn the essays into verse and then, after he had forgotten the originals, turn his rhyming versions back into prose. "By comparing my work afterwards with the original, I discovered my faults and amended them," he wrote.[40] Sometimes he even fancied that he had improved on the prose of Joseph Addison, who cofounded the *Spectator* with his friend Richard Steele in 1711.

An essayist, poet, politician, and dramatist, Addison wrote the play *Cato*, based on the last days of Cato the Younger and his resistance to the tyranny of Caesar. Franklin and George Washington greatly admired the play, arguably the most influential drama of the American Revolution. (In addition to Patrick Henry's rallying cry "Give me liberty or give me death," it also inspired the patriot Nathan Hale's last words, "I regret that I have but one life to give for my country.") Franklin used an excerpt from the play as an epigraph for his virtues project, along with his quotation from Cicero. Addison was also a classicist who translated the Greek and Roman moral philosophers. His goal in founding the *Spectator*, he announced in one of the first issues, was "to enliven Morality with Wit, and to temper

Wit with Morality." Addison proposed to free readers from partisan ha-
treds and set them down the path to self-improvement, with "Writings as
tend to the wearing out of Ignorance, Passion, and Prejudice."[41]

The *Spectator*, in other words, was the antithesis of social media. Most
of the weekly essays began with a quotation in Latin from a Roman poet
or philosopher to emphasize the weekly lesson about moderating the
passions. *Spectator* No. 408, published on June 18, 1712, features a special
guest columnist, the poet Alexander Pope, who begins with a Latin quotation from Cicero: "We should keep our passions from being exalted
above measure, or severely depressed." He then sums up the essence of
the civic republican creed: "The Actions of Men follow their Passions
as naturally as Light does Heat, or as any other Effect flows from its
Cause; reason must be employed in adjusting the Passions, but they must
ever remain the Principles of Action."[42] At the same time, the *Spectator*
warned of the difficulty of subduing reason with passion. "Reason should
govern Passion, but instead of that, you see, it is too often subservient to
it," Richard Steele wrote in *Spectator* No. 6.[43]

In his own *Spectator* essays, Addison returned repeatedly to the classical idea that the soul has higher and lower faculties or powers, and
we need to strengthen our higher faculties of reason and prudence so
that they can control our lower faculties of pleasure seeking and desire.
Spectator No. 624, published on November 24, 1714, uses the phrase "the
pursuit of happiness." "Mankind is divided into two Parts, the Busie and
the Idle," Addison writes. "The Busie World may be divided into the
Virtuous and the Vicious. The Vicious again into the Covetous, the Ambitious, and the Sensual. The idle Part of Mankind are in a State inferior
to any one of these." All the rest—namely, the virtuous and the busy—
"are engaged in the Pursuit of Happiness."[44] Franklin relied on the style,
the sensibility, and the content of the *Spectator* in composing columns
under a series of pseudonyms he invented for himself as a journeyman
printer. He wrote as "Silence Dogood" for his brother James's newspaper,
the *New-England Courant*; as the "Busy Body" for the *American Weekly
Mercury*, and, most famously, as "Richard Saunders" for *Poor Richard's*

Almanack. Many of Franklin's essays, like Addison's, began with a Latin quotation from Cicero, Virgil, or Horace, and then a morality tale illustrating the connection between the pursuit of virtue and the pursuit of happiness. Franklin followed the *Spectator* in emphasizing the need to use reason to subdue passion. "If *Passion* drives, let *Reason* hold the reins," he wrote in *Poor Richard's Almanack*.[45]

When Franklin founded the *Almanack* in 1732, he reprinted aphorisms from English anthologies of moral maxims, such as the clergyman Thomas Fuller's 1726 compilation *Directions, Counsels, and Cautions Tending to Prudent Management in Affairs of Common Life*. Fuller begins with a Pythagorean introduction exhorting his son to read and reflect on each of the numbered maxims in the book, drawn from "the Wisdom of the Antients and Moderns," to jot down in a memorandum book the ones that strike him as useful, and to set aside time each day to meditate on the maxims in turn. By applying the maxims in his daily life, Fuller tells his son, he cannot fail of being *"Wise and Good, Useful and Happy."*[46]

Franklin took Fuller's maxims and, in many cases, improved them. The most famous of the Poor Richard aphorisms, for example, is "Early to bed and early to rise, makes a man healthy, wealthy and wise."[47] This is Franklin's snappier version of Fuller's more lugubrious maxim number 1325: "Use thy self to rise and go to bed early. This may seem like a frivolous Precept, because it respects such common Matters; but if it be well observed, it will contribute very much toward the rendering of a Life long, useful and happy."[48] And it represents a shift in emphasis from Fuller's classical and Christian notion—that virtue is its own reward—toward Franklin's American notion that self-improvement and self-discipline will also lead to health and wealth.

What was the connection between Franklin's philosophical and spiritual journeys? In addition to Cicero, he chose as a motto for his virtues project what he called a verse from "the Proverbs of Solomon, speaking of wisdom or virtue: 'Length of days is in her right hand, and in her left hand riches and honor. Her ways are ways of pleasantness, and all her paths are peace.'"[49] Cabanis writes that when Franklin read these lines, it "was like a ray of light to him. So, it depends on man if he lives long and acquires enough wealth to be happy! He determined to be a living example of this proverb, on both counts."[50]

Cabanis understates the significance of the "ray of light" that Franklin found in the Book of Proverbs—namely, that happiness depends on our own virtuous works and deeds, and not simply on faith in God's saving grace. In Franklin's youth, the debate over whether salvation could be achieved by good works or faith alone was the central theological dispute in England and America. Franklin was born in Boston in 1706, at a time when the old Puritan dogmas were still vigorously enforced from the pulpit of the Second Church in Boston, presided over by Increase Mather and his son Cotton. Following Puritan orthodoxy, the Mathers insisted that all human beings are predestined by God for heaven or for hell. Predestination meant that your ultimate fate was sealed by God at birth, and your salvation could come not by your good works but only by your faith in God's saving grace. Even a lifetime of faith and good works couldn't save you if God had chosen to assign you to hell rather than heaven. Franklin recalls reading in his father's library Cotton Mather's *Essays to Do Good*, a stern self-help manual that ties itself in knots trying to explain why people should devote themselves to a life of virtuous self-improvement, given the fact that our ultimate fate is predestined by God, regardless of our good works on earth. The basic idea was that, since "good works follow, they do not precede justification," devoting yourself to a life of good works could be viewed as reassuring evidence that you had already been predestined by God for ultimate salvation.

Franklin found this theological hair splitting unconvincing, and he made his debut as a journalist with a series of essays mocking Mather. The satire was triggered by a controversy over vaccinations. In 1721 Boston had been seized by a smallpox epidemic, and the city was divided about whether or not to inoculate healthy people with a small bit of pus from infected people. Mather, whose wife and three children had earlier succumbed to measles, was pro-inoculation. He had learned about the treatment from Onesimus, a Black man he held in bondage, who had been successfully inoculated several years earlier.[51] Once smallpox returned to Boston, Mather and other members of the educated elite became enthusiastic proponents, reflecting the best scientific evidence arriving from Britain, where Queen Caroline was also a supporter. In ridiculing Mather, Franklin, who was a scientific provincial at the time, sided with the eighteenth-century equivalent of anti-vaxxers.

In August 1721, at the height of the smallpox epidemic, James began publishing the *New-England Courant*, which ran a series of essays attacking the Mathers, Harvard, the clergy, and the Boston elite for their pro-inoculation sympathies. Benjamin Franklin recalled hearing his brothers' friends discussing their work at James's printing shop; under a pseudonym, he submitted an essay introducing himself as a self-educated orphan who had lost both of her parents after immigrating from London. The pseudonym he chose, Silence Dogood, was a cruel mockery of Cotton Mather, who had just published a sermon called "Silentarius," or "The Silent Sufferer," mourning the loss of his newborn daughter to smallpox. "Dogood" was an allusion to Mather's book *Bonifacius*, whose English title was *Essays to Do Good*.[52] The satire became even more biting as Silence Dogood revealed herself in subsequent essays to be a lusty widow who consorted with prostitutes and may have been one herself.

Although he never owned up to the pseudonym during his lifetime, Franklin seems to have felt abashed by his youthful ridicule of Cotton Mather. Years later, in 1784, he wrote an appeasing letter to Samuel Mather praising the "Vigour" and "Usefulness" of his father's sermons. Franklin also recalled some advice about the dangers of pride that Cotton Mather gave him in 1723, exhorting him to "Stoop! Stoop!" as he was taking his leave through a narrow passage with a low ceiling beam. "Not immediately understanding what he meant, I hit my Head hard against the Beam. He then added, *Let this be a Caution to you not always to hold your Head so high; Stoop, young Man, stoop—as you go through the World—and you'll miss many hard Thumps*."[53] The story seems like a gracious attempt by an older and wiser Franklin to apologize for his youthful arrogance. But it in no way signaled Franklin's acquiescence to Mather's unbending Puritan theology.

In fact, at the time of his encounter with Mather, Franklin was moving in the opposite direction. As he told Cabanis, he had been reading "a few good English authors" on the connection between virtue and happiness: John Locke; the Earl of Shaftsbury; and Anthony Collins's *A Discourse of Free-Thinking*, published in 1713.[54] A friend of Locke, Collins attacked superstition, religious dogma, and the King James Bible, arguing that there was no reason to believe the literal truth of the New Testament, since its authors repeatedly misquoted passages from the Old Testament or selectively quoted them out of context. (Thomas Paine, the pamphleteer of the Revolution, would later make the same argument in *The Age of Reason*, enumerating the selective quotations so relentlessly that Jefferson advised him not to publish.) Collins praised ancient philosophers such as Cicero and Seneca for recognizing that happiness can be obtained only by virtuous living according to the dictates of reason and conscience, rather than by blind faith.

According to Cabanis, Franklin "was so shaken by his reading of Collins that he undertook to discuss all the questions of dogma in short essays."[55] In 1725, Franklin published a few copies of an essay called "A Dissertation on Liberty and Necessity, Pleasure and Pain," which he wrote in response to the Anglican cleric William Wollaston's *The Religion of Nature Delineated*. Wollaston argued that morality can be discerned without relying on the authority of revealed religion, because moral good is the affirmation of a true proposition and moral evil its denial. As a result, he wrote, "natural religion . . . in its truest definition is: 'The pursuit of happiness by the practice of reason and truth.'"[56] (Franklin may have typeset the phrase "the pursuit of happiness" when he helped to print a new edition of the book in the 1720s.) At the same time, Wollaston wrote, both religious and moral truths could be deduced by "right reason," like Euclid's mathematical axioms. Unconvinced by some of Wollaston's arguments about the "self-evident" compatibility of reason and religion, Franklin questioned the immortality of souls, the possibility of free will to choose virtue or vice, and the claim that a providential God rewards virtue and punishes evil.[57] Knowingly or not, he had reached the same conclusion that Collins expressed to the American educator Samuel Johnson on another occasion: that because all human actions are determined by fate and necessity, there is no possibility of a providential, interventionist God.[58] Franklin came to regard this essay, he wrote in his *Autobiography*, as one of the "errata of my life,"[59] and Cabanis says that in "question[ing] the foundation of morals," Franklin "quickly acknowledged that he had been wrong." As Cabanis put it, "Few Philosophers are as certain as he was of the existence of an intelligent being who animates the universe. . . . As for practical morality, he constantly repeated that it was the only reasonable choice for individual happiness as well as the only guarantee of general happiness."[60]

We don't know precisely what persuaded Franklin to return to his original idea that individuals are free to choose to live virtuous lives, which will be rewarded (but not predestined) by the Creator, in this life or the next. But by 1728, he had composed for his own private use a prayer to the Deity he called his "Articles of Belief and Acts of Religion," which included the following statement of first principles: "I Believe there is one Supreme most perfect Being, Author and Father of the Gods themselves," Franklin wrote. "Next to the Praise due, to his Wisdom, I believe he is pleased and delights in the Happiness of those he has created; and since without Virtue Man can have no Happiness in this World, I firmly believe he delights to see me Virtuous, because he is pleas'd when he sees me Happy."[61] And by 1731, he had composed the following creed to be preached by his proposed United Party for Virtue, containing, in his view, "the essentials of every known religion":[62]

That there is one God Father of the Universe.

That he [is] infinitely good, Powerful and wise.

That he is omnipresent.

That he ought to be worshipped, by Adoration Prayer and
   Thanksgiving both in publick and private.

That he loves such of his Creatures as love and do good to others:
and will reward them either in this World or hereafter.

That Men's Minds do not die with their Bodies, but are made more
happy or miserable after this Life according to their Actions.

That Virtuous Men ought to league together to strengthen the
Interest of Virtue, in the World: and so strengthen themselves in
Virtue.

That Knowledge and Learning is to be cultivated, and Ignnorance
dissipated.

That none but the Virtuous are wise.

That Man's Perfection is in Virtue.[63]

Franklin's mature views about the connection between virtue and
happiness were also deeply influenced by the sermons of John Tillotson,
whom he first encountered in Boston. Tillotson was the spiritual mentor
of Franklin's local preacher, Ebenezer Pemberton, who became pastor
of the Old South Meeting House in 1707. Rejecting Cotton Mather's
harsh insistence that faith alone could save, Pemberton quoted, often
verbatim, from Tillotson's collected sermons, which were published in
London the same year.

Tillotson, who served as archbishop of Canterbury under the joint
monarchs William and Mary, was for nearly a century the most popular
preacher in England and America.[64] Franklin later recommended his
sermons as models of moral instruction for American youth.[65] And the
young John Adams, as a Harvard student in 1758 preparing for the min-
istry, spent many days transcribing the works of Tillotson.[66] He was the
leader of the English latitudinarians, ministers who insisted that virtuous
conduct, rather than rigid adherence to religious dogma, was the most
prudent way of pursuing human happiness. A word search for "pursuit
of happiness" in the 1707 edition of Tillotson's collected sermons reveals
the following passage: "And this error every man commits, who pursues
happiness by following his own inclination, and gratifying his irregular
desires."[67]

As the scholar Jacob Blosser has argued, Tillotson's sermons repeatedly stressed the practical benefits on earth of "virtuous happiness."[68] Following classical wisdom, Tillotson maintained that "[t]he capacity and Foundation of all Felicity must be laid in the inward Frame of our Minds."[69] And, in a practical theme that Franklin popularized, Tillotson insisted that practicing virtue would make men healthy, wealthy, and wise. Getting angry and losing your temper, by contrast, would ruin your health and reputation, and earn you the contempt of others.

In 1751 Franklin set out to devise a curriculum for the Academy of Philadelphia, which would evolve forty years later into the University of Pennsylvania. Unlike the other founding trustees of the academy, who wanted to emphasize purely classical studies in Greek and Latin, Franklin preferred moral instruction rooted in the classics with a practical twist, so that students could apply the teachings of Cicero and Seneca to their daily lives. He found the answer in a minister, philosopher, and educator named Samuel Johnson. One of the first tutors at Yale College, Johnson would go on to become the first president of King's College, which became Columbia University. And Johnson, more than any other American philosopher of his time, helped to popularize the phrase "pursuit of happiness."

Unlike the British essayist Dr. Samuel Johnson, with whom he was often confused, the American Samuel Johnson belonged to a group of Yale faculty members who had been expelled from the college during the "great apostasy" of 1722, when they embraced the Episcopalian, rather than Presbyterian, policy on ordination into the Church. (The doctrinal details aren't important for our purposes, except that they led Johnson and his fellow apostates to travel to London, where they were warmly welcomed into the Church of England.) His life was changed in 1714, the year of his Yale graduation, by "a well chosen library of new books" sent to Yale from England by the royal agent for the colony. "He had then all at once the vast pleasure of reading the works of our best English poets, philosophers and divines," Johnson recalled, such as William

Shakespeare, John Milton, John Locke, and Isaac Newton, as well as the sermons of liberal clergymen such as Tillotson. "All this was a flood of day to his low state of mind," and allowed him to reject the rigid Calvinism of his youth in favor of an emphasis on John Locke's reason and Francis Bacon's empiricism.[70]

On his return to America, Johnson continued his missionary work, spreading the doctrine of liberal Anglicanism rather than orthodox Puritanism in his pamphlets and sermons. And he worked to complete the philosophical treatise he had begun while an undergraduate at Yale: an attempt to synthesize all the doctrines of human knowledge by combining classical learning with the new insights of the Enlightenment. In 1729 Johnson met and befriended Bishop George Berkeley, the famous British idealist philosopher who argued that reality consists only of the mind and its ideas, and that we can know only our ideas about material objects, not the objects themselves. (The British Samuel Johnson famously responded to Berkeley's claim by kicking a large stone and declaring, "I refute him thus.") Berkeley had settled in Rhode Island while awaiting money from the British Crown to establish a college in Bermuda to educate the colonists. The money never arrived, and so Berkeley returned to England. But he continued to advise the American Samuel Johnson, who inscribed in his own hand a quotation from Berkeley on the title page of his *Elementa Philosophica*, which Benjamin Franklin first printed in 1752.[71]

Johnson's book, which he called "a new system of morality," was the first philosophy textbook published in America. And it closely follows William Wollastan's definition of "the pursuit of happiness" as aligning our thoughts and actions with the self-evident moral and spiritual truths of the universe, all of which are accessible by reason. Johnson's definition of "the Religion of Nature," which he calls morality itself, is identical to Wollastan's: "the pursuit of our true happiness by thinking, affecting and acting, according to the laws of truth and right reason."[72] To emphasize the connection, Franklin's 1752 printing of Johnson's textbook includes a prayer from Wollaston.

Franklin not only printed the textbook but also became its enthusiastic champion. In 1750, as Franklin was founding the Academy of Philadelphia, he invited Johnson to be its first professor of moral philosophy.[73] The following year, he sent Johnson a draft curriculum adopting his textbook as its centerpiece. "Dr. Johnson's *Ethices Elementa*, or first Principles of Morality, may now be read by the Scholars, and explain'd by the Master, to lay a solid Foundation of Virtue and Piety in their Minds," Franklin wrote.[74]

In 1753 Franklin traveled to Connecticut to meet with Johnson, accompanied by William Smith, a Scottish educational reformer. They discussed their joint project of creating "new model" colleges that would teach Johnson's nondenominational moral philosophy in English, rather than Calvinist theology in Latin and Greek. Soon after, Johnson became the first president of King's College in New York City, and Smith became the first president of the College of Philadelphia, both of which used Johnson's textbook. According to Neil C. Olsen, about half the college graduates in America between 1743 and 1776 were taught a version of Johnson's nondenominational moral philosophy (with the other half taught orthodox Calvinist theology),[75] and more than half of the men who contributed to the Continental Congress that passed the Declaration of Independence were connected in some way to Johnson's, Franklin's, and Smith's "practical idealism, as taught in their new model American colleges."[76]

In addition to serving as a kind of moral textbook for the American Revolution, Johnson's book is a practical how-to manual for what he repeatedly calls "the pursuit of happiness." He begins his *Introduction to Philosophy* with the following definition, which might have been written by Aristotle or the Stoics: "Philosophy is the study of truth and wisdom . . . in the pursuit of true happiness."[77] After following the classical division of philosophy into three branches—rational, natural, and moral—he then defines the practical branch of moral philosophy as "the art of pursuing our highest happiness by the universal practice of virtue."[78]

Johnson wrote the sections on governing the passions as a kind of advice manual to his son, William Samuel Johnson, a Founding Father who served in the first Continental Congress, signed the Constitution as a delegate from Connecticut, and succeeded his father as president of King's College. Children, Samuel Johnson writes, "should, from the beginning, be taught and inured to the practice of self-denial, and the moderation and restraint of their appetites and passions."[79] The particular mental faculties we can deploy are our "powers of reason and conscience," to ensure "that they might preside over our passions." Johnson equates our powers of reason with our innate moral sense, or intuitive sense of right or wrong, which gives us not only the right but the duty "of seeking and persuing our own preservation and well-being or happiness" by thinking and acting according to the laws of truth and reason.[80] Like Wollaston and the Stoics, in other words, Johnson defined the pursuit of happiness as thinking and acting according to the laws of truth and reason, aligning our lives with God, nature, and reason itself.

Johnson recited the standard Stoic wisdom that virtue is the only true path to happiness. "God's glory must consist in our pursuing our own happiness"[81] by avoiding sin and following the path of virtue, he writes. He enumerated a series of duties that we owe to ourselves, "which are called Human Virtues, and may be comprehended under the general term, temperance, or a right government of all my powers, appetites and passions." We can fulfill these duties, Johnson stresses, by cultivating the individual virtues of prudence, moderation, sobriety, chastity, meekness, patience, fortitude, contentment, frugality, and industry.[82] (This covers most of the virtues on Franklin's list.)

Johnson also emphasized the importance of controlling our "ruling passion," borrowing a phrase from Alexander Pope, who introduced the idea of a "ruling passion" in his widely read poem "An Essay on Man."[83] According to Pope, each person has a ruling passion that explains the inconsistency in our conduct by allowing our self-love to conquer our powers of reason. And in his *Reflections on Courtship and Marriage* (1746), Franklin had quoted Pope's famous couplet as a warning against allowing the "love of money" to be our ruling passion when we choose a mate:

The ruling Passion, be it what it will,

The ruling Passion conquers Reason still.[84]

Samuel Johnson's moral textbook wasn't his last word on the pursuit of happiness. Around 1764, he published a fictional dialogue, or "Rhapsody," called *Raphael, or the Genius of the English America.* An angel called Raphael, representing "the guardian or genius of New England," visits a philosopher called Aristocles, representing Johnson.[85] (Aristocles of Messene had attempted to synthesize all of Greek moral philosophy.) Raphael helpfully reminds Aristocles that "[t]he natural obligation to virtue is founded in the necessity that God and nature lays under us to desire and pursue our own happiness."[86]

In their most inspiring joint venture, Johnson and Franklin worked together to extend their educational philosophy of self-improvement to Black as well as white students. The project represented a significant evolution in Franklin's thinking on the question of equal rights for all. Franklin arrived in London in 1757 with two enslaved men—Peter and King—and had initially maintained that education for Black people, which he supported, could never make them the intellectual equals of whites. But in 1760 he was elected to the Bray Society, founded by a British clergyman committed to educating Black people in the American colonies. With funding from the society, Franklin helped to establish schools for the education of Black youth in Williamsburg, Virginia, Newport, Rhode Island, and New York City, and he appointed the American Samuel Johnson to run the New York school.[87] When Franklin returned to America, he visited the school in Philadelphia and was favorably impressed. "I was on the whole much pleas'd, and from what I then saw, have conceiv'd a higher Opinion of the natural Capacities of the black Race than I had ever before entertained," he wrote to the secretary of the Bray Society in London. "Their Apprehension seems as quick, their Memory as strong, and their Docility in every Respect equal to that of white Children." After the visit, Franklin vowed, "I will not undertake to justify all my Prejudices, nor to account for them."[88]

By 1781, Franklin's household no longer included enslaved labor. In 1787, the year of the Constitutional Convention, he accepted the presidency of the Philadelphia Society for the Abolition of Slavery, founded by Quaker abolitionists, and sought public support for a plan to educate and employ "those who have been restored to freedom," with the goal of promoting "the public good and the happiness of these our hitherto too much neglected fellow-creatures."[89] And in February 1790, two months before his death, Franklin forwarded an antislavery petition to the First Congress, at the very beginning of the American experiment. "That mankind are all formed by the same Almighty being, alike objects of his Care & equally designed for the Enjoyment of Happiness," the Petition begins, invoking the language of the Declaration of Independence, "the Christian Religion teaches us to believe, & the Political Creed of America fully coincides with the Position." The petition then quotes the language of the preamble to the Constitution, insisting that "*the blessings of liberty* . . . ought rightfully to be administered, *without distinction of Colour*, to all descriptions of People." It concludes by calling on Congress to "countenance the *Restoration of liberty* to those unhappy Men, who alone, in this land of Freedom, are degraded into perpetual Bondage," in the process "removing this *Inconsistency from the Character of the American People*."[90] For the mature Franklin, it was obvious that the promise of the Declaration—that all men are equally entitled to the pursuit of happiness—meant what it said.

In 1757, three years after he published Johnson's textbook, Franklin drafted a last will and testament. He divided the bulk of his estate, including his library, his house on Market Street, the income from his printing business, and his share in the Library Company of Philadelphia among his wife, Deborah, his son, William, and his daughter, Sarah, each of whom received £1,000. There were smaller bequests to his sister Jane Mecom and her son Benjamin, as well as some unexpected beneficiaries. ("My Electrical Apparatus I give to Yale College at New-haven in Connecticut.") Most strikingly, however, Franklin concluded by thanking

God for giving him "a Mind, with moderate Passions" to which he attributed his happiness and success in overcoming "Ambition, Avarice
and Superstition, common Causes of much Uneasiness to Men."[91]

This "evenness of temper," as he called it in his *Autobiography*, proved
to be crucial in allowing Franklin to play the role of moderator and
conciliator throughout a series of important diplomatic assignments: in
London before the American Revolution and in Paris after it. His judgment, of course, sometimes failed him: in 1774, during his service as a
colonial agent to London, he rashly publicized letters that he had somehow obtained between the royal governor of Massachusetts, Thomas
Hutchinson, and Lieutenant Governor Andrew Oliver, suggesting a
conspiracy to deprive the colonists of their liberties. Franklin was hauled
before the British Privy Council to justify his actions and was humiliated
in a slashing public cross-examination by the king's solicitor general. The
experience radicalized Franklin and led him to return to America in a
revolutionary spirit. He was soon elected as a delegate to the Continental Congress, where he would serve, with John Adams and Thomas Jefferson, on the committee that drafted the Declaration of Independence.

Franklin overcame his youthful overconfidence, however, and expressed his humility in his final speech to the Constitutional Convention on September 17, 1787. "[T]he older I grow, the more apt I am to
doubt my own judgment, and to pay more respect to the judgment of
others," he emphasized. Although "there are several parts of this Constitution which I do not at present approve," Franklin confessed, in his
long life, he had "experienced many instances of being obliged by better
information" to change his opinions. It was amazing, he said, to find the
proposed Constitution "approaching so near to perfection as it does."[92]

He closed by emphasizing the connection between the happiness of
the people and the virtue of the government. "Much of the strength &
efficiency of any Government in procuring and securing happiness to
the people, depends on opinion, on the general opinion of the goodness
of the Government, as well as of the wisdom and integrity of its governors." And he hoped that all the delegates would sign the Constitution

despite any reservations, in the spirit of humility. "On the whole, Sir, I cannot help expressing a wish that every member of the Convention who may still have objections to it, would with me, on this occasion doubt a little of his own infallibility—and to make manifest our unanimity, put his name to this instrument."[93] In Franklin's final appeal for humility at the Constitutional Convention, he connected the Declaration's promise of private happiness with the Constitution's promise of public happiness.

When he called on each of his fellow delegates to "doubt a little of his own infallibility," Franklin may have had in mind one Founder with whom he clashed more openly than any other: John Adams. Although Adams was not at the convention (he was on diplomatic duty in London while Jefferson was in Paris), Franklin had called him, in one of history's more memorable put-downs, "[a]lways an honest man, often a great one, but sometimes absolutely mad."[94] After serving on the committee that drafted the Declaration of Independence, Adams and Jefferson had shared a bed in a crowded inn on Staten Island in September 1776, during a visit to the British general Lord Howe, leading to a famous disagreement about whether to keep the window open or shut. (As Franklin explained his theory of why people never caught colds through contact with cold air, Adams fell asleep.) But Adams seethed with envy at the man he called "the Grand Franklin," who embodied the diplomatic success, polish, and global celebrity that Adams lacked. "His whole Life has been one continued Insult to good Manners and to Decency," Adams wrote to the Boston politician James Warren in the 1780s, adding that Franklin's reputation for honesty and wisdom were exaggerated.[95] In what may have been an act of psychological projection, the envious Adams insisted repeatedly that Franklin was, in fact, envious of him. Writing to Warren's brilliant wife, the historian and poet Mercy Otis Warren, in 1807, Adams said that Franklin had never forgiven him for being chosen first among the five peace commissioners who were in Paris to negotiate the end of the Revolutionary War. "Jealousy And Envy engender Malice and Revenge," Adams declared, writing about himself in the third person. "Franklin found that John Adams possessed more of the Confidence of his Country than himself."[96]

Violating his own strictures against envious gossip, Adams suggested that Franklin was an adulterer, noting that the king of France had become exasperated with a French duchess who was constantly fawning over "the Grand Franklin, for reasons which I could detail, from probable Conjecture." The king, according to Adams, "Sometimes Smiled, Sometimes Snickered" and "gave Secret orders to have a Chamber Pot made of the finest materials and most exquisite Workmanship, with the most exact Portrait of the Grand Franklin painted on the Bottom of it" so that the duchess in her bedchamber should "have the Satisfaction of contemplating the Image of her Great Philosopher and Politician whenever she had occasion to look at it." At another house in Paris, Adams heard, the guests had passed around a portrait where "America was represented as a Virgin naked and as beautifull," and "the grand Franklin, with his bald head, with his few long scattering straight hairs" was depicted "in the Act of debauching her behind her back. Can you imagine any Ridicule more exquisite than this both upon America and Franklin?"[97]

In fact, it was Adams who feared nothing more than ridicule, and, in his calmer moments of self-awareness, he acknowledged that his ruling passion was vanity. Like Franklin, Adams was committed to Pythagorean self-accounting. He struggled throughout his life to overcome his vanity, which he called "self-love," and to cultivate the humility that Franklin came closer to achieving.

Notes on Epictetus's *Enchiridion*

Some things, not others, under our control
Desire, choice, aversion are our own
If honor, wealth or office you extol
You're helpless once external goods have flown

Test all harsh thoughts by this exacting rule:
It's out of your control? Indifferent be
When strangers bray on cell phones like a mule
Your choice to keep your mind's tranquility

At life's banquet, free guests await each dish
Calmly accepting food when it's passed round
Not seeking things to happen as they wish
But wishing things to happen as they're found

Avoid all contests, every day and hour
Where victory is not within your power

Three

HUMILITY

John and Abigail Adams's Self-Accounting

I n December 1758, at the age of twenty-three, John Adams was alarmed to find his parents in the middle of what he called "A conjugal Spat." His father, Deacon John Adams, had invited an impoverished young Black woman named Judah to live with the Adams family at public expense. Since she came from a broken home and couldn't support herself, he explained, the town of Braintree, Massachusetts, would support her instead. "I won't have all the Towns Poor brought here, stark naked, for me to clothe for nothing," his mother, Susanna Adams, objected. As Adams recorded the scene in his diary, his father "continued cool and pleasant a good while, but had his Temper roused at last" and "resolutely asserted his Right to Govern." As the fight went off the rails, his brother Peter observed that Judah was crying. "[A]ll was breaking into a flame," Adams recalled. He left the room and started reading Cicero "to compose myself."[1]

Once Cicero helped him calm down, Adams reflected about the

Roman philosopher's lessons on the importance of controlling violent passions, at home and in public. Observing that his mother's "rages" and "raves" had no effect in persuading his father, he concluded that "Cool Reasoning upon the Point with my Father" would have been more likely to produce a meeting of minds. "Passion, Accident, Freak, Humour, govern in this House," Adams wrote. "I feel a fluttering concern upon my mind."[2]

It had been a trying month, and Adams turned to Cicero repeatedly to ease his nerves. The day before his parents' fight, he had lost his first legal case—involving a neighbor's horse that had broken into his client's field and trampled his crops. As Adams reproached himself for his handling of the case, he read Cicero's *Catiline Orations* aloud.[3] Adams had first encountered Cicero as a fourteen-year-old schoolboy, and he was so fond of his textbook of Cicero's orations in Latin that he wrote "John Adams Book 1749/50" several times on the title page.[4] In his diary between 1756 and 1759, the years he was teaching school and studying law after his graduation from Harvard, Adams gives us psychological insight into his own internal struggles to lead a virtuous life by applying the teachings of Cicero, Epictetus, and other classical moral philosophers. Adams's diary is remarkable for its self-awareness; a combination of a Pythagorean and Puritan self-accounting book of his soul. Its central theme is Adams's struggle to use his powers of reason to overcome his turbulent passions. "He is not a wise man and is unfit to fill any important Station in Society, that has left one Passion in his Soul unsubdued," Adams wrote.[5]

The central passion Adams struggled to subdue was vanity. Cultivating humility was a lifelong struggle for Adams, who was famously ridiculed as one of the most self-regarding men of his age. His monarchical pretensions as Washington's vice president led him to suggest that the president of the United States should be addressed "His Elective Majesty"; he himself was mocked as "His Rotundity." He constantly seethed with envy that he wasn't receiving enough credit for his role in the American Revolution, insisting that he had played a more central role in drafting the Declaration of Independence than he actually did. He was given to outbursts of temper—according to Jefferson, Adams as president was so frustrated by opposition from his cabinet that he yelled obscenities at his colleagues while pacing around the cabinet room and "dashing and trampling his wig on the floor."[6] As we will see, Adams's hypersensitivity to being disrespected and unappreciated led to famous political falling-outs with his close friends and Revolutionary associates, Jefferson and Mercy Otis Warren. But what makes Adams so human and endearing is that he ultimately overcame his vanity and wounded pride sufficiently to reconcile with both Warren and Jefferson. In the end, through daily efforts to control his temper, Adams wore his heart on his sleeve and worked throughout his long life to subdue his vanity and ambition in order to achieve the tranquility of mind that he learned from Cicero was the secret of happiness.

"Vanity I am sensible, is my cardinal Vice and cardinal Folly," Adams wrote in his diary in May 1756. "[W]ithout the strictest Caution and watchfulness over my self," he was in "continual danger" of being led astray.[7] In July he once again lamented his vanity, which he attributed to "Love of Fame." "No Accomplishments, no Virtues are a sufficient Attonement for Vanity, and a haughty overbearing Temper in Conversation," he wrote. Adams also resolved to guard himself against the related vices of envy, boasting, and gossip. Confessing himself to have been guilty "to a very heinous Degree" of "censorious Remarks upon others" and ostentatious displays of his learning and wit in company, he resolved to avoid envious remarks and "never to shew my own Importance or Superiority, by remarking the Foibles, Vices, or Inferiority of others."[8]

By subduing his vanity, Adams hoped to achieve the humility prized by the classical and Christian wisdom literature. "Oh! that I could . . . conquer my natural Pride and Self Conceit . . . acquire that meekness, and humility, which are the sure marks and Characters of a great and generous Soul, and subdue every unworthy Passion," Adams wrote in February 1756. "How happy should I then be, in the favour and good will of all honest men, and the sure prospect of a happy immortality!"[9]

In adding humility at the end of his list of thirteen virtues, Franklin had given the example "Imitate Jesus and Socrates." Cicero, too, invoked Socrates as a model of humility. "[I]t is a fine thing to keep an unruffled temper, an unchanging mien, and the same cast of countenance in every condition of life," he writes in *On Duties*; "this, history tells us, was characteristic of Socrates."[10]

Adams viewed self-improvement as a lifelong quest, and, like Franklin, he was inspired by Pythagoras's *Golden Verses* to develop a rigorous daily reading schedule and to practice self-accounting before bed. "Let me practice the Rule of Pythagoras," he wrote in 1760, in order to "be better able to shew that no Time has been lost." He then quoted, in Greek, the lines from *Golden Verses* that had inspired Franklin's virtue project.[11] In the Pythagorean spirit, and as he began a new year as a schoolteacher—work that he found arduous and exhausting—Adams resolved "not to neglect my Time as I did last Year." Instead, he would rise with the sun and read every morning, studying the Bible from Thursday through Sunday and "some Latin author the other 3 mornings." Noon and nights would be reserved for English authors. "May I blush whenever I suffer one hour to pass unimproved," Adams wrote. Like Franklin, Adams decided to use every moment of the day to improve himself. "I will strive with all my soul to be something more than Persons who have had less Advantages than myself," he wrote in 1756.[12] "I think it necessary to call my self to a strict account, how I spend my Time, once a week at least."[13]

Following the wisdom of the Stoics, Adams also resolved during this period to cultivate humility by disciplining his own thoughts and judgments about the world, rather than worrying about the world's judgments about him. He used to dread encounters with the legal giant James Otis and his law tutor James Putnam because "I suspected they laughed at me" with "satirical and contemptuous smiles," he confessed in 1759. But philosophers such as Cicero taught him to act in "Contempt of Fortune, Fame, Beauty, Praise, and all such Things." Adams had no money, he noted, but

he would work to cultivate "an easy Heart" and "a quiet Mind." Quoting
two Latin phrases that appear in *On Duties*, Adams reminded himself that
"*Animi Magnitudo and Rerum humanarum Contemptio*"—that is, greatness of soul and contempt for human affairs—"are alone secure of Happiness." Cicero was popularizing the arguments of the Stoic Epictetus,
who argued that we should avoid judging others or taking offense at their
judgments of us. Because we can't know or control someone else's motives, thoughts, or actions, we should instead focus on controlling our
own. "Oh Stoicks you are wise," Adams wrote.[14]

In addition to reading the Stoic philosophers in Greek and Latin,
Adams encountered them in a treatise on happiness by the English politician and grammarian James Harris, which he told Thomas Jefferson
was "one of the first pieces of morals I ever read." (When Adams later
met Harris, who had been elevated to the House of Lords, Harris told
him that the famous essayist Lord Chesterfield had been surprised to
learn that he had written about virtue and happiness. "[W]hat the devil
has the House of Lords to do with either Happiness or Virtue!" Chesterfield exclaimed.)[15] A summary of classical moral philosophers, primarily
Socrates, Cicero, and Epictetus, Harris's dialogue is notable for arguing
that the good life comes not from arriving at any fixed point in obtaining
happiness but from the steady self-improvement that comes from the
pursuit itself. "[A] *Life*, whose *Pursuings* and *Avoidings* are governed by
these *Virtues*"—the "FOUR GRAND VIRTUES" of "PRUDENCE, TEMPER-
ANCE, FORTITUDE, *and* JUSTICE"—is "that *True and Rational Life*, which
we have so long been seeking," Harris wrote. And our "Happiness [is]
dependent, not on the *Success*, but on the *Aim*," because, as any sportsman
will tell you, "the *Joy* [is] in the *Pursuit*."[16]

Throughout his life, Adams used his diary to record his dreams. And
in January 1759 he dreamt of the most famous choice in classical mythology: Hercules's choice between Virtue and Vice. As described by
Socrates in Xenophon's *Memorabilia*, Hercules as a young man encountered two women. One summoned him to a path of easy pleasure—she
was known by some as Happiness, but her real name was Vice. The other

pointed to a path of high and noble deeds. Her name was Virtue, and hers was the path to "the most blessed happiness."[17] As Adams wrote in his diary, "The other night, the Choice of Hercules came into my mind," and Virtue addressed him, asking: "Which, dear Youth, will you prefer? a Life of Effeminacy, Indolence and obscurity, or a Life of Industry, Temperance, and Honour?" Virtue then advised him to rise and mount his horse at dawn, and then return to his study and "bend your whole soul to the Institutes of the Law," allowing "no Girl, no Gun, no Cards, no flutes, no Violins, no Dress, no Tobacco, no Laziness, decoy you from your Books." Virtue also admonished him to "keep your Law Book or some Point of Law in your mind at least 6 Hours in a day," and to "study Seneca, Cicero, and all other good moral Writers," as well as the French philosopher Baron de Montesquieu, the British philosopher Lord Bolingbroke, and "all other good, civil Writers." The goal of this reading was to learn about the effects of different forms of government on "public and private Happiness."[18]

The fable of the choice of Hercules made such an impression on Adams that, after the signing of the Declaration of Independence, he proposed it as a model for the seal of the United States. As Adams wrote to his wife, Abigail, in August 1776, "I proposed the Choice of Hercules," with "Virtue pointing to her rugged Mountain, on one Hand," and "Sloth, glancing at her flowery Paths of Pleasure, wantonly reclining on the Ground, displaying the Charms both of her Eloquence and Person, to seduce him into Vice."[19] After concluding "this is too complicated a Group for a Seal or Medal, and it is not original,"[20] Adams wisely abandoned his proposal.

In the same diary entry where he recorded his dream about the choice of Hercules, Adams noted that he had been reading Benjamin Franklin's *Reflections on Courtship and Marriage,* a how-to manual for young people choosing a mate. Franklin's themes, written in the form of letters to a friend, are obvious from his table of contents. "*Unhappy Marriages* are often occasioned from the *Headstrong Motives* of *ungoverned Passion*," Franklin wrote. "All litigious *Wranglings,* and capricious *Contentions*, should be carefully avoided" in marriage, and we should "cultivate Dispositions *of reciprocal Condescension*" and *"Uniformity* in our Tempers."[21]

It's not surprising that Adams was dreaming of choices involving virtue and marriage, for around this time, he was falling in love. He had recently met Hannah Quincy, the daughter of Josiah Quincy, the wealthiest and most respected citizen in Braintree. Beautiful and flirtatious, Hannah was also being courted by Adams's close friends the clockmaker Richard Cranch and the physician Bela Lincoln. At the moment, Adams was her favorite, and he recorded his infatuation in a series of diary entries in January 1759. Franklin's courtship manual had emphasized the importance of sincerity in courtship, but Adams worried that Hannah was disguising her true temper and was not what she appeared. "She is apparently frank, but really reserved, seemingly pleased, and almost charmed, when she is really laughing with Contempt," he wrote. "Her face and Hart have no Correspondence."[22] The courtship progressed to the point that Adams walked with Hannah through "Cupid's Grove," a Braintree pleasure garden, which further quickened his tender passions. But in the spring, when Adams found himself alone in a room with Hannah and was about to propose, her cousin Esther and Adams's friend Jonathan Sewall "broke in upon H. and me and interrupted a Conversation that would have terminated in a Courtship [and] a Marriage." The accident of the interruption, Adams wrote, cleared the way for his friend Bela Lincoln to propose successfully to Hannah, and their marriage "delivered me from very dangerous shackles, and left me at Liberty."[23]

Adams didn't remain at liberty for long. In the summer of 1759, soon after he broke off his courtship of Hannah, he met Abigail Smith at the home of her father, Reverend William Smith. A liberal Congregationalist minister, Smith opposed the rigid Puritan doctrines of predestination by faith. He emphasized instead the importance of reason, morality, and good works. But Adams's initial impression of both Smith and his daughters was not favorable. Parson Smith, he wrote, "is [a] crafty de-signing Man.—He watches Peoples Looks and Behaviour. . . . I caught him, several times, looking earnestly at my face."[24]

Noting that Smith had a knack for criticizing, judging, and mak-ing fun of others, Adams didn't know at the time that this was precisely the kind of uncharitable behavior that her father enjoined Abigail and her siblings to avoid. In fact, Abigail recalled, Parson Smith frequently told his children "never to speak ill of any Body" and "to make Things rather than Persons the Subjects of Conversation."[25] Adams worried that Abigail, like her father, might be an uncharitable gossip. "Polly and Nabby are Wits," Adams wrote in his diary, referring to Abigail and her seventeen-year-old sister, Elizabeth, by their nicknames, and suggesting that one of them may have made a joke at his expense. Are the Smith Girls "either Frank or fond, or even candid"? he wondered. "Not fond, not frank, not candid."[26]

Today the word *candid* means frank and honest, but in the eigh-teenth century, it had a different meaning: kind, charitable, and impar-tial. "To prove this, let Facts be submitted to a candid world," Thomas Jefferson wrote in the Declaration of Independence, expressing the hope that the world would read the Declaration in a charitable spirit, with absence of malice.[27] Samuel Johnson's 1755 dictionary defines *candour* as "[s]weetness of temper; purity of mind; openness; ingenuity; kindness."[28] In this sense, *candor* meant the harmonious temper that was necessary for the pursuit of happiness. And in the mid-eighteenth century, a time when partisan debate was becoming increasingly acrimonious, political writers frequently expressed the hope that their readers would evaluate their arguments in a "spirit of candour." In *The Federalist Papers*, writing about the presidency, Alexander Hamilton declared that no part of the proposed Constitution "has been inveighed against with less candor or criticised with less judgment."[29]

When Adams worried that Abigail was "not fond, not frank, not can-did," he may also have gotten his trilogy of virtues from the 1712 volume of the *Spectator*, which he read in 1756. In *Spectator* No. 449, Addison

offers an ideal woman, Fidelia (the Latin word for faithful), whose fondness for her father leads her to a life of constant self-improvement. She
speaks with "a Frankness that always attends unfeigned Virtue," while
her home is marked by "Conversation without Mention of the Faults of
the Absent."[30] In another essay, Addison called this last virtue "the spirit
of Candour, rather than that of Cavilling," with the "purpose to palliate little Errors."[31] Adams defined the virtues he hoped for in a wife in
terms identical to Addison. "Fondness is doting Love," Adams wrote in
his diary. "Candor is a Disposition to palliate faults and Mistakes, to put
the best Construction upon Words and Actions, and to forgive Injuries.
Simplicity is a direct, open, artless, undisguised, Behaviour."[32]

Adams was also an admirer of Adam Smith, the Scottish political economist famous today for writing *The Wealth of Nations* but more
famous in his own time as a moral philosopher. In 1790 Adams recommended that his son John Quincy read "a sett of Scotch Writers" whose
"Speculations in Morals Politicks and Law" are "more luminous than
any other I have read": Henry Home (Lord Kames), James Stewart, and
"Adam Smith &c both his Theory of Moral Sentiments and his Wealth
of Nations."[33] In *The Theory of Moral Sentiments*, Smith wrote about how
candor, or a spirit of charity, could counteract the contrary influences of
self-love and selfish passion by helping us put ourselves in the position
of the "indifferent spectator"—a kind of objective third-party mirror—
of our own actions. "When we are about to act, the eagerness of passion
will seldom allow us to consider what we are doing with the candour
of an indifferent person," Smith wrote. "The violent emotions which at
that time agitate us, discolour our views of things, even when we are
endeavouring to place ourselves in the situation of another." By contrast,
"When the action is over, indeed, and the passions which prompted it
have subsided, we can enter more coolly into the sentiments of the indifferent spectator." As a result, "we can now examine our own conduct
with his candour and impartiality."[34]

As for Abigail, Adams soon learned that she was fond, frank, and
candid after all. In addition to her willingness to be charitable about

Adams's lifelong struggles with his own self-regard, Abigail Adams was one of the most brilliant women of her time. She also shared Adams's views about virtue, self-control, the importance of mutual learning and growth, and the centrality of friendship as the basis for a happy marriage. In their letters, Abigail and John soon addressed each other as "my dearest friend" and signed with affection, using the classical pseudonyms "Diana" and "Lysander." Diana was the Roman goddess of hunting and the moon; Lysander, the Spartan admiral who defeated the Athenian fleet and won the Peloponnesian War. But in 1775, on the eve of the Revolutionary War, Abigail changed her signature to Portia. One tradition holds that Portia, the heroic wife of Brutus, nobly took her own life after her husband lost a battle to Mark Anthony and then committed suicide. By embracing this rigorous model of Roman fortitude, Abigail signaled her conviction that women were just as capable of embodying all of the classical virtues as men. "Dont you think me a Courageous Being?" she wrote to John in 1764, confessing that the only capacity in which she feared him was as a critic. "Courage is a laudable, a Glorious Virtue in your Sex, why not in mine?"[35]

Unlike John, Abigail was not permitted to receive a Harvard education. Although there were academies in Massachusetts that admitted women, her father, according to the conventions of the day, had denied all three of his daughters the classical training that he granted William, his son. But Abigail was a voracious reader: she quoted by memory in her letters from a remarkable range of writers, including Pope, Shakespeare, John Dryden, and the French historian Charles Rollin's widely read *The Ancient History*.[36] In her fifties, she expressed gratitude to Adams's friend Richard Cranch, who became her brother-in-law when he married her sister Elizabeth. "I shall feel ever gratefull to the kind hand who formd My early Years to a Love of Letters," she wrote, "Who inspired me with a taste for reading and put into my hands Books Suited to my capacity, and led me on step by step until I was capable of judging for myself." She also thanked Adams, "a Lover of Literature, who confirmd my taste, and gave Me every indulgence that Books could afford."[37] But she always regretted her lack of formal education and became a powerful advocate for the equal education of women. "If we mean to have Heroes, Statesmen and Philosophers," Abigail wrote to John in August 1776, "we should have learned women."[38]

John and Abigail Adams achieved a true intellectual and romantic friendship, the harmony of minds and temperaments that Franklin described in his book on marriage as the model of conjugal happiness. It's remarkable how much of their long correspondence, which began in 1762 and ended with Abigail's death in 1818, involves their mutual quest to govern their emotions. "Patience my Dear! Learn to conquer your Appetites and Passions!" Adams wrote to Abigail in one of his first letters, in April 1763. The injunction "Know thyself," he said, "came down from Heaven," adding that "the Government of ones own soul requires greater Parts and Virtues than the Management of Kingdoms." "Know Thyself," of course, was the injunction of the ancient oracle at Delphi, attributed to Plato and Pythagoras. And the idea that the government of the passions is more important than the management of Kingdoms comes straight from the Bible. ("He that is slow to anger is better than the mighty," says the proverb that Abigail loved to quote, "and he that ruleth his spirit than he that taketh a city.") Adams's reference, however, is to the Stoics. "Did you ever read Epictetus?" he asked Abigail. "He was a sensible Man."[39]

Born into slavery in 55 BC, Epictetus was one of the greatest Stoic moral philosophers. He was said to be disabled because of abuse by his master, which he endured with the remarkable mental self-discipline that became the touchstone of his philosophy. Abigail Adams read Elizabeth Carter's 1757 translation of the works of Epictetus (which also appears on Jefferson's reading list). According to Carter's introduction, "It is reported, that when his Master put his leg to the Torture, *Epictetus*, with great Composure, and even smiling, observed to him: 'You will certainly break my Leg:' which accordingly happened; and he continued, in the same Tone of Voice—'Did not I tell you, that you would break it?'"[40]

Freed by his master after the death of the Roman emperor Nero, Epictetus spent the end of his life in exile. Living in poverty and simplicity, he taught his disciples about the importance of controlling the passions through reason. The core principle of his philosophy appears in the first sentences of the *Enchiridion*, a compilation by his student Arrian of his essential teachings. "Some things are under our control, while others are not under our control," Epictetus wrote. "Under our control are conception, choice, desire, aversion, and, in a word, everything that is our own doing; not under our control are our body, our property, reputation, office, and, in a word, everything that is not our own doing."[41] This passage, famously known as the dichotomy of control, is a pillar of Stoic philosophy. It emphasizes that all external goods—such as wealth or fame—can be taken away from us, since they depend on fortune or the reaction of others. We can lose all our money in a bad investment or our reputation in a single tweet. To achieve freedom, tranquility, and happiness, we should free ourselves from the attempt to control external events and focus instead on controlling the only thing within our control: namely, our own thoughts, desires, and emotions. "Whoever, therefore, wants to be free, let him neither wish for anything, nor avoid anything, that is under the control of others," Epictetus taught, "or else he is necessarily a slave."[42]

At his most rigorous, Epictetus insisted that we should be calm even when faced with the sickness or death of loved ones, since we have no power to bring them back to life. Instead, we should live in the present, expressing gratitude for the happy experiences we shared and cultivating our present relationships. "Do not seek to have everything that happens happen as you wish, but wish for everything to happen as it actually does happen, and your life will be serene," he wrote.[43]

The Stoic advice to overcome all grief and anxiety about the health of our loved ones was too much for Abigail, who responded by invoking a Stoic philosopher of her own. In August 1763, when John failed to visit her, she said that she confessed to an "uneasiness" of mind that resulted from a concern that he might be unwell. "Seneca, for the sake of his Paulina, was careful and tender of his health," Abigail wrote. "The health and happiness of Seneca she says was not dearer to his Paulina than that of Lysander to his Diana."[44] The reference was remarkably apt: In his letter "on care of health and peace of mind," Seneca expressed appreciation to "my dear Paulina, who always urges me to take care of my health." He was leaving the city to recover from a fever and was grateful for her concern. Paulina had taught him, he said, the value of compassion for those we love, and therefore he would take care of himself out of a concern for her feelings rather than his own. "I am beginning, in my solicitude for her, to be solicitous for myself," Seneca wrote.[45]

Abigail used Paulina's concern for Seneca's health to illustrate the value of cultivating empathy for the well-being and happiness of others. "There is a tye more binding than Humanity, and stronger than Friendship, which makes us anxious for the happiness and welfare of those to whom it binds us," Abigail wrote to John. "It makes their Misfortunes, Sorrows and afflictions, our own. Unite these, and there is a threefold cord," and "by this cord I am not ashamed to own myself bound."[46] The beautiful image of the "threefold cord," which comes from the book of Ecclesiastes, was one of Abigail's favorites. Here she applies it to sum up the philosophy of Seneca, who wrote, "The first thing which philosophy undertakes to give is fellow-feeling with all men; in other words, sympathy and sociability."[47] She also distills the central lesson of the so-called commonsense philosophers and writers of the eighteenth century, including her favorite novelist, Samuel Richardson, who insisted that our moral sense leads us to take pleasure not only in our own happiness but also that of others.

All three of Richardson's most famous novels—*Pamela; or, Virtue Rewarded*; *Clarissa—or, the History of a Young Lady*; and *The History of Sir Charles Grandison*—appear on Jefferson's reading list. In his novels, Richardson sought to show how cultivating our virtue and controlling our temper can help promote our own happiness and the happiness of others. Richardson offered characters like Pamela as paragons of virtue for his readers to imitate, in the hope that "by an Emulation of her Sweetness, Humility, Modesty, Patience, and Industry," they could "attain some faint Hope of arriving, in time, within View of her Happiness."[48]

Richardson presented readers with popularized Stoicism, and his characters display their virtues by controlling their tempers. "There was command of temper!" Lady Grandison exclaims when she catches herself before losing her own. "I thought, at the instant of Epictetus and his snapt leg. Was I not as great a Philosopher?"[49] In addition to being admired by British novelist Jane Austen, the novel was Abigail Adams's favorite. Abigail would later write that the more she read of Richardson's books, "the more I am led to love and admire the author." His books, she said, elevate the human mind "to the contemplation of truth and virtue, and . . . teach it that it is capable of rising to higher degrees of excellence than the mere gratification of sensual appetites and passions."[50]

In April 1764, as part of their mutual quest for self-improvement, Abigail and John decided to enumerate each other's faults. Epictetus, in his *Discourses*, had endorsed the daily practice of self-accounting recommended in *Golden Verses*. "Also allow not sleep to draw nigh to your languorous eyelids, Ere you have reckoned up each several deed of the daytime: 'Where went I wrong? Did what? And what to be done was left undone?'" he wrote, quoting Pythagoras. "Starting from this point review, then, your acts, and thereafter remember: Censure yourself for the acts that are base, but rejoice in the goodly."[51]

In the Pythagorean spirit, Abigail's list of John's faults included the charge that his formidable reserve intimidated others. "An intolerable forbiding expecting Silence, which lays such a restraint upon but moderate Modesty that tis impossible for a Stranger to be tranquil in your presence," as she put it. "What say you to that charge? Deny it not, for by experience I know it to be true." Abigail advised John to read Richardson's *Charles Grandison* for an example of a perfectly virtuous man who put everyone at ease. "Sir Charles call'd forth every one's excellencies, but never was a thought born in Lysanders presence." She then absolved John of other charges that others made against him—for instance, that he was an "Unsociable Being" given to "Haughtiness." In her view, Adams had neither haughtiness nor ill nature in his disposition, "but for Saucyness," she concluded flirtatiously, "no Mortal can match him."[52]

John replied with a "[c]atalogue" of Abigail's "Faults, Imperfections, [or] Defects." Some were tongue in cheek, such as his criticizing her for qualities that he clearly valued, such as a "Habit of Reading, Writing and Thinking," which he jokingly called qualities "inexcusable in a Lady." More serious was his upbraiding her for an excessive "Modesty, Sensibility, [or] Bashfulness," which he attributed to her country upbringing, leading to prudish blushes at any departures from decency and propriety. The only criticism that got a rise out of Abigail was his claim that she would "very often hang your Head like a Bulrush" so that "you appear too short for a Beauty" and her habits of "sitting with the Leggs across" and "of Walking, with the Toes bending inward."[53] Abigail responded with impressive good humor, saying that she would persist in her modesty, while avoiding hypocrisy and formality. As for her posture, "a gentleman has no business to concern himself about the Leggs of a Lady," and her pigeon toes "can be cured only by a Dancing School."[54]

In the same diary entry where he recorded his first meeting with Abigail, John had quoted Seneca's Stoic definition of happiness from his book on the importance of overcoming anger. "The Felicis Animi immota Tranquilitas, the immovable Tranquility of a happy Mind," Adams wrote in 1759, "unmoved by Perils of Water or of fire, unmoved by any Losses, Accidents, by Loss of Wealth, of fame, of friends [is a] Happy Mind indeed." He added, "Cant a Mind be called happy, unless its Tranquility, its Ease, its Rest, is immovable, invincible."[55] As he and Abigail prepared to marry, Adams expressed confidence that she would help him achieve Seneca's definition of happiness, one that he would quote throughout his life:

But you who have always softened and warmed my Heart, shall restore my Benevolence as well as my Health and Tranquility of mind.
You shall polish and refine my sentiments of Life and Manners, ban-
ish all the unsocial and ill natured Particles in my Composition, and
form me to that happy Temper, that can reconcile a quick Discernment with a perfect Candour.[56]

In the same letter, Adams reproached himself for his own lack of
candor in gossiping about one of their mutual acquaintances, who had
spent the other evening in company "engaged in the nobler Arts of smutt,
Double Ententre, and Mimickry of Dutchmen and Negroes." Although
the ethnic impersonations were offensive, Adams worried that in trading gossip, he had violated the Stoic injunction to work on controlling
our own judgments about others, rather than others' judgments of us. "I
see nothing but Faults, Follies, Frailties and Defects in any Body, lately,"
Adams acknowledged. "People have lost all their good Properties or I my
Justice, or Discernment."[57]

In her response on October 4, 1764, Abigail said that her own mind
had been "really discomposed" by his gossip. She had found the best path
to mental tranquility was "never to say a severe thing because to a feeling heart they wound to[o] deeply to be easily cured." The philosopher
who laughed at the follies of mankind, she said, referring to the Stoic
Democritus, passed through life "with more ease and pleasure, than he
who weept at them." In the same letter, she agreed to Adams's mother's
suggestion that they take on Judah as a servant in their new home—the
same woman whose boarding had caused the argument between Adams's parents. Abigail had already sent many of her belongings to Braintree by cart, and she said the rest of them would be ready in about a week.
"I hope by that time, that you will have recoverd your Health, together
with your former tranquility of mind," Abigail wrote. "And—then Sir
if you please you may take me."[58] On October 25, 1764, in her father's
church in Weymouth, John and Abigail were married.

·   ·   ·

Around the same time that John and Abigail were exchanging tender passions, protests against Britain's taxation without representation were igniting the American Revolution. John Adams began spending time with two people he credited with kindling the fire: James Otis and his brilliant sister, Mercy Otis Warren. James had been a member of the panel of legal eminences who examined Adams for his admission to the bar, and Adams admired him for the depth of his classical learning.[59] Otis had been tutored at home in Greek and Roman philosophy and literature by his uncle, the Yale-trained minister John Russell. He then completed his classical studies at Harvard, where he graduated twelve years before Adams. He inscribed his name into American history with his 1761 speech denouncing the British writs of assistance, which allowed Crown officials to break into people's houses without a warrant and search for evidence of smuggled goods. Adams was in the courtroom as Otis spoke, and years later, he recorded his impressions of what he called the scene of the "first Act of opposition" to the arbitrary claims of Great Britain.[60] Asserting that "the rights of man in a state of nature" were "inherent and inalienable," Otis insisted that no one could be deprived of life, liberty, or property without consent.[61] "Otis was a flame of fire!" Adams recalled of the speech, which lasted five hours. In Adams's view, "then and there the Child Independence was born."[62]

Otis helped inspire the Revolutionary-era slogan "No taxation without representation." And he was striking among the founding generation in clearly and unequivocally asserting that all human beings—Black and white, men and women—were born free and equal, with the same natural rights. "The Colonists are by the law of nature free born, as indeed all men are, white or black," Otis wrote in *The Rights of the British Colonies Asserted and Proved*, a 1764 pamphlet calling the enslavement of "those of any color . . . the most shocking violation of the law of nature."[63] In the same pamphlet, Otis asserted that all men and women are created equal. "Are not women born as free as men?" he asked. "Would it not be infamous to assert that the ladies are all slaves by nature?"[64]

Otis proved his devotion to the equal rights of women by sharing his classical education with Mercy. While James studied the classics with Reverend Russell, Mercy would listen outside the door. She begged her father to be allowed to join her uncle and brother in their studies together, and he eventually relented. James enthusiastically supported his sister's thirst for learning, as they studied Greek and Roman history and literature and Shakespeare, Pope, Milton, and Dryden.[65] But Otis's ability to learn and grow with his sister soon came to an end. He had a psychological disorder that led to increasingly erratic behavior over the course of the 1760s. In 1768, as the Massachusetts Legislature was voting on the election of Governor Thomas Hutchinson to serve in the upper chamber, Otis ran across the assembly room, alarming his colleagues by shouting gibberish.[66]

More dangerously, Otis published a letter in the *Boston Gazette* attacking two royal customs commissioners as "superlative blockheads" and warning that unless one of them, John Robinson, stopped misrepresenting him, he had "a natural right . . . to break his head."[67] The very next day, Otis returned to the British coffeehouse, where he met Robinson, who demanded a gentleman's satisfaction and grabbed his nose. When Otis responded by striking him with a cane, Robinson hit Otis's head with his own walking stick, possibly causing permanent brain damage. As Mercy described the incident, Otis "was suddenly assaulted in a public room, by a band of ruffians armed with swords and bludgeons," led by Robinson. "The lights were immediately extinguished, and Mr. Otis covered with wounds was left for dead." Although the injuries did not prove mortal, the consequences were "tenfold worse than death," Mercy continued. "The future usefulness of this distinguished *friend* of his country was destroyed, reason was shaken from its throne, genius obscured, and the great man in ruins lived several years."[68] By early 1770, after British soldiers killed five colonists during the Boston Massacre, Adams recorded that Otis had become "raving Mad," firing guns and breaking the windows of the Massachusetts Statehouse.[69]

As Otis's powers of reason failed—and his family had him declared incompetent—his sister took his place as the scourge of British tyranny. In 1770 she wrote a moving poem lamenting her brother's illness called "A Thought on the Inestimable Blessings of Reason, Occasioned by its Privation to a Friend of Very Superior Talents and Virtues." Summing up the essence of classical philosophy, she implored the divine to allow her to continue to use her powers of reason to live in harmony with nature:

That thou this taper should preserve
From reason's laws let me n'er swerve,
But calmly, mistress of my mind
A friend to virtue and mankind.[70]

In 1772 Mercy anonymously published in the Massachusetts Spy newspaper her first political satire, The Adulateur. Using classical pseudonyms, she depicted the conflict in a mythical land called "Servia" between the evil "Rapatio" (representing the imperious Massachusetts royal governor Thomas Hutchinson) and patriots including her brother (whom she called "Brutus") and John Adams ("Hortensius"). Just as Hutchinson's house and papers had been attacked by an angry mob in 1765 protesting against the Stamp Act, Rapatio vows to take revenge on his patriot foes, who have destroyed his property. The play ends with Brutus praising the citizens for their virtuous determination to resist the corruption of Rapatio and his courtiers.

In October 1773 Mercy sent John Adams some private verses calling for the mobilization of republican virtue to counter the corruption of Hutchinson and his relatives. "Does prejudice, and passion, Rule Mankind. / Are there no springs that actuate the Mind, / Whose deep Maeanders, have some Nobler source, / Than Vain self Love; to Guide their Winding Course," she wrote.[71] The satire and the poem were such a success that they led John to offer Mercy an important assignment. On December 16, 1773, a group of rebels disguised as Mohawk Indians ceremonially dumped British tea into Boston Harbor to protest the hated tea tax. The following week, John Adams wrote to James Warren asking Mercy to commemorate the Boston Tea Party in verse. "I wish to See a late glorious Event, celebrated, by a certain poetical Pen, which has no equal that I know of in this Country."[72] Mercy obliged in February 1774, sending a verse to Abigail Adams that developed John's suggestion of a classical satire centered around Neptune, the ancient Roman god of the sea.[73] But while John had suggested focusing on the sons of Neptune, Mercy wrote her poem about his divine daughters instead. "For Females have their Influance over kings," she wrote of the deities who resolve to dump tea in the ocean, "Nor wives, nor Mistresses, were useless things."[74]

John Adams had the piece printed, and it was well received. With his encouragement, Mercy Otis Warren then wrote a series of satires and plays over the next two years, expressing her belief that, like the Romans, the American people were in danger of being corrupted by luxury and greed to surrender their ancient liberties to tyrannical officials of the Crown. Just as individuals could become slaves of passions such as greed, avarice, and ambition, so could societies allow themselves to be enslaved by demagogic rulers who enticed them to exchange their austere virtues for lives of comfortable subservience. To avoid the fate of citizens of the Roman Republic, who surrendered their liberties to the demagogic Caesar, Americans needed to reaffirm the classical virtues of simplicity, self-mastery, frugality, temperance, and fortitude.

Mercy expressed her views on the relationship between public and private virtue and happiness in a letter to her friend Hannah Winthrop in January 1774. "I believe the grandeur, magnificence and wealth of States seldom promotes, either the virtue or happiness of individuals;-where there is the most simplicity of life and manners there is most felicity." She looked forward to a "happy state, such an equal government, [as] may be considered by some as an Utopian dream"—an America whose rulers are not "prompted by avarice or ambition to infringe the natural rights of their fellow men."[75]

Mercy dramatized this classical vision of Roman virtue in a series of satirical plays that followed *The Adulateur*, including *The Defeat* (1773) and, most notably, *The Group*, written at the end of 1774, months before the Battle of Lexington and Concord. *The Group* depicted a Tory conclave of Americans loyal to the British Crown, corrupted by royal bribes and indifferent to the suffering they were inflicting on the virtuous patriots. The Tories gather in a library full of scandalous literature—including Governor Hutchinson's *The History of Massachusetts*, Thomas Hobbes's *Leviathan*, and the Dutch philosopher Bernard Mandeville's 1714 pamphlet *The Fable of the Bees: Or, Private Vices, Publick Benefits*. The fable depicts a hive of bees that collapses when it abandons its devotion to pleasure-seeking self-interest and instead decides to be governed by virtue and sacrifice on behalf of the common good. "Bare Virtue can't make Nations live / In Splendor; they, that would revive / A Golden Age, must be as free, / For Acorns, as for Honesty," Mandeville infamously wrote.[76] In the same spirit, the characters in the group, all modeled on well-known Massachusetts Tories, openly affirm their devotion to placing their own greedy self-interest above the self-sacrifice of patriots like Brutus and the brave multitude, who would rather die than exchange their liberty for royal bribes.

In January 1775 Mercy wrote to John Adams, whom she called one of "the Worthy Guardians of our Freedom and Happiness," asking his opinion of *The Group*. She wondered whether he thought it was consistent with the spirit of "Candour and Charity" for any author—and, in particular, a woman—to write such pointed satires of corrupt public officials.[77] Adams wrote back on March 15 to praise her satirical genius in the most glowing terms. "Of all the Genius's which have yet arisen in America, there has been none, Superiour, to one, which now shines, in this happy, this exquisite Faculty," Adams wrote.[78]

"Aim at an exact Knowledge of the Nature, End, and Means of Government," Adams wrote in his diary in 1759, in the same entry where he recorded his dream of the choice of Hercules. "Compare the different forms of it with each other and each of them with their Effects on public and private Happiness."[79] And in April 1776, as independence approached, Adams made his first sustained effort to sum up what he had learned from the ancient and modern philosophers about the relationship between public and private happiness. As he recalled, "In January, 1776, Mr. George Wythe, of Virginia, passing an evening with me, asked me what plan I would advise a colony to pursue, in order to get out of the old government and into a new one."[80] That month, Adams had already begun to collect his thoughts about the connection between government and the pursuit of happiness in his draft of a Proclamation by the General Court of Massachusetts, which declared, "As the Happiness of the People *alone*, is the sole End of Government, So the Consent of the People is the only Foundation of it, in Reason, Morality, and the natural Fitness of things."[81] Adams developed his thoughts further in a longer draft he gave to Wythe, who happened to be Thomas Jefferson's law professor. Wythe, in turn, gave them to Richard Henry Lee, who in June 1776 would draft the Continental Congress's resolution calling for independence from Great Britain. In April Adams's *Thoughts on Government* were published in Philadelphia by John Dunlap, who would print the first copy of the Declaration of Independence three months later.

"Upon this point all speculative politicians will agree," Adams wrote, "that the happiness of society is the end of government, as all divines and moral philosophers will agree that the happiness of the individual is the end of man. From this principle it will follow, that the form of government, which communicates ease, comfort, security, or in one word happiness to the greatest number of persons, and in the greatest degree, is the best."[82]

What were Adams's sources for these conclusions, which he summed up by noting that "the divine science of politicks is the science of social happiness"?[83] Adams's diary records that in 1759 he read Francis Hutcheson, the Irish moral philosopher who was one of the founders of the Scottish Enlightenment. The claim that the government that communicates the greatest happiness to the greatest number of persons paraphrases Hutcheson's famous formulation from *An Inquiry into the Original of Our Ideas of Beauty and Virtue* (1726): "that Action is best, which procures the greatest Happiness for the greatest numbers."[84]

Adams's conclusion that "the Happiness of the Society must be the fundamental Law of every Government" relies on the Swiss natural law theorist Jean-Jacques Burlamaqui, who wrote in his *Principles of Natural and Politic Law* (1747) that "the felicity of the people is the end of government."[85] When Adams took his oral examination for admission to the bar in 1758, he was asked which books he had read about "the Law of Nature and Nations." "Burlamaqui, sir," Adams replied.[86] Burlamaqui, who taught natural law at the University of Geneva, was another of the most influential philosophers of happiness read by the American Founders. According to Burlamaqui, men are created by nature "all equal, all free and independent of each other," and they form governments and renounce natural liberty "in hopes, that under the protection and care of their sovereign, they should meet with solid happiness." This means that all laws passed by government should "be ultimately designed for [our] happiness, which reason makes [us] necessarily pursue."[87]

Adams had other sources for his conclusion that "all speculative politicians will agree, that the happiness of society is the end of government." He owned a copy of Edward Wortley Montagu's *Reflections on the Rise and Fall of the Ancient Republicks* (1759), which he cited in 1776.[88] Montagu, a Whig politician, studied free states in ancient times and concluded that they were founded on "this just and benevolent plan, that the safety and happiness of the whole community was the only end of all government."[89] He went on to show how the corruptions of five ancient republics could provide lessons for modern Britain. Adams synthesized these points into his conclusion that unlike most monarchies, which are founded on fear, and aristocracies, which are founded on honor, republican governments, which he defined as "an Empire of Laws, and not of men," are founded on virtue. For this reason, a republican government is "better calculated to promote the general happiness than any other form."[90]

Adams was channeling Aristotle's warning that governments based entirely on one part of society—the one, the few, or the many—could degenerate into a corrupt form. Monarchy, based on rule by the one, could degenerate into tyranny. Aristocracy, based on rule by the few, could degenerate into oligarchy. And what Aristotle called "polity," or a mixed regime based on rule by the many, could degenerate into democracy, or rule by the mob. The best governments, Adams insisted, separated the three "powers of society" with the goal of preserving liberty.[91] "Liberty depends upon an exact Balance, a nice Counterpoise of the Powers in the state," he wrote in his 1772 Notes for an Oration in Braintree. "The best Governments in the World have been mixed."[92] Adams insisted on the importance of mixing and balancing the three social orders—represented in England by the king, the lords, and the people—until the end of his life. "The fundamental Article of my political Creed," Adams wrote in a letter to Thomas Jefferson, "is, that Despotism, or unlimited Sovereignty, or absolute Power is the same in a Majority of a popular Assembly, and Aristocratical Counsel, an oligarchical Junto and a single Emperor."[93] For this reason, in his *Thoughts on Government*, he recommended a complicated system of checks and balances: the popular house would elect an aristocratic council, and the two bodies, in turn, would elect a governor, with all three bodies subject to annual elections. Adams insisted that annual elections would teach the people's representatives "the great political virtues of humility, patience, and moderation, without which every man in power becomes a ravenous beast of prey."[94]

At the same time, Adams worried that the people might lack the virtue necessary to sacrifice their self-interest for the public good, or res publica. He turned to classical Rome to suggest protective measures that the new government could pass to encourage virtue, including term limits, an independent judiciary, publicly funded education, and sumptuary laws to promote frugality—in other words, laws that restricted the extravagant purchases of food, drink, and luxurious dress. "The very mention of sumptuary laws will excite a smile," Adams, who was still a Puritan, wrote in *Thoughts on Government*. "Whether our countrymen have wisdom and virtue enough to submit to them I know not. But the happiness of the people might be greatly promoted by them."[95]

Adams had faith that, through self-restraint and education, the people could cultivate the habits of personal self-government necessary for political self-government. "Laws for the liberal education of youth," he insisted, would inspire "good humour, sociability, good manners, and good morals." Adams's conclusion was that by promoting virtue through education, a republic could fulfill its primary end: to increase the happiness of the people. "That elevation of sentiment, inspired by such a government, makes the common people brave and enterprizing," he wrote. "That ambition which is inspired by it makes them sober, industrious and frugal. You will find among them some elegance, perhaps, but more solidity; a little pleasure, but a great deal of business—some politeness, but more civility." Compared with a monarchy or an aristocracy, virtuous citizens in the virtuous new republic would imagine themselves living "in Arcadia or Elisium"—in other words, in paradise.[96]

And what about the education of women? This was a topic that John and Abigail Adams began to discuss with Mercy and her husband, James Warren, after they first met as couples at the Warrens' house in 1773. In July Abigail wrote to thank Mercy for the kind reception she and John had received and also to ask her opinion of a parenting manual they had discussed during their visit, *On the Management and Education of Children*, by "the Honourable Juliana-Susannah Seymour." Presented as "a series of letters written to a young niece," the widely circulated book was, in fact, written by an enterprising man, the English botanist and actor John Hill. It offers advice about the need for mothers to cultivate the characters of their young daughters and sons, teaching them by example how to use their powers of reason to control anger and other unproductive emotions. Praising Mercy's own attentions to her "well ordered family," Abigail copied out a poem about the importance of teaching self-mastery to daughters as well as to sons. (The "Parent who vast pleasure find's / In forming of her childrens minds. . . . Each Boisterous passion to controul / And early Humanize the Soul.")[97]

Mercy thanked Abigail for "the ingenious Mrs. Seymours treatise on Education," which she acknowledged was "Generally admired." As for her own child-rearing advice, she lamented the fact that the "mighty task of cultivating the minds and planting the seeds of Virtue in the infant Bosom" was "almost wholly left to our uninstructed sex."[98] However, inspired by her own classical reading and education, she agreed with Abigail that girls and boys should be educated on equal terms. Although in ancient Rome, as in colonial America, women were under the legal dominion of their husbands and fathers, the Stoic Seneca had recognized the equal intellectual capacities of men and women. As he wrote in his letters of consolation to a female friend named Marcia, who was mourning the death of her son: "[W]ho would say that nature has dealt grudgingly with the minds of women, and stunted their virtues? Believe me, they have the same intellectual power as men, and the same capacity for honourable and generous action. If trained to do so, they are just as able to endure sorrow or labour."[99]

In her famous letter urging John to "Remember the Ladies" in the design of the new government, Abigail Adams encouraged her husband to repudiate English law, which gave husbands unlimited control over their wives. "In the New Code of Laws which I suppose it will be necessary for you to make I desire you would Remember the Ladies, and be more generous and favourable to them than your ancestors," she wrote after Congress declared independence in 1776. Stressing that "all Men would be tyrants if they could," she warned that "[i]f perticuliar care and attention is not paid to the Laidies we are determined to foment a Rebelion, and will not hold ourselves bound by any Laws in which we have no voice, or Representation." If men would be happy, they would use the lawmaking power to ensure women's equal happiness, and "willingly give up the harsh title of Master for the more tender and endearing one of Friend."[100]

Adams's reply was disappointingly glib. "As to your extraordinary Code of Laws, I cannot but laugh," he wrote. "We know better than to repeal our Masculine systems."[101] Abigail lamented his dismissive tone in a letter to Mercy Otis Warren. "He is very sausy to me in return for a List of Female Grievances which I transmitted to him [and] I think

I will get you to join me in a petition to Congress," she wrote on April 27, 1776. "In return he tells me he cannot but Laugh at My Extrodonary Code of Laws." Abigail resolved to tell her husband that, in advocating for her sex, "I have only been making trial of the Disintresstedness of his Virtue, and when weigh'd in the balance have found it wanting."[102]

Although Mercy did not reply to this protest, Abigail refused to abandon her advocacy for equal education. "If you complain of neglect of Education in sons, What shall I say with regard to daughters, who every day experience the want of it," she wrote to John in August 1776, lamenting that she felt out of her depth in educating their children because of the deficiencies in her own education. "If we mean to have Heroes, Statesmen and Philosophers, we should have learned women," she insisted.[103] On the question of education, John concurred enthusiastically. "Your Sentiments of the Importance of Education in Women, are exactly agreable to my own," he wrote.[104]

As independence approached, John Adams demonstrated his respect for the equal rights of women by seeking Mercy Otis Warren's advice about the most fundamental question of the day: What kind of government would best promote virtue and happiness? Adams said he thought republics best, but he acknowledged "one Difficulty" on the horizon. "There is So much Rascallity, so much Venality and Corruption, so much Avarice and Ambition, such a Rage for Profit and Commerce among all Ranks and Degrees of Men even in America, that I sometimes doubt whether there is public Virtue enough to support a Republic," he wrote her at the beginning of 1776.[105] Mercy replied on March 10, expressing similar concerns. Like Adams, she favored a republic to a monarchy but feared "that American Virtue has not yet Reach'd that sublime pitch" necessary to sustain it.[106]

After the Revolution, Adams and Warren split on the question of whether the American people had sufficient virtue to sustain a republic, and the fissure cost them their friendship for a time. In the 1780s and 1790s, Adams became increasingly pessimistic about the people's capacity to put the public good ahead of their selfish interests. In 1787, while serving as the first American ambassador to London, Adams watched in horror as mob violence broke out in western Massachusetts and a group of debtors, led by the Revolutionary War veteran Daniel Shays, attacked a courthouse to avoid paying their debts. As a principal drafter of the Massachusetts Constitution of 1780, which he designed to check democratic excesses with an independent judiciary, an aristocratic Senate, and a strong governor, Adams now despaired that education might never eradicate the inequalities he perceived among men.

The same year that the Constitutional Convention was convening in Philadelphia, Adams published from London his *Defence of the Constitutions of Government of the United States of America*, a rambling and pessimistic collection of essays questioning the premise of the Declaration of Independence: that all men are created equal. "Was there, or will there ever be, a nation, whose individuals were all equal, in natural and acquired qualities, in virtues, talents, and riches?" he asked. In every American state, he insisted, "there are inequalities which God and nature have planted there, and which no human legislator ever can eradicate."[107] Adams was responding in particular to the Pennsylvania Constitution's democratic decision to create a one-house state legislature, which he thought was a bad idea and would consolidate power in the mob. Adams's proposed solution was to double down on the separation of powers, arguing for a lower house composed of the common people and an upper house composed of the gentry, checked by a strong executive.

In the 1790s Adams grew even more pessimistic about the possibility that the mass of citizens had an equal capacity to cultivate public and private virtue. Recognizing his struggles to overcome his vanity, he became convinced that the "desire of the attention, consideration, and congratulations of our fellow men" was the "great leading passion of the soul," which nature had inscribed into its "texture and essence."[108] (Once again projecting his own vices onto others, Adams accused "the Grand Franklin" of vanity as well.) He was especially struck by Adam Smith's chapter in *The Theory of Moral Sentiments*, "Of the Origin of Ambition, and of the Distinction of Ranks," which emphasized that all people have a powerful desire to win the admiration and avoid the contempt of others. "Our obsequiousness to our superiors" results from our admiration of "the passions of the rich and the powerful," Smith wrote, and the result is "distinction of ranks" throughout society.[109] According to the historian Gordon Wood, it was Adams's reading of Smith that led him to conclude that the best way to regulate human ambition was to make the offices of government hereditary.[110] After trying "all possible experiments of elections of Governors and Senates," Adams wrote in one of his *Discourses on Davila*, published in 1790, history suggested that "hereditary succession was attended with fewer evils than frequent elections."[111] This conclusion, along with his high-handed behavior after his election as president in 1796, led to charges that Adams was a closet monarchist, which would lead to his break with Mercy Otis Warren and Thomas Jefferson—and to defeat in the election of 1800.

Adams made things worse by treating Mercy carelessly. When he took office as George Washington's vice president, she asked him to find a position for her husband in the new government. Instead of explaining that he lacked control over patronage, Adams announced pompously that his virtue precluded him from granting political favors; he then went out of his way to criticize her husband for supporting Shays's Rebellion.[112] Put off by Adams's manner as well as his politics, both Warrens became Jeffersonian Republicans, whose main claim in the election of 1800 was that President Adams and the Federalist Party had become secret defenders of monarchy.

In 1805 Mercy published her three-volume *History of the Rise, Progress and Termination of the American Revolution,* which argued that Adams had "forgotten the principles of the American revolution." It included only five pages on Adams, but it cut him to the quick, accusing him of abandoning republicanism for monarchy and allowing ambition to overcome his virtue. "Mr. Adams was undoubtedly a statesman of penetration and ability; but his prejudices and his passions were sometimes too strong for his sagacity and judgment," she wrote. After his return from

England as American ambassador, he had "unfortunately for himself and his country bec[o]me so enamoured with the British constitution" that he developed a partiality for monarchy, which was "inconsistent with his former professions of republicanism." When he succeeded George Washington as president, Mercy charged, Adams displayed "[p]ride of talents and much ambition" that "had a powerful tendency to shake the republican system through the United States."[113]

In the spirit of "candor and forgiveness of injuries," Mercy emphasized that despite "any mistakes or changes in political opinion, or errors in public conduct, Mr. Adams, in private life, supported an unimpeachable character." She praised "his habits of morality, decency and religion," which "rendered him amiable in his family, and beloved by his neighbours." But Mercy suggested that because of the betrayal of republican principles, "party feuds have thus divided a nation." Her conclusion: "influenced by the most malignant and corrupt passions," citizens were losing sight "of the sacred obligations of virtue" and risked being seduced by "artful or ambitious men who may subvert the system which the inhabitants of the United States judged to be most conducive to the general happiness of society."[114]

Mercy Otis Warren expressed hope that readers would pursue her *History* "with kindness and candor . . . in consideration of her sex, the uprightness of her intentions, and the fervency of her wishes for the happiness of all the human race."[115] But kindness and candor were not the emotions that Adams exhibited when a copy of Mercy's book arrived in Braintree. On July 11, 1807, Adams wrote to "Mrs. Warren" with agitation and wounded pride. He had read most of her history, he said, and would not allow "misunderstanding," "Resentment," or "hostility" to convert an "ancient Friend" into an "Enemy." Nevertheless, he had a few errors to correct. Mercy had written that his "Passions and Prejudices were sometimes too strong for his Sagacity and Judgment," and "I will not, I cannot say that this is not true," Adams confessed. But "I can and will say with the Utmost sincerity, that I am not conscious of having ever in my life taken one public Step or performed one public

Act from Passion or Prejudice, or from any other Motive than the Public Good."[116]

Adams also took strong exception to Mercy's claim that he had a "Partiality for Monarchy." He had always favored a "mixed Elective Government in three Branches." He rejected the hereditary monarchy and aristocracy of the British constitution, whose principles he had otherwise learned to admire from writers on government, including Montesquieu, Bacon, Bolingbroke, and Sidney, as well as from James Otis, James Warren, and Mercy herself. Could she substantiate her claim that he was a secret monarchist? He awaited her reply "with impatience."[117]

Mercy replied as soon as she received Adams's letter, on July 16. She had tried to write her history with "truth and candor," she said, but Adams had not responded in the same spirit of "candor and friendship" with which he once viewed her compositions. "Your warmest friends and acquaintances" would never contradict her claim that he was subject to "passions and prejudices like other men," and she had personally heard him "advocate for Monarchic Government."[118]

At this point, Adams became unhinged. He unleashed a series of letters boasting that others had testified to his honesty, integrity, and central role in American history. He had heard from Warren's friend John Dickinson and "many other sources" at the Constitutional Convention that his book *A Defence of the Constitutions of Government* "had produced an entire Revolution in the Sentiments of the Convention, and influenced the Members to agree to the Constitution that was adopted." In addition, he boasted, the general principles of his book had influenced "Mr Jay, Mr Madison, and Mr Hamilton" when they wrote *The Federalist Papers*.[119] Mercy's own brother, James Otis, had testified, "many years before I was a Representative that John Adams would one day be the greatest Man in North America." And Adams insisted that his 1774 resolutions had been the basis for the principles that Jefferson inserted into the Declaration of Independence. "All these little Anecdotes you will Say are Proofs of my 'Pride of Talent,'" Adams wrote. "Be it so. Make the most you can of them Mrs Warren."[120]

Adams protested that he never believed he had "any Talents beyond mediocrity," and if "I could be proud of any Thing it would be Industry." But he couldn't help adding his "great Satisfaction in believing" that he had "made greater Sacrifices, than any Man among my Contemporaries living or dead, in the Service of my Country." Could Mercy name any man who had "Suffered and Sacrificed So much?" Adams asked. "You may call this Pride or Vanity or Self Sufficiency, or vain Glory or what you please. But it is the Truth."[121]

Adams was especially outraged to hear that Mercy's husband, James Warren, said he had been corrupted by power. "Corrupted! Madam!" he exclaimed. "What Provocation, what evidence, what Misrepresentation" could have prompted Warren "to utter this execrable Calumny?" Adams recalled that when their mutual friend Elbridge Gerry, a Massachusetts Anti-Federalist, asked a French nobleman "whether he thought Mr John Adams might not be corrupted," the chevalier replied, "one might as well attempt to corrupt Jesus Christ."[122] And he accused Mercy of corruption, in turn, suggesting that she had turned against him because he had denied her husband an appointment as tax collector for the Port of Plymouth.

All of this was too much for Mercy Otis Warren, and Adams's gossiping about the king of France making a chamber pot with Benjamin Franklin's face on it was, as it were, the final straw. She upbraided Adams for his "vindictive" feelings, "paroxysms of rage," and "fall from decency and dignity" in relating the "obscene anecdote."[123] On August 27 she'd had enough. "The lines with which you concluded your late correspondence cap the climax of rancor, indecency, and vulgarism," she wrote. "Yet, as an old friend, I pity you, and as a Christian, I forgive you." Still, she concluded indignantly, Adams would have to acknowledge his injurious treatment and offer a sign of reconciliation "before I can again feel that respect and affection towards Mr. Adams which once existed in the bosom of Mercy Warren."[124]

Adams did not apologize for his letters, and he and Warren had no contact for the next six years. But in 1812, after learning about Adams's reconciliation with Thomas Jefferson, Mercy resolved to repair her relationship with Adams as well. She asked Elbridge Gerry to offer an olive branch to Abigail. Reports that a Republican congressman had been assaulted in August by a Federalist mob on Mercy's front steps quickened Abigail's sympathy. Abigail visited Mercy, now an octogenarian patriot, in Plymouth in September, accompanied by her daughter and granddaughter. The visit, after years of separation, was sufficiently successful that Mercy sent Abigail a locket of her hair as a token of friendship. After initial hesitation on John's part, Abigail reciprocated by sending a locket containing strands of her own hair intertwined with that of John and Mercy. This moving gesture opened the door for John Adams gingerly to resume his correspondence with Mercy. In September 1813 he sent her a respectful memorial that he had written on the death of Franklin in 1789.

After a friendly exchange of old memories, Mercy asked John for a favor. "Do you remember who was the author of a little pamphlet entitled *The Group*?" she asked on July 10, 1814, referring to the Revolutionary satire she had written years ago at his request. A friend of hers who recently visited the Boston Athenæum had seen it among a bundle of other pamphlets, with a notice on the title page asserting that it had been written by someone called Samuel Barrett. Adams was one of the two people alive who could contradict this "false assertion."[125]

Adams wrote back five days later. He would swear on his Bible that "there was but one person in the world, male or female," who could have written *The Group*. "And that person was Madam Mercy Warren."[126] Adams then rode into Boston and walked with determination into the Athenæum. As he wrote to Mercy on August 17, "I have certified in the book in the Athenæum that to my certain Knowledge, The Group was written by Mrs: Warren."[127] Visitors to the Athenæum today can see his signature on the pamphlet. It is testament to Adams's ability to overcome his powerful vanity and easily wounded pride, as well as to his candor, capacity for forgiveness, and, in the end, humility. He would show a similar capacity for growth in his friendship, break, and reconciliation with Thomas Jefferson.

Notes on Seneca's "On Saving Time"

I wake today too late and with a gasp
Find Sun already rising into clouds
I must hold every moment in my grasp
Sun reemerges as I write; it glows

While we postpone our tasks, life passes by
Tune in and focus on the present hour
Happy the man who knows each day we die
Nothing is ours but time; let's seize its power

Sun rises each day to eternity
One day is all our days' equivalence
So every day should regulated be
As if it rounded out our existence

Time is a loan repaid by industry
By squandering it, what fools these mortals be!

Four

INDUSTRY

Thomas Jefferson's Reading List

A round 1758, at the same time John Adams was copying passages from Cicero into his diary, the young Thomas Jefferson was copying into his own diary another passage from Cicero—the same one that he would send to a group of Maine students nearly sixty years later as the epitome of his philosophy about the pursuit of happiness:

Therefore the man, whoever he is, whose soul is tranquillized by restraint and consistency and who is at peace with himself, so that he neither pines away in distress, nor is broken down by fear, nor consumed with a thirst of longing in pursuit of some ambition, nor maudlin in the exuberance of meaningless eagerness—he is the wise man of whom we are in quest, he is the happy man.[1]

It's not a surprise that Jefferson found the passage meaningful. His father, Peter Jefferson, had died the previous year, and Jefferson took consolation in Cicero's words, which the Roman philosopher and states-man had written to console himself after his only daughter, Tullia, died in childbirth around 45 BC. Cicero had visited his longtime friend Atticus in the early weeks of his bereavement and read the works of Greek philoso-phy in Atticus's library in search of guidance about how to overcome his grief. In letters he sent to Atticus from his villa in Tusculum, in the Alban hills of Italy, Cicero lamented that "my sorrow is too much for any conso-lation. Nay, I have done what certainly no one ever did before me: tried to console myself by writing a book." But writing all day could provide only a temporary respite, for "the violence of my grief is overpowering."[2]

Jefferson was devoted to his father, and his own grief must have been overpowering as well. He acquired his lifelong habits of self-improvement through disciplined reading from Peter Jefferson, whose own "educa-tion had been quite neglected," Jefferson recalled, "but being of a strong mind, sound judgment, and eager after information, he read much and improved himself."[3] In the spirit of self-reliance, his father told him, "Never ask another to do what you can do yourself."[4] (Relying on en-slaved labor to support their lifestyles, Peter Jefferson and his son did not honor the injunction.) On his deathbed, Peter Jefferson gave his son two other edicts, which he took seriously: that he receive a proper classical education and that he never neglect physical exercise.[5] Jefferson, who began studying Greek and Latin at age nine, recalled later: "If I were to decide between the pleasures derived from the classical education which my father gave me, and the estate left me, I should decide in favor of the former."[6]

Jefferson's career after he wrote the Declaration of Independence is well known: governor of Virginia, secretary of state under George Washing-ton, vice president under John Adams, and a president who doubled the size of the United States with the Louisiana Purchase. He put none of these distinctions on his tombstone, listing only his authorship of the Declaration and the Virginia Statute for Religious Freedom, and his founding the University of Virginia. Those three achievements, the ones he considered the most significant, were united by Jefferson's faith in what he called "the illimitable freedom of the human mind," based on his commitment—in theory if not always in practice—"to follow truth wherever it may lead, nor to tolerate any error so long as reason is left free to combat it."[7] Jefferson's unwavering faith in the power of reason to vanquish passion began with his classical education.

Jefferson learned from Cicero the overriding importance of pursuing happiness by cultivating a "soul . . . tranquillized by restraint and consistency." But to achieve a sense of being "at peace with himself," Jefferson compartmentalized his own contradictions so carefully that his personality might be compared to a Chinese box. Others have used different metaphors to describe Jefferson's determination to conceal his inner conflicts even from himself—from Chief Justice John Marshall, who called him "the great lama of the Mountain" to the historian Joseph Ellis, who referred to him as an "American Sphinx."[8] Jefferson shrank from the perturbations of personal and political life by withdrawing whenever possible to the classical temple he built for himself at Monticello, where he indulged the Ciceronian ideal of a tranquil life of reading and gentleman farming, devoted to cultivating his books and his garden.

Jefferson achieved this classical idyll only because of his lifelong exploitation of enslaved labor, despite his repeated insistence that slavery violated the principles of equal liberty he enshrined in the Declaration of Independence. Jefferson denounced other enslavers for their unwillingness to abandon the lifestyle that slavery made possible because of their avaricious addiction to luxury and comfort. But he refused to acknowledge that he was guilty of precisely the same hypocrisy by constructing his life around self-justifying illusions—telling himself that the light-skinned slaves in his own house were servants, for example, rather than his own children by Sally Hemmings, whom he also held in bondage. For Jefferson, inner tranquility required self-rationalization as well as self-mastery, and the cost of his relentless quest for psychological order was his lack of self-awareness.

In this sense, Jefferson's personality was very different from that of Adams. If Adams invited conflict, Jefferson avoided it. If Adams struggled openly to overcome his vanity, Jefferson cultivated airs of republican simplicity. If Adams projected onto the mass of humanity his own egoistic desire for fame and attention, Jefferson projected onto the mass of humanity his illusions about his own benevolence and good feeling. Adams regarded the mass of people as prone to selfishness and vice, while Jefferson idealistically imagined them inclined to virtue. But Jefferson read the same classical and Enlightenment moral philosophers that Adams and Franklin did, and he took from those philosophers the same Pythagorean determination to use every moment of the day industriously—cultivating his mind, body, thoughts, and faculties in order to achieve the mental tranquility he was determined to maintain at all costs.

"Determine never to be idle," he wrote his daughter Martha from Marseilles, France, in May 1787. "No person will have occasion to complain of the want of time, who never loses any. It is wonderful how much may be done, if we are always doing."[9] Writing again two weeks later from the Canal of Languedoc, where he was sailing, Jefferson told his daughter that if she ever was bored, it was her own fault. (My mother gave me the same excellent advice.) He was determined, he said, to see both his daughters "developing daily those principles of virtue and goodness which will make you valuable to others and happy in yourselves" as well as "acquiring those talents and that degree of science which will guard you at all times against ennui," or boredom, which Jefferson called "the most dangerous poison of life." According to Jefferson, "[a] mind always employed is always happy. This is the true secret, the grand recipe for felicity. The idle are the only wretched." Warning Martha to practice the harpsichord and avoid gambling, he stressed that in a world with so many useful and amusing employments, "it is our own fault if we ever know what ennui is."[10]

In a 1785 letter to his nephew Peter Carr, Jefferson emphasized his father's advice about the importance of industry, which required daily

physical as well as mental exercise. "Encourage all your virtuous dispositions, and exercise them whenever an opportunity arises, being assured
that they will gain strength by exercise as a limb of the body does, and
that exercise will make them habitual," Jefferson wrote. "Give about two
[hours] every day to exercise; for health must not be sacrificed to learning. A strong body makes the mind strong." As to the specifics of exercise, Jefferson recommended shooting and long walks in the afternoon.
And in the Pythagorean spirit of mindful living in the moment, he advised Carr to focus his attention on nature during his hikes rather than
allowing himself to be distracted by unproductive thoughts. "The object
of walking is to relax the mind," Jefferson wrote. "You should therefore
not permit yourself even to think while you walk. But divert your attention by the objects surrounding you."[11]

Jefferson requested frequent accountings of his nephew's progress.
"I am anxious to hear from you, to know how your time is employed,
and what books you read," Jefferson wrote to Carr in 1783 when the
thirteen-year-old was beginning his studies with Jefferson's own tutor,
Reverend James Maury, whom Jefferson had praised as a "correct classical scholar." Cautioning Carr to "never waste a moment" and to submit
to Maury's "strict discipline" with "resolution" and "resignation," Jefferson said, "[y]ou will find it contribute to your happiness in the end."[12]

Jefferson's most systematic attempt to codify his life lessons about
industry, virtue, and happiness came in his list of twelve virtues, which he
called "cannons of conduct in life." He sent the list to his granddaughter
Cornelia Jefferson Randolph and later shared the list with friends starting in 1817:

1. never put off to tomorrow what you can do to-day.
2. never trouble another with what you can do yourself.
3. never spend your money before you have it.
4. never buy a thing you do not want, because it is cheap, it will
    be dear to you.
5. take care of your cents: Dollars will take care of themselves!

6. pride costs us more than hunger, thirst and cold.

7. we never repent of having eat[en] too little.

8. nothing is troublesome that one does willingly.

9. how much pain have cost us the evils which have never happened!·

10. take things always by their smooth handle.

11. think as you please, & so let others, & you will have no disputes.

12. when angry, count 10. before you speak; if very angry, 100.[13]

Jefferson includes most of Franklin's original twelve virtues on his list. Although it's not clear whether he read Franklin, we know that both men were inspired by Cicero's *Tusculan Disputations*. In the reading list Jefferson had drafted for Robert Skipwith in 1771, he suggested books he might assemble for a private library. He revised the list in 1773 for Bernard Moore, a friend's son who was heading for law school, specifying not only the books to be read but also the time of day they should be studied. Jefferson noted that "the faculties of the mind, like the members of the body, are strengthened & improved by exercise."[14] He then set out a challenging, ten-hour-a-day reading schedule that seems to have been modeled on Jefferson's own Pythagorean reading schedule as a student. It was divided into five parts.

1. From dawn until eight in the morning, Jefferson suggested "Physical studies"—including agriculture, chemistry, anatomy, zoology, and botany—followed by ethics, religion, and natural law, including the following works. Under ethics and natural religion: Locke's *An Essay Concerning Human Understanding* and *Some Thoughts on the Conduct of the Understanding in Search of the Truth*; Cicero's *De Officiis (On Duties)*, *Tusculan Disputations*, *De Senectute (On Old Age)*, and *The Dream of Scipio*; Seneca's *Philosophica*; Lord Kames's *Essays on the Principles of Morality and Natural Religion*, and—an important addition from his

original list—Francis Hutcheson's *A Short Introduction to Moral Philosophy*.

2. From eight until noon, Jefferson recommended reading law, including *Coke's Institutes*, Lord Kames's *Principles of Equity*, and Sir William Blackstone's *Commentaries on the Laws of England*.

3. From noon to one came politics, including Locke's *Two Treatises on Civil Government* and Algernon Sidney's *Discourses Concerning Government*.

4. In the afternoon, Jefferson recommended reading history: English, American, and ancient history in Greek and Latin, as well as Edward Gibbon's *The History of the Decline and Fall of the Roman Empire*.

5. After dark came belles lettres, rhetoric, criticism, and oratory, including Shakespeare (to "learn the full powers of the English language") and the orations of Demosthenes and Cicero. Jefferson recommended learning the habits of deliberation by preparing orations on hypothetical cases, working with "any person in your neighborhood engaged in the same study" with "each of you" taking "different sides" of the same case.

6. And then to bed.[15]

From Jefferson's reading list, we can reconstruct which books of moral and political philosophy he had in mind when he said that the Declaration was an attempt to "harmoni[ze] sentiments of the day," reflected in books and essays by authors such as Aristotle, Cicero, Locke, and Sidney. He was referring to Aristotle's *Ethics* and *Politics*, Cicero's *Tusculan Disputations* and *On Duties*, Locke's *Two Treatises on Civil Government* and *An Essay Concerning Human Understanding*, Sidney's *Discourses Concerning Government*, as well as other well-known books of moral and political philosophy such as Blackstone's *Commentaries*. All of these books share the same understanding of happiness as a quest that requires the pursuit of virtue.

If we review the books in the "ethics and natural religion" section of Jefferson's reading list, we can reconstruct his original understanding of the pursuit of happiness. Let's begin, as Jefferson did, with Cicero. *Tusculan Disputations* made a profound impact on Jefferson, who read it in Latin. Of the classical authors Jefferson copied around the time of his father's death into his commonplace book of quotations he found especially significant, Cicero was the only philosopher—the rest are Latin poets.[16] By reading Cicero's advice book through Jefferson's eyes, we can watch his turns of mind as he works through the ancient wisdom about the need for emotional self-control in the face of grief, loss, and misfortune.

First, some background on the author, which Jefferson would have learned from Plutarch's *The Life of Cicero*. In addition to coming to terms with his recent divorce and the death of his daughter, Marcus Tullius Cicero was at an especially vulnerable point in his political career, having recently returned to Rome in the middle of the civil war between Pompey and Julius Caesar. In fact, Cicero wrote nearly all of his important philosophical works during the burst of productivity that coincided with his withdrawal from political life from 46 to 43 BC. As Plutarch relates, he was called Cicero, the Latin word for *chickpea*, because the vent at the end of his nose resembled a chickpea. He was famous in his youth for his learning in philosophy, poetry, oratory, and law, developing a reputation as the best poet and orator of Rome. He studied Greek philosophy in Athens, embracing many of the Stoic doctrines. He then continued his studies in Alexandria, Egypt, where his teacher foretold that he would transfer the glories of oratory and philosophy from Greece to Rome. According to Plutarch, the Greek oracle at Delphi told Cicero to make "his own genius, and not the opinion of the people the guide of his life." Nevertheless, his ambition was kindled by his successful defense in Sicily of a group of young Roman noblemen accused of neglecting their military duties. His powerful speeches helped bring about their acquittal. On returning to Rome, however, he was distressed to find that his reputation hadn't preceded him and tried to get his ambition under control, recognizing that the pursuit of glory had no fixed end. "He was always excessively pleased with his own praise," Plutarch writes, "and continued to the very last to be passionately fond of glory; which often interfered with the prosecution of his wisest resolutions."[17]

Cicero made his name in Rome with his flamboyant prosecution of Gaius Verres, a corrupt governor of Sicily (his speech "Against Verres" is a model of controlled sarcasm), and, at the age of forty-two, he was elected consul, the highest elected office in Rome. Trusted but not loved by both the oligarchs and the people, he claimed to have saved the Roman Republic when he unmasked a conspiracy by the debauched politician Lucius Sergius Catilina, or Catiline. Dramatically interrogating the traitor before his Senate colleagues (who refused to sit next to Catiline in disgust), Cicero then read to the Senate Catiline's letters identifying his co-conspirators and their violent plans. (His *Catiline Orations* were widely studied during the American Revolution as a model for the defense of republican liberty.) Cicero then persuaded the Senate to condemn Catiline and his fellow conspirators to death, over the objection of Julius Caesar, who advocated clemency.

This harsh verdict would come back to haunt Cicero when he became entangled in the politics that would ultimately lead to the fall of the Roman Republic. The tribune Publius Clodius Pulcher, a populist demagogue, sought to have him put to death for having executed the Catiline conspirators without a trial. After being assaulted by a mob hurling stones and excrement as he walked through the streets of Rome, Cicero fell into depression and went into exile. Eventually recalled by the Senate, Cicero distinguished himself as governor of Cilicia, where he was praised for his financial honesty and defense of civil rights. But on returning to Rome in 49 BC, he repeatedly picked the wrong side in the battles leading up to the fall of the republic. He sided with Pompey over Caesar, who, after defeating Pompey the following year, pardoned Cicero for his error.

It was during this period of political uncertainty that Cicero's daughter died, and he wrote *Tusculan Disputations*, which became one of the most widely read attempts to popularize Stoic philosophy of all time. Its five chapters teach us how to have contempt for worldly things and to look on death as a blessing rather than an evil; to bear pain, grief, and other "perturbations of the mind" with fortitude; to moderate all our other passions; and to understand that virtue alone is necessary for a happy life.

One of the first passages that Jefferson copied into his diary poses the central question of Cicero's first chapter, "On Contempt of Death": "What satisfaction can there be in living, when day and night we have to reflect that at this or that moment we must die?"[18] Cicero notes Plato's famous division of the soul into three parts: reason, passion, and desire. Happiness, Cicero says (following Pythagoras, Plato, and Aristotle), occurs when we apply our powers of reason to calm and moderate our turbulent and violent passions and desires, liberating ourselves from our bodily pains and anxieties by controlling the only thing we can control: namely, our thoughts.

At the beginning of chapter 2, "on bearing pain," Jefferson copied out a passage expressing the standard Stoic argument that because death is inevitable, no one who fears death can be happy.[19] Cicero emphasizes that moral philosophy, "the medicine of our souls," can help free us from all groundless apprehensions, desires, and fears.[20] Its effects will be strongest, he says, among those who are able to practice the four classical virtues. Prudence, the foundation of all virtues, will help us avoid unproductive thoughts, emotions, and labor. Temperance will ensure that we do nothing to excess. Justice will prevent us from discovering the secrets of others, betraying our friends and colleagues, and shirking our duties to others. And courage will ensure that we despise death and pain, acting with "greatness of soul, resolution, patience, and contempt for all worldly things."[21]

At the beginning of chapter 3, which deals with overcoming grief, Jefferson copied out a passage that would become central for the Scottish Enlightenment philosophers, who repeatedly used the phrase "the pursuit of happiness." Cicero writes that we are born with an innate moral sense that is "natural to our constitutions" and, if allowed to mature, would "naturally conduct us to a happy life."[22] What prevents us from cultivating the seeds of virtue are what Cicero calls the "perturbations of the mind"—including anger, envy, and lust for revenge. Those who are overcome by anger, Cicero writes, have lost command over themselves; they are said "not to be masters of themselves" because "they are not under the government of reason." Soundness of mind depends on "a certain tranquility and steadiness," qualities inconsistent with a perturbed mind or a disordered body.[23] Jefferson was struck by Cicero's comparison of mental commotion to the violent motions of a storm and copied out the following passage. "We are not sprung from rock, but our souls have a strain of tenderness and sensitiveness of a kind to be shaken by distress as by a storm."[24]

In chapter 4, "On Other Perturbations of the Mind," Cicero writes that he will follow Pythagoras and Plato, who divided the mind into two parts: the rational, which was the source of "tranquility," and the irrational, which housed "the turbid motions of anger and desire."[25] When our temporary perturbations of the mind harden into habits or dispositions, they can become permanent character traits, which Cicero compares to diseases of the body. Like the body, the mind is said to be healthy when its judgments, rooted in reason, and emotions and desires, rooted in passion, are aligned harmoniously. "And this union is the virtue of the mind, which, according to some people, is temperance itself."[26] This leads to the passage that Jefferson copied and shared throughout his life: Cicero's definition of the wise and happy man as one "whose soul is tranquillized by restraint and consistency and who is at peace with himself."

Around a year after Cicero completed *Tusculan Disputations*, on the Ides of March in 44 BC, Brutus and other Roman senators assassinated Julius Caesar. Although Cicero wasn't involved in the conspiracy, Brutus called Cicero's name while lifting the bloody dagger from Caesar's body and implored him to restore the republic. This understandably earned him the enmity of Marc Antony, who became Cicero's main rival for the leadership of Rome. Attacking Antony in a series of speeches known as the *Philippics*, Cicero praised and flattered Caesar's adopted son, Octavian, later known as Caesar Augustus. But after Antony and Octavian reconciled, Octavian turned on Cicero and condemned him to death. Cicero's servants tried to carry him to safety in a litter, and, as his assassins caught up to him, Plutarch emphasizes Cicero's fortitude, self-control, and calm acceptance of his fate. By Antony's command, his assassins cut off the hands that had written the *Philippics*. And then, as Cicero bravely bared his neck for the final blow, they cut off his head. With his fortitude in death, Cicero had achieved his own ideal of the happy man at peace with himself, tranquilized by his own mental consistency.

The Roman Republic fell shortly after, but Cicero's reputation as a moral philosopher continued to rise. He was admired by the Church fathers: Saint Augustine credited Cicero's writing on natural law for his own conversion to Christianity. The rediscovery of Cicero's letters by the Italian poet Petrarch in the fourteenth century helped to spark the Italian Renaissance. And Cicero exerted a profound impact on the founding generation. Although he was only the eleventh most cited writer during the founding era, between 1760 and 1805, he was the second most cited classical writer, after Plutarch, who was tenth on the list. The top four were Montesquieu, Locke, the British legal commentator William Blackstone, and the Scottish philosopher David Hume, all of whom frequently cited Cicero.[27] In his *Discourse on Cicero* (1717), Montesquieu praises him for defending republican liberty and inspiring people to practice the habits of virtue rather than merely preaching them.[28] And in *Some Thoughts Concerning Education*, written in 1693, John Locke recommends that young students who are learning the habits of virtue need read only two books on morality and ethics: the Bible and Cicero's *On Duties*. Reading Cicero, Locke says, will inform a student "in the principles and precepts of virtue, for the conduct of his life."[29] And, following Cicero, Locke defines the "foundation of all virtue" as the principle "that a man is able to deny himself his own desires, cross his own inclinations, and purely follow what reason directs as best, though the

appetite lean the other way."[30] Both of Locke's most famous books—
An Essay Concerning Human Understanding and *Two Treatises on Civil
Government*—begin with epigraphs from Cicero.

We don't know when, precisely, Jefferson read Locke and the other Enlightenment philosophers on his recommended reading list, since a fire
in 1770 at his mother's house, Shadwell, destroyed nearly his entire library. In 1760, however, he matriculated at William & Mary College
and began his studies with Dr. William Small of Scotland, an assignment that Jefferson later called "my great good fortune, and what probably fixed the destinies of my life." Through daily conversations with
Small, who was appointed to the chair in natural philosophy soon after
Jefferson arrived, the future president received his "first views of the expansion of science, and of the system of things in which we are placed."
Small then introduced Jefferson to his most intimate friend on the faculty, George Wythe, with whom Jefferson would study law and who
"continued to be my faithful and beloved mentor in youth, and my most
affectionate friend through life."[31] Wythe would go on, with his favorite
student, to sign the Declaration of Independence in 1776.

Both Small, educated in Scotland, and Wythe, who grew up in Virginia, were scholars of the classics and the Scottish Enlightenment. Small
graduated from the University of Aberdeen in 1755, three years after
Thomas Reid, a founder of the Scottish commonsense school of moral
philosophy, had been appointed a professor there. Wythe's library, which
he bequeathed to Jefferson upon his death, includes most of the works
of moral philosophy that Jefferson put on his reading list, including the
works of Cicero, Locke's *Essay Concerning Human Understanding*, and
Lord Kames's *Essay on the Principles of Morality and Natural Religion*.[32]
Whenever he read Locke, Jefferson came to admire him extravagantly.
In 1789 he asked the painter John Trumbull to copy portraits of Bacon,
Locke, and Newton for him, "as I consider them as the three greatest men that have ever lived, without any exception, and as having laid
the foundation of those superstructures which have been raised in the

Physical and Moral sciences."[33] But in 1823, toward the end of his life, he denied a charge by his fellow Declaration signer Richard Henry Lee that he "copied [the Declaration] from Locke's Treatise on government." While he may have been influenced by his previous reading and reflection, he wrote to James Madison, "I know only that I turned to neither book or pamphlet while writing it."[34]

Given the linguistic similarities between the Declaration and Locke's *Second Treatise of Government* on the right of revolution, Jefferson's denial has seemed, to many, hard to credit.[35] Locke's discussion of what he calls "a pursuit of happiness," however, occurs not in the *Second Treatise*, which is an essay on how we form governments, but in *An Essay Concerning Human Understanding*, which is an essay on how we form our ideas about reality. Locke insisted that our ideas and beliefs are not innate, as rationalists like the French philosopher René Descartes insisted, and are also not the result of original sin or divine grace, as maintained by the old Puritan faith. Instead, we are born as blank slates and our character and personality are entirely the products of the "association of ideas" we receive from our external environment as perceived by our senses.[36] As Locke put it, the mind originally was "a white paper, void of all characters, without any ideas," and it was eventually "furnished" by "experience."[37]

The phrase "a pursuit of happiness" occurs in chapter 21 of the *Essay*, in a discussion of what Locke, following Cicero, calls the "powers" or "faculties" of the mind.[38] Section 50 of that chapter is called "A Constant Determination to a Pursuit of Happiness No Abridgment of Liberty." Section 51 continues: "The Necessity of Pursuing True Happiness, the Foundation of Liberty."[39] These sections are central to Locke's discussion of our power to use our faculties of reason and judgment to master the emotions that lead to uneasiness of mind. Our will is not entirely free, since it is determined by our desires, which Locke (following Cicero) defines as "an uneasiness of the mind for want of some absent good."[40] But although we don't have the freedom to determine our desires, we do have the freedom to decide to act on our desires or not. For Locke,

virtue and—by extension—happiness aren't about eliminating our passions but about dealing with them realistically by focusing on our long-
term interests rather than our short-term desires. According to Locke,
the "successive uneasiness of our desires" often misleads us into "pursuing trifles"—that is, short-term gratification—instead of the infinitely
greater good that will lead to our long-term happiness.[41] When our
minds are possessed by any "extreme disturbance" or "violent passion,"
such as anger, he says, "we are not masters enough of our own minds"
to "consider thoroughly" our true interests. Locke defines liberty as the
freedom to deploy our powers of reason to think twice before acting on
our "impetuous uneasiness." By avoiding "a too hasty compliance with
our desires" and through "the moderation and restraint of our passions,"
we can pursue the choices on which "true happiness depends."[42]

To the degree that Locke suggested that all human beings have an
equal capacity to cultivate virtue and happiness based on their experiences and reason, his philosophy was appealing to critics of the divine right of kings on both sides of the Atlantic. Locke himself became
a critic of the Restoration monarchy of Charles II, as did his mentor,
the first Earl of Shaftesbury, whom he served as a physician while living in his house. Shaftesbury was a proprietor of the English colony of
Carolina, later divided into North and South, and Locke drafted the
Fundamental Constitutions of Carolina in 1669. After Shaftesbury, or
possibly Locke, wrote essays critical of King Charles, the earl was imprisoned for treason in the Tower of London, but then escaped to Holland. Locke followed him in exile in 1684, returning to England only
after the Catholic-leaning King James II was overthrown and replaced
by the Protestants William and Mary in 1689. That year, his three most
influential works—*An Essay Concerning Human Understanding*, the *Two
Treatises on Civil Government*, and *A Letter Concerning Toleration*—were
published anonymously.

Although Lockean sensationalism was attractive to the American colonists as they formulated their own opposition to King George III,

Jefferson and others worried that individuals would be unable to process all the sensations bombarding them from their chaotic environment without some kind of internal moral compass. Also, was unaided reason sufficient to allow most men to subdue their selfish passions? Locke's answer—that people would behave virtuously because the Bible promised future rewards and punishments—wasn't entirely satisfying to those who doubted the Scripture's literal truth. For this reason, Jefferson and others were attracted by Scottish commonsense philosophers, who argued that we are not born as entirely blank slates. Instead, our minds have a hardwired "moral sense" that can aid our reason in helping us to overcome our selfish impulses and act benevolently toward others.

The commonsense philosophers were part of the Scottish Enlightenment, a movement of scientists, writers, political scientists, and artists who insisted on the centrality of human reason rather than received authority as the touchstone of truth. Centered in Edinburgh, leading thinkers of the movement included Adam Smith, David Hume, and the poet Robert Burns. They focused on virtue and self-improvement, defending a version of Christianity that was compatible with practical reason while acknowledging the importance of conscience and intuition. The commonsense philosophers were led by Francis Hutcheson, who wrote in his *Inquiry into the Original of Our Ideas of Beauty and Virtue* that when we compare the moral qualities of actions, "we are led by our moral Sense of Virtue."[43] In other words, Hutcheson resurrected Cicero's idea that our minds have an innate "moral sense," or conscience, which disposes us to act benevolently toward others. Cicero and the Stoics had referred to common sense, meaning the moral ideas that all people hold in common, without the need for sophisticated reason.[44] Hutcheson and the Scottish commonsense philosophers agreed that morality was, in part, a matter of sentiment or feeling rather than purely the result of a reasoned calculation of costs and benefits, pleasure and pain.

Hutcheson summed up his argument about the moral sense in his *A Short Introduction to Moral Philosophy* (1747), a book Jefferson added to his reading list. This clearly written self-help book begins with epigraphs from Pythagoras, Plato, Epictetus, and Cicero, and acknowledges "how much of this compend is taken from the works of others, from Cicero and Aristotle." Of all Cicero's books, Hutcheson recommends *Tusculan Disputations* as the best place to study Cicero's "doctrine concerning *virtue*, and the *supreme good*, which is the principal and most necessary part of ethicks." Following Aristotle, he defines happiness as "a constant activity according to the highest virtue in a prosperous course of life."[45]

Hutcheson's uses of the phrases "pursuing happiness" and "pursue the greatest happiness" occur in a definition of the faculty of mind that he, like Cicero, calls the Will—the source of all of "our desires pursuing happiness and eschewing misery."[46] "[T]here constantly appears, in every rational being, a stable essential propensity to desire its own happiness," Hutcheson writes, and "the mind while it is calm, and under no impulse of any blind appetite or passion, pursues that one [desire] which seems of most importance." But if our minds are agitated by "certain vehement turbulent Impulses"—namely, "the keener passions of lust, ambition, anger, hatred, envy, love, pity, delight or fear," we may blindly pursue them without deliberating about whether or not they are likely to further our "previous calm desire of happiness." Hutcheson's conclusion is that, with the help of our moral sense, or conscience, we can ensure that our "calm affections" will ultimately outweigh our violent passions because they "pursue the greatest happiness of the whole system of sensitive nature."[47]

Hutcheson also uses the phrase "pursue Happiness" in his *Inquiry into the Original of Our Ideas of Beauty and Virtue*. In defining our innate "moral sense," he writes that if anyone asks "'how we can be mov'd to desire the Happiness of others, without any View to our own?' It may be answer'd, 'That the same Cause which determines us to pursue Happiness for our selves'" leads us to feel benevolence for others. He then defines the difference between alienable and unalienable natural rights, which Jefferson made famous in the Declaration of Independence. A natural right comes from God or Nature, and it can be alienated, or transferred, to government for two reasons—first, if the transfer is within our power, and second, if it would serve some valuable purpose. The rights of conscience are unalienable for both reasons. First, it's not in our power to transfer our freedom of thought to others. "The Right of private Judgment, or of our inward Sentiments, is unalienable," Hutcheson writes, "since we cannot command ourselves to think what either we our selves, or any other Person pleases." Second, "it can never serve any valuable purpose" to make people worship God in any way that seems to them displeasing.[48] Because our thoughts and opinions cannot be commanded by others, Hutcheson concludes, our rights to life, liberty, and the pursuit of happiness are also unalienable, as long as our actions do not harm others. (By contrast, the right to property is an alienable natural right, which is why Jefferson substituted "the pursuit of happiness" for "property" in the Declaration.) "The private rights of individuals are pointed out by their senses and natural appetites, recommending and pursuing such things as tend to their happiness," Hutcheson writes, "and our moral faculty or conscience, shows us, that each one should be allowed full liberty to procure what may be for his own innocent advantage or pleasure."[49]

Jefferson would invoke the same principles in his original draft of the Virginia Statute for Religious Freedom, which he drafted in October 1776, when he returned from Philadelphia. Under Virginia's colonial religious code, all dissenters were required to support and attend the established Anglican Church. Presbyterians and Baptists could be arrested for practicing their faith or preaching the gospel. Quakers, Jews, and other dissenters could be denied the freedom to marry or to have custody of their children. Jefferson proposed not only to disestablish the Anglican Church and remove all criminal punishments for dissent but also to prohibit all compelled support for religion of any kind. When Patrick Henry proposed a general tax to support teachers of the Christian religion, James Madison mobilized popular opposition to persuade the legislature to pass Jefferson's religious freedom bill in 1785. The original draft of the bill is the single best guide to Jefferson's and Madison's original understanding of the First Amendment, which they believed allowed the government to punish "overt acts against peace and good order" but denied it all power to "intrude . . . into the field of opinion."[50]

"Well aware that the opinions and belief of men depend not on their own will, but follow involuntarily the evidence proposed to their minds," Jefferson began, "Almighty God hath created the mind free, and manifested his supreme will that free it shall remain by making it altogether insusceptible of restraint."[51] In other words, Jefferson agreed with Hutcheson that freedom of conscience is, by definition, an unalienable right—one that can't be surrendered or alienated to government—because our opinions are the involuntary result of the evidence contemplated by our reasoning minds. We can't give presidents, priests, professors, or fellow citizens the power to think for us, even if we wanted to, because we are endowed by our Creator with the capacity to reason and therefore can't help thinking for ourselves. Madison supported Jefferson—and relied explicitly on Hutcheson—in his "Memorial and Remonstrance Against Religious Assessments" in 1785, where he called the right to freedom of conscience "in its nature an unalienable right." As Madison explained, "It is unalienable, because the opinions of men, depending only on the evidence contemplated by their own minds cannot follow the dictates of other men." Madison added, "It is unalienable also because . . . [i]t is the duty of every man to render to the Creator such homage and such only as he believes to be acceptable to him."[52]

In addition to providing a central inspiration for the Declaration of Independence and the First Amendment, Hutcheson's work deeply influenced the Founders, culminating in Thomas Paine's best-selling political tract *Common Sense*. But it also provoked a philosophical rejoinder by David Hume (1711–1776), another giant of the Scottish Enlightenment who appears on Jefferson's reading list. Hume believed that Hutcheson had overstated the degree to which the moral sense could aid our powers of reason in disposing us to behave virtuously. "We speak not strictly and philosophically when we talk of the combat of passion and of reason," Hume wrote in *A Treatise of Human Nature*. "Reason is, and ought only to be the slave of the passions, and can never pretend to any other office than to serve and obey them."[53]

•   •   •

The practical question of whether the moral sense is powerful enough to guide most people in their pursuit of happiness was central to the debate between Adams and Jefferson in the 1780s and 1790s about the connections among virtue, democracy, and the size of government. Jefferson, influenced by Hutcheson, Paine, and the commonsense school, insisted that virtue was ultimately a question of feeling rather than reason, and although virtue could be cultivated by education and sociable interactions, all men were equally endowed with the capacity to experience benevolent feelings toward their fellow men. For this reason, strong government wasn't necessary to restrain people's worst impulses, as the ancient Greeks and Romans had maintained; people could cultivate their social dispositions and benevolent feelings in the private sphere. Virtue in Sparta had flowed from participation in government; in the eighteenth-century republic, virtue would flow from participation in commerce and society.

John Adams disagreed entirely. "Society cannot exist without Government, in any reasonable sense of the Word," he wrote to his son Thomas in 1803. "[C]an you conceive of any thing which can be properly called Society, which signifies a Series of Acts of Sociability without Government?"[54] Adams held fast to the old Roman view that "Government is nothing more than Authority reduced to practice," and that visible authority—in the form of a strong executive—was necessary to restrain people's violent passions and promote public virtue.[55]

Jefferson's optimism about the capacity of ordinary people to achieve personal and political self-government was centrally shaped by the third Scottish philosopher on his reading list: Henry Home, known as Lord Kames (1696–1782). In his *Essays on the Principles of Morality and Natural Religion*, first published in 1751, Kames carved out a middle ground between Hutcheson and Hume. He agreed with Hume that "A principle of universal benevolence does certainly not exist in man."[56] Nevertheless, Kames agreed with Hutcheson that our "moral sense" does give us an intuitive sense of our rights and responsibilities without the need for complicated abstract reasoning. Kames defined the purpose of the "moral sense" as "the voice of God within us, regulating our appetites and passions."[57] In other words, we are hardwired to act well based on our feelings rather than our reasoning, although our conscience, like our reason, can be improved through education. Kames's book ends with a prayer of thanksgiving to the Deity for inclining us toward benevolence and virtue: "While man pursues happiness as his chief aim, thou bendest self-love into the social direction."[58]

Jefferson summed up the essentially democratic understanding of our hardwired moral sense that he distilled from Kames in a letter he sent to his nephew Peter Carr from Paris on August 10, 1787. As the Constitutional Convention was winding down across the ocean in Philadelphia, Jefferson wrote to Carr, who was preparing for university, that it would be a waste of time to attend lectures in moral philosophy. Because the rules of moral conduct could not be reduced to a science, he would do better to read good books instead:

> The moral sense, or conscience, is as much a part of man as his leg or arm. It is given to all human beings in a stronger or weaker degree, as force of members is given them in a greater or less degree.... This sense is submitted indeed in some degree to the guidance of reason; but it is a small stock which is required for this: even a less one than what we call Common sense. State a moral case to a ploughman and a professor. The former will decide it as well, and often better than the latter, because he has not been led astray by artificial rules. In this branch therefore read good books because they will encourage as well as direct your feelings.[59]

Jefferson then suggested that his nephew read Kames's essays, along with the other works of moral philosophy that had become a staple of his reading list, including Cicero's *Philosophies* and Locke's *Essay Concerning Human Understanding*. And he also recommended another writer on his original reading list: Laurence Sterne, whose work Jefferson praised as "the best course of morality that ever was written."[60] An Anglo-Irish

priest, Sterne is best known for his novel *The Life and Opinions of Tris-
tram Shandy, Gentleman.* In the reading lists he sent to Robert Skipwith
and Bernard Moore, however, Jefferson recommended not only *Tris-
tram Shandy* and another novel, *A Sentimental Journey*, but also a seven-
volume set of "Sterne's sermons," first collected in 1760.[61]

The first sermon in the collection is called "Inquiry After Happiness,"
and it begins with the following words: "The GREAT PURSUIT of man is
after happiness: it is the first and strongest desire of his nature." After
reviewing the unproductive ways of pursuing happiness by seeking immediate gratification ("The epicure . . . hearing the object of his pursuit
to be happiness [knows] of no other happiness than what is seated immediately in the senses . . . [and] in the indulgence and gratification of the
appetites"), Sterne reveals the "true secret of all happiness": "there can be
no real happiness without religion and virtue, and the assistance of GOD's
grace and Holy Spirit to direct our lives in the true pursuit of it."[62]

Having reviewed the books on Jefferson's reading list, we can understand in a new light the list of twelve virtues that he sent to his granddaughter after his retirement from politics. It's notable how closely
Jefferson's "cannons of conduct" track not only Franklin's list of virtues
but also the lessons of classical moral philosophy about the pursuit of
happiness. The warning that pride costs us more than hunger comes
from Cicero's lessons about humility. Never repenting of eating too little
is a Pythagorean injunction, as are the warnings about doing things willingly and not wasting time. The reminder to cultivate tranquility and not
worry about evils that we can't control is straight from *Tusculan Disputations.* Never troubling others to do what you can do yourself came from
his father, Peter. The advice about counting to ten before speaking when
you're angry is a fine example of Ciceronian moderation. Taking things
by the smooth handle is a version of the Ciceronian injunction of justice,
which holds that we should do good to others and treat all people according to their due.

What's most striking about Jefferson's original list of twelve virtues
for the pursuit of happiness is that three of them refer to frugality and

avoiding needless luxury: "never spend your money before you have it"; "never buy a thing you do not want, because it is cheap, it will be dear to you"; "take care of your cents: Dollars will take care of themselves!" The exclamation point seems significant. If frugality was one of the classical virtues, greed—or, to use the Latin word, *avarice*—was one of the classical vices. Frugality was always the virtue that Jefferson failed to cultivate, and avarice his cardinal sin. And when he wrote his list of twelve virtues during his retirement, his own extravagant borrowing was beginning to catch up with him. Jefferson's addiction to luxury called to mind a Roman emperor more than a Greek philosopher: the historian Garry Wills describes "a buying spree in France that was staggering in its intensity," as he gilded Monticello with Houdon busts and Marie Antoinette armchairs.[63] Jefferson's lifelong inability to pay his bills influenced his famous letter to James Madison insisting that because "the earth belongs in usufruct to the living," no men can impose their personal or national debts—or their laws or constitutions—on the generations to follow.[64] Unfortunately, when it came to his own children, including those he held in bondage, this was advice that Jefferson failed to follow.

Notes on Seneca, "The True Good as Attained by Reason"

Divine Reason that shines within my mind
Grant me resolve your light to cultivate
All other prayers with nature unaligned
This one alone well-tempered minds can sate

When God created man and biospheres
With man alone he shared bright reason's glow
The happy soul no pain or pleasure fears
Content with goods his own mind can bestow

Of sense's pleasures, any could surcease
All outside gifts snatched back by Fortune's hooks
Wisdom alone, through reason, can increase
The fountain of pure wisdom flows through books

In clear or clouded sky, mind's light adorning
Moon at night and Sun's eternal Morning

Five

FRUGALITY

James Wilson and George Mason's Debts

A lthough Thomas Jefferson's reading list tells us which books of Aristotle, Cicero, Locke, and Sidney he relied on to draft the Declaration, his draft contains no footnotes to point us toward particular passages that influenced his original understanding of the pursuit of happiness. But Jefferson also read the writings on happiness of other signers of the Declaration and the Constitution, which do contain footnotes or easily traced sources. Two documents in particular influenced Jefferson directly: James Wilson's *Considerations on the Nature and the Extent of the Legislative Authority of the British Parliament* and George Mason's Virginia Declaration of Rights. By following Wilson's and Mason's footnotes, we can get an even more precise sense of Jefferson's intellectual debts—that is, the classical and Enlightenment sources for particular phrases in the Declaration. And by reconstructing the lives of two of the most influential and least remembered Founders, we can understand how the same vice that tainted Jefferson's legacy—an

avaricious addiction to living beyond his means—also tainted the lega-
cies of Wilson and Mason.

James Wilson's words and thoughts were central influences on both
the Declaration of Independence and the Constitution. It was his brilliant and original insight that We the People of the United States have
the sovereign power and that "*all* LEGITIMATE AUTHORITY," as he put it
in a report for Congress in 1776, is based on the "*sacred Authority of the
People.*"[1] At the Constitutional Convention, he championed a president
and Congress entirely elected by popular vote. Wilson was also arguably
the best educated of all the Founders, having studied in Scotland with
the students of Hutcheson, Kames, Reid, and other great philosophers
of happiness.

The son of a farmer, Wilson was born in 1742 in the Scottish shire
of Fife. He grew up in the village of Caskardy, a few miles east of the
University of St. Andrews, where he would matriculate fifteen years later
in 1757, the same year that Jefferson was copying out consoling passages
from Cicero. His tutors came from the University of Edinburgh, the
home of Lord Kames and his protégé David Hume. In 1759, while Wilson was in college, Benjamin Franklin embarked on a tour of Scotland;
the cities of Edinburgh, Glasgow, and St. Andrews feted and honored
him. In Edinburgh, he spent several days with Kames and his family and
later wrote to his host, "the Time we spent there, was Six Weeks of the
densest Happiness I have met with in any Part of my Life."[2] Franklin
also met Adam Smith, who argued that moral sentiments, or "empathy,"
could encourage individuals to act in accordance with conscience.[3] Finally, Franklin visited the University of St. Andrews, where he received
the honorary doctorate of letters that led him to insist, for the rest of
his life, on being called Dr. Franklin. Although Wilson was one of only
forty undergraduates during Franklin's visit to St. Andrews, there was no
public ceremony and no evidence that the two men met there.

They did, however, soon meet in Philadelphia, where Wilson arrived to make his fortune in 1765. With his St. Andrews education,
Wilson was quickly appointed a tutor at the College of Philadelphia,

which Benjamin Franklin was building into a national university, and his success in teaching Greek and Latin and the natural law theories of Hutcheson and the Dutch jurist Hugo Grotius led him to be awarded an honorary master's degree from the college in 1766, "in regard to particular learning and merit."[4] Wilson then studied law with John Dickinson, who became known as the "penman of the Revolution" for his *Letters from a Farmer in Pennsylvania* expressing vehement opposition to the British Townshend Acts, which imposed hated taxes on imported goods such as glass, paper, and, most famously, tea.

In 1768 Wilson turned to journalism, writing a series of essays for the *Chronicle* using the pseudonym "The Visitant." His subject, as it happens, was the pursuit of happiness. The first article, published on February 1, began: "Our happiness, which is the final end of our existence, and the mark at which we aim, though sometimes injudiciously, cannot be obtained without being acquainted with those sentiments and affections, which are to enjoy that happiness." Quoting the injunction of the Delphic Oracle, "Know then thyself," Wilson insisted that happiness depended on psychological self-awareness—namely, an objective evaluation of our immediate desires and a deliberate consideration of whether they would serve our long-term interests.[5] Following the teaching of his Scottish tutors, Wilson stressed that "the most *important* moral truths are discovered not by *reasoning* but by that act of the mind I have called *perception*."[6] In other words, certain moral truths were self-evident, or easily perceived by our common sense. Still, Wilson emphasized in his opening essay, we could improve our moral judgments—and our pursuit of happiness and the good life—by studying human nature, either by reading history or by observing the way other people, men and women, behave in society.

Wilson tried to appeal to the *Chronicle*'s female readership by focusing on what men could learn from the conversation of women. "I prefer the company of a fine woman to that of a philosopher," he wrote. "[T]he sentiments of a sensible woman, arise in an easy and natural way from matters of common observation."[7] For this reason, Wilson said that conversations were "best when they are composed of near an equal number of both sexes," since they combined "an agreeable mixture of sense and delicacy."[8] Wilson was a bachelor on the marriage market, and the Visitant series sometimes reads like an anonymous dating profile. ("I must inform my fair reader, that I *admire* the beauties of her *person*, though I am *enslaved* by the virtue of her *mind*.") Nevertheless, Wilson viewed women as fully equal to men in capacities of reason, and he lamented the practice of denying women the same access to education. It was unfortunate, he said, that accomplished women were stigmatized as "sentimental, learned, and bookish." "[F]emale education," he asserted, "is in a great measure formed" on a "very bad" principle: "that the cultivation of the mind is of less importance than the external accomplishments of person and behavior."[9] Wilson insisted that women should be as free to cultivate their minds as men.

As soon as he finished the Visitant essays, Wilson turned his attention from private to public happiness. His law tutor, John Dickinson, in his *Letters from a Farmer*, had conceded Parliament's authority to regulate British trade with the colonies, but not the colonies' internal commerce. Wilson was the first to argue that Parliament lacked the constitutional authority to regulate the colonies' internal *or* external affairs. He introduced the argument in his pamphlet on the legislative authority of the British Parliament, which he wrote in 1768 but ultimately decided, for political reasons, not to publish until 1774. Here is Wilson's first draft of the crucial paragraph about the pursuit of happiness, complete with his handwritten footnotes:

> All Men are naturally equal, and naturally free. No one therefore has a Right to any Authority over another without his Consent. All lawful Government then must be founded on the Consent of those who are subject to it. Such Consent was given with a View to ensure and increase the Happiness[10] of the governed above what they could enjoy in an independant and unconnected State of Nature. It

could be given only with this View;[11] for no Man can himself devote himself to Misery:[12] This would be to Counteract the benefecient Intent of his Creation, and to trample upon the first Great Law of Nature. The unavoidable Consequence of this Deduction is that the Happiness of the Society must be the fundamental Law[13] [14] of every Government.[15]

Let's follow Wilson's footnotes one by one. The first (above the word *Happiness*) is to Algernon Sidney's discussion, in his *Discourses Concerning Government*, of how our common ideas of liberty come from nature. Sidney's conclusion: "that man is naturally free; that he cannot justly be deprived of that liberty without cause, and that he doth not resign it, or any part of it, unless it be in consideration of a greater good, which he proposes to himself."[16] In the margins of the manuscript, Wilson copied out another passage from Sidney: "The law of every instituted power, is to accomplish the end of its institution."[17]

The next paragraph reinforces the point, emphasizing that because the Creator intended us to pursue happiness as individuals, we can only consent to join governments that increase our happiness as a society. To support his conclusion that liberty is an unalienable right, because "no Man can devote himself to Misery," Wilson copies out in the margins a closely paraphrased sentence from the Whig political theorist Robert Molesworth, who wrote in "An Account of Denmark as it Was in the Year 1692": "No people can give away the Freedom of themselves and their Posterity: such a donation ought to be esteemed of no more validity than the gift of a child or of a madman. People can no more part with their legal Liberties, than Kings can alienate their Crowns." And Wilson's citation for the proposition that "the Happiness of the Society must be the fundamental Law of every Government" is to Jean-Jacques Burlamaqui, who concluded that "the felicity of the people is the end of government."[18]

Finally, Wilson reaches his crucial conclusion that because the happiness of society is the first law of every government, the people have a moral and natural right to insist that the legislature observes it. For the proposition that the law of nature is unalterable and must regulate the legislature itself, Wilson first cites John Locke's argument in *The Second Treatise of Government* that "the municipal laws of countries ... are only so far right, as they are founded on the law of nature, by which they are to be regulated and interpreted."[19] Earlier in the same discussion of the state of nature, Locke includes the famous words that Jefferson echoes in the Declaration: Writing of "the equality of men by nature," he declares, "The state of nature has a law of nature to govern it, which obliges every one: and reason, which is that law, teaches all mankind, who will but consult it, that being all equal and independent, no one ought to harm another in his life, health, liberty, or possessions."[20]

In addition to Locke, Wilson also cites William Blackstone, who appears on Jefferson's reading list and whose monumental *Commentaries on the Laws of England* had been published just a few years earlier, in 1765. The first comprehensive attempt to codify the common law, as it evolved over centuries in opinions by British judges, Blackstone's *Commentaries* were often cited as a legal authority in the founding era, because they were relatively portable (in four volumes) and relatively easy to read.

Wilson closely paraphrases the following sentence from Blackstone's discussion of the laws of nature: "The Law of Nature is superior in obligation to any other." The previous paragraph contains the following crucial passage. The Creator, Blackstone writes, "has so intimately connected, so inseparably interwoven the laws of eternal justice with the happiness of each individual" that he has "reduced the rule of obedience to this one paternal precept, 'that man should pursue his own true and substantial happiness.'" According to Blackstone, "This is the foundation of what we call ethics, or natural law," which is "binding over all the globe in all countries, and at all times"—and superior to all human laws. Blackstone says that our powers of reason will help us pursue "our own substantial happiness" as opposed to rushing to gratify our immediate desires. But because we often find that our "reason is corrupt" and our "understanding is full of ignorance and error," we need the assistance of "revealed or divine law . . . found only in the holy scriptures."[21]

There is one final source that Blackstone, Locke, and Burlamaqui all have in common: Cicero. The Latin epigraph for Locke's *Second Treatise* is Cicero's maxim "Let the safety of the people be the supreme law."[22] Burlamaqui says that Cicero's maxim should be the "chief end" of any sovereign's actions.[23] And Blackstone invokes Cicero to argue that legislatures can't punish conduct that wasn't illegal at the time it was committed.[24] All three sources also adopt Cicero's basic definition of virtue: namely, that we have not only a right but also a duty to pursue happiness by using our powers of reason to temper and moderate our violent passions and emotions. "You ask, for example, whether the moderation of the passions be a duty imposed upon us by the law of nature?" Burlamaqui asks. "In order to give you an answer, I inquire, in my turn, whether it is necessary to our preservation, perfection, and happiness?" Citing Cicero, Burlamaqui concludes, "[U]ndoubtedly it is."[25]

On July 4, 1788, a Grand Federal Procession marched through Philadelphia to celebrate the Adoption of the US Constitution. Seventeen thousand spectators watched five thousand prominent citizens march behind a float adorned by an eagle representing the Constitution. The parading citizens wore costumes to signify their ranks as bankers and merchants or artisans and mechanics, with the bricklayers holding trowels and the shoemakers garbed in white aprons. The Constitution float was a thirteen-foot-high American eagle pulled by six horses, followed by a golden replica of the text, signed by the people. Ten Federalist worthies marched behind the giant eagle, with James Wilson representing Pennsylvania. The men of different sizes and shapes struggled to hold aloft their golden state flags while linking their arms to celebrate their unity, proceeding unsteadily but successfully.

This impressive spectacle convened at eight o'clock in the morning at Third and South Streets, blocks from the house where, nine years earlier, an angry mob of working-class artisans had turned on Wilson and his fellow members of the merchant class for their refusal to impose price controls on staples such as flour and wood during the inflation that raged during the Revolutionary War. On October 4, 1779, the armed mob, led by the artist Charles Willson Peale, had paraded four merchants through the streets. Shouting "Get Wilson!" the militiamen then attacked his house on Third and Walnut, where Wilson had barricaded himself, his wife, and other merchants upstairs for safety. The rabble stormed the front door, set fire to the first floor, and killed a young Captain, Robert Campbell, who had shouted or shot at them through an upstairs window. At least five other men were also killed in the fight. Only the arrival of the president of the Pennsylvania Supreme Executive Council, accompanied by the City Troop of Light Horse, ended the attack on what became known as "Fort Wilson."[26]

Nine years later, all was forgiven between the merchant and artisanal classes, and the peaceful crowd watched mostly in silence, exemplifying the classical republican virtue of "rational joy."[27] They were especially impressed by the float carrying the "Grand Federal Edifice," or "new roof" of the Union—a thirty-six-foot-high neoclassical temple supported by thirteen columns. Its designer was none other than the now mollified Peale, who had also planned the parade and provided helpful advice on the costumes. At twelve thirty, the procession came to rest at an estate on Bush Hill, and James Wilson mounted the Grand Federal Edifice to deliver a special oration on happiness he had prepared for the occasion. Alas, due to confusion about the timing, the ships in the harbor began to fire their gun salutes during his address, making his words almost inaudible. But Wilson gamely exhorted his audience about the central connection between virtue and happiness.

"If we would be happy, we must be active," he declared, adding a few thoughts about the "virtues and manners" necessary to justify the festivities and support the Constitution. "Frugality and temperance" were "simple but powerful virtues" and, as the fall of Rome demonstrated, "the sole foundation, on which a good government can rest with security." Next was industry. "The industrious alone constitute a nation's strength," since in a well-constituted society, "each gains from all, and all gain from each." By contrast, the enemies of liberty included "licentiousness," with "her motions . . . regulated by dark ambition, who sits concealed behind the curtain," always followed by "despotism." Since all power stemmed from "the original movement of the people at large," Wilson said, "publick happiness" would turn on citizens having the virtue to select representatives who were "wise and good." "A progressive state is necessary to the happiness of perfection of man," Wilson concluded with a flourish. "[L]et our progress in every excellence be proportionately great . . . while liberty, virtue, and religion go hand in hand, harmoniously protecting, enlivening, and exalting all! Happy country! May thy happiness be perpetual!"[28]

Alas, perpetual happiness was not Wilson's fate. He had an unrealistically romantic view of the capacity of the people, including himself, to achieve perfection. And, failing to follow his own advice about the importance of frugality, he was undone by his own avarice. A compulsive speculator in western lands, his credit went bad in the periodic economic panics of the 1790s. In April 1789, overcome with ambition, Wilson broke with protocol by boldly writing to President Washington and asking to be appointed chief justice of the United States. "[My] Aim rises to the important office of Chief Justice of the United States," Wilson wrote, with apologies for his indelicacy in raising the subject. "But how shall I now proceed? Shall I enumerate Reasons in Justification of my high Pretensions? I have not yet employed my Pen in my own Praise."[29] Washington, aware of Wilson's chaotic finances, appointed John Jay as chief justice instead but nominated Wilson as an associate justice in September.

Risky land speculation was a common vice among the Founders: George Washington himself bought vast tracts of western land on credit and tried to sell it at higher prices. Still, Wilson was distinguished by the recklessness and scale of his borrowing. In 1780 he had invested in the Illinois-Wabash Company, one of the largest land investors in America, encompassing sixty million acres. With a possible holding of more than a million acres, he was the largest individual shareholder.[30] Wilson set out to recruit European investors in the western lands he had bought on credit, so that they could provide the hard currency he needed to pay off his mortgages.

Through rose-colored glasses, as always, Wilson wrote a hyperbolic prospectus in the early 1790s promising that the lands would be settled by European immigrants transported by humane officers on clean ships. After resting from the "Fatigues of the Voyage," they would then be escorted to the best tracts of his western lands, where they would find "a House already built, a Garden already made, an Orchard already planted, a Portion of Land already cleared, and Grain already growing or reaped." The "reasonable Prices" they would pay for the land, livestock, and "farming Utensils of the best Kinds and Construction" ensured that both the settlers and the land investors would benefit from what Wilson called "the first Axiom in this Plan—*never to be in Want of Money.*"[31] Despite the extravagant promises of this get-rich-quick scheme, it's not clear that Wilson's prospectus reached a single European investor.

In 1792 William Duer, one of Wilson's fellow land speculators, failed on a massive scale—he had borrowed millions of dollars from "merchants, tradesmen, widows, and orphans" to buy government bonds, and when he was unable to sell them abroad, he lost more than $2 million, bringing down Philadelphia and New York merchant banks and real estate prices, and causing a financial panic.[32] As a sitting Supreme Court justice, Wilson had to rush back to Philadelphia from Connecticut, where he was hearing cases on circuit, to try to get his financial affairs in order. He held on for the moment, since his creditors were in no rush to force the sale of increasingly worthless lands, but was forced to take out new loans to hold off his creditors.

Justice Wilson's reputation for living beyond his means became so notorious that, in 1793, while he was hearing cases in Boston, his idealistic charge to the grand jury about the responsibilities of citizens to participate equally in American democracy by finding facts fairly and interpreting laws neutrally was criticized as hypocritical by the Federalist press. "It is said that a Charge has been delivered 'replete with the happiness of *equal* government,'" wrote the *Federal Gazette* in Philadelphia. "This idea comes with an ill grace from a man, who parades our streets with a coach and four horses, when it is known his exorbitant salary enables him to make this *flashy parade*, and the money is taken from the pockets of the industrious part of the community."[33]

During the same visit, the fifty-one-year-old justice fell in love with eighteen-year-old Hannah Gray, a relative of Mercy Otis Warren, and he proposed to her on their second meeting. The whirlwind courtship became the talk of Boston: a young John Quincy Adams wrote to his brother Thomas that "the wise and learned Judge & Professor Wilson, has fallen most lamentably in love with a young Lady in this town, under twenty; by the name of Gray. He came, he saw, and was overcome." According to Adams, Wilson "was smitten at meeting with a first sight love—unable to contain his amorous pain, he breathed his sighs about the Streets; and even when seated on the bench of Justice, he seemed as if teeming with some woful ballad to his mistress eye-brow." As Adams predicted, "the happy consort of the happy judge" soon followed Wilson to Philadelphia, where the couple renovated a splendid new house, even corresponding with Thomas Jefferson about buying a custom-made bookcase he had constructed at Monticello.[34] Hannah's influence may also have helped persuade Wilson to grant freedom to Thomas Purcell, an enslaved man who had long managed Wilson's household, as a new year's gift at the end of 1793.[35] Unlike Mason and Jefferson, Wilson did not rely on a large enslaved population to maintain his lavish lifestyle.

At this point, however, it was too late. Another financial panic beginning in 1796 brought the land speculators of Philadelphia to their knees. Over the course of six weeks, more than sixty people went to jail for debt, including Robert Morris, the so-called financier of the Revolution, a signer of both the Declaration and the Constitution, and founder of the US financial system. Morris was also one of Wilson's unlucky business partners, who expressed the fear that Wilson's chaotic affairs "will make the Vultures more keen after me."[36] Wilson's son from his first marriage,

Bird, collected his father's salary as a justice to pay his father's rent but was unable to sell his properties, finding that they had already been sold. Wilson and Hannah hid from their creditors at a tavern in Bethlehem, Pennsylvania, frantically trying to put their affairs in order. Justice Wilson then made his way to Burlington, New Jersey, where a creditor overtook him, and he was thrown in jail.[37] After his release, he fled south to Edenton, North Carolina, hoping to bring order to his southern lands.

But Wilson owed money to Pierce Butler, the vain son of a baronet, a former senator, and one of the largest slaveholders in the United States. As a delegate for South Carolina at the Constitutional Convention, Butler had introduced the Fugitive Slave Clause, giving federal protection to the enslavers. In March 1798 the vengeful Butler began legal proceedings against Justice Wilson for the unpaid debt, and Wilson was arrested and thrown in jail again. On his release, he took refuge at the dingy Horinblow Tavern, where Hannah found him raging against those who had begun to speculate on his estate. "I have been hunted—I may be hunted—like a wild beast," he wrote to his lawyer on May 12. Nevertheless, Wilson refused to turn over his properties to a trust for general distribution to his creditors in bankruptcy, since this would "exclude me from performing the duty, and feeling the pleasure, of doing full and effectual justice for all." For Wilson, duty and pleasure were always intertwined. Blinkered with unrealistic optimism until the end, he found "reason to believe that the season is approaching when my exertions may be crowned with the most abundant success." With a poignant nod to the classical virtue of industry, he stressed that "my life has not been a life of idleness or indolence."[38] In July Wilson suffered an attack of malaria and then a stroke. On August 21, with Hannah mopping his brow in the tavern as he railed against his creditors, Justice Wilson died.

In addition to Wilson's pamphlet, Thomas Jefferson had at least one other source in mind as he wrote the Declaration of Independence: George Mason's Virginia Declaration of Rights. A Virginia aristocrat,

George Mason IV was one of the most influential and underappreci-
ated Founders, one of three delegates to the Constitutional Convention
who refused to sign the Constitution because it didn't contain a Bill
of Rights. The Virginia Declaration of Rights, which Mason drafted,
also served as James Madison's primary source when he drafted the
Bill of Rights in 1789. Mason, like Jefferson, derived his libertarian
principles from his classical reading. He was the oldest son of a wealthy
landowner whose estate included more than two dozen enslaved people
and eight thousand acres.[39] His father died in 1735, when he was ten,
and his mother ensured that, like Thomas Jefferson, he was privately
tutored in Latin and the classics by a Scottish clergyman; he also read
deeply in the extensive library of his uncle, who ordered books for him
from London. Mason's own library included many of the classic texts
of moral and political philosophy that Jefferson read as well: Cicero's
Morals, Locke on government and education, and Sidney on government. It also included Addison's *Spectator*, Blackstone's *Commentaries*,
Plutarch's *Lives*, Pope's *Works*, Rollin's *Ancient History*, the Greek playwright Euripides (whom Mason quoted in Latin) and the Roman historians Sallust and Livy.[40]

In May 1776, when the Continental Congress in Philadelphia asked
the colonies to form new governments, the Virginia Convention appointed Mason, James Madison, and others to draft a new Constitution
and Bill of Rights. Writing in Raleigh Tavern in Williamsburg, Mason
produced the first draft of the Virginia Declaration of Rights, whose
preamble includes language that Jefferson would include in the Declaration of Independence almost word for word:

> That all men are born equally free and independant, and have cer-
> tain inherent natural Rights, of which they can not by any Compact,
> deprive or divest their Posterity; among which are the Enjoyment of
> Life and Liberty, with the Means of acquiring and possessing Prop-
> erty, and pursueing and obtaining Happiness and Safety.[41]

We can see how closely Jefferson mirrored this language in his rough draft of the Declaration of Independence, before it was edited by Adams and Franklin:

> We hold these truths to be sacred & undeniable; that all men are cre-
> ated equal and independant, that from that equal creation they derive
> rights inherent & inalienable, among which are the preservation of
> life, & liberty, & the pursuit of happiness.[42]

Jefferson was sensitive to the charge of plagiarism. Nearly fifty years later, he wrote to a correspondent who, like many readers, was surprised by the similarities between Jefferson's and Mason's bills of particu-lars against King George III. Jefferson said that he had sent his own draft constitution for Virginia from Philadelphia to Williamsburg in 1776, along with a preamble justifying separation from Great Britain. Although Jefferson's constitution arrived too late, he said, the Virginia House liked his preamble and inserted it into the final document. "Thus my preamble became tacked to the work of George Mason," Jefferson explained defensively, going on to praise Mason as "one of our really great men, and of the first order of greatness."[43]

Nevertheless, when the Virginia Convention began to debate Ma-son's Declaration of Rights on May 29, one delegate objected to the phrase "All men are born equally free and independant, and have certain inherent natural rights," on the grounds that it could be interpreted as a call to abolish slavery or to encourage insurrections by the enslaved. The delegates debated the issue until June 3, when they modified the lan-guage in the following way: "That all men are by nature equally free and independent, and have certain inherent rights, of which, when they enter into a state of society, they cannot, by any compact, deprive or divest their posterity."[44] The legalistic addition hardly resolved the inconsistency of slavery and natural law—How could enslaved people be prevented from entering into a state of society?—but it sufficiently muddled the issue by implying that enslaved people were not *in* a state of society and therefore (paradoxically) were not owed their natural rights. The language passed without further amendment.

One obvious source for Mason's claim that "All men are born equally free and independant" is Locke's *Second Treatise*, which declares that "all" are "equal and independent." Another is *Cato's Letters*, a four-volume series of "essays on liberty" by the Whig polemicists, who chose the pseudonym "Cato" as a tribute to the Roman patriot. First published in the *London Journal* in 1720 and reprinted in colonial newspapers in the 1770s, *Cato's Letters* were the most widely read and influential efforts to synthesize the classical liberalism of John Locke and the civic republicanism of the Italian political philosopher Niccolò Machiavelli with the libertarianism of Whig defenders of England's Glorious Revolution of 1688.

"[L]iberty is the unalienable right of all mankind," Trenchard and Gordon put it in Letter 59. The same essay continues, "All men are born free; liberty is a gift which they receive from God himself." Emphasizing that "[n]o man has power over his own life, or to dispose of his own religion," Cato maintains that he "cannot consequently transfer the power of either to any body else" or "give away the lives and liberties, religion or acquired property of his posterity."[45] As a result, Trenchard and Gordon conclude, the people's "happiness and security . . . are the very ends of magistracy."[46]

Mason's phrase in article 15 of the Virginia Declaration about "the blessings of liberty" is a quotation from *Cato's Letters* as well. Letter 25 concludes that the "blessings of liberty" make the people "great and happy," while tyranny and despotic power lead to slavery, which makes the people "little, wicked, and miserable."[47] Mason and other Founders repeatedly compared themselves to slaves of the king while refusing to free the human beings they themselves held in bondage. They would inscribe the phrase "blessings of liberty" into the preamble to the Constitution, without extending those blessings to the enslaved.

In their letters, which compare the corruption of Britain to the fall of Rome, Trenchard and Gordon begin by denouncing the South Sea

Bubble scandal, when the British stock market crashed in 1720 after the government created a private corporation at inflated share prices to float its war debt. Quoting Cicero's maxim "*Salus populi suprema lex esto*," they declare, "That the benefit and safety of the people constitutes the supreme law, is an universal and everlasting maxim in government."[48] And they return to a series of themes that Mason would synthesize into the core principles of the American Revolution: that in Caesar's Rome and George's Britain, wicked ministers had corrupted the people by playing on their "prevailing passions"—namely, "avarice and ambition."[49]

Several of *Cato's Letters* include extensive quotations from Algernon Sidney, the Whig Revolutionary whose *Discourses Concerning Government* Jefferson had identified as one of his main inspirations as well. Sidney was an English politician who had opposed the execution of Charles I and was later executed for plotting against Charles II, due largely to the libertarian principles he embraced in the *Discourses*, which helped to inspire the Glorious Revolution in 1688 and the American Revolution in 1776. The *Discourses* oppose the divine right of kings and defend the idea that kings can rule only with the consent of the people, who have a right to alter and abolish government whenever it becomes corrupt or tyrannical. "Whilst every man fears his neighbour," Sidney writes of the need to establish government by popular consent, "he must live in that perpetual anxiety which is equally contrary to that happiness, and that sedate temper of mind which is required for the search of it."[50] Trenchard and Gordon also quote Machiavelli's famous maxim, in his *Discourses on Livy*, that for republics to exist for a long time, they need to return frequently to the principles of frugality and virtue on which they were founded. "Machiavel tells us that no government can long subsist, but by recurring often to its first principles; but this can never be done while men live at ease and in luxury; for then they cannot be persuaded to see distant dangers, of which they feel no part."[51] Drawing on *Cato's Letters*, Machiavelli, and Sidney, Mason's 15th Article in the Virginia Declaration makes explicit the connection between the classical virtues and the pursuit of happiness:

That no free government, or the blessings of liberty, can be preserved
to any people but by a firm adherence to justice, moderation, temperance, frugality, and virtue and by frequent recurrence to fundamental
principles.[52]

Mason did better than Wilson and Jefferson in following his own
advice about the importance of frequent recurrence to the virtue of frugality. He refused to overextend himself in land speculation, declining
to buy his uncle's plantation in retirement, and paid off his debts to his
British creditors by the time of his death in 1792. But Mason's avarice
took another and more pernicious form: his refusal to abandon his lavish
lifestyle at Gunston Hall, his colonial plantation, which could be sustained only by enslaved labor. At the time of his death, he held seventy-
five-thousand acres along the Potomac River and in Kentucky, $50,000
of property, $30,000 in receivable accounts, and three hundred enslaved
human beings.[53] Mason, unlike Jefferson, died solvent. But both of them
denounced the immorality of slavery in theory while continuing to ex-
ploit it in practice, because they were addicted to the lifestyle that enslaved labor made possible. In this regard, the only difference among
Mason, Wilson, and Jefferson was that Mason was better at managing
his finances. And, as we will see in the next chapter, the combination
of Jefferson's avarice and his endless capacity for self-rationalization led
him not only to refuse to free the men, women, and children he held in
bondage but to deny the talents of the most eminent African American
female poet of the age.

On VIRTUE.

BY PHILLIS WHEATLEY

O Thou bright jewel in my aim I strive
To comprehend thee. Thine own words declare
Wisdom is higher than a fool can reach.
I cease to wonder, and no more attempt
Thine height t'explore, or fathom thy profound.
But, O my soul, sink not into despair,
Virtue is near thee, and with gentle hand
Would now embrace thee, hovers o'er thine head.

Fain would the heav'n-born soul with her converse,
Then seek, then court her for her promis'd bliss.
Auspicious queen, thine heav'nly pinions spread,
And lead celestial Chastity along;
Lo! now her sacred retinue descends,
Array'd in glory from the orbs above.
Attend me, Virtue, thro' my youthful years!
O leave me not to the false joys of time!
But guide my steps to endless life and bliss.

Greatness, or Goodness, say what I shall call thee,
To give an higher appellation still,
Teach me a better strain, a nobler lay,
O Thou, enthron'd with Cherubs in the realms of day!

Six

SINCERITY

Phillis Wheatley and the Enslavers' Avarice

I n the fall of 1772, eighteen men acclaimed as "the most respectable Characters in *Boston*" determined that Phillis Wheatley, an enslaved African poet in her late teens, had, in fact, written her own poems.[1] The panel of examiners included Thomas Hutchinson, the colonial governor of Massachusetts; John Hancock, who would soon become president of the Continental Congress; and Samuel Mather and Ebenezer Pemberton Jr., the sons of the rival ministers who had vied for the soul of the young Benjamin Franklin. The panel had been convened at the request of John Wheatley, a Boston merchant who had purchased Phillis from the enslaver John Avery in 1761 when she arrived in Boston Harbor on the slave ship *Phillis*, the source of her name. His wife, Susanna Wheatley, was a follower of the evangelical minister George Whitefield, who set off a wave of religious enthusiasm in colonial America. Although a defender of slavery, Whitefield preached to the enslaved and campaigned against their cruel treatment.

Inspired by Whitefield's spirit, Susanna decided to give seven-year-old Phillis a classical education alongside the Wheatleys' twins, Mary and Nathaniel. Tutored in part by Mary, Phillis studied the Bible and the Greek and Roman poets and moral philosophers, including Virgil, Ovid, Horace, and Terence, as well as English poets such as Alexander Pope and John Milton. "Without any Assistance from School Education, and by only what she was taught in the Family, she, in sixteen Months Time from her arrival, attained the English Language, to which she was an utter Stranger before, to such a Degree, as to read any, the most difficult Parts of the Sacred Writings, to the great Astonishment of all who heard her," John Wheatley wrote in a letter to the publisher of her first book of poems. "She has a great Inclination to learn the Latin Tongue, and has made some Progress in it."[2]

Phillis Wheatley began to write classically influenced poetry in 1765, four years after she arrived in America in chains. She gained international attention in 1770 at the age of seventeen with the publication of her ode on the death of George Whitefield, whose preaching she may have heard months before. In the poem, she praised Whitefield's appeal for divine grace to dwell in the hearts of all human beings, white and Black alike. Based on the success of the ode to Whitefield, a London printer agreed to publish a collection of her poems. In light of skepticism that a Black woman could have produced works of such genius, however, he specified that a group of white authorities would have to attest to their authenticity.

The result was what Professor Henry Louis Gates Jr. has called the "Trials of Phillis Wheatley," in which he imagines that the young poet was examined on the depth of her classical learning. Although we don't know precisely what she was asked, Professor Gates imagines questions such as "Who was Apollo?" and "Name the Nine Muses."[3] (In fact, no actual "examination" by the review board took place.)[4] Wheatley, in any event, passed with flying colors, and the board of poetic examiners signed the following jarring statement, which the London publisher reproduced at the beginning of Wheatley's *Poems on Various Subjects, Religious and*

Moral: "WE whose Names are under-written, do assure the World, that the POEMS specified in the following Page, were (as we verily believe) written by PHILLIS, a young Negro Girl, who was but a few Years since, brought an uncultivated Barbarian from *Africa*, and has ever since been, and now is, under the Disadvantage of serving as a Slave in a Family in this Town. She has been examined by some of the best Judges, and is thought qualified to write them."[5]

Informed by the classical sources that inspired the verses of Benjamin Franklin and Mercy Otis Warren, Wheatley's poems explore the same themes about the connection between virtue and happiness. Her 1766 poem "On Virtue" begins: "Attend me, *Virtue*, thro' my youthful years! / O leave me not to the false joys of time! / But guide my steps to endless life and bliss."[6] Her "Thoughts on the Works of Providence" examines the central classical theme of how, in our dreams, passion can triumph over reason: "On pleasure now, and now on vengeance bent, / The lab'ring passions struggle for a vent. / What pow'r, O man! thy *reason* then restores, / So long suspended in nocturnal hours?"[7] Wheatley also addresses her unique status as an African poet, emphasizing that the classical Roman playwright Terence "was an *African* by birth" and asserting her right to join the same literary tradition.[8] And in one poem, addressed to the 2nd Earl of Dartmouth, the British secretary of state for North American affairs, she connects Americans' desire to be free from enslavement by Britain to her own desire to be free from enslavement by Americans:

> *I, young in life, by seeming cruel fate*
> *Was snatch'd from Afric's fancy'd happy seat:*
> *What pangs excruciating must molest,*
> *What sorrows labour in my parent's breast?*
> *Steel'd was that soul and by no misery mov'd*
> *That from a father seiz'd his babe belov'd:*
> *Such, such my case. And can I then but pray*
> *Others may never feel tyrannic sway?*[9]

Encouraged by the favorable verdict of her Boston examiners, Phillis Wheatley set off for London, accompanied by Nathaniel Wheatley, the son of her enslavers. She had arranged to meet with her British publisher and her patron, Selina Hastings, Countess of Huntingdon, an acolyte of George Whitefield who had supported the publication of other Black writers on religious themes. While she was at sea, the publicity campaign for her book was hitting the press. "The Book here proposed for publication displays perhaps one of the greatest instances of pure, unassisted genius, that the world ever produced," read a notice that appeared in London. By the time she arrived there on June 17, 1773, Wheatley was already an international celebrity—"the most famous African on the face of the earth," Professor Gates calls her, "the Oprah Winfrey of her time."[10] She met the Earl of Dartmouth, who gave her five guineas to buy the complete works of Alexander Pope, and the future Lord Mayor of London, who gave her a folio edition of Milton's *Paradise Lost* printed in silver ink. A meeting with King George III was promised but never materialized.

Wheatley also met the British antislavery campaigner Granville Sharp, who took her to the Tower of London and showed her the lions, panthers, and royal christening fountain. And she received a special visit from Benjamin Franklin, who was spending nearly two decades, from 1757 to 1775, in London as an agent for the American colonies. "Upon your Recommendation I went to see the black Poetess and offer'd her any Services I could do her," Franklin wrote to a relative whom Susanna Wheatley had encouraged to arrange the visit. "Before I left the House, I understood her Master was there and had sent her to me but did not come into the Room himself, and I thought was not pleased with the Visit." Although Franklin noted, "I have heard nothing since of her," Wheatley was sufficiently satisfied with the visit to propose dedicating her second book of poetry to Franklin.[11]

Nathaniel Wheatley may have been uncomfortable arranging an interview with Franklin because of his uncertainty about whether or not Phillis would agree to return to America with him. In 1772 Lord

Mansfield issued a landmark opinion in the *Somerset* case, holding that an enslaved person brought to England from America could not be forced by his or her enslaver to return to the colonies. The decision was widely viewed as having ended slavery in England, and it suggested that Nathaniel couldn't force Phillis to return to America against her will. It's possible, as the scholar Vincent Carretta speculates, that Phillis agreed to return to the Wheatleys to care for ailing Susanna in exchange for a promise that the family would free her upon arrival.[12] Whatever their motives, John and Susanna Wheatley did indeed grant Phillis her freedom by October 18, 1773, a month after her return to Boston. She received the first copies of her book the following January and moved back into the Wheatleys' house to care for Susanna, who died three months later.

Wheatley's genius was recognized not only by Franklin but also by the Commander in Chief of the Continental Army. In October 1775, six months into the Revolutionary War, Phillis wrote a poem praising General George Washington's classical virtue ("Fam'd for thy valour, for thy virtues more, / Hear every tongue thy guardian aid implore"). She sent it to Washington at army headquarters in Cambridge, Massachusetts, along with a cover note that drove the point home. "Your being appointed by the Grand Continental Congress to be Generalissimo of the armies of North America, together with the fame of your virtues, excite sensations not easy to suppress," she wrote.[13] Washington replied in February 1776, "with great respect," as he put it. He apologized for the delay caused by "a variety of important occurrences, continually interposing to distract the mind and withdraw the attention." Thanking Wheatley "most sincerely for your polite notice of me, in the elegant Lines you enclosed," and professing himself unworthy of them, Washington added that "the style and manner exhibit a striking proof of your great poetical Talents." He closed by inviting Wheatley to visit him if she found herself in Cambridge or near army headquarters. "I shall be happy to see a person so favoured by the Muses, and to whom nature has been so liberal and beneficent in her dispensations," Washington concluded.[14]

Washington's desire to see Wheatley's encomium to him published was genuine. Days before replying to her, he had shared her poem and cover letter with Colonel Joseph Reed, noting that he had thought of publishing the poem "with a view of doing justice to her great poetical Genius," but had laid it aside, "not knowing whether it might not be considered rather as a mark of my own vanity than as a Compliment to her."[15] Reed took the hint and arranged for the poem's publication in the spring.

Encouraged by Washington's endorsement, Wheatley continued to write poems suggesting that the revolution would end all forms of enslavement in America. After General David Worcester was killed in battle in 1777, Wheatley wrote an ode to his death that she sent to his widow the following year. In it, she pointed out the hypocrisy—also noted by English reviewers of her first book—of a colony that demanded freedom for white people but failed to extend the same freedom to Black people:

> But how, presumptuous shall we hope to find
> Divine acceptance with th' Almighty mind—
> While yet (O deed ungenerous!) they disgrace
> And hold in bondage Afric's blameless race?
> Let virtue reign—And thou accord our prayers
> Be victory our's, and generous freedom theirs.[16]

Wheatley listed the poem in a series of advertisements she took out in the *Boston Evening Post* proposing a second book of poetry in 1779, but despite her stated intention to dedicate the book to Benjamin Franklin, there weren't enough subscribers. Meanwhile, her own fortunes had turned. With the death of John Wheatley, who left her nothing in his will, she struggled to make ends meet. In April 1778 she married John Peters, a free Black man who seems to have changed jobs and struggled with debt. They had two children who died as infants. In January 1784 she published her last poem, "Liberty and Peace," celebrating the end of the American Revolution. Her husband then abandoned her after the birth of their third child, who died in December. The same month, at the age of thirty, Phillis Wheatley died alone.

Although George Washington and Benjamin Franklin responded enthusiastically to Phillis Wheatley's poetry, Thomas Jefferson had a very different reaction. The year after Wheatley's death, Jefferson in Paris published his *Notes on the State of Virginia*, a long response to a set of twenty-three "queries" about America posed to him by the secretary of the French legation to the United States in 1780. In Query 14, on the administration of justice, Jefferson questions the quality of Phillis Wheatley's poems. Discussing "physical and moral" difference between Black and white people, Jefferson reveals the intensity of his racism. He suggests that Blacks are less capable of reason and deliberation than whites because "their existence appears to participate more of sensation than reflection.... Comparing them by their faculties of memory, reason, and imagination, it appears to me that in memory they are equal to the whites; in reason much inferior ... and that in imagination they are dull, tasteless, and anomalous."[17]

Jefferson wasn't finished. "Some have been liberally educated," he acknowledges, in contrast to "[t]he Indians, with no advantages of this kind, [who] . . . astonish you with strokes of the most sublime oratory; such as prove their reason and sentiment strong, their imagination glowing and elevated. But never yet could I find that a black had uttered a thought above the level of plain narration; never saw even an elementary trait of painting or sculpture." He then acknowledges Wheatley's poetry as her own but denies the ability of any Black person to write good poetry. "Misery is often the parent of the most affecting touches in poetry. Among the blacks is misery enough, God knows, but no poetry." In Jefferson's view, the love of Black people "is ardent, but it kindles the senses only, not the imagination. Religion, indeed, has produced a Phyllis Whately [*sic*]; but it could not produce a poet. The compositions published under her name are below the dignity of criticism."[18]

Having declared Black people to be intellectually inferior, dismissed Wheatley's poetry, and misspelled her name, Jefferson contrasts her art with that of Roman slaves:

We know that among the Romans, about the Augustan age espe-cially, the condition of their slaves was much more deplorable than that of the blacks on the continent of America.... Yet notwithstand-ing these and other discouraging circumstances among the Romans, their slaves were often their rarest artists. They excelled too in science, insomuch as to be usually employed as tutors to their master's chil-dren. Epictetus, Terence, and Phaedrus, were slaves. But they were of the race of whites. It is not their condition then, but nature, which has produced the distinction.[19]

Jefferson's opinion that Black people "are inferior in the faculties of reason and imagination" is a "suspicion only," he hastens to add, and requires more scientific investigation. He would be glad to be proved wrong. After all, Jefferson goes on, "[t]his unfortunate difference of col-our, and perhaps of faculty" might be viewed as "a powerful obstacle to the emancipation of these people," since emancipation would lead to miscegenation. This was a distressing prospect, since "[m]any of their advocates, while they wish to vindicate the liberty of human nature, are anxious also to preserve its dignity and beauty." In Rome, Jefferson con-tinued, "The slave, when made free, might mix with, without staining the blood of his master," while in America, enslaved people, once freed, would have to be "removed beyond the reach of mixture" with white people.[20]

Jefferson's racism was jarring even by the standards of his time— Washington and Franklin expressed no such animus toward Wheatley or other Black poets. And his statements about the dangers of miscege-nation are astonishing, especially when we realize that he was writing about himself and his own children. Based on DNA tests conducted in 1998, historians now agree that Jefferson was the father of at least six children by Sally Hemings, whom he held in bondage and who was the half sister of his deceased wife, Martha Wayles Skelton Jefferson.[21] (Hemings was the daughter of John Wayles, Martha's father, and Betty Hemings, whom Wayles held in bondage.) Four of Jefferson's children with Sally Hemings lived until adulthood: a daughter, Harriet, and sons Beverly, Madison, and Eston. When twenty-year-old Harriet and twenty-four-year-old Beverly ran away together in 1822, Jefferson freed his daughter but not his son. In his will, Jefferson provided for the freedom of Eston and Madison when they turned twenty-one, but he failed to free Sally Hemings, who remained in bondage. In his will, he also freed Sally's brother John Hemings and two other Hemings relatives, but not their wives and children, who were sold to pay Jefferson's debts.

Jefferson repeatedly denigrated the intellectual capacities of Black people and declined to acknowledge his own children. Yet throughout his life, he maintained that slavery violated the equal liberty with which all people are endowed by the Creator in the state of nature. He claimed to support the "total emancipation" of enslaved people—but always at some unspecified point in the future. In his *Notes*, Jefferson insisted that he had supported a bill "[t]o emancipate all slaves born after passing the act." It contained an amendment, he wrote, stipulating that when "the females should be eighteen, and the males twenty-one years of age . . . they should be colonized to such place as the circumstances of the time should render most proper." In other words, Jefferson believed that enslaved people should be educated and then emancipated, but only on the condition that they be deported to another nation as a "free and independent people."[22]

Jefferson's theoretical support for Black people's total emancipation was based not only on a concern for the natural rights of Black people but also a concern for the moral improvement and happiness of white people. "There must doubtless be an unhappy influence on the manners of our people produced by the existence of slavery among us," he writes in Query 23, discussing customs and manners. "The whole commerce between master and slave is a perpetual exercise of the most boisterous passions, the most unremitting despotism on the one part, and degrading submissions on the other." Since "a parent" will generally be unable to restrain "the intemperance of passion toward his slave," he will offer a bad example for his white "children," who will "see this, and learn to imitate it; for man is an imitate animal," Jefferson declares. In his view, slavery brings out "the worst of passions" in enslavers, and no child who observed his parents dealing with slaves could remain "undepraved." This failure of personal self-government will also lead to failures of democratic self-government, since, by "permitting one half the citizens thus to trample on the rights of the other," statesmen will transform whites into despots and Blacks into enemies. Jefferson's conclusion is that enslaving Black people is bad for the morals, virtue, and industry of white people: "With the morals of the [white] people, their industry also is destroyed," since "in a warm climate, no man will labour for himself who can make another labour for him."[23] Here, in a moment of self-awareness, he is taking to heart his father's injunction to work for yourself.

Jefferson's very next sentence is his famous warning of divine retribution for the sin of slavery. After stressing that liberties may be insecure once people no longer view them as a gift from God, he prophesies that "they are not to be violated but with his wrath." He goes on to warn of the slave insurrections that he feared throughout his life. "Indeed I tremble for my country when I reflect that God is just: that his justice cannot sleep forever: that considering numbers, nature and natural means only, a revolution of the wheel of fortune, an exchange of situation is among possible events; that it may become probable by supernatural interference!" Jefferson's prediction of "supernatural interference" on behalf of the enslaved, from someone who otherwise doubted miracles and the possibility of God's intervention in human affairs, is striking. Warming to his subject, Jefferson ends by endorsing voluntary total emancipation as a way of avoiding a slave rebellion and democratic revolution.[24]

Despite his repeated calls for "a total emancipation" of enslaved Americans at an unspecified date in the future, Jefferson during his lifetime freed only eight of the nearly two hundred enslaved human beings he held in bondage at Monticello, his five-thousand-acre estate. And as the historian Paul Finkelman has noted, all eight were members of the Hemings family and therefore were Jefferson's relatives by blood, marriage, or both.[25] Some of the enslaving Founders from Virginia, however, were willing to practice as well as preach the principles of the Declaration of Independence. For example, George Wythe, Jefferson's favorite law professor, not only emancipated all of his slaves during his lifetime but also made arrangements for their support and livelihood.[26] Though George Washington waited until his death, he provided in his will that all of the people he held in slavery should be freed on the death of his wife, Martha. At the same time, other Virginia enslavers—such as James Madison and George Mason—maintained the same hypocritical position that Jefferson did, professing a desire for the abolition of slavery in theory but refusing, even after death, to free their own enslaved population in practice.

Jefferson was insincere about inconveniencing himself to achieve his stated goal of abolishing slavery because he enjoyed the lifestyle that enslaved labor made possible and was unwilling to give it up. His insincerity—let's call it hypocrisy—was unusually dramatic among the enslaving Founders, because of his addiction to living beyond his means and his capacity for rationalization. In moments of candor, however, Jefferson acknowledged that it was simple avarice that led southern enslavers who recognized that slavery was immoral to refuse to emancipate their own slaves. In 1785 Benjamin Franklin gave Thomas Jefferson a copy of the British abolitionist Richard Price's *Observations on the Importance of the American Revolution*, which denounced the slave trade as "shocking to humanity, cruel, wicked, and diabolical."[27] In thanking Price for his observations, in August 1785 Jefferson predicted that slavery would gradually be abolished in all states except the Carolinas and Georgia. In all slaveholding states, Jefferson said, there was an "interesting spectacle of justice in conflict with avarice and oppression." In the northern states, where there were "few slaves," Jefferson said, slaveholders "can easily disencumber themselves of them" without personal financial sacrifice. By contrast, in the southern states, he predicted that "the bulk of the people will approve" Price's sentiments "in theory and find a respectable minority ready to adopt it in practice," while the majority "have not the courage to divest their families of a property which however keeps their consciences inquiet." Jefferson then invited Price to address the students of William & Mary about the immorality of slavery, enlisting the support of his own tutor, George Wythe, whom Jefferson called "one of the most virtuous of characters, and whose sentiments on the subject of slavery are unequivocal." Jefferson expressed confidence that Price's influence on the thinking of the young men of Virginia "would be great, perhaps decisive."[28]

While Jefferson was addressing the avarice of enslavers in general, everything he wrote applied to his own behavior. Because of his remarkable capacity for self-rationalization, however, Jefferson refused to acknowledge his own insincerity while denouncing the hypocrisy of his fellow enslavers. In Query 14 of *Notes on the State of Virginia*, he acknowledged the fact that slaveholders were "actuated by sordid avarice," as "a powerful obstacle to the emancipation of these people."[29] And yet Jefferson could never overcome his own avarice. He not only relied on enslaved labor to maintain his lavish lifestyle but also trafficked in slaves throughout his lifetime to pay his debts. To keep his creditors at bay, he sold at least eighty-five slaves in the decade between 1784 and 1794 alone. And in his will, Jefferson concluded brutally that he couldn't afford to free his slaves and had to sell them instead, preferring to separate husbands from wives and mothers from children than to impose his debts on his own children. Despite Jefferson's avaricious calculation, his debts were so crushing that, six months after his death, on January 15, 1827, all of his possessions, including the Monticello estate and "130 valuable negroes," were sold at auction to the highest bidders.[30]

The Founder who most resembled Jefferson on slavery—opposing it in theory and relying on it in practice—was his fellow Virginia aristocrat

George Mason. Like Jefferson, Mason combined a lifelong crusade to denounce and abolish the international slave trade with a lifelong dependence on enslaved labor. And, like Jefferson, Mason drew on his classical education in an unsatisfactory attempt to reconcile his own avarice in exploiting enslaved labor with his claim that importing more enslaved people would corrupt the morals of Americans in the future.

In 1754 Mason began to build Gunston Hall, a majestic estate on more than five thousand acres overlooking the Potomac River in Fairfax County, not far from George Washington's Mount Vernon. When construction began, the estate included 22 enslaved people; nearly thirty years later, the number had increased to 128, making him one of the most significant enslavers in the county, second only to Washington, who held 188 people in bondage.[31] Over the same period, as their tobacco harvests became exhausted, Mason and other Virginia planters shifted their focus to wheat, reducing the need for enslaved labor in the field. Since the enslaved population tripled over the same period, Virginians perceived no need to import more enslaved people from Africa. Mixing expediency and principle, Jefferson and other leading Virginians became fierce opponents of the international slave trade and called for the ultimate abolition of slavery in the distant future. On this point, they found no contradiction between their avarice and their virtue.

In December 1765, in response to the Stamp Act, Mason turned to Roman history in his first recorded opposition to the international slave trade. Passed by the British Parliament earlier that year, the Stamp Act was another spark that kindled the Revolution. To pay for the British troops stationed in colonies, Parliament required everyone who used various papers, documents, or even playing cards to pay a tax, represented by a stamp. Virginians' refusal to pay the tax threatened to shut down the court system. As they prepared to dispense with imported luxuries, Virginia landowners had a more immediate concern: collecting rents from delinquent tenants before the courts closed their doors. In December Mason sent George Washington a proposal for the Virginia Legislature that would allow landlords to collect their rents. To support his self-interested case, Mason began by arguing that leasing lands was more beneficial to the community than settling them with slaves, and he attacked the international slave trade for discouraging white migration. Like Jefferson, Mason was more focused on the economic and moral effects of slavery on white people than on Black people. He decried "the ill Effect such a Practice has upon the Morals & Manners of our People: one of the first Signs of the Decay, & perhaps the primary Cause of the Destruction of the most flourishing Government that ever existed was the Introduction of great Numbers of Slaves—an Evil very pathetically described by the Roman Historians."[32]

Stung by the American boycott of British goods, Parliament repealed the Stamp Act in March 1766 but then flexed its muscles by passing—on the very same day—the Declaratory Act, which asserted Parliament's power to legislate for the colonies "in all cases whatsoever."[33] In the years that followed, as Parliament passed a series of punishing new taxes, Mason, Washington, Jefferson, and Patrick Henry continued to agitate for the end of the international slave trade. In July 1774, during a meeting at the Fairfax Court House chaired by Washington, the inhabitants of Fairfax County considered twenty-four resolutions written by Mason. The seventeenth resolution declared that "during our present Difficulties and Distress, no Slaves ought to be imported into any of the British Colonies on this Continent, and We take this Opportunity of declaring our most earnest Wishes to see an entire Stop for ever put to such a wicked cruel and unnatural Trade."[34] The following month, a statewide convention of delegates across Virginia adopted more resolutions by Mason, pledging that "we will neither ourselves import, nor purchase, any Slave, or Slaves, imported" from Africa, the West Indies, or any other place, and also pledging to end all imports from Great Britain, except for medicine.[35] Jefferson repeated his denunciation of King George III for vetoing efforts by the colonies to end the international slave trade in a draft paragraph of the Declaration of Independence that was deleted by the Continental Congress: "[H]e has waged cruel war against human nature itself, violating it's most sacred rights of life & liberty in

the persons of a distant people who never offended him, captivating &
carrying them into slavery in another hemisphere, or to incure miserable
death in their transportation thither."[36] In 1778, after the Declaration of
Independence, Governor Thomas Jefferson and the Virginia House of
Burgesses finally joined together to ban the importation of all enslaved
persons into the state.

Mason's most fervent defense of what he called in the Virginia Declaration of Rights "the blessings of the liberty" was at the Constitutional
Convention, where he argued that Congress should have the power to
put an immediate end to the international slave trade. With a gesture to
the classical virtues, he began by asserting, "This infernal traffic originated in the avarice of British Merchants." He complained that "The
British Govt. constantly checked the attempts of Virginia to put a stop
to it." Mentioning the danger of slave insurrections in Greece and Sicily,
he noted that Maryland, Virginia, and, effectively, North Carolina, had
already banned the importation of slaves, but that these bans would be
in vain if South Carolina and Georgia could continue to import slaves.
He then indicted slavery for discouraging industry and virtue and, like
Jefferson, predicted divine retribution:

> Slavery discourages arts & manufactures. The poor despise labor
> when performed by slaves. They prevent the emigration of Whites,
> who really enrich & strengthen a country. They produce the most
> pernicious effect on manners. Every master of slaves is born a petty
> tyrant. They bring the judgment of heaven on a Country.[37]

By the time Mason delivered his speech on August 22, the convention was impatient to conclude. And South Carolina and Georgia
made clear that they would agree only to give Congress the power to
ban the international slave trade in twenty years. As a result, the convention adjourned without considering Mason's proposal to include a
Bill of Rights, which, he said, "would give great quiet to the people"
and "with the aid of the State declarations . . . might be prepared in

a few hours."[38] Writing to Jefferson in May 1788, Mason complained that supporters of the Constitution had cobbled together majority support "during the last Week of the Convention" based on "a Compromise between the Eastern, and the two Southern States"—he meant Georgia and South Carolina—"to permit the latter to continue the Importation of Slaves for twenty odd Years; a more favourite Object with them than the Liberty and Happiness of the People."[39] There was no doubt that, for Mason and Jefferson, slavery was inconsistent with the pursuit of happiness. But, in a remarkable act of projection, they blamed British merchants for the same avarice that prevented them from freeing the human beings they held in bondage.

The other great compromise over slavery at the Constitutional Convention was brokered by James Wilson. In his lectures on law, delivered at the University of Pennsylvania in 1791, Wilson drew on his classical training to conclude that "the Roman law was not, in every age of Rome, the law of slavery." Surveying the ancient authorities, he declared unequivocally that slavery violated natural and common law. "Slavery, or an absolute and unlimited power, in the master, over the life and fortune of the slave, is unauthorized by the common law," he wrote. "Indeed, it is repugnant to the principles of natural law that such a state should subsist in any social system."[40] And in his speech defending the Constitution at the Pennsylvania Ratifying Convention, Wilson praised as one of the "lovely" features and "delightful" prospects of the Constitution the fact that, after "the lapse of a few years . . . congress will have the power to exterminate slavery from within our borders."[41]

Despite Wilson's typically Panglossian claim that Congress might end slavery entirely—rather than simply banning the international slave trade—Wilson himself did nothing at the Constitutional Convention to hasten slavery's demise. It was Wilson, in fact, who proposed the infamous formula that counted slaves as three-fifths of a person for purposes of determining representation in Congress. Borrowing the three-fifths formula from one that Congress had used in 1783 to raise revenue from the states, Wilson was trying to mediate between the delegates who wanted to count enslaved people fully in a state's total population and those who wanted to exclude them entirely.[42] Speaking in favor of the three-fifths formula, Wilson admitted that he "did not well see on what principle the admission of blacks in the proportion of three-fifths could be explained." If they were admitted as citizens, "[t]hen why are they not admitted on an equality with White Citizens?" If they were admitted as property, "then why is not other property admitted into the computation?" He thought these "difficulties," however, had to be "overruled by the necessity of compromise."[43] Taking a more principled position, Gouverneur Morris, the most outspoken antislavery delegate to the Convention, denounced the three-fifths compromise for giving the enslavers of South Carolina and Georgia more political power than the citizens of Pennsylvania or New Jersey, who viewed "with a laudable horror, so nefarious a practice." Calling slavery "a nefarious institution" that brought "the curse of heaven on the States where it prevailed," Morris insisted that he "never would concur in upholding domestic slavery."[44]

Wilson, Mason, and Jefferson all received a kind of karmic comeuppance for the avarice that led them to betray their own ideals of frugality and universal justice for all. Because of his ignominious death as a fugitive on the run from his creditors, Wilson, who arguably had more influence on the Constitution than any other Founder, is all but forgotten today. As for Jefferson, his shining achievement in distilling the principles of the American mind is tainted by his failure to live up to those principles in practice. It would take a less philosophical Founder—George Washington—to exemplify better the principles of pursuing happiness through self-control that Jefferson eloquently expressed but never fully achieved.

Notes on Cicero's *On Duties*

Our spirits include appetite and reason
Reason commands and appetite obeys
Self-controlled characters find cohesion
When passion is calmed by reason's ukase

All moral right arises from what's true
Or strong and great within a noble soul
Or what renders to every man his due
Be Moderate: the source of self-control

Courageous souls are fearless for what's right
All brave men must at the same time be good
Their fortitude scorns praise in outward sight
Embracing risk of danger as they should

Why anger, desire, and fear? All men are brothers
Be self-controlled and calm, and think of others.

Seven

RESOLUTION

George Washington's Self-Command

I n March 1783, at his headquarters in Newburgh, New York, General Washington faced the possibility of mutiny. Congress owed the Revolutionary army years of back pay, and soldiers were plundering local farmers for rations. Anonymous letters circulated among the troops, including one urging them to lay down their arms and leave "an ungrateful Country to defend itself," as Washington noted with alarm. It was an inflection point for the American Revolution: Washington had every incentive to cast himself as a Caesar, siding with the soldiers over the democratically elected Congress. The army could have descended into a military dictatorship, or Washington might have been toppled in a military coup. Instead, he chose to appeal to the soldiers who favored democracy and deliberation over force and ambition. The anonymous call to mutiny, he told his troops, was "addressed more to the feelings & passions, than to the reason & judgment of the Army."[1]

Washington was famous for his self-command—"Fam'd for thy

valour, for thy virtues more," as Phillis Wheatley had put it—and throughout his career as a soldier and statesman, he led by controlling his emotions. But when he read the letter urging his troops to "suspect the man who should advise to more moderation & longer forbearance," he became, according to a major who observed the scene, "sensibly agitated."[2] With a keen sense of the theatrical, Washington summoned his troops to convene in a wooden structure known as the Temple of Virtue, which had been specially constructed for Masonic meetings and modest dances. As he prepared to deliver his carefully drafted remarks, the general was guided by his favorite play, Joseph Addison's *Cato*, which he had encouraged his officers to perform for his forty-sixth birthday fifteen years before during the Battle of Valley Forge. An ode to the virtues of the Roman Republic, the play described how Cato the Younger had preferred suicide rather than submit to Caesar's tyranny. It included a phrase spoken by the character of Marc Antony that inspired Washington as he prepared to address his troops: "Thy steady temper, Portius, Can look on guilt, rebellion, fraud, and Caesar, In the calm lights of mild philosophy."[3]

Drawing on the same mild Stoic philosophy that he had studied in his youth, in particular the letters of Seneca, Washington steadied his temper as he mounted the podium. He called on the army to "express your utmost horror & detestation" of anyone who was plotting "to overturn the liberties of our Country, & who wickedly attempts to open the flood Gates of Civil discord, & deluge our rising Empire in Blood." By seeking "to take advantage of the passions," he said, the "secret Mover of the Scheme" wanted to prevent the soldiers from "giving time for cool, deliberative thinking" and "composure of Mind." Instead, Washington urged the troops to give Congress more time, recognizing that deliberations are always slow in large bodies that have to reconcile competing interests. The troops could attain "the last stage of perfection to which human nature is capable of attaining," Washington said, by giving the world an example of "patient virtue."[4]

At this point, according to another observer, Major Samuel Shaw,

Washington told the troops he would read them a letter that gave him confidence that Congress would pay them in the end. As he struggled to put on his reading glasses, he observed "that he had grown gray in their service, and now found himself growing blind." According to Shaw, "There was something so natural, so unaffected, in this appeal" that the soldiers wept. Shaw had seen Washington in many circumstances: "calm and intrepid where the battle raged, patient and persevering under the pressure of misfortune, moderate and possessing himself in the full career of victory." But Washington never appeared more truly great than at this moment. In Shaw's view, he had attained the "last stage of perfection" that he was urging his troops to emulate.[5] Moved by the example of Washington's self-mastery, the troops heeded his appeal for patience and waited for Congress to make them whole. And later that year, Congress finally gave the soldiers what amounted to full pay for five years.

Washington had averted mutiny by inspiring the troops to display the same mastery of emotions that he attempted to embody. At every stage of his career—as a young surveyor, army officer, commander in chief of the Continental army, president of the Constitutional Convention, and president of the United States—he struggled mightily to control his temper. As he put it in a letter to a friend in 1799, just months before he died, he had "endeavoured as far as human frailties & perhaps strong passions would enable him" to discharge his duties to "his Maker & fellow-men," without courting popularity.[6]

The most striking feature of Washington's daily efforts to control his "strong passions" is that, more often than not, he succeeded. Washington's classical reading also helped him draw the connection between personal self-government and political self-government. Like individuals, he believed, groups of citizens could be happy only if they used their powers of reason and conscience to control their selfish passions. When individuals failed to exercise self-control, they were plagued by anxiety; when groups failed to exercise self-control, they descended into factions and mobs. In both cases, emotional self-regulation was the key to individual and collective happiness. Throughout his career, however, Washington worried that Americans would abandon the virtue they had displayed in the Revolutionary era. He was unsure, in other words, whether his fellow citizens could control their tempers even as he struggled impressively to control his own.

"[P]erhaps the strongest feature in his character was prudence," Thomas Jefferson wrote of Washington, "never acting until every circumstance, every consideration was maturely weighed; refraining if he saw a doubt, but, when once decided, going through with his purpose whatever obstacles opposed." Noting that Washington was "incapable of fear," Jefferson added that "his integrity was most pure, his justice the most inflexible I have ever known," and, "on the whole, his character was, in it's mass perfect." But Washington's perfection of character was the result of a lifelong battle to control his temper. "[H]is temper was naturally irritable and high toned; but reflection & resolution had obtained a firm and habitual ascendancy over it," Jefferson emphasized. "[I]f ever however it broke it's bonds, he was most tremendous in his wrath."[7]

John Adams, whose relationship with Washington was based more on envy than filial devotion, agreed with Jefferson about the general's self-mastery. "He had great Self Command," Adams wrote to Benjamin Rush, the visionary physician who signed the Declaration of Independence, ticking off a list of Washington's ten "Talents." "It cost him a great Exertion sometimes, and a constant Constraint, but to preserve so much Equanimity as he did, required a great Capacity. Whenever he lost his temper as he did Sometimes, either Love or fear in those about him induced them to conceal his Weakness from the World."[8]

Adams also observed that Washington possessed "a tall Stature," "[a]n elegant form," "graceful Attitudes and Movements," "a large imposing Fortune," "the Gift of Silence," and was "[s]elf taught"—all talents that Adams himself lacked.[9] In fact, Washington acquired his lifelong determination to perfect his character from his parents and his youthful reading in classical moral philosophy. His father, Augustine Washington, had received a fine classical education at the Appleby School in the north of England, and he sent his two sons from his first marriage, Lawrence and Augustine Jr., to Appleby as well. But Augustine died in 1743, when George was eleven, and his mother, Mary Ball Washington, decided to educate him at home.[10]

Washington had a fraught relationship with his mother: his biographer Ron Chernow speculates that the "hypercritical" Mary "produced a son who was overly sensitive to criticism and suffered from a lifelong need for approval," cultivating the "extreme self-control of a deeply emotional young man who feared the fatal vehemence of his own feelings, if left unchecked." His "boyhood struggle" to "master his temper and curb his tongue," in dealing with his "querulous" mother, Chernow suggests, was "the genesis of the stoical personality that would later define him."[11]

Whatever the influence of his emotional struggles with his mother, Washington's Stoicism was also shaped by the classical philosophy that he read in his father's library. In 1787, in a remarkably formal letter to his mother, who was short of money, he advised her to reduce her expenses by renting out her plantation to her nephew and living with one of her children (but not him). He then proceeded to lecture her about how happiness can be achieved only through tranquility of mind, in words that could have been copied from a Stoic textbook: "Happiness depends more upon the internal frame of a persons own mind—than on the externals in the world," he instructed his mother, and "if you will pursue the plan here recommended I am sure you can want nothing that is essential—the other depends wholy upon your self."[12]

Where did Washington learn this Stoic wisdom? The book of classical moral philosophy that influenced him most was Seneca's *Morals*, a collection of essays on how to lead a good life. (Washington, who didn't read Greek or Latin, owned the 1746 translation by Roger L'Estrange, which appears on Jefferson's reading list.) One of the most accessible of the classical moral philosophers, Seneca wrote a series of short and easily understood "moral epistles"—letters to a friend on topics such

as "On Anger," "On Saving Time," and "On a Happy Life." Born in
Spain around 4 BC, he was raised in Rome and distinguished himself
as senator, where his eloquence aroused the jealousy of the wicked Emperor Caligula, and he barely escaped death. After exile on the island
of Corsica, he was recalled to Rome by Agrippina, wife of Emperor
Claudius, who appointed him as moral tutor to her son, soon to become
the debauched Emperor Nero. Despite Seneca's instruction, Nero became as dissolute as Caligula once he ascended to the imperial throne.
After Seneca was accused (probably falsely) of supporting a conspiracy
to kill Nero in AD 65, his vengeful pupil ordered him to kill himself,
and he complied serenely, cutting his wrists and bleeding to death in a
warm bath.

Despite his unfortunate end, Seneca explored the connection between happiness and virtue more clearly than any Roman philosopher
since Cicero, who, a century earlier, had also bravely accepted death at a
wicked ruler's command. Washington's edition of *Morals* includes Seneca's book "On a Happy Life," which begins with the following words:

> There is not anything in this world, perhaps, that is more talked of,
> and less understood, than the business of a happy life. It is every
> man's wish, and design, and yet not one of a thousand that knows
> wherein that happiness consists. We live, however, in a blind and
> eager pursuit of it; and the more haste we make in a wrong way, the
> further we are from our journey's end.[13]

In addition to including the phrase about "happiness" and the "eager
pursuit of it," Seneca's essay, in the translation that Washington read,
goes on to say that we should "govern ourselves by *reason*" and defines
happiness, in terms similar to the Cicero passage that Jefferson and
Franklin often quoted:

> The true felicity of life is to be free from perturbations; to understand
> our duties toward God and man, to enjoy the present, without any

anxious dependence upon the future. Not to amuse ourselves with either hopes or fears, but to rest satisfied with what we have, which is abundantly sufficient; for he that is so, wants nothing. . . . Tranquillity is a certain equality of mind, which no condition of fortune can either exalt or depress. Nothing can make it less, for it is the state of human perfection.[14]

Washington used similar language when he called on the mutinous soldiers at Newburgh to be guided by "reason and judgement" rather than "feelings and passions" and to give the world an example of "the last stage of perfection to which human nature is capable of attaining."

Washington's translation of Seneca includes his epistle "On True Courage," which Washington famously displayed on the battlefield, calmly leading the charge toward the enemy with musket balls flying around him. "Fortitude *is* (properly) the contempt of all hazards according to reason," Seneca writes. "A brave Man . . . looks upon himself as a citizen and soldier of the world" and "is more ambitious of being reputed good than happy."[15] Washington established his reputation for contempt of all hazards during the Battle of Monongahela in 1755, where he fought the French as a volunteer aide to the British general Edward Braddock. Although the battle led to Braddock's death and a British defeat, Washington distinguished himself by riding fearlessly on horseback into the line of fire as bullets swirled around him. "Because of his height, he presented a gigantic target on horseback, but again he displayed unblinking courage and a miraculous immunity in battle," Ron Chernow writes. "When two horses were shot from under him, he dusted himself off and mounted the horses of dead riders."[16] Washington showed similar courage during the Revolutionary War, when he became famous for near misses with death during his charges on horseback into enemy fire. In 1778, during the Battle of Monmouth Court House, his white horse died from under him because of the heat. His aide walked up with a chestnut mare, which Washington rode instead. "I never saw the general to so much advantage. His coolness and firmness were admirable," his aide Alexander Hamilton enthused. "[H]e directed the whole with the skill of a Master workman."[17]

Seneca's collection includes another epistle on "The Blessings of a Virtuous Retirement." Washington may have kept it in mind during his career-defining decisions to retire voluntarily both as general of the Army and as president of the United States, rather than emulating the Roman emperors who anointed themselves supreme commander for life. When Washington fulfilled his promise to retire at the end of the war, Thomas Jefferson attributed his greatness to his self-abnegation. "[T]he moderation and virtue of a single character has probably prevented this revolution from being closed as most others have been by a subversion of that liberty it was intended to establish," Jefferson wrote to Washington in 1784.[18] In modestly stepping aside from the army and, later, the presidency, Washington embraced the example of Cincinnatus, the Roman military and political hero to whom he was often compared. A former senator, Cincinnatus was living in exile as a gentleman farmer when his fellow citizens offered him complete control over the state. Twice appointed supreme dictator of Rome, Cincinnatus renounced power as soon as he had achieved his military objectives in a matter of days. He then returned to his farm, becoming a symbol of civic virtue, modesty, and humility.

In February 1784 the Chevalier de Chastellux, who had fought with the Americans at Yorktown, remarked to Washington that he hoped to visit him someday at Mount Vernon, "where I am told, your excellency is retired like an other Cincinnatus."[19] Washington welcomed the analogy, once again invoking Addison's *Cato*. For Washington, as for Cincinnatus, Cato, and Seneca, the "serenity of mind" that came from the "calm lights of mild philosophy" was more valuable than the "glory" and "fame" pursued by the "Soldier" and the "Statesman," respectively.[20] "It is for young men to gather knowledge, and for old men to use it," Seneca wrote, advising that old men in retirement should use their time mindfully for daily self-improvement. "[A]nd judge of your improvement, not by what you speak, or by what you write, but by the firmness of your mind, and the government of your passions."[21] Seneca emphasized that "he that spends his time well, even in a retirement, gives a great example."[22]

Seneca expanded on the importance of time management in his memorable essay "On Saving Time." "What man can you show me who places any value on his time, who reckons the worth of each day, who understands that he is dying daily?" he wrote to his protégé Lucilius. "[H]old every hour in your grasp. Lay hold of to-day's task, and you will not need to depend so much upon to-morrow's. While we are postponing, life speeds by. Nothing, Lucilius, is ours, except time."[23] Washington took the advice to heart, maintaining a regimented schedule from his youth through his retirement years.

In his diary, Washington kept a detailed account of his daily activities under the heading "Where and how my time is Spent."[24] Throughout his life, he kept the unvarying hours of a farmer, rising before sunrise and devoting hours before breakfast to reading, correspondence, inspecting his horses, and private prayer. After a breakfast of corn cakes and tea, he mounted his horse and rode twenty miles to make a survey of his farms, supervising the construction and inspecting the field work. He returned for a midday dinner, the most substantial meal of the day, which began at exactly two forty-five in the afternoon with the sounding of the dinner bell. After a few hours in his library, he had a light supper and would read aloud to his family before bed at nine o'clock.[25] Washington's legendary punctuality was expressed in his love of timepieces: he placed a sundial at the center of his lawn at Mount Vernon and, as president, enjoyed visiting his watchmakers in Philadelphia. Washington's unvarying schedule—a habit he shared with Jefferson—allowed him to be remarkably productive throughout his life. Parson Weems, in his famous hagiography *The Life of Washington* (1800)—the one that invented the legend of young Washington chopping down the cherry tree—writes that he divided every day into four parts: "sleep, devotion, recreation, and business."[26] "[O]f all the virtues that adorned the life of this great man,"

Weems declares, "there is none more worthy of our imitation than his admirable INDUSTRY."[27]

Washington's edition of Seneca also includes the book *On Anger*. Seneca argues that anger is an unproductive passion: by dividing human beings from one another, it prevents us from pursuing our divine duty to live in harmony with divine Reason. "Anger is not only a vice, but a vice point blank against nature," Seneca writes, "for it divides instead of joining, and, in some measure, frustrates the end of Providence in human society." Seneca includes several chapters on how to prevent anger by avoiding rash judgments, techniques of emotional self-regulation that Washington devoted his life to cultivating. "There is hardly a more effectual remedy against anger than patience and consideration," Seneca suggests. "There is no encountering the first heat and fury of it, for it is deaf and mad. The best way is (in the beginning) to give it time and rest."[28] Washington deployed the technique of delaying responses to allow his passion to cool so successfully that he seldom lost control of himself in public.

Washington's emotional self-control was so legendary, in fact, that the few moments when he lost his temper are more notable than the many when he kept it. On Christmas Eve 1776, the day before Washington and the Continental army crossed the Delaware River and defeated Hessian soldiers at the Battle of Trenton, Washington learned that another general, Adam Stephen, had exchanged fire with the Hessians in the course of a scouting expedition into enemy territory. Washington was furious that Stephen might have tipped off the enemy and dressed him down in the presence of his troops. "You, sir, may have ruined all my plans by having put them on their guard," Washington exclaimed.[29] The public display of anger shocked the soldiers, who had never seen Washington lose his self-control. The next day, the general composed himself and displayed such fortitude in leading his troops across the icy river that he restored the morale of the army, launching a ten-day campaign that would culminate in victory at the Battle of Princeton.

Two years later, during the Battle of Monmouth, Washington lost

his temper when his deputy, Major General Charles Lee, failed to no-
tify him of a decision to retreat. "What is the meaning of this, sir?"
Washington demanded indignantly. "I desire to know the meaning of
this disorder and confusion!" Lee was so surprised by Washington's un-
accustomed outburst that he stammered in amazement, "Sir? Sir?"[30]
Once again, Washington's outburst shocked observers because it was
so unusual.

During his political career, Washington lost his temper in public
only on a few memorable occasions, usually when he felt disrespected
by Congress. On August 5, 1789, after the Senate rejected the president's nomination of Benjamin Fishburn to become a naval collector for
the Port of Savannah, Washington unexpectedly appeared at the Senate
chamber in New York City's Federal Hall, took the chair offered to him
by a surprised Vice President Adams, and inquired why the senators had
rejected his nominee. The next day, the Senate appointed a committee
to meet with Washington about the proper "mode of communication . . .
in the formation of treaties." After the committee insisted on oral communications, Washington once again repaired to the upper chamber to
receive the Senate's advice about treaties with Native Americans in the
South. As Washington sat in the presiding officer's chair, the senators
struggled to hear his written questions and asked for more time to study
them. "This defeats every purpose of my coming here," Washington exclaimed angrily, and stalked out of Congress "with a discontented air."[31]
He never returned.

For the most part, Washington displayed his temper only to his most
trusted deputies, such as Alexander Hamilton, whom he regarded like
a son, and who bore the brunt of his outbursts. As James Madison recorded in his journal in 1783, "Mr. Hamilton said that he knew Genl.
Washington intimately & perfectly, that his extreme reserve, mixed
sometimes with a degree of asperity of temper both of which were said
to have increased of late, had contributed to the decline of his popularity." But Hamilton assured the small group of colleagues, who had met
in a private house to discuss Congress's inability to pay the army, that

Washington's "virtue his patriotism & his firmness" would "never yield to any dishonorable or disloyal plans," and "that he would sooner suffer himself to be cut into pieces."[32]

Washington also learned techniques of anger management from Matthew Hale's *Contemplations Moral and Divine*, which his mother read aloud to him in his youth and which he kept in his library until he died.[33] Hale was a seventeenth-century English jurist whose works on the common law were so influential that they continue to be cited by the US Supreme Court today (including in *Dobbs v. Jackson Women's Health Organization* overturning *Roe v. Wade* in 2022, where Hale's misogyny also came under scrutiny).[34] He was widely read during the founding era for his advice book about how to live a virtuous life. After endorsing Aristotle's definition of happiness (tranquility of mind, obtained through the pursuit of virtue), Hale offers practical advice about how to master your passions and control your temper. "Carry always a Jealousy over thy Passion, and a strict Watch upon it," Hale exhorts in his essay "On the Moderation of Anger." "Take up this peremptory Resolution and Practice: *I will not be angry, tho' an Occasion be administered.*" To calm ourselves when we feel ourselves being seized by anger, Hale suggests the following reflections: "It puts me into a Perturbation, and makes me unuseful for my self or others, while the Distemper is upon me: It breaks and discomposeth my Thoughts, and makes me unfit for Business; it disorders my Constitution of Body, till the Storm be over." Hale recommends that we reason and deliberate with ourselves to cool the passion of anger, asking whether there's any good end that can be achieved by it. For example, he suggests, "Witness our Anger with Cards and Dice, when their Chances please us not; which shews the Unreasonableness and Frenzy of this Passion."[35]

Washington may have recalled Hale's advice on one of the few occasions he was observed laughing boisterously in public. During a game of whist, an English card game, with his Revolutionary War aide David Cobb, Washington watched his opponents, a clergyman and a physician, become increasingly agitated by their bad luck. As the clergyman proceeded to lose each hand, his partner swore so vigorously that the clergyman refused to continue unless the physician controlled himself. Finally, the physician abandoned the effort. He threw down his cards, stuck his head up the chimney, and cursed uncontrollably. According to Cobb, Washington laughed so hard that he wept.[36]

In addition to Seneca and Matthew Hale, young Washington encountered popularized versions of classical moral philosophy in the *Spectator*, which he read as avidly as Franklin, and in the *Gentleman's Magazine*, an English periodical whose motto was "*E Pluribus Unum*." One of his surviving schoolboy exercises includes a poem from the *Gentleman's Magazine* called "True Happiness," which Washington copied out from the February 1734 issue when he was about fourteen. It includes the standard Stoic advice about how to achieve happiness by cultivating moderation and tranquility of mind:

> *These are the* things *which once posses'd*
> *Will make a life that's truly* bless'd, . . .
> *A quiet* wife, *a quiet* soul,
> *A* mind *as well as* body *whole;*
> Prudent *simplicity,* constant *friends,*
> *A* diet *which no* art *commends,*
> *A* merry *night without much* drinking,
> *A* happy *thought without much* thinking.[37]

Under the guidance of his tutor, the Reverend James Marye, Washington encountered a more substantial collection of moral aphorisms in the well-known "Rules of Civility and Decent Behaviour in Company and Conversation," which he also copied out in his 1745 exercise book. "The Rules of Civility" was first published in English in a mid-seventeenth-century English advice manual, Francis Hawkins's *Youths Behaviour, or, Decency in Conversation Amongst Men*, which is based, in turn, on a late-sixteenth-century treatise by French Jesuits about the art of conversation.[38] Widely available today in National Park gift shops (and often misattributed to Washington himself), the 110 "Rules of Civility" include excellent advice about how to behave in polite company. (Rule 2: "When in Company, put not your Hands to any Part of the Body, not usualy Discovered.") But in addition to helpful tips about good table manners (Rule 16: "Do not Puff up the Cheeks, Loll not out the tongue"), the rules include important advice about how to deploy our powers of reason to moderate our passions. "Let your Conversation be without Malice or Envy, for 'tis a Sig[n o]f a Tractable and Commendable Nature," declares Rule 58. "And in all Causes of Passion [ad]mit Reason to Govern." Rule 83 reinforces the point: "When you deliver a matter do it without Passion & with Discretion, howev[er] mean [the] Person be you do it too."[39]

Derived from the same classical sources that inspired Benjamin Franklin's thirteen virtues, many of the Rules of Civility could have been written by Franklin himself. But what Washington seems to have found especially useful was their practical advice for controlling the public display of emotions. The rules emphasize the importance of anger management and cultivating a tranquil disposition: "Be not Angry at Table whatever happens & if you have reason to be so, Shew it not but on a Chearfull Countenance especially if there be Strangers," Rule 105 counsels. "Good Humour makes one Dish of Meat a Feas[t]." And they also advise the importance of "Think[ing] before you Speak" (Rule 73), listening to different points of view, and not being "obstinate in your own Opinion" (Rule 69), and working to ensure that every conversation is an exercise in civil dialogue rather than partisan acrimony (Rule 86).[40]

Although founded on classical wisdom, the Rules of Civility also reflect the Christian natural law tradition articulated by Saint Thomas Aquinas, the thirteenth century Italian theologian. Citing Aristotle, Cicero, and other classical sources, Aquinas and other medieval theologians agreed that human beings can discover rules of moral conduct through the exercise of right reason, and they called this moral faculty "conscience."[41] Rule 110 encapsulates this wisdom: "Labour to keep alive in your Breast that Little Spark of Ce[les]tial fire Called Conscience."[42] Washington nobly defended freedom of conscience throughout his career, combining personal piety in the Anglican tradition with a commitment to defending the rights of all to worship freely according to the dictates of their own reasoning minds.

Washington sent inspiring letters defending freedom of conscience to many members of the religious denominations who wrote congratulating him on his election as the first president of the United States in January 1789, including Quakers, Baptists, and Jews. "All possess alike liberty of conscience and immunities of citizenship," he wrote in his famous letter to the Hebrew Congregation in Newport, Rhode Island. "It is now no more that toleration is spoken of, as if it was by the indulgence of one class of people, that another enjoyed the exercise of their inherent natural rights. For happily the Government of the United States, which gives to bigotry no sanction, to persecution no assistance requires only that they who live under its protection should demean themselves as good citizens." Washington went on in the beautiful letter to quote the Old Testament's book of Micah, asking the "father of all mercies" to help all Americans to become virtuous citizens so that we could be "everlastingly happy."[43]

Washington's classical reading also helped him draw the connection between personal and political self-government and happiness. He believed that groups of citizens, like individuals, could be happy only if they controlled their tempers and moderated their violent passions. When individuals failed to exercise self-control, they were plagued by anxiety; when groups failed to exercise self-control, they descended into partisan factions. In 1764 Washington made a list of the books in his library at Mount Vernon. It includes the classical moral philosophers and historians on Jefferson's reading list, including Seneca and Plutarch. It also includes the English writers in the Independent Whig tradition that inspired all the Founders, including the *Spectator* by Addison and *Cato's Letters* by Trenchard and Gordon.[44] The English Whigs cited classical historians such as Livy, who argued that ancient Rome had flourished when its citizens combined self-restraint and austerity with virtue and public spirit and had fallen when the expansion of empire created an addiction to what they called Asiatic luxury, resulting in factions, division, strife, and civil war. *Cato's Letters* invoked the example of Rome, where demagogues had encouraged factions and played them against one another to shore up their own absolute power. According to the English writers, history itself repeated before and after the decade-long English Civil War between Royalists and Parliamentarians in the mid-seventeenth century. The rise of religious factions led to the execution of Charles I in 1649, and the rise of political factions after the Restoration of Charles II in 1660 allowed designing ministers to pursue their own corrupt self-interest rather than the public good.

Following the classical writers, *Cato's Letters* defined a faction as any group animated by passion rather than reason, devoted to self-interest rather than the public good. "When the publick passions" were "well regulated and honestly employed," this is called "the art of governing," and when they are "knavishly raised and ill employed, it is called faction, which is the gratifying of private passion by publick means," Trenchard and Gordon wrote.[45] Influenced by his youthful reading of *Cato's Letters* and the *Spectator*, Washington displayed a single-minded focus on the dangers of "party spirit" or "faction" as the greatest threat to public happiness throughout his career, from his generalship in the army, to the Constitutional Convention, to his Farewell Address as president.

In the army, Washington was challenged by a group of senior officers who questioned his leadership and sought to replace him. Led by Brigadier General Thomas Conway, the group was known as the Conway Cabal. Instead of confronting Conway publicly, which would have risked splitting loyalties, Washington, when presented with evidence of Conway's criticisms, returned the damning letter to Conway without comment—a display of soft power that he often deployed against those who plotted against him. "My caution to avoid anything that could injure the service prevented me from communicating, but to very few of my friends, the intrigues of a faction," Washington wrote in 1778 to Patrick Henry, who had passed along another anonymous letter questioning his leadership.[46]

Washington made the connection between public and private virtue and happiness repeatedly in his career. In his Farewell Address to the officers and soldiers of the army in 1783, he said that their "future happiness" depended on their cultivating the "private virtues of economy, prudence and industry" in "civil life," just as they had displayed the public virtues of "valour, perseverance and enterprise ... in the Field."[47] And the same year, in his farewell letter to the people of the States, he said that "four things" were necessary for their "political happiness" and "social happiness": an "indissoluble Union," a "sacred regard to public Justice," a "proper Peace Establishment," and the cultivation of private virtue, which he defined as "[t]he prevalence of that pacific and friendly disposition among the people of the United States, which will induce them to forget their local prejudices and policies" and "to sacrifice their individual advantages to the interest of the community."[48]

Washington ended his farewell letter by quoting once again the book of Micah, praying that God "would incline the hearts of the Citizens" toward "Charity, humility & pacific temper of mind, which were the Characteristicks of the Divine Author of our blessed Religion."[49] For Washington, like Franklin, the injunction to imitate Jesus and Socrates by cultivating "humility" and a "pacific temper of mind" was key to public and private happiness.

Washington's confidence that Americans would, in fact, find the emotional and spiritual self-discipline to govern their tempers, as individuals and citizens, waxed and waned with the fate of America itself. As the Revolutionary War approached, Washington repeatedly exhorted Americans that the only way to defeat the British was to practice "public virtue," which he defined as the control of selfish interests in the service of the public good. In 1769, when he learned that colonists in

Philadelphia and Annapolis had set up associations to protest British taxes by boycotting British goods, he wrote a letter to George Mason suggesting that Virginia should follow their lead. In particular, Washington emphasized that refusing to buy British goods until the taxes were repealed would free Virginia landowners from the cycle of debt that had trapped even the wealthiest Founders. Jefferson, Mason, and Washington himself lived on borrowed money—and enslaved labor—to support their lavish lifestyles, and Washington suggested that the boycott would give them an excuse to reduce their expenses without losing face among their rich neighbors.

"The extravagant & expensive man . . . is thereby furnished with a pretext to live within bounds, and embraces it," Washington wrote to Mason, adding that "prudence dictated œconomy to him before, but his resolution was too weak to put it in practice."[50] During the early years of the conflict with Britain, Washington was optimistic that citizens would be able to overcome their avarice and that the "non-Importation Scheme," as he called the boycott, would succeed. "I think, at least I hope, that there is publick Virtue enough left among us to deny ourselves every thing but the bare necessaries of Life to accomplish this end," he wrote in 1774.[51]

The greatest threat to public virtue, Washington emphasized, was American greed, which led speculators and war profiteers to circumvent the boycott or sell supplies to the army at monopoly prices. During and after the encampment of Valley Forge, he warned repeatedly that avarice would lead to "inevitable ruin" unless Americans recovered their willingness to sacrifice for the common good. "[N]othing therefore in my Judgment can save us but a total reformation in our own conduct," he wrote to Mason in March 1779. "Speculators—variant tribes of money makers—& stock jobbers of all denominations . . . continue the War for their own private emolument, without considering that their avarice, & thirst for gain must plunge every thing (including themselves) in one common ruin."[52] In November he lamented to his younger brother John Augustine Washington the "decay of public virtue with which people were inspired at the beginning of this contest."[53] The same month, he told Henry Laurens, who had just served as president of the Continental Congress, that "alas, virtue & patriotism are almost kicked out! Stock Jobbing—Speculating—engrossing . . . seems to be the great business of the day—and of the multitude—whilst a virtuous few struggle— lament—& suffer in silence—tho' I hope not in vain."[54] Given Washington's own land speculation, his anxiety may have been an exercise in projection.

After the war, Washington warned once again that the greatest threat to the virtue of the new republic was not greed but factions. He worried that the loose union of the thirteen states established by the Articles of Confederation was too weak to force the states to pay their fair share of the war debt or to raise an army for the common defense. "[S]omething must be done" to amend the Articles, Washington wrote to John Jay in 1786, "or the fabrick must fall. It certainly is tottering!"[55] Washington attributed the failure of the Articles of Confederation to the fact that factions were threatening civil war. Like other Founders, he was especially alarmed in 1786 by Shays's Rebellion, a group of four thousand rebels in western Massachusetts who mobbed the courts in protest against economic policies that made it hard for them to pay their debts. "What stronger evidence can be given of the want of energy in our governments than these disorders?" Washington wrote to James Madison in November 1786.[56]

Convinced by Madison and Hamilton to come out of retirement and chair the Constitutional Convention in Philadelphia, Washington led through silence and self-mastery rather than bombastic self-assertion. It was the simple force of his self-disciplined presence—his willingness to show up and to preside impartially—that allowed the warring factions, representing states big and small, enslaving and free, to reach compromises in the interest of creating a more perfect union. When Washington was unanimously elected president of the convention, he accepted the appointment with self-possessed modesty. "[I]n a very emphatic manner," James Madison recorded, Washington "thanked the Convention for the honor they had conferred on him; reminded them of the novelty of the scene of business in which he was to act, lamented his want of better qualifications, and claimed the indulgence of the House towards the involuntary errors which his inexperience might occasion."[57]

Washington's most important contribution to the Constitution was the fact that everyone knew he would be elected the first president. The fact that the delegates trusted him allowed them to create a stronger national executive than they had been willing to accept in their state constitutions. And after the Constitution was ratified, Washington was indeed unanimously elected to the presidential chair. "[T]here is no truth more thoroughly established," President Washington declared in his first inaugural address in April 1789, than the "indissoluble union between virtue and happiness." He thanked God for allowing the American people to converge around a Constitution that gave them "opportunities for deliberating in perfect tranquility, and dispositions for deciding with unparalleled unanimity on a form of Government, for the security of their Union, and the advancement of their happiness."[58] In a letter to the Pennsylvania Legislature in September, he praised "[t]he virtue, moderation, and patriotism which marked the steps of the American People" in framing and adopting the Constitution. It should be the "highest ambition of every American to extend his views beyond himself," he said, and our success in acting in the public interest rather than pursuing our own selfish interests would determine whether or not We the People would "gain respect abroad and ensure happiness and safety to ourselves and to our posterity."[59]

At the beginning of his presidency, as the country united around his nationalist policies, Washington was initially optimistic about the ability of Americans to sustain public virtue. In July 1791 he wrote to the Marquis de Lafayette, the French aristocrat who commanded American troops in the Revolutionary War, that he had just returned from a three-month tour of the southern states. He contrasted their tranquility, virtue, and happiness with the terror that was seizing France. "Industry and economy have become very fashionable in those parts, which were formerly noted for the opposite qualities," Washington observed. He was especially pleased that Congress had rallied around his Treasury Secretary Alexander Hamilton's report on public credit, which called for full payment of all national debts, and had passed the Bank Bill of 1791, establishing a national bank. "The complete establishment of our public credit is a strong mark of the confidence of the people in the virtue of their Representatives, and the wisdom of their measures," Washington emphasized."[60]

That tranquility began to unravel, however, at the end of Washington's first term, as his own cabinet broke into polarized factions. From the beginning, Washington had presided over cabinet meetings with studious neutrality, much as he presided over the army and the Constitutional Convention. He had the confidence to seek advice from strong advisors with diverse perspectives and would ask Hamilton, who favored the Union, and Jefferson and Madison, who favored the states, to draft different versions of policy papers in his name. (In most cases, he sided with Hamilton.)

Exemplifying the virtue of self-disciplined silence, Washington weighed his words carefully and avoided sharing his opinions in the heat of the moment. "Never be agitated by *more than* a decent *warmth*, & offer your sentiments with modest diffidence," he wrote to his nephew Bushrod Washington, who studied law under James Wilson and would later fill his seat on the Supreme Court. "[O]pinions thus given, are listened to with more attention than when delivered in a dictatorial stile."[61] Delaying decisions until he had thoughtfully considered all points of view, Washington displayed a deliberative prudence that allowed him to master his temper and take the long view. Hamilton observed that Washington "consulted much, pondered much, resolved slowly, resolved surely," in contrast to the impetuous Adams.[62] Jefferson agreed that "no judgment was ever sounder" than Washington's; his mind "was slow in operation, being little aided by invention or imagination, but sure in conclusion." Like all of Washington's advisors, Jefferson especially praised his practice of listening to divergent points of view, "where hearing all suggestions, he selected whatever was best."[63]

Washington was willing to listen to private criticism from trusted subordinates, especially Hamilton, but he displayed a thin-skinned sensitivity to criticism in public. And toward the end of his first term, he encountered growing criticism from the rise of the factions he feared most. After their defeat over the Bank Bill, Jefferson and Madison became convinced that Hamilton was a pro-British "monocrat" scheming to expand federal power in ways that could entrench a monarchical presidency, threaten states' rights, and allow the northern states to interfere with protections for slavery in the South. After a tour of New York and New England to drum up political opposition, Jefferson and Madison invited one of Hamilton's fiercest critics, Philip Freneau, editor of the *National Gazette* in Philadelphia, to work for Jefferson in the Department of State. Soon the two factions began to organize as informal political parties, with the partisans of Jefferson and Madison calling themselves Democratic-Republicans, and those of Hamilton and Washington calling themselves Federalists.

By the end of his first term, Washington was so distressed by sniping from Freneau and the Republican press that he decided not to seek a second term. He asked Madison to draft a farewell address emphasizing the need for civil discourse and nonpartisan unity. Madison obliged by sending Washington a draft that expressed the hope that "the happiness of the people of America" would be maintained by a virtuous avoidance of partisan sniping and "indiscriminate jealousies."[64] Hamilton talked him into running for reelection, but the continued criticism led to one of Washington's most memorable explosions.

In August 1793 Thomas Jefferson recorded Washington's reaction to one of Freneau's screeds published soon after his reelection. It depicted his death on the guillotine, along with that of Justice James Wilson. "The Presidt. was much inflamed, got into one of those passions when he cannot command himself," Jefferson wrote. He "[ra]n on much on the personal abuse which had been bestowed on him," ranting "[t]hat he had rather be on his farm than to be made *emperor of the world* and yet that they were charging him with wanting to be a king."[65] After an awkward silence, the cabinet meeting resumed.

As Washington approached the end of his second term, he asked Hamilton to prepare a new draft of his Farewell Address. Sending Hamilton the version Madison had written four years earlier, Washington added his own edits that showed how rattled he was by the partisan sniping. "[S]ome of the Gazettes of the United States have teemed with all the Invective that disappointment, ignorance of facts, and malicious falsehoods could invent, to misrepresent my politics & affections; to wound my reputation and feelings," the president wrote, adding that he would not take "notice of such virulent abuse" but would instead "pass them over in utter silence."[66] Hamilton wisely omitted Washington's outburst and instead produced the final draft of the address, which the president published in the Philadelphia newspapers on September 19, 1796. Drawing on his own classical education, Hamilton ghostwrote for Washington one of the greatest American statements of personal and political happiness.

Reading Washington's Farewell Address through the lens of the classical moral philosophers, we can understand it as a message to the American people about how to pursue happiness. "I[t] is of infinite moment, that you should properly estimate the immense value of your national Union, to your collective & individual happiness," Washington declared. He then emphasized that the people could be happy, as individuals and as a nation, only if they maintained a nonpartisan attachment to the Union by using their powers of reason to master their selfish passions. Washington warned against "the baneful effects of the Spirit of Party," or political factions. "This spirit, unfortunately, is inseparable from our nature, having its root in the strongest passions of the human Mind," Washington explained. In addition to agitating the community "with ill founded jealousies and false alarms," Washington warned, the Spirit of Party "kindles the animosity of one part against another, foments occasionally riot & insurrection," and "opens the door to foreign influence & corruption."[67]

Only virtuous self-mastery, Washington concluded, could ensure that Americans avoided the partisan entanglements at home and abroad that would threaten their "private & public felicity." The two "Pillars of human happiness," he emphasized, were "Religion and morality." Washington and Hamilton, more conventionally Christian than Jefferson, warned against the "influence of refined education on minds of peculiar structure"—here they seemed to have Jefferson in mind—who maintained that "morality can be maintained without religion." Washington concluded with a rhetorical question about whether Americans could sustain the virtue necessary for their continued happiness. "Can it be, that Providence has not connected the permanent felicity of a Nation with its virtue?" he asked. "Alas! is it rendered impossible by its vices?"[68]

After leaving the presidency with a mixture of gratitude and relief, Washington returned to Mount Vernon. There he resumed his structured schedule, rising at dawn, reading and attending to correspondence in a dressing gown before breakfast, and then taking a morning tour of the plantation on horseback. Besieged by visitors demanding political favors and free meals, he worried openly that he was unable to pay his debts and cover his expenses. The financial burden of keeping up Mount Vernon overcame him, and, with great reluctance, Washington was forced to take out bank loans. In the last months of his life, he decided to sell two houses he had built in the new capital city of Washington.

Despite these financial challenges, Washington in his last will and testament committed a final act that distinguished him from all the other enslaving Founders: he not only freed his own slaves but also provided for their education and support. The emancipation would take place on the death of his wife, he explained, although he "earnestly wished" it could happen sooner, because he had no power to liberate the dowager slaves Martha had inherited. He also claimed that the emancipation of some but not all of Mount Vernon's enslaved population would require breaking up marriages, resulting in "the most painful sensations, if not disagreeable consequences." Washington provided that, while they were waiting for freedom, the older slaves "shall be comfortably cloathed & fed by my heirs" and the younger ones "taught to read & write."[69] At a time when Black literacy was seen as a growing threat to white supremacy—by 1831, Virginia law would ban meetings to teach free Black people to read or write—Washington's faith in the ability of all people to cultivate their faculties through education was notable.

In the same Enlightenment spirit, Washington set aside funds in his will for the support of "a Free school" in Alexandria, Virginia, for the purpose of educating "Orphan children," as well as the children of "other poor and indigent persons" who could not afford to educate themselves. And he made a separate bequest for the endowment of a national university, to be established in the District of Columbia. Washington explained that it had long been his "ardent wish" to support the creation of a national university, which would discourage "local attachments and State prejudices" in the future leaders of America by bringing together "youth of fortune and talents from all parts" of the country.[70] At the end of 1796, in his last public appearance as president, Washington told Congress that "a primary object of such a national institution should be, the education of our Youth in the science of *Government*," adding that "[i]n a Republic, what species of knowledge can be equally important?"[71]

In his will, he tried to make that vision a reality. By teaching literature, arts, and sciences, and "the principles of Politics & good Government," and bringing together students from diverse backgrounds across the United States for conversation and friendship, the national university would discourage partisanship and faction, allowing future leaders to "free themselves in a proper degree from those local prejudices & habitual jealousies" that "are never failing sources of disquietude to the Public mind."[72] For Washington, as for Jefferson, public education was the key to cultivating public virtue. But while Jefferson saw the purpose of the university he created in Charlottesville as the cultivation of individual boys "of best genius" who would serve the state of Virginia, Washington saw the purpose of the national university he hoped to create as the cultivation of nationally minded leaders who would serve the United States of America.[73] Washington ended his final speech to Congress by expressing hope "that the virtue and happiness of the People may be preserved; and that the Government, which they have instituted, for the protection of their liberties, may be perpetual."[74]

How happy was Washington at the end of his life? In 1799 he worried about the rise of factions that were threatening the Union he had worked so hard to establish and perfect. When Jefferson and Madison drafted the Virginia and Kentucky Resolutions asserting the rights of states to object to federal laws they considered unconstitutional, such as the Alien and Sedition Acts, which allowed President Adams to jail his critics, Washington urged Patrick Henry to run for the Virginia General Assembly and to defend the Union against what he perceived to be the threat of civil war. "Vain will it be to look for Peace and happiness, or for the security of liberty or property, if Civil discord should ensue," he wrote to Henry at the beginning of 1799. Washington was afraid, he confessed, "that the tranquillity of the Union, and of this State in particular, is hastening to an awful crisis."[75]

Increasingly alarmed about the rise of partisan passion, Washington was unable to avoid it himself. In May he wrote to Bushrod, who had recently been confirmed to the Supreme Court, that the election of the Federalist candidates to Congress, John Marshall and Henry Lee, were "grateful to my feelings," although he wished "both of them had been Elected by greater majorities." He emphasized that there should be "no relaxation on the part of the Federalists. We are sure there will be none on that of the Republicans, as they have very erroneously called themselves."[76]

Washington died on December 14, 1799, uncertain about whether the American people had enough virtue and self-control to preserve their happiness by resisting the lure of factions. His two deputies who

were most responsible for the framing of the Constitution—Hamilton
and Madison—were also most responsible for the rise of the Federalist and Democratic-Republican Parties. And they would come to very
different conclusions about whether or not the people were capable of
personal and political self-government.

Notes on Aristotle's *Eudemian Ethics*

The happy soul tames passion with reason
Passions are feelings that bring pleasure or pains
Our faculties to feel them in season
Based on habits that character obtains

Virtues are habits of moderation
Use reason to follow the middle way
All thoughts and actions in balanced station
Vice comes when excess or shortfalls outweigh

The first habit of virtue is courage
Recklessness and cowardice are its vices
Habits of temperance the gods encourage
Free from avaricious sacrifices

In Virtue passions find the golden mean
Not in surfeit or dearth but in between

Eight

MODERATION

James Madison and Alexander Hamilton's
Constitution

J ames Madison traveled to Philadelphia in 1787 with Athens on
his mind. Madison had spent the year before the Constitutional
Convention reading two trunkfuls of books on the history of failed
democracies, sent to him from Paris by Thomas Jefferson. Madison was
determined, in drafting the Constitution, to avoid the fate of those "ancient and modern confederacies," which he believed had succumbed to
rule by demagogues and mobs.[1]

Madison's reading convinced him that direct democracies—such as
the assembly in Athens, where six thousand citizens were required for a
quorum—unleashed populist passions that overcame the cool, deliberative reason prized above all by Enlightenment thinkers. "In all very numerous assemblies, of whatever characters composed, passion never fails
to wrest the sceptre from reason," he argued in *The Federalist Papers*, the
essays he wrote with Alexander Hamilton and John Jay to build support

for the ratification of the Constitution. "Had every Athenian citizen been a Socrates, every Athenian assembly would still have been a mob."[2]

Born into an enslaving family—his father was one of the most substantial landowners in Orange County, Virginia—Madison served in the Virginia House of Delegates and the Continental Congress before helping to organize the Constitutional Convention. On his way to Philadelphia, Madison remembered that Athenian citizens had been swayed by crude and ambitious politicians who had played on their emotions. The demagogue Cleon was said to have seduced the assembly into becoming more hawkish toward Athens's opponents in the Peloponnesian War, and even the reformer Solon canceled debts and debased the currency. In Madison's view, history seemed to be repeating itself in America. After the Revolutionary War, he had observed in Massachusetts "a rage for paper money, for abolition of debts, for an equal division of property." That populist rage had led to Shays's Rebellion, the riots that helped convince Washington and other elites that it was time for the Articles of Confederation to be replaced in order to create a government restrained enough to protect liberty but strong and deliberative enough to resist foreign threats and the mob. Madison referred to impetuous mobs as factions, which he defined in "Federalist No. 10" as a group "united and actuated by some common impulse of passion, or of interest, adverse to the rights of other citizens, or to the permanent and aggregate interests of the community."[3] Factions arise, he believed, when public opinion forms and spreads quickly. But they can be dissolved if the public is given time and space to consider long-term interests rather than short-term gratification.

According to classical theory, republics could exist only in relatively small territories, where citizens could know one another personally and assemble face-to-face. Plato would have capped the number of citizens capable of self-government at 5,040. Madison, however, thought Plato's small-republic thesis was wrong. He believed that the ease of communication in small republics was precisely what had allowed hastily formed majorities to oppress minorities. "Extend the sphere" of a territory,

Madison wrote, "and you take in a greater variety of parties and interests; you make it less probable that a majority of the whole will have a common motive to invade the rights of other citizens; or if such a common motive exists, it will be more difficult for all who feel it to discover their own strength and to act in unison with each other."[4] Madison predicted that America's vast geography and large population would prevent passionate mobs from mobilizing. Their dangerous energy would burn out before it could inflame others.

James Madison died at Montpelier, his Virginia estate, in 1836, one of the few Founding Fathers to survive into the democratic age of President Andrew Jackson. Madison supported Jackson's efforts to preserve the Union against nullification efforts in the South but was alarmed by his populist appeal in the West. What would Madison make of American democracy today, an era in which Jacksonian populism looks restrained by comparison? Madison's worst fears of mob rule have been realized—and the cooling mechanisms he designed to slow down the formation of impetuous majorities have broken.

The polarization of Congress in the twenty-first century, reflecting an electorate that has not been this divided since around the time of the Civil War, has led to ideological warfare between parties that directly channels the passions of their most extreme constituents—precisely the type of factionalism the Founders abhorred. The executive branch, meanwhile, has been transformed by the spectacle of tweeting presidents, though the presidency had broken from its constitutional restraints long before the advent of social media. During the election of 1912, the progressive populists Theodore Roosevelt and Woodrow Wilson insisted that the president derived his authority directly from the people. Since then, the office has moved in precisely the direction the Founders had hoped to avoid: presidents now make emotional appeals, communicate directly with voters, and pander to the mob. Twitter, Facebook, and other platforms have accelerated public discourse to warp speed, creating virtual versions of the mob. Inflammatory posts based on passion travel further and faster than arguments based on reason. Rather than encouraging deliberation, mass media undermine it by creating bubbles and echo chambers in which citizens see only those opinions they already embrace.

We are living, in short, in a Madisonian nightmare.[5] Nevertheless, if the republic of Twitter seems like the antithesis of the republic of reason, Madison and Hamilton also point a possible way forward. Their great contribution in *The Federalist Papers* was to apply insights of faculty psychology, or the psychology of using reason to control our emotions, to the drafting and preservation of constitutions. And their conclusion, following the classical and Enlightenment moral philosophers, was that personal self-government is necessary for political self-government. Just as individuals can use their powers of reason to achieve psychological happiness, so can groups of citizens use their powers of reason to achieve political happiness. Constitution makers, they insisted, should seek to cultivate the same harmony in the state as individuals seek to cultivate in their minds. Ultimately, they believed that individual citizens have a responsibility to think for themselves, mastering their own passions, resisting groupthink, and taking the time for sober second thoughts in order to achieve private and public happiness.

The new republic mirrored the human mind, Madison and Hamilton believed, and was vulnerable to the same anxieties and perturbations. Individuals could become unsettled by violent passions such as anger, envy, ambition, and avarice; and they would most likely succumb to these passions when in large groups. By encouraging decisions based on long-term reason rather than short-term passions, the Constitution promised to achieve its broader goal of promoting what Madison and Hamilton repeatedly call "the happiness of the people" or "public happiness."

As the historian Daniel Walker Howe observes in his essay "The Political Psychology of *The Federalist*," Madison and Hamilton treated self-interest as a selfish passion when it was directed at short-term gratification but as rational when it took the long view.[6] In his invaluable book on the faculty psychology of the Founders, Howe further notes that just as the mind has faculties of reason, prudence, and passion, so, according to *The Federalist*, the state includes a small group of natural aristocrats (who govern based on reason), a larger group of people who can discern their enlightened self-interest (prudence), and still larger masses of people driven by a desire for immediate gratification (passion).[7] The separation of powers in government should be designed to mirror the separate faculties of the human mind, recognizing that long-term wisdom, tranquility, and happiness require careful checks and balances among the faculties.

In other words, the Founders believed that harmony that results from a well-tempered Constitution mirrors the harmony of a well-tempered mind. But instead of balancing the monarchy, aristocracy, and democracy, as ancient Constitutions had done, the American Constitution would balance the legislative, executive, and judicial branches, each of which corresponded to a different faculty of the mind. The executive branch, with the power of the sword, wielded force; the legislative branch, with the power of the purse, possessed will; and the judicial branch, as Hamilton wrote in "Federalist No. 78," had "neither FORCE nor WILL, but merely judgment," corresponding to the faculty of conscience that could resist the impulses of unreasonable passion.[8] By the same token, the president could check the impulsive passions of Congress with the veto, just as the more aristocratic Senate could cool the passions of the more democratic House. The goal of all these institutional checks was to slow down deliberation so that large groups of people could achieve the same long-term thinking in the body politic that individuals sought to achieve through virtuous self-mastery.[9]

The Federalist Papers are a how-to manual for achieving public happiness. In "Federalist No. 62," Madison writes that "[a] good government implies two things: first, fidelity to the object of government, which is the happiness of the people; secondly, a knowledge of the means by which that object can be best attained."[10] According to *The Federalist*, the "happiness of the people" requires security against foreign threats, standing armies, factions, and conflicts among the states. It also requires the same harmony among the powers of government that individuals seek to cultivate among the faculties of their own minds. Writing of "the true means by which the public happiness may be promoted," Hamilton explains that it sometimes requires the president to resist the momentary passions of the people rather than inflaming them. "The republican principle demands that the deliberate sense of the community should govern the conduct of those to whom they entrust the management of their affairs; but it does not require an unqualified complaisance to every sudden breese of passion, or to every transient impulse which the people may receive from the arts of men, who flatter their prejudices to betray their interests," he writes in "Federalist No. 71."[11]

Because Hamilton had more trouble than Madison and Washington in deploying reason to tame his passions, he was the one who became the subject of a Broadway musical. His efforts to overcome his disadvantaged background, as a self-taught genius from Saint Croix who wrote his way out of poverty and illegitimacy, fired his ruling passion to win fame and glory, and to inscribe his name, like a sunbeam, on the history of the world. Like Madison, Hamilton served as a delegate at the Constitutional Convention and became more partisan after spending eight years in the Washington administration as the first secretary of the Treasury. His first big break was an essay he published at the age of seventeen describing a hurricane that tore through Saint Croix; it created such a sensation that local business leaders raised funds to send Hamilton to North America to continue his education. Arriving in New York Harbor in 1773, Hamilton crammed for the entrance exam of the College of New Jersey (now Princeton University), reading Cicero's orations in Latin and Homer in Greek. He impressed the college president, John Witherspoon, but failed to persuade the trustees to accept his bold proposal that he be allowed to complete his education in two years rather than three, as Madison had done two years earlier.

Undaunted, Hamilton set off across the Hudson River to be tutored in moral philosophy at King's College (now Columbia University) by President Myles Cooper, a British loyalist. We have a sense of

Hamilton's Pythagorean daily schedule at college from a stern list of "Rules for Philip Hamilton" that he sent to his son after Philip's graduation from Columbia in 1800: "rise not later than" six in the morning; "read Law" until nine; at the office until an afternoon dinner; after dinner, read law until five; from seven to ten, more reading and study; and then to bed.[12] The King's College curriculum at the time centered on the classics, including Virgil, Ovid, Cicero, Epictetus, Pliny, Horace, Aristotle, Plato, Xenophon, Aeschylus, and Euripides.[13] Hamilton's college essays suggest he also read the same moral and political philosophers as the other Founders: Locke, Montesquieu, Hobbes, and Hume, as well as the legal writers Hugo Grotius, Samuel von Pufendorf, and Emmerich de Vattel.[14] After the Battle of Lexington and Concord in 1775, he enlisted with other King's College graduates in a new artillery company forming in New York to defend liberty, and his paybook records the books that fired his imagination in the field.

The most influential of all was Plutarch's *Lives*. Hamilton took fifty pages of notes recording excerpts from Plutarch's paired biographies of the great Greek and Roman heroes of antiquity, focusing on four lives in particular: Romulus, founder of Rome; Numa Pompilius, his successor; Theseus, founder of Athens; and, above all, Lycurgus, lawgiver of Sparta. Plutarch's *Life of Lycurgus* was one of the most widely cited of the *Lives* in the founding era, and Hamilton and Madison both invoked it in *The Federalist Papers*. It tells the story of the legendary constitution maker of Sparta, who is said to have embodied military virtue and personal self-discipline. Hamilton took notes on Lycurgus's constitutional innovations, including his establishment of a Senate that, like ballast to a ship, preserved the state in a "just equilibrium," preventing it from leaning too far "towards an absolute monarchy" or a "pure demockracy."

"Amongst the many Alterations which Lycurgus made," Plutarch writes, in a passage Hamilton copied, "the first and most important was the establishment of the Senate, which having a power equal to the Kings" constantly restrained the monarchy "within the bounds of equity and moderation."[15] To ensure equality, Lycurgus divided all the property of Sparta into nine thousand evenly distributed lots, allowing distinctions based on envy to give way to those based on merit. He outlawed luxury as well as gold and silver currency, which ended all avarice, lawsuits, theft, and poverty. He also commanded all the Spartans to eat simple fare at common tables, where they learned the habits of personal and political moderation.

In addition to recording Lycurgus's constitutional innovations, Hamilton was especially drawn to Plutarch's accounts of how the young men and women of Sparta paraded naked through the streets. To make the women "more robust and capable of a vigorous offspring," Plutarch writes, in another passage Hamilton copied, Lycurgus ordered them to exercise; then, "he ordained that at certain solemn feasts and sacrifices the virgins should go naked as well as the young men and in this manner dance in their presence."[16] (According to Plutarch, "These public processions of the maidens, and their appearing naked in their exercises and dancings, were incitements to marriage.") To further encourage thoughts of matrimony, bachelors were forbidden from voting, and unwed soldiers were forced to sing humiliating songs in public. All men were expected to live not for themselves but for their country, sacrificing their private interests for the public good. Having established the happiness and virtue of the state, Lycurgus administered a solemn oath to the commons, kings, and senators, to keep the constitution in perpetuity. He then decided to end his life by starving himself to death, in order to give the citizens a final example of virtuous self-denial. According to Plutarch, Lycurgus thought "that the happiness of a state, as of a private man, consisted chiefly in the exercise of virtue, and in the concord of the inhabitants; his aim, therefore, in all his arrangements, was to make and keep them free-minded, self-dependent, and temperate."[17]

Madison, too, grew up reading Plutarch and the *Spectator*, and, with the benefit of a private tutor, he learned Latin, Greek, and French. He also read the other staples of Jefferson's reading list: Locke's *An Essay Concerning Human Understanding* and Montesquieu's *The Spirit of the Laws*.

His commonplace book includes selections he copied from five works that especially impressed him in his teens, including *Abstracts from the Memoirs of Cardinal de Retz*, the French cardinal who emphasized the importance of prudence in holding public offices and the dangers of uniting church and state. "All the World is, & will be for ever decieved in things which flatter their Passions," Madison paraphrased de Retz. (The cardinal's arrest in 1652 for political infighting during the French civil wars proved his point.) Madison also copied selections from the essays of the French philosopher Michel de Montaigne, including his observations about how turbulent passions could be cooled over time. "Our passions are like Torrents which may be diverted, but not obstructed," Madison copied. "Time is the Sovereign Physician of our Passions." Madison was also drawn to the Abbé du Bos's *Critical Reflections on Poetry and Painting*, including his thoughts about how our taste for pleasure is shaped not by reason but by passion. "Even Gentlemen of Sense & Honour are fond of Gaming, & chiefly of Hazard," Madison paraphrased du Bos, "not from Avarice, but merely from the violent Emotion of the Passions."[18]

In 1769, at the age of eighteen, Madison entered the College of New Jersey, where he immersed himself in the psychology of the faculties, and was more successful than Hamilton would be in persuading Dr. Witherspoon, the college president, to let him graduate early. An evangelical Protestant, Witherspoon had attended the University of Edinburgh, where he studied the leading thinkers of the Scottish Enlightenment, Francis Hutcheson and Thomas Reid. Although he questioned Hutcheson's claim that humans are inherently benevolent because of their instinctive moral sense—Witherspoon emphasized man's sinful nature, which could be redeemed only by God's saving grace—the clergyman brought to the college a commitment to teaching the basic principles of Reid's faculty psychology: namely, that human minds have faculties, or powers, including the mechanical, the animal, and the rational. Mechanical faculties include our involuntary reflexes; animal faculties include our physical appetites, desires, and passions (or emotions); and rational faculties include our conscience (or moral sense) and our prudence (or self-interest).[19] According to Reid, human beings had a duty to use their rational faculties to moderate their passionate ones, checking impulsive desires with sober second thoughts. Madison would later extrapolate from these Enlightenment philosophers the importance of designing a government so that the passions checked and balanced one another rather than rigidly separating the three branches of government, as classical philosophy had advised.

Witherspoon taught moral philosophy to Madison and eight other Princeton graduates who later served as delegates to the Constitutional Convention. He was the only clergyman to sign the Declaration of Independence in July 1776 as a delegate to the Continental Congress; two months earlier, he had delivered a sermon on "The Dominion of Providence over the Passions of Men," in which he argued that "the cause in which America is now in arms is the cause of justice, of liberty, and of human nature." Emphasizing that "our civil and religious liberties" were the foundations for our "temporal and eternal happiness," Witherspoon urged his audience to practice the classical virtues of industry, fortitude, temperance, and prudence. "This certainly implies not only abstaining from acts of gross intemperance and excess, but a humility of carriage, a restraint and moderation in all your desires," he declared. The same "self-denial" necessary to achieve independence in politics "is also necessary to make you truly independent in yourselves."[20]

Madison threw himself into his studies with Witherspoon at Princeton, sleeping only three hours a night, by some estimates, and completing the four-year course in two years. After graduation, he stayed on for several months to study Hebrew. We know the authors Madison read in Witherspoon's course on politics and government, because he sent a list of them to his friend and classmate William Bradford, in 1773. Madison's list included Hutcheson's *A System of Moral Philosophy* and Montesquieu's *The Spirit of the Laws*, as well as works by Locke, Sidney, Grotius, and Pufendorf. It also includes the collected essays of David Hume, which Hamilton cited in the final *Federalist Paper*, No. 85, and which shaped Madison's thinking about public opinion and factions in "Federalist No. 10."[21]

Hume was cited so often at the Constitutional Convention that some delegates spoke as if they had committed his essays to memory.[22] His essays, which also appear on Jefferson's reading list, include popular summaries of how the Stoic, Epicurean, Platonist, and Skeptical schools of classical philosophy approached the "pursuit of happiness," a phrase that Hume uses twice in his essays. It is not true that "every man, however dissolute and negligent, proceeds [unerringly] in the pursuit of happiness," Hume wrote in his chapter on the Stoics. Even the most "polished citizen" is "inferior to the man of virtue, and the true philosopher, who governs his appetites, subdues his passions, and has learned, from reason, to set a just value on every pursuit and enjoyment."[23] In his chapter on the Skeptics (a Greek philosophical school that emphasized inquiry rather than claims about ultimate truth), Hume poses and then answers the following question: "When we reflect on the shortness and uncertainty of life, how despicable seem all our pursuits of happiness?"[24] The Skeptic's solution is not to pursue riches or other external pleasures but to cultivate the more durable "passion for learning" that allows us to govern our own minds. "[T]he passions, which pursue external objects, contribute not so much to happiness, as those which rest in ourselves; since we are neither so certain of attaining such objects, nor so secure in possessing them."[25]

All governments are founded on opinion, Hume argued: since the governed always possess the force of numbers, the authority of the governors must rest on public opinion about their right to govern or their ability to protect the public interest. But people's judgments about the public interest can be distorted by political parties or factions. "Factions may be divided into PERSONAL and REAL," Hume wrote—that is, into those "founded on personal friendship or animosity among such as compose the contending parties, and into those founded on some real difference of sentiment or interest." Following Hume, Madison, in "Federalist No. 10," also divided factions into those based on passion and those based on interest.

As the scholar Douglass Adair famously noted, Madison's thinking about factions was especially influenced by Hume's 1777 essay "Idea of a Perfect Commonwealth."[26] Hume emphasized that small assemblies were more likely to be governed by reason than large ones, which were liable to be misled by passion. "[A]ll numerous assemblies, however composed, are mere mob, and swayed in their debates by the least motive," Hume wrote.[27] (Compare Madison: "In all very numerous assemblies, of whatever characters composed, passion never fails to wrest the sceptre from reason."[28]) Hume provided an answer, however, to Montesquieu's claim that republics could flourish only in small territories where representatives would best understand the interests of their constituents. In Hume's view, republics in large territories were "more difficult to form," but, once established, were less susceptible to "tumult and faction." The various parts of a large republic would be "so distant and remote" that it would be "very difficult" for factions to use "intrigue, prejudice, or passion, to hurry" the representatives "into any measures against the public interest."[29] In "Federalist No. 10," Madison distilled this idea in his famous sentence about how, in an extended republic, it's less probable that a majority will be inclined to invade the rights of a minority or, if a motive exists, to discover its strength and to act in unison.[30]

Hume had expressed skepticism about whether reason was sufficiently strong to cool our passions. "Reason is and ought only to be the slave of the passions," he declared provocatively. Madison and Hamilton, however, were more optimistic. In Madison's view, public opinion could be cooled and refined by enlightened representatives, whose distance from their constituents ensured that they could act based on reason rather than passion. In a republic, Madison wrote in "Federalist No. 10," the delegation of government to a small number of elected representatives would "refine and enlarge the public views, by passing them through the medium of a chosen body of citizens whose wisdom may best discern the true interest of their country."[31] In "Federalist No. 63," Madison wrote that "temperate and respectable" representatives would save the people from their most selfish impulses, preventing "the people stimulated by some irregular passion, or some illicit advantage, or misled by the artful misrepresentations of interested men" from making short-term decisions they would later come to regret. "What bitter anguish would not the people of Athens have often escaped if their government had contained so provident a safeguard against the tyranny of their own passions?" he asked.[32] For this reason, Madison argued against frequent direct appeals to the people as a way of resolving constitutional disputes. Because popular deliberations are inevitably "connected with the spirit of pre-existing parties," he wrote in "Federalist No. 49," "the *passions* therefore not the *reason*, of the public, would sit in judgment." But in a well-tempered government, reason should always prevail over passion: "[I]t is the reason of the public alone that ought to controul and regulate the government. The passions ought to be controuled and regulated by the government."[33]

Although enlightened representatives might be able to cool public passions, Madison and Hamilton recognized that "[e]nlightened statesmen will not always be at the helm."[34] Despite their idealism about the possibility of self-government, they were also realists who acknowledged that citizens would not always send the most virtuous men to office, and that elected officials might not always act in the most virtuous ways. After all, "If men were angels, no government would be necessary. If angels were to govern men, neither external nor internal controls on government would be necessary," Madison wrote in "Federalist No. 51." "In framing a government," he emphasized, "[y]ou must first enable the government to control the governed; and in the next place, oblige it to control itself."[35]

For this reason, Madison and Hamilton turned to the second of their institutional checks for the problem of faction: the separation of powers, or, as Hamilton called them, the "counteracting passions."[36] The idea that rival passions could counteract one another arose in the seventeenth century, in the philosophy of Francis Bacon and Baruch Spinoza, and it was developed in the eighteenth by Scottish Enlightenment philosophers such as Hutcheson and Hume. The basic idea was that passions or emotions could not be eliminated but that the violent passions of the mind could be moderated or tempered when they were balanced against calmer ones. "Nothing can oppose or retard the impulse of passion but a contrary impulse," Hume wrote. When violent passions clash within the mind, he suggested, they might eventually cool into calmer ones, allowing us to pursue our true interests rather than be misled by our immediate desires: "What we call strength of mind implies the prevalence of the calm passions above the violent."[37]

In a famous passage, Madison defends the separation of powers by invoking the principle of counteracting passions. "Ambition must be made to counteract ambition," he wrote in "Federalist No. 51." "The interest of the man must be connected with the constitutional rights of the place."[38] Madison assumed that the president, Congress, and the judiciary would resist encroachments by the other branches on their powers because of their ambition to maintain their own power and prestige. Another application of the theory of counteracting passions comes in "Federalist No. 72," where Hamilton talks about the president being restrained by the clashing forces of avarice and ambition within his own mind. Imagine a greedy president who is tempted to behave corruptly. If he thought his time in office was short, he might take everything he could get; but if he thought he might extend his time in office by winning reelection fair and square, he would try to serve the public interest rather than his own selfish interest, in order to increase his chances of being reelected. "His avarice might be a guard upon his avarice," Hamilton writes.[39]

In "Federalist No. 1," Hamilton says that the Constitution will be a test of whether groups of people can govern themselves by reason rather than passion—whether, as he puts it, societies "are really capable or not of establishing good government from reflection and choice, or whether they are forever destined to depend, for their political constitutions, on accident and force." He then identifies "[a] torrent of angry and malignant passions" that will be "let loose" by the partisan debate over the Constitution. In particular, he singles out "[a]mbition, avarice, personal animosity, party opposition, and many other motives not more laud-able."[40] In addition to ambition and avarice, a series of other malignant passions occur throughout *The Federalist Papers*, including pride, vanity, envy, jealousy, fear, resentment, self-love, and love of power.[41]

Hamilton and Madison explain repeatedly how malignant passions can usefully clash with one another, exhausting themselves in the pro-cess, so that decisions motivated by self-interest will ultimately coincide with the public interest. For example, Hamilton writes in "Federalist No. 84," envy will ensure that state governors and legislators act like sentinels policing the conduct of the president and Congress; the "rival-ship of power" will ensure that the states let the people know about any threats to their interest from the national government.[42] In "Federalist No. 57," Madison writes that in addition to unselfish motives such as duty and gratitude, "selfish" motives—among them ambition, pride, and vanity—will bind a representative to his constituents. "His pride and vanity attach him to a form of government which favors his pretensions and gives him a share in its honors and distinctions."[43]

Enlightenment thinkers placed more emphasis on commerce than on classical virtue as the key to happiness. Adam Smith emphasized that when individuals pursue their selfish economic interests, domestic and international harmony may result as if by an "invisible hand."[44] For Madison and Hamilton, too, when harmful passions collide, they can be converted into productive ones: useful vanity will seek honor and use-ful pride, and ambition will seek "the love of fame," which Hamilton called "the ruling passion of the noblest minds," and which can come only when the selfish interests of our representatives coincide with their devotion to the public interest.[45] Hamilton assumed, for example, that ambition for reelection would lead a president to act virtuously.

At the end of his life, however, Hamilton was more pessimistic than Madison about the future of America because he believed the fed-eral government—and, in particular, the presidency—wasn't powerful enough to resist populist passions. Hamilton focused single-mindedly on promoting what he called "energy in the executive" ever since the

Constitutional Convention, where he delivered a notorious speech on June 18 calling for a president who would be elected for life. "The general government must, in this case, not only have a strong soul but *strong organs* by which that soul is to operate," Hamilton wrote in his notes for the speech, invoking Aristotle, Cicero, and Montesquieu for the proposition that the "British constitution" had the "best form" in mixing a king, hereditary lords, and elected Commons. For Hamilton, "There ought to be a principle in government capable of resisting the popular current" because of the "unreasonableness of the people" in all cases where there is a "strong public passion." Warning that "[d]emagogues will generally prevail," Hamilton insisted that the few, represented by an aristocratic Senate and the many, represented by a popular House, had to be separated. "And if separated, they will need a mutual check," Hamilton wrote. "This check is a monarch."[46]

Stunning the convention with his proposal of a monarchical president elected for life, Hamilton explained, "The advantage of a monarch is this—he is above corruption—he must always intend, in respect to foreign nations, the true interest and glory of the people." In his speech, Hamilton also proposed that the Senate, too, should be elected for life, meaning that only the House would face periodic elections. And he added that the states should be effectively obliterated, with their powers absorbed by the general government. All of this was designed to ensure a federal government strong enough to resist the populist whims of democratic mobs. "Gentlemen say we need to be rescued from the democracy. But what the means proposed?" Hamilton asked. "A democratic assembly is to be checked by a democratic senate, and both these by a democratic chief magistrate." According to Hamilton, this democratic solution would be "feeble and inefficient."[47] In this sense, Hamilton was less forward thinking than Madison, who creatively applied the principles of faculty psychology, or the view that the mind has separate powers of reason, will, and emotion, to check and balance the three branches of government rather than separate them entirely.

• • •

For the rest of his career, Hamilton faced charges from his political opponents that he wanted to restore a monarchy to America. (The fact that he preferred an elected monarch to the hereditary one was hardly a convincing answer.) And in his remarkable performance during and after the election of 1800, Hamilton demonstrated that his conception of the presidency was so lofty that he believed only George Washington could fill it. "Vanity and Jealousy exclude all counsel," Hamilton wrote at the beginning of 1800, lamenting that Washington's recent death at the age of sixty-seven had removed a control on the excesses of democracy and faction. "Passion wrests the helm from reason."[48] But his focus on the need for a monarchical president to check the excesses of democracy were in part a projection of his own character. Hamilton, more than any other Founder, was possessed by a driving ambition and status anxiety that fueled his rise and then his fall. His lack of self-control landed him in a sex scandal that ended his political career. And his hypersensitivity to slights led to a duel with Aaron Burr that ended his life.

Anyone who has seen the *Hamilton* musical knows the story of the Reynolds pamphlet, in which Hamilton revealed to the world, in 1797, his extramarital affair with a woman named Maria Reynolds, and the hush money he paid to her abusive husband, James Reynolds, to defend himself against charges of illegal speculation that would have harmed the Federalist Party. The pamphlet extinguished his chances of running for president in 1800 and set in motion the series of events that would end in the fateful duel.

In the election of 1800, Hamilton couched his support for a strong presidency in the guise of his opposition to the newly formed Democratic-Republican Party led by Jefferson and Madison. Hamilton disavowed the Jeffersonian charge that he was heading a "Monarchical party meditating the destruction of State & Republican Government." Hamilton's own political creed, he said, was simple: "I desire *above all things* to see the *equality* of political rights exclusive of all *hereditary* distinction firmly established by a practical demonstration of its being consistent with the order and happiness of society." On this question—whether republican (in other words, democratically elected) governments could promote happiness—the jury was still out. He was "*affectionately* attached" to the republican theory, Hamilton said, but "[i]t is yet to be determined by experience whether it be consistent with that *stability* and *order* in Government which are essential to public strength & private security and happiness." If the spirit of "faction and anarchy" proved that republican government engendered "disorders in the community," the "demagogues who have produced the disorder will make it for their own aggrandizement. This is the old Story." Hamilton insisted that he had no plans to play the demagogue, adding, "If I were disposed to promote Monarchy & overthrow State Governments, I would mount the hobby horse of popularity." He believed, however, that "there are men acting with Jefferson & Madison" who were indeed demagogues. As for Jefferson himself, Hamilton read him as "[a] man of profound ambition & violent passions."[49]

Given his fervent opposition to Vice President Jefferson, it would have made sense for Hamilton to support John Adams in the election of 1800, the first partisan presidential contest in American history. And yet Hamilton announced early on that "my mind is made up" and that he would never support Adams "even though the consequence should be the election of *Jefferson.*" By Hamilton's perverse logic, "If we must have an *enemy* at the head of the Government, let it be one whom we can oppose & for whom we are not responsible, who will not involve our party in the disgrace of his foolish and bad measures."[50] Accordingly, in an act of political madness and personal spite, shortly before Election Day, Hamilton savaged Adams in a lengthy essay, "Letter from Alexander Hamilton, Concerning the Public Conduct and Character of John Adams, Esq., President of the United States." The gist of Hamilton's attack was that Adams was too conciliatory in his desire to avoid war with France. The disparaging remarks about his character focused on what Hamilton called "the disgusting egotism, the distempered jealousy, and the ungovernable indiscretion of Mr. Adams's temper." For Hamilton, Adams's "ill humors and jealousies" had "divided and distracted the supporters of the Government," and his reelection might cause the Government to "totter, if not fall."[51] Hamilton hoped that the Electoral College would abandon Adams and choose instead his running mate, Charles Cotesworth Pinckney of South Carolina, a Revolutionary War officer, signer of the Constitution, and slaveholder.

After the explosive election, Adams and Pinkney lost to Jefferson and his running mate, Aaron Burr, who tied with seventy-three electoral votes each. The election was then thrown into the House, lame duck and Federalist, where each state had one vote. Neither Jefferson nor Burr could secure a majority of states on the first thirty-five ballots, where most Democratic-Republicans supported Jefferson and most Federalists, Burr. Hamilton declared that if Burr were elected, he would overthrow the Constitution and establish a military dictatorship. "He is as unprincipled & dangerous a man as any country can boast; as true a *Catiline* as ever met in midnight conclave."[52] According to Hamilton, Burr had to be resisted because of his selfish egoism: "Burr loves nothing but himself; thinks of nothing but his own aggrandizement, and will be content with nothing short of permanent power in his own hands."[53]

Fearing that Burr would use "atrocious" means to entrench his own power, Hamilton warned, "The truth is that under forms of Government like ours, too much is practicable to men who will without scruple avail themselves of the bad passions of human nature."[54] Accordingly, Hamilton helped persuade several Federalists to switch their votes, throwing the election to Jefferson. By invoking Catiline, the Roman revolutionary who attempted to overthrow the republic in the plot denounced by Cicero, as well as comparing Burr to Napoléon Bonaparte, Hamilton may not have been hyperbolic: after the election, Burr did indeed ally himself with the High Federalists from New England who proposed to secede from the Union, and in 1807 he was arrested on charges of plotting to annex Spanish and U.S. territories in Mexico and Louisiana with the goal of creating an independent republic. Although prosecuted by President Jefferson, Burr was subsequently acquitted of treason.

Hamilton viewed the Jeffersonian Republicans as the only political party in America: in his view, he and other High Federalists were not a party but a collection of disinterested individuals devoted to national principles. In his own eyes, he could, in good conscience, support Jefferson over both Adams and Burr because Jefferson represented the lesser evil. His opponents, he acknowledged, saw things differently, accusing Hamilton of opposing Adams because he was disappointed at not being appointed commander in chief of the army. The truth is that Hamilton's behavior reflected a mix of complicated motives and clouded his political judgment in ways that ultimately led to the fatal interview with Burr. Although not a model of self-awareness, Hamilton devoted the four years that remained to him to wondering whether the federal government was energetic enough to constrain populist passions.

In particular, Hamilton zeroed in on the question that Madison introduced in *The Federalist Papers*: Could public opinion be educated to resist the flattery of demagogues and embrace the virtuous reason necessary for private and public happiness? In a visit to the Grange, Hamilton's estate in upper Manhattan, months before the duel in 1804, the Chancellor of New York, James Kent, found Hamilton contemplating the most ambitious intellectual work of his life: a "full investigation of the history and science of civil government, and the practical results of various modifications of it upon the freedom and happiness of mankind." In other words, Hamilton wanted to write a history of the effect of public and private institutions on the pursuit of happiness. As Kent put it, "The impending election exceedingly disturbed him, and he viewed the temper, disposition, and passions of the times as portentous of evil, and favorable to the sway of artful and ambitious demagogues." Hamilton told Kent he hoped to apply Lord Francis Bacon's inductive philosophy, which became the basis for the modern scientific method, to investigate the effect of various institutions throughout history on "the freedom, the morals, the prosperity, the intelligence, the jurisprudence, and the happiness of the people."[55]

Two years earlier, in a letter to the politician James Bayard, Hamilton had a more specific proposal for the kind of institution he thought could educate public opinion to be guided by reason rather than passion. "Nothing is more fallacious than to expect to produce any valuable or permanent results, in political projects, by relying merely on the reason of men," Hamilton wrote. "Men are rather reasoning tha[n] reasonable animals for the most part governed by the impulse of passion." His Republican adversaries had understood this, "For at the very moment they are eulogizing the reason of men & professing to appeal only to that faculty, they are courting the strongest & most active passion of the human heart—*Vanity!*" In order to help the Federalists "carry along with us some strong feelings of the mind," Hamilton proposed to create a new private association devoted to preventing changes to the Constitution except through the amendment process. He proposed to call it the Christian Constitutional Society, and its goals would be: "The support of the Christian Religion" and "The support of the Constitution of the United States." The society would achieve these goals by distributing free pamphlets in the press, promoting the election of "*fit* men" through all legal means, and establishing vocational schools and immigrant aid societies in the large cities. In a passage he marked "especially confidential," Hamilton said he wanted to focus in particular on the large cities, where the Republicans had plans in the last election to "seize the Government" if a clear winner hadn't emerged.[56]

The historian Ron Chernow justly concludes: "The society was an execrable idea that would have grossly breached the separation of church and state and mixed political power and organized religion."[57] Hamilton, however, believed that he was focused on the education of public opinion, not on public aid to the Church. And Hamilton's notion that Christian and constitutional principles could reinforce each other in promoting public happiness is consistent with his turn, at the end of his life, toward faith as the foundation for his own private happiness. Although never drawn to organized worship, Hamilton in his final years pronounced himself convinced of the authenticity of the Christian religion and urged his wife, Eliza, to "[a]rm yourself with resignation," after her mother died in 1803. "In the later period of life," he continued prophetically, "misfortunes seem to thicken round us and our duty; and our peace both require that we should accustom ourselves to meet disasters with christian fortitude." Resignation to the will of providence, Hamilton told Eliza, was the best way to achieve the classical virtues of "prudence and fortitude."[58]

Hamilton's fatal interview the following year was the culmination of his long-standing political rivalry with Burr, which was inflamed by the election of 1800. After Jefferson decided to drop him as a running mate for vice president four years later, Burr ran for governor of New York, and Hamilton campaigned against him. In June 1804, seven weeks after his defeat in the election, Burr received a copy of a New York newspaper that had published a letter asserting that Hamilton had expressed a "despicable opinion" of him. Burr demanded an apology, and Hamilton, overcome by self-righteous passion, refused. The day before the fatal duel, on July 10, 1804, Hamilton wrote to Eliza in an attempt to calm both of their fears. "I charge you to remember that you are a Christian," he implored, and as he lay dying the following day, he repeated the injunction: "Remember, my Eliza, you are a Christian."[59] In the achingly sad letter he wrote for Eliza to read after his death, Hamilton said that "[t]he consolations of Religion, my beloved, can alone support you," concluding that "[w]ith my last idea; I shall cherish the sweet hope of meeting you in a better world." Hamilton had two dying wishes: the preservation of the Union and eternal happiness in the hereafter. "I humbly hope from redeeming grace and divine mercy, a happy immortality."[60]

Although Hamilton didn't know it, James Madison had been preparing extensive notes for a writing project on the same topic that occupied Hamilton when he died: How could public opinion be educated and refined to pursue happiness by reason rather than passion? In early 1791, soon after completing *The Federalist Papers*, Madison holed up in his rented home at Fifth and Market Streets in Philadelphia—he was staying in the aptly named Mrs. House's boardinghouse—to begin what became his essays on government for the *National Gazette*. Madison told Jefferson it was a "little task," but it was the most ambitious philosophical project of his career.[61] Once again consulting books from Jefferson's library, Madison immersed himself in classical and Enlightenment sources—his footnotes include Aristotle, Montesquieu, Benjamin Franklin, and the French academic Jean-Jacques Barthelemy. In a multivolume fictional narrative about life in the golden age of Greece, Barthelemy explored the question of how public opinion could be cooled and harmonized so that it supported a stable republic.[62]

In the 1780s and 1790s, at the recommendation of Jefferson, who was in Paris, Madison studied a series of French Enlightenment writers on the new science of public opinion, including not only Barthelemy but also the Marquis de Condorcet. These thinkers agreed that a class of enlightened scientists, scholars, and journalists—Condorcet called them the "literati"—could use the new technology of the mass market printing press to refine popular opinion, which was based on passion, into a more stable and durable public opinion based on reason. In his *Outlines of an Historical View of the Progress of the Human Mind*, published in 1795, Condorcet summed up his views about the role of the press in promoting public reason. "[I]s it not the press that has freed the instruction of the people from every political and religious chain?" he asked. Once the "learned of all nations" could take advantage of a "common medium of communication," they could appeal to the universal reason of the masses, establishing "a new species of tribune . . . where all the advantage is on the side of truth."[63]

Condorcet was confident that the new media would lead to the spread of universal reason, overcoming prejudice, suspicion, partisan attachments, and vast distances. He was also confident that the literati, by diffusing complicated facts, figures, and scientific investigations, could inspire their fellow citizens to be governed by facts rather than by prejudices. "To the press we owe those continued discussions which alone can enlighten doubtful questions," he wrote. Thanks to the press, it would be impossible for tyrants or demagogues to promulgate fake news or to persuade people to believe falsehoods. "We shall accordingly see reason triumphing over these vain efforts," he predicted.[64]

Taking up Condorcet's question of how to promote public opinion based on reason rather than passion, Madison began his "Notes for the *National Gazette* Essays" in 1791 by listing various influences on government. He included circumstantial factors, such as the size of the territory and external threats, as well as intangible influences such as public opinion itself. "Public opinion sets bounds to every Government and is the real sovereign in every free one," Madison declared. And following Condorcet, Madison emphasized the role of the press in influencing public opinion. Any technology that "facilitates a general intercommunication of sentiments & ideas among the body of the people"—such as newspapers, roads, and commerce—"is equivalent to a contraction of the orbit within wch. the Govt. is to act," Madison recognized. As such, the communication of ideas could "favor liberty in a nation too large for free Government" by uniting individuals in far-flung territories around a shared devotion to basic constitutional principles. At the same time, the communication of ideas could hasten the "violent death" of liberty in too small a territory, where face-to-face mobs could quickly form.[65]

Madison's central insight in his "Notes" was that the press could contribute to what he called a "commerce of ideas" by slowly diffusing the cool voice of reason across the land, counteracting the disadvantages of large territories without resurrecting the turbulence and passion of small ones.[66] By promoting slow deliberation on a wide scale, between constituents and their representatives and among the people themselves, new communications technology could achieve over a large territory the same harmony and balance that individuals sought to cultivate in their own minds.

In Madison's time, new media technologies, including what he called "a *circulation of newspapers through the entire body of the people*," were already closing the communication gaps among the dispersed citizens of America.[67] The popular press of the eighteenth and early nineteenth centuries was highly partisan; for example, the *National Gazette*, where

Madison would publish his thoughts on the media, was, since its founding in 1791, an organ of the Democratic-Republican Party and often
attacked the Federalists viciously. But newspapers of the time were also
platforms for elites to make thoughtful arguments at length, and had
faith that citizens would take the time to read complicated arguments—
including the essays that became *The Federalist Papers*—allowing level-
headed reason to spread slowly across the new republic.

Madison followed Condorcet in expressing faith that a class of
enlightened journalists and public officials, whom he, too, called the literati, could serve as "cultivators of the human mind," using the new media
to teach the public how to pursue happiness through reason rather than
passion. As Madison put it in a crucial passage: "The class of literati is
not less necessary than any other. They are the cultivators of the human
mind—the manufacturers of useful knowledge—the agents of the commerce of ideas—the censors of public manners—the teachers of the arts
of life and the means of happiness."[68] When he wrote about the literati, Madison had in mind elite journalists such as Benjamin Franklin's
Poor Richard or his own essays in *The Federalist*; the modern equivalent
would be essays in the *Atlantic* or the *New Yorker*. Madison was confident that the literati could teach the public to converge around shared
principles—such as a national attachment to republicanism, the Constitution, and the Bill of Rights—rather than descending into "prejudices,
local, political, and occupational, that may prevent or disturb a general
coalition of sentiments."[69]

In 1791 Madison ended his *National Gazette* essays full of optimism
that, with the help of the literati and a free press, public opinion would
converge around a shared devotion to republican principles, including
popular elections and free speech. And in the turbulent decades that
followed, Madison maintained his basic optimism in the possibilities for
calming the American mind. In March 1836, months before his death,
Madison wrote a letter about the growing signs of "instability . . . [t]he
besetting infirmity of popular Govts.," which the Constitution had been
designed to remedy. The tenure of senators, he said, had been intended as

an "obstacle" to that instability, but growing calls that senators obey the instructions of their constituents threatened to make the Senate a more popular body. In his long life, he wrote, he had seen other threats to the constitutional balance of power that were leading the "Federal & State Governments to encroach" on each other's authority, including with regard to the expanding size of the Union and multiple political parties.[70]

Despite these "vicissitudes," Madison said, "I am far however from desponding of the great political experiment in the hands of the American people." Until the end, Madison retained his faith in new media technologies, emphasizing that he continued to expect that public opinion would be harmonized by "the Geographical, commercial & social ligaments, strengthened as they are by mechanical improvements, giving so much advantage to time over space." Madison acknowledged signs of an "ill omen," as the clouds of Civil War began to gather, but said that future threats to the Union could be "greatly mitigated if not removed" by Congress or by constitutional amendment "whenever, if ever, the public mind may be calm & cool enough for that resort."[71]

Today, of course, the idea that new media technologies might be deployed by an enlightened class of literati to calm and refine public opinion seems quaint. In an age of social media, the opposite dynamic occurs, as journalists, scholars, and public officials pander to the most extreme and passionate voices on social media rather than slowly diffuse reason across the land. Madison believed the print media should promote cool deliberation; the social media model is "enrage to engage." At the same time, new media are undermining the speed bumps of time and space that Madison thought would make it difficult for mobs to mobilize and act impulsively. The passions, hyper-partisanship, and split-second decision-making that Madison and Hamilton feared from large, concentrated groups meeting face-to-face have proved to be even more dangerous from exponentially larger, dispersed groups that meet online.

In addition to speeding up public discourse, media polarization has also allowed geographically dispersed citizens to isolate themselves into virtual factions, which today we call echo chambers, communicating only with like-minded individuals and reinforcing shared beliefs. Far from being a conduit for considered opinions by an educated elite, social media platforms spread misinformation and inflame partisan differences. As new technologies allow virtual mobs to form instantaneously, they encourage citizens and representatives to define themselves by their membership in red or blue bubbles rather than by their independent deliberations about what the public interest requires. As likes and retweets based on emotion take the place of complicated arguments based on reason, we are seeing public opinion heated and fractured in ways the Founders most feared.

The Founders themselves disagreed about whether or not the press could refine public opinion and promote the civil dialogue necessary for a moderate, well-tempered, and more perfect Union. When John Adams, for example, read Condorcet's *Progress of the Human Mind*, with its paean to the calming powers of a free press, he scribbled in the margins: "There has been more new error propagated by the press in the last ten years than in an hundred years before 1798."[72] Jefferson, by contrast, placed the book on the later editions of his reading list. But although they disagreed about whether or not the American mind could be calmed by the cool light of reason, Adams and Jefferson provided a model of civil dialogue and the ability of friendship to triumph over partisanship in the correspondence they resumed in 1812, leading to their moving and improbable reconciliation.

Notes on the Bhagavad Gita, Book 2, Self-Realization

The wise see the eternal Self in all
They have renounced every selfish desire
Not once disturbed by grief or pleasure's call
They live free from lust and fear and anger

Always act without selfish attachment
Or desire for the fruits of your actions
Desire can burn to anger; detachment
Allows an even mind's satisfactions

Reality lies in the eternal
Not in the impermanent we're seeing
Train body, mind, senses, thoughts internal
And unite with the Self in all being

Renounce selfish desires of "I," "mine," "me"
Enjoy freedom and immortality

Nine

TRANQUILITY

Adams and Jefferson's Reconciliation

On March 4, 1801, Thomas Jefferson's Inauguration Day, John Adams left the White House at four in the morning rather than wait for his successor to take the oath of office—perhaps because he wasn't invited or because he was still seething. A few hours later, Jefferson walked from his boardinghouse to the US Capitol, was sworn in at noon by Chief Justice John Marshall, and, in a barely audible voice in the Senate Chamber, proceeded to give one of the greatest inauguration speeches in American history.

Applying the psychology of happiness to the new Constitution, Jefferson began by acknowledging the same connection between personal and political self-government that Washington, Madison, and Hamilton had all emphasized. "Sometimes it is said that man cannot be trusted with the government of himself. Can he then be trusted with the government of others?" Jefferson was confident that history would answer in the affirmative because Americans had "a due sense of our equal right to the use of our own faculties, to the acquisitions of our own industry, to honor and confidence from our fellow citizens." If private happiness for Jefferson required the freedom to cultivate mental tranquility, public happiness required that citizens be "free to regulate their own pursuits of industry and improvement."[1]

Now that the election was over, Jefferson said, he was confident that all citizens would accept the results and "unite in common efforts for the common good." And he expressed optimism that the American public could continue to govern itself by reason rather than passion. "[E]very difference of opinion is not a difference of principle," he said. "We are all republicans; we are all federalists. If there be any among us who would wish to dissolve this Union, or to change its republican form, let them stand undisturbed as monuments of the safety with which error of opinion may be tolerated, where reason is left free to combat it."[2]

Despite Jefferson's gracious inaugural address, he had no contact with Adams between the end of March 1801 and May 1804, when Abigail Adams wrote to console the president on the death of his daughter. Replying that he considered only one act of his predecessor "personally unkind"—namely, Adams's appointment of midnight judges in the last hours of his presidential term—Jefferson emphasized that both Republicans and Federalists agreed about the public good but disagreed about how to promote it.[3] According to Jefferson, Republicans were more concerned about educating public opinion and Federalists about checking public opinion through the separation of powers. "One [party] fears most the ignorance of the people; the other the selfishness of rulers independant of them."[4] Abigail's wary attempt at rapprochement failed to heal the wounds of the election of 1800, which were still raw.

It took the intervention of their mutual friend Benjamin Rush to reunite the estranged patriots. In 1811 Jefferson sent his correspondence with Abigail Adams to Rush, as evidence of his desire to bury the hatchet. The same year, he heard that Adams had told another friend, "I always loved Jefferson, and still love him." "[T]his is enough for me,"

Jefferson told Rush, and asked him to effect a reconciliation.[5] In December Rush urged Adams "to receive the Olive branch which has thus been offered to you by the hand of a Man who still loves you. Fellow labourers in creating the great fabric of American Independence . . . embrace— embrace each Other!"[6]

What followed was a remarkable correspondence that lasted until their deaths on the same day, July 4, 1826, the fiftieth anniversary of the Declaration of Independence. In their letters, they returned repeatedly to a spiritual theme: namely, the common teachings of the ancient Eastern and Western wisdom traditions about the pursuit of happiness. In Adams's view, these common teachings of the Christians, Greeks, and Jews about happiness could be traced back to Pythagoras, who was said to have encountered them during his travels in Egypt and India. In the correspondence, Jefferson called himself an Epicurean, and Adams expressed respect for the Hindu Vedas. Drawing on these ancient sources, both Adams and Jefferson concluded that happiness consists in tranquility of mind and that it can be found not in the success or failure of our efforts to achieve inner harmony but from the pursuit itself.

On January 1, 1812, Adams sent Jefferson a peace offering of his own. The gift, which Adams called "two Pieces of Homespun," was a two-volume set of lectures that his son John Quincy Adams had delivered two years earlier when he became the Boylston Professor of Rhetoric and Oratory at Harvard.[7] At the end of January, Jefferson thanked Adams for the books, which he called "a mine of learning & taste."[8] His thoughts turned immediately to the theme that would come to dominate their correspondence: how to pursue happiness by leading a good life. Jefferson reported that, in retirement, he had returned to his youthful schedule of disciplined daily exercise and reading in classical and Enlightenment history and philosophy. "I am on horseback 3. Or 4. Hours of every day . . . I walk little however; a single mile being too much for me." Jefferson asked Adams for a similar update, a letter, "full of egotisms, & of details of your health, your habits, occupations & enjoiments."[9]

"I walk every fair day. Sometimes 3 or 4 miles," Adams replied. "Ride now and then but very rarely more than ten or fifteen Miles." Adams apologized for his handwriting, explaining that he had been struggling with "a kind of Paralytic affection of the Nerves, which makes my hands tremble." He told Jefferson he wished he had spent more time reading the scientists Newton and Euclid than the historians Tacitus and Thucydides, as well as political philosophers such as Plato, Aristotle, Sidney, and Bolingbroke. He was "heartily weary" of recollecting history, Adams said, "for I am not weary of Living." Day by day, he emphasized, he was focused on living in the present, and he found himself happy as a result. "Whatever a peevish Patriarch might Say, I have never yet Seen the day in which I could say I have had no Pleasure; or that I have had more Pain than Pleasure."[10]

Adams then introduced a central topic of their correspondence: the similarities and differences between happiness teachings of the Eastern and Western wisdom traditions. He had recently received two books about mystic prophets, and he wanted to learn more about the Shawnee prophet Tenskwatawa, a younger brother of Tecumseh, the Shawnee chief who had called for Native Americans to return to their traditional ways. Jefferson responded that he remembered Tenskwatawa from his administration and had read accounts of traditional Native American spiritual practices that claimed they descended from the Jews. In Adams's view, however, the spiritual system of Native Americans seemed to resemble less the "Genuine System of Judaism" than the philosophy of "Plato, [who] borrowed his doctrines from oriental and Egyptian Philosophers, for he had travelled both in India and Egypt."[11] (In fact, Plato studied in Egypt but almost certainly did not travel in India.)

Adams said he was interested in a work that would compare the moral principles of all the major wisdom traditions. "I have not Seen any Work which expressly compares the Morality of the old Testament with that of the New in all their Branches: nor either with that of the ancient Philosop[h]ers," he told Jefferson.[12] In particular, Adams noted that the British polymath Joseph Priestley had planned to write a book comparing the philosophies of Socrates and Jesus, but Adams feared he had died before completing it. A chemist, natural philosopher, and theologian, Priestley was acclaimed in his lifetime for discovering oxygen and carbonated water. Priestley's support for the American and French Revolutions forced him to flee an English mob that burned down his house in 1791; he settled in Northumberland, Pennsylvania, where he supported Jefferson over Adams in the election of 1800 and held Unitarian services in his home.

Happiness, Priestley argued, was a quest for individual perfection by living according to the divine laws of the universe, and the "good and happiness of the . . . majority of the members of any state" was the standard by which states should be judged.[13] (The nineteenth-century utilitarian philosopher Jeremy Bentham wrote later that Priestley had inspired his famous declaration "[T]he greatest happiness of the greatest number is the foundation of morals and legislation.")[14] Priestley died in Pennsylvania in 1804, a year after completing *Socrates and Jesus Compared*, the book that Adams awaited. "It is with great pleasure I can inform you that Priestley finished the comparative view of the doctrines of the Philosophers of antiquity, and of Jesus, before his death," Jefferson wrote to Adams in August 1813, promising to forward a copy from Philadelphia.[15] The topic had long been of interest to Jefferson, who had begun his own comparison of the moral philosophy of Socrates and Jesus years earlier. Like Priestley, Jefferson's "Syllabus" found "the merits of the doctrines of Jesus" vastly superior to those of the ancient philosophers—in particular, "Pythagoras, Socrates, Epicurus, Cicero, Epictetus, Seneca, Antoninus." Of the ancient philosophers, Jefferson wrote: "Their precepts related chiefly to ourselves, and the government of those passions which, unrestrained, would disturb our tranquility of mind." Jefferson said that "in this branch of Philosophy they were really great." But, he concluded, "In developing our duties to others, they were short and defective," since they failed to inculcate "peace, charity, & love to our fellow men."[16]

As for the Jews, Jefferson also found their moral principles inferior to those of Jesus. "Their system was Deism, that is, the belief of one only god. But their ideas of him, & of his attributes, were degrading & injurious," Jefferson wrote. "[T]heir Ethics were not only imperfect, but often irreconcileable with the sound dictates of reason & morality, as they respect intercourse with those around us: & repulsive, & anti-social, as respecting other nations."[17] (Here Jefferson sounds as anti-Semitic as he was racist.) "[I]t was the reformation of this 'wretched depravity' of morals which Jesus undertook," Jefferson wrote to Adams in October 1813. By contrast, Jefferson found the "system of morals" presented by Jesus "the most perfect and sublime that has ever been taught by man." Using a razor and glue, Jefferson had cut and pasted selections from the New Testament that he felt represented the pure moral teachings of Jesus, stripped of the "corruptions" and "mysticisms" of his followers.[18]

Adams, showing far more open-mindedness than Jefferson, focused on the similarities among the wisdom traditions rather than their differences. "It appears to me that the great Principle of the Hebrews was the *Fear* of God: that of the [Greeks and Romans] *Honour* the Gods, that of Christians, the *Love* of God," he wrote to Jefferson in September 1813. Nevertheless, Adams suggested, the moral principles of all three religions could be found in the *Hymn to Zeus* by Cleanthes, an ancient Stoic, which Adams translated from the Greek as follows: "Most glorious of immortal beings! Though denominated by innumerable names and titles, always omnipotent! Beginning and End of Nature! Governing the Universe by fixed Laws? Blessed be thy name!"

"What think you, of this translation? Is it too Jewish? Or too Christian?" Adams asked Jefferson.[19] In fact, he insisted, it contained the common wisdom of all the world religions: that there is one God, and we should adore God with all our heart, soul, and mind. In Adams's view, Cleanthes's *Hymn* expressed the moral principles common to Jews, Christians, Muslims, and Greeks alike.

Adams's synthesis wasn't limited to the Greek and Abrahamic religions. Showing a remarkable interest in tracing the core principles of
all the world religions back to a common source, Adams suggested that
the Greek religion was influenced by the Old Testament, and that both
the Jews and the Greeks, in turn, were influenced by the religions of ancient Egypt and India. Adams said that the Roman moral philosophers,
including Cicero, Seneca, and Plutarch, must have seen or heard the
Septuagint, the Greek translation of the Hebrew Bible. "Will any Man
make me believe that Cæsar, that Pompey, that Cicero, that Seneca, that
Tacitus, that Dionisius Hallicarnassensis, that Plutarch, had never Seen
nor heard of the Septuagint?" Adams asked. "Why, might not Cleanthes
have Seen the Septuagint?"[20]

In Adams's view, the common principles of the Christians, Greeks,
and Jews could be traced back to Egypt and India, but the records had
been lost with the Destruction of the Library at Alexandria. Adams said
this was an intentional act of sabotage, akin to the destruction of the
Tower of Babel, by Christian, Jewish, Greek, and Roman sects determined to preserve their own mystical authority. "I believe that Jews Grecians Romans and Christians all conspired, or connived At that Savage
Catastrophy," Adams wrote.[21] "[T]he Spirit of Party has destroyed ... every
Thing that could give Us true light and a clear insight of Antiquity," including records of the celebrated laws passed by disciples of Pythagoras
five hundred years before Christ.[22]

Adams said he was determined to explore the roots of Greek moral
philosophy in the Hindu scriptures, and he wanted to reconstruct
Pythagoras's travels in India. "To return to Priestley. . . . Why has he not
given Us a more Satisfactory Account of the Pythagorean Phylosophy
and Theology?" Adams asked Jefferson in December 1813. "Priestley
ought to have told Us that Pythagoras passed twenty Years, in his Travels in India, in Egypt, in Chaldea, perhaps in Sodom and Gomorrah,
Tyre and Sydon. He ought to have told Us that in India he conversed
with the Brahmans and read the Shast[r]a, 5000 Years old, written in
the Language of the sacred Sanscrists with the elegance and Sentiments

of Plato." (Adams's claims, reflecting what people believed at the time, were supported by the standard biographies of Pythagoras he would have read, including Thomas Stanley's 1687 *The History of Philosophy*.) Adams said there was no "[t]heology more orthodox or Phylosophy more profound than in the Introduction to the Shast[r]a," the sacred commentaries on the Hindu Vedas. He then quoted two "Sublime" doctrines from the Vedas that he insisted Pythagoras had learned in India and taught to his disciples: "God is one, creator of all, Universal Sphere, without beginning, without End. God governs all the Creation by a general Providence, resulting from his eternal designs," Adams wrote. "Search not the Essence and the nature of the Eternal, who is one; your research will be vain and presumptuous. It is enough that, day by day, and night by night, you adore his Power, his Wisdom and his Goodness, in his Works."[23]

As it happens, these two principles (God is One and Love God and his Works) are similar to the two commandments from the Old Testament that Jesus said were the foundation of all the laws and prophecies of the New Testament. "The first of all the commandments is, Hear, O Israel; The Lord our God is one Lord: And thou shalt love the Lord thy God with all thy heart, and with all thy soul, and with all thy mind, and with all thy strength," Jesus said, according to the book of Mark. "And the second is like, namely this, Thou shalt love thy neighbour as thyself."[24]

Adams distilled the common teaching of the Greek and Roman philosophers and the Old and New Testaments into a single sentence: "The fundamental Principle of all Phylosophy and all Christianity is "REJOICE ALWAYS IN ALL THINGS."[25] Adams said this wisdom also expressed the essence of his own faith, which he summed up in the following words: "He who loves the Workman and his Work, and does what he can to preserve and improve it, Shall be accepted of him."[26] In a subsequent letter, Adams repeated his personal creed to Jefferson in similar terms. "Allegiance to the Creator and Governor of the Milky Way and the Nebulæ, and Benevolence to all his Creatures, is my Religion," he wrote.[27]

For Jefferson, too, virtue consisted in benevolence to all. "[T]he essence of virtue is in doing good to others,"[28] Jefferson wrote to Adams in October 1816, adding that he was convinced that our moral sense, or instinct to do good, was innate rather than acquired. In this sense, he sided with Hutcheson, rather than with Locke and Hobbes, although, unlike Hutcheson, he seemed to believe that doing good to others was somehow compatible with slavery. "I agree perfectly with you," Adams replied. After "50 or 60 years" of reading, "my moral or religious Creed" could be summed up "in four short Words: 'Be just and good.'"[29]

Adams had been reading another book by Priestley comparing "the Institutions of Moses, with those of the Hindoos and other ancient Nations," which he called a "work of great labour, and not less haste."[30] The marginal notes that Adams scribbled in his own copy of Priestley's book return to one of his favorite themes: that Priestley was too quick to dismiss the claims that the moral principles of all the world religions could be traced back to Hinduism. "This conclusion is loose, like the Reasoning from which it is drawn," Adams scrawled on page 23.[31] Adams told Jefferson he was disappointed that Priestley hadn't discussed the Indian influences on Pythagoras's "prohibition of Beans So evidently derived from India." The original Hindu Vedas, including the Upanishads, hadn't yet been located, or "not yet translated into any European Language," but once they were, Adams believed they would show the Hindu influence on Western moral philosophy to be decisive.[32]

Adams was correct. Priestley appears to have read the first English translation of the Bhagavad Gita, which had been published in 1785. The translation makes clear that Priestley was wrong to conclude that the Hindu emphasis on the union of the tranquil soul with God has "no connection whatever with real devotion or virtue"—namely, with "the due government of the passions, and consequently a proper conduct in life," as Priestley put it.[33] In fact, the Gita contains the central lesson about the pursuit of happiness that Adams and Jefferson had learned from Pythagoras's *Golden Verses* and Cicero's *Tusculan Disputations*: that we are what we think, and life is shaped by the mind; that happiness requires virtue, and virtue requires the cultivation of daily habits of self-mastery and mental tranquility; that we should think and act mindfully rather than impulsively, using our powers of reason to moderate our ego-based passions; and that we should do good for its own sake rather than acting with any expectations about the reactions of others.

"A man is said to be confirmed in wisdom when he forsaketh every desire which entereth into his heart, and of himself is happy, and contented in himself," says the Charles Wilkins translation of the Gita, in words that sound almost identical to Cicero's definition of the happy man: "His mind is undisturbed in adversity, he is happy and contented in prosperity, and he is a stranger to anxiety, fear, and anger." The Gita emphasizes that we should find happiness within our minds rather than in the external world. "So the man is praised, who, having subdued all his passions, performeth with his active faculties all the functions of life, unconcerned about the event." From beginning to end, the Gita stresses the importance of abandoning expectations about the fruits of our action, focusing instead on thinking and acting rightly for its own sake, since the only thing we can control is our own thoughts and behavior. "Practical men, who . . . forsake the fruit of action, obtain infinite happiness."[34] The Gita emphasizes the importance of finding mental happiness and tranquility through the daily practice of moderate habits of eating and drinking and meditation. "[H]e who hath gotten the better of his passions; and having obtained this spiritual wisdom, he shortly enjoyeth superior happiness."[35]

In a remarkable synchronicity, on December 25, 1813, Adams compared the Hindu and Stoic wisdoms by quoting to Jefferson a passage from the book that Jefferson himself cited as the best guide to the pursuit of happiness: Cicero's *Tusculan Disputations*. The tranquil and self-mastered mind, Cicero suggested, in the passage Adams quoted, has no reason to fear death. ("Dying I shun: of being dead I nothing reck[on].")[36] Although there is no evidence that John Adams meditated, he recognized that the Hindu injunction to abandon expectations about the fruits of our action anticipated the Stoic doctrine of the dichotomy of control. As Cicero put it, the archer can practice aiming the arrow as well as possible, but once he releases the bow, can't control the gusts of wind that may divert the arrow from its course. Through his own deep reading, Adams had discovered that both the Hindus and the Stoics emphasize that happiness consists not in the success or failure of our efforts, which is beyond our control, but in the pursuit itself. When we master our thoughts and overcome unproductive emotions such as anger, jealousy, and fear, we achieve an inner peace, harmony, and tranquility that the Gita calls sattva and Aristotle calls ataraxia. It's the inner tranquility that results from knowing that we've done our best to align with the light.

Jefferson agreed with Adams that the goal of the pursuit of happiness was tranquility of mind, although at the end of his life, he declared himself to be not a Stoic but an Epicurean. He shared his mature reflections on happiness in an exchange with Adams in the spring of 1816 about whether both men considered themselves happy. Adams declared he would live his eighty years again. "[T]his is upon the whole a good World. There is ten times as much pleasure as pain in it," Adams wrote— and asked Jefferson if he would do the same.[37]

"You ask if I would agree to live my 70. Or rather 73. Years over again?" Jefferson replied. "[T]o which I say Yea. I think with you that it is a good world on the whole, that it has been framed on a principle of benevolence, and more pleasure than pain dealt out to us." In a revealing passage, Jefferson said that a lifetime of reflection had convinced him that "the perfection of the moral character is, not in a Stoical apathy, so hypocritically vaunted, and so untruly too, because impossible, but in a just equilibrium of all the passions."[38]

As a result, Jefferson had concluded that he was an Epicurean. "[T]he summum bonum with me is now truly Epicurean, ease of body and tranquility of mind; and to these I wish to consign my remaining days," he declared.[39] Now that he was retired, Jefferson found the best way to cultivate tranquility of mind was through Epicurus's council of moderating desire and taking pleasure in all things, rather than the unrealistic Stoic advice to overcome our desires entirely. "As you say of yourself, I too am an Epicurean," he wrote to his friend William Short in 1819. "I consider the genuine (not the imputed) doctrines of Epicurus as containing every thing rational in moral philosophy which Greece & Rome have left us."[40] Jefferson sent Short a syllabus he had prepared twenty years ago on the moral doctrines of Epicurus:

Happiness the aim of life.
Virtue the foundation of happiness.
Utility the test of virtue.[41]

For Epicureans, Jefferson stressed, the highest good "is to be not pained in body, nor troubled in mind." And "to procure tranquility of mind we must avoid desire & fear the two principal diseases of the mind."

Virtue consists in	1. Prudence.	2. Temperance.	3. Fortitude.	4. Justice
to which are opposed	1. Folly.	2. Desire.	3. Fear.	4. Deciept.[42]

Although the Stoics, including Cicero, had caricatured the Epicureans as impulsive pleasure seekers, this was one of their "calumnies," Jefferson objected. In fact, Epicurus advocated the rational pursuit of pleasure through mindful self-mastery and the contraction of our desires. For this reason, Jefferson advised Short to avoid indolence and to practice the virtue of industry. "[Y]ou are not a true disciple of our master Epicurus, in indulging the indolence to which you say you are yielding," Jefferson wrote. "[O]ne of his canons, you know, was that 'that indulgence which prevents a greater pleasure, or produces a greater pain, is to be avoided.'" Jefferson warned Short that "your love of repose will lead, in it's progress, to a suspension of healthy exercise, a relaxation of mind, an indifference to every thing around you, and finally to a debility of body and hebetude of mind, the farthest of all things from the happiness which the well regulated indulgences of Epicurus ensure."⁴³ Until the end of his days, Jefferson wrote letters to his daughters and his friends about the importance of improving their faculties through industrious exercise of body and mind, never ceasing in the daily pursuit of self-improvement. But Jefferson himself never succeeded in contracting his desires for lavish living sufficiently to support his lifestyle by his own industry rather than by enslaved labor.

Jefferson, having declared himself a well-regulated Epicurean rather than an apathetic Stoic, asked Adams to answer the standard Stoic question that Cicero had posed in *Tusculan Disputations*: What are the uses of Grief? "[T]here are, I acknolege, even in the happiest life, some terrible convulsions," Jefferson wrote to Adams. "I have often wondered for what good end the sensations of Grief could be intended. All our other passions, within proper bounds, have an useful object."⁴⁴ In May 1816 Adams replied that, in his view, grief was a sign of the self-command advocated by the Stoics: "Did you ever See a Portrait or a Statue of a great Man, without perceiving Strong Traits of Paine, & Anxiety? These Furrows were all ploughed in the Countenance, by Grief," Adams wrote. He agreed with the English jurist Sir Edward Coke that only "Sad Men" were fit to be legislators—"aged Men, who had been tossed and buffeted in the Vicissitudes of Life, forced upon profound Reflection by Grief and disappointments and taught to command their Passions & Prejudices." Adams agreed with Jefferson that "Stoical Apathy is impossible," but he insisted that "Patience and Resignation and tranquility may be acquired by Consideration in a great degree, very much for the hapiness of Life."⁴⁵

Adams then quoted a passage from Seneca's essay "On Anger" that summed up his own mature understanding of the relationship between grief and happiness:

Grief drives Men into habits of Serious Reflection Sharpens the Understanding and Softens the heart; it compels them to arrouse their Reason, to assert its Empire over their Passions Propensities and Prejudices; to elevate them to a Superiority over all human Events; to give them the Felicis Annimi immotan tranquilitatem ["the imperturbable tranquility of a happy mind"]; in short to make them Stoicks and Christians.[46]

Nearly sixty years earlier, while he was courting Abigail, Adams had copied the same passage from Seneca about the "imperturbable tranquility of a happy Mind" in his Harvard diary. "The Felicis Animi immota Tranquilitas, the immovable Tranquility of a happy Mind, unmoved by Perils of Water or of fire, unmoved by any Losses, Accidents, by Loss of Wealth, of fame, of friends, &c," he wrote. "Happy Mind indeed." After a lifetime of reflection, in other words, Adams and Jefferson agreed that the pursuit of happiness was the goal of life, tranquility of mind the key to the pursuit of happiness, and moderation of the passions the key to tranquility of mind.

Like Hamilton and Madison, however, they disagreed about whether Americans as a whole could achieve the personal self-government necessary for political self-government on a large scale. In other words, they were unsure whether Americans could find the self-mastery necessary to sustain the republican experiment. At the end of his long life, Adams had concluded that all utopian claims about human perfectibility were unrealistic. In the *Progress of the Human Mind*, Condorcet had insisted that "[t]he time will therefore come when the sun will shine only on free men who know no other master but their reason."[47] Condorcet was confident that "nature has set no term to the perfection of human faculties; that the perfectibility of man is truly indefinite."[48] All nations, he believed, would eventually follow America in being ruled by reason rather than passion, and, eventually, force and prejudice would lose their power, inequality would be abolished, and reason would shine across the globe.

Adams found all this to be idealistic claptrap. "I am a Beleiver in the probable improvability and Improvement the Ameliorabi[li]ty and

Amelioration in human Affaires: though I never could understand the
Doctrine of the Perfectability of the human Mind," he wrote to Jefferson
in 1814.[49] This appeared to him like the Hindu claim that Brahmans,
through rigorous studies, could so perfect their self-control that they
could become omniscient and merge with the Divine. The fundamental premise of Adams's political creed, he told Jefferson, was that most
powerful forces in society would always seek absolute power, and absolute power was "[e]qually arbitrary, cruel bloody and in every respect,
diabolical," whether wielded by "a Majority of a popular Assembly, and
Aristocratical Counsel, an Oligarchical Junto and a single Emperor."[50]
In Adams's view, human reason and conscience were no match for
human passions and "Power must never be trusted Without a Check."[51]
The only way to prevent the clashing interests in society from trying to
dominate one another through force was to separate powers entirely.

Jefferson, by contrast, agreed with Condorcet that the eighteenth
century had seen the steady diffusion of the cool light of reason and morality, as public opinion was slowly enlightened, monarchies were toppled, and representative government spread across Europe. Jefferson was
confident that the public mind could be perfected by education. "[N]o
government can continue good but under the controul of the people,"
and the American people had to be educated for self-government, as
citizens were in ancient Rome. "[T]heir minds were to be informed, by
education, what is right & what wrong, to be encouraged in habits of
virtue," Jefferson wrote. Only education could "render the people a sure
basis for the structure of order & good government."[52]

The disagreement between Adams and Jefferson on the perfectibility of the human mind mirrored that between Hamilton and Madison,
and between the Federalists and the Republicans more generally. Taking
the Federalist position, Adams doubted that virtue could be taught on
a wide scale. "[H]ave you ever found in history one single example of a
Nation thoroughly Corrupted—that was afterwards restored to Virtue,"
Adams asked. "To return to the Romans—I never could discover that
they possessed much Virtue, or real Liberty."[53] In Rome, aristocrats such

as Caesar, feigning frugality and virtue, had acquired popularity among the people and had extended the republic into a vast empire until it was felled by riches and luxury.

In the same letter, Adams expressed concern about the growing crisis over whether to admit Missouri to the Union as a slave state or free state. "The Missouri question I hope will follow the other waves under the Ship and do no harm," Adams wrote.[54] Jefferson was more pessimistic about the Missouri crisis, which he feared might presage a Civil War. Aligning himself with the most extreme Southern defenders of slavery, Jefferson insisted that Congress had no power to ban slavery north of Missouri. In April 1820, a month after Congress passed the Missouri Compromise, which admitted Missouri as a slave state and Maine as a free state, an angry and radicalized Jefferson wrote to a friend that "the Missouri question . . . like a fire bell in the night, awakened and filled me with terror. I considered it at once as the knell of the Union." Having once opposed the expansion of slavery, Jefferson now supported it, on the grounds that the "diffusion" of the enslaved "over a greater surface would make them individually happier."[55] (Jefferson's perverse and absurd logic was that a larger enslaved population meant less work for individual slaves. Of course, he was neglecting the fact that the children of the enslaved would themselves be born into bondage, and so the enslaved population would grow exponentially.)

Jefferson's reflections on the Missouri crisis revealed a badly frightened man. Although he claimed (as always) to support a "general emancipation" in the distant future, Jefferson expressed pessimism that slavery could end unless the South was peacefully persuaded to abandon it. "A geographical line, coinciding with a marked principle, moral and political, once concieved and held up to the angry passions of men, will never be obliterated." In a remarkable expression of despair, Jefferson expressed doubt that the Union would survive. "I regret that I am now to die in the belief that the useless sacrifice of themselves, by the generation of '76 to acquire self government and happiness to their country, is to be thrown away by the unwise and unworthy passions of their sons, and that my only consolation is to be that I live not to weep over it."[56]

As the political scientist Dennis Rasmussen argues, many of the Founders by their end of their lives had become disillusioned for different reasons about the future of the American experiment. "Washington became disillusioned above all because of the rise of parties and partisanship, Hamilton because he felt that the federal government was not sufficiently vigorous or energetic, Adams because he believed that the American people lacked the requisite civic virtue for republican government, and Jefferson because of sectional divisions that were laid bare by conflict over the spread of slavery," Rasmussen writes.[57]

Despite Jefferson's fears that sectional divisions would destroy the Union, he maintained some tranquility of mind in his final years by trusting that he would find happiness in the hereafter. Although he never attempted to understand the mysteries of how souls transmigrated from one world to the next, he was consistent in his belief in an afterlife. "I have thought it better, by nourishing the good passions, & controuling the bad, to merit an inheritance in a state of being of which I can know so little, and to trust for the future to him who has been so good for the past," he wrote in 1801.[58] And he maintained his belief in the afterlife until the end. When Abigail Adams died in October 1818, Jefferson wrote movingly to John Adams expressing confidence that he would be reunited with his wife in a future state. "[I]t is of some comfort to us both that the term is not very distant," he wrote, when they would ascend "in essence to an ecstatic meeting with the friends we have loved & lost and whom we shall still love and never lose again."[59] Jefferson also sustained his disciplined daily schedule of reading, writing, and exercise until the end. After breaking his arm at the age of seventy-eight, he recovered quickly, and his handwriting remained firm. In 1822 he calculated the number of letters he had received two years earlier and found the total to be 1,267, "many of them requiring answers of elaborate research."[60] The industrious daily schedule that he began as a young student remained unchanged, his lifestyle supported as always by enslaved labor. Adams doubted that he had ever received a fourth as many letters in his busiest year.

In 1820 Jefferson, who always guarded his emotions, wrote movingly to Adams about his true feelings for his friend. "I am sure that I really know many, many, things, and none more surely than that I love you with all my heart, and pray for the continuance of your life until you shall be tired of it yourself."[61] And in their final year on earth, both men reaffirmed that their friendship transcended politics, as Jefferson warmly congratulated Adams on the election of his son John Quincy to the presidency. "I sincerely congratulate you on the high gratific[atio]n which the issue of the late election must have afforded you," Jefferson wrote in February 1825. "[I]t must excite ineffable feelings in the breast of a father to have lived to see a son to whose educ[atio]n and happiness his life has been devoted so eminently distinguished by the voice of his country."[62] The same day, Jefferson had written to his preferred candidate, William Crawford, who served as Treasury secretary under Presidents Madison and Monroe, saying how disappointed he was in the election results. To John Adams, however, he expressed confidence that Americans would rally around his son, who had been elected by the House of Representatives after no candidate won a majority of the Electoral College.

Jefferson ended his affectionate letter by wishing Adams "nights of rest to you and days of tranquility," which was his definition of the pursuit of happiness.[63] "I am certainly very near the end of my life," Adams responded in his penultimate letter to Jefferson, in January 1826. He then repeated Socrates's advice about keeping calm in the face of death, which Cicero embraced in *Tusculan Disputations*. Adams contemplated death "without terror or dismay," he said, because either it was followed by a transmigration to the afterlife or it was the end ("aut transit, aut finit"). If it was the end, "which I cannot believe, and do not believe," then he would "never know it, and why should I dread it," and if it was a transmigration to the afterlife, "I shall ever be under the same constitution and administration of Government in the Universe and I am not afraid to trust and confide in it."[64] Months later, on July 4, 1826, the old friends died within hours of each other, each believing the other still lived. John Quincy Adams was defeated for reelection three years later but would devote his life to exemplifying the ideals of the Declaration of Independence in ways that Jefferson could only imagine.

Notes on Marcus Aurelius's *Meditations*

Four habits of thought to erase from your mind:
This thought is unnecessary or destructive
This isn't what you truly think; you find
Your mortal makes your divine part unproductive

Work for three things: proper understanding;
unselfish action and truthful speech
And if you find yourself in a crash landing
Accept it calmly, as the sages teach

Do the work with patience and industry
Find fulfillment in what you're doing now
Free from fear or hope of publicity
Your life will be happy if all your words are true

Life is short, and that's all there is to say
Unrestrained moderation: the only way

Ten

CLEANLINESS

John Quincy Adams's Composure

I n the two volumes of "homespun" lectures that his father had sent
Thomas Jefferson, John Quincy Adams summed up the classical
wisdom on the importance of self-control. For Aristotle and Cicero,
Adams wrote in his Harvard lectures, "the management of the passions
was considered as including almost the whole art of oratory."[1] "[P]erfect
and unalterable self command," Adams said, was the hallmark of virtuous living as well as persuasive public speaking. "If it be true of mankind
in general, that he who ruleth his spirit is greater than he that taketh
a city," Adams said, quoting one of his mother's favorite proverbs, "self
dominion" was especially important for public speakers. "Let no man
presume to bespeak an ascendency over the passions of others, until he
has acquired an unquestioned mastery over his own."[2]

Adams kept this advice in mind throughout his remarkable career, which took him from diplomatic service in Europe to serving as
a congressman, secretary of state, and president of the United States.

After he left the White House, he returned to the House of Representatives. There he became Congress's leading opponent of slavery, which he eloquently denounced as inconsistent with the ideals of the Declaration of Independence. And his lifelong commitment to self-improvement and moral growth reflects his deep reading throughout his life in Stoic philosophy—in particular the works of Epictetus, Cicero, and the philosophical emperor Marcus Aurelius. "I believe much, very much in the usefulness of the Stoic Philosophy, to promote the pursuit of happiness as well as the practice of virtue," John Quincy wrote to his father in 1811. "[I]t is of all the antient systems of philosophy, that which is most congenial to the still wiser and more perfect doctrine of Christianity." Adams told his father that Epictetus "prepares us most effectually for the evils of life," while Marcus Aurelius "guards us most carefully against its prosperities." He was grateful that, in the first decades of his career, he found himself drawing on "Marcus–Aurelius' lessons of Temperance more than of Epictetus's school of Fortitude." Nevertheless, he frequently consulted both philosophers throughout his life and always found himself returning to the works of Cicero—particularly *Tusculan Disputations*. Adams dismissed the criticism that followers of Stoicism often violated its stern precepts because, as he put it, "human Passions, are often too mighty for their control." "To say that the sensitive part of our nature is too frail for the government of its rational part," he wrote, "is to take the exception for the rule."[3]

From the age of eleven until he died at eighty-one, Adams kept a diary of his daily attempts to pursue happiness through Stoical self-mastery. And the diary, which many consider the most revealing diary ever kept by an American president, is a model of Benjamin Franklin's system of daily moral self-accounting. "A Diary is the Time Piece of Life, and will never fail of keeping Time, or of getting out of order with it," Adams wrote to his son George Washington Adams in 1827. "A Diary if honestly kept is one of the best preservatives of Morals. A man who commits to paper from day to day the employment of his time, the places he frequents, the persons with whom he converses, the actions with which he is occupied, will have a perpetual guard over himself. His Record is a second Conscience."[4]

Adams's diary reflects the relentless pressure that he exerted on himself in his quest for self-discipline and self-improvement. Like his father, John Quincy had a hot temper and struggled to control it. He achieved self-mastery only with great effort, showing to the world a granite imperturbability that concealed his own roiling emotions. Throughout Adams's life, he battled depression, or what he called "melancholy," as he took himself to task for falling short of his own impossible ideals. Adams's diary reflects the conflicting imperatives of the wisdom literature—to pursue moral perfections and mental tranquility at the same time. These conflicting impulses led Adams to heights of self-reproach whenever he failed to practice the classical virtues, beating himself up for every black spot that he imagined himself recording on Franklin's chart.

But if Adams was the most self-critical of the Founders' sons, he was also the one most committed to the quest for lifelong growth. His father never overcame his vanity; Thomas Jefferson his avarice; Alexander Hamilton his ambition. By contrast, Adams's daily commitment to moral self-accounting led him to transcend his youthful pragmatism and political ambition and to become one of the leading antislavery voices of his time.

For both the elder and the younger Adams, keeping a diary was necessary for self-reflection and self-discipline. Adams's diary for 1785 begins with a maxim from Voltaire ("Indolence is sweet, its consequences bitter"), and the virtue he upbraided himself most frequently for failing to sustain was industry.[5] But no one accused Adams of indolence aside from Adams himself. He started keeping the diary in 1779, at the age of eleven, as he set off to France for the second time, to accompany his father, who had been appointed by Congress to join Benjamin Franklin as an envoy. Young Adams dined frequently with Franklin (whose habits his father found disorganized, despite Franklin's professed devotion to order) and attended French boarding school with Franklin's grandson, Benjamin Franklin Bache. He spent seven years abroad, studying at the

University of Leyden in Holland, serving as private secretary and French interpreter to the American envoy to Russia, and assisting his father and Thomas Jefferson as they negotiated treaties with Great Britain and across Europe. Returning to the United States to matriculate at Harvard, he gave the Phi Beta Kappa oration and, in 1791, wrote a series of essays under the pseudonym "Publicola" responding to Jefferson's attacks on his father's *Discourses on Davila*. The essays went viral and kindled his hunger for a literary career.

In 1792, as he was studying law, Adams published a series of essays attacking as unconstitutional a Massachusetts law banning theatrical performances. The following year, at the age of twenty-five, he atoned for his imagined laziness by writing "a very decent flourish upon the passions" and the importance of overcoming them by self-discipline, comparing himself to the debauched Catiline in Virgil's epic *The Aeneid*.[6] To his exacting mind, none of these achievements seemed adequate. "I am not satisfied with the manner in which I employ my time," Adams wrote in his diary on May 26, 1792. "It is calculated to keep me forever fixed in that state of useless and disgraceful insignificancy which has been my lot for some years past."[7]

He was "[a]t an age bearing close upon 25," Adams noted, but still found himself "as obscure, as unknown to the world, as the most indolent, or the most stupid of human beings." Adams reminded himself that achieving a "respectable reputation" was "within my own powers," but he would never fulfill his potential "without such a steady, patient and persevering pursuit of the means adapted to the end." He quoted the poem about the choice of Hercules between Virtue and Vice that was his father's favorite fable. Only "Labour and Toil" could prevent "my Time" from being "loitered away in stupid laziness," he wrote. "[M]y character is (under the smiles of heaven) to be the work of my own hands."[8]

Adams was, as always, too hard on himself. And he inherited from his parents the habit of beating himself up for not living up to his potential—for wasting time and losing his temper. "You must curb that impetuosity of temper, for which I have frequently chid you, but which properly directed may be productive of great good," Abigail wrote to him in January 1780.[9] He was in Paris with his father and, at the age of thirteen, was beginning to notice women in the streets. Abigail warned him that vice was lurking on every corner. "Passions are the Elements of life," but "Elements which are subject to the controul of Reason," she wrote. "Who ever will candidly examine themselves will find some degree of passion, peevishness or obstinancy in their Natural tempers." She warned her son that he had been born with a naturally hot temper, but he could use his powers of reason to subdue it. "The due Government of the passions has been considered in all ages as a most valuable acquisition," Abigail wrote. She then quoted the proverb that Adams would quote years later in his Harvard lectures: "He that is slow to anger is better than the Mighty, and he that ruleth his Spirit than he that taketh a city."[10]

In particular, Abigail Adams emphasized to her son the destructive power of anger. "This passion unrestrained by reason cooperating with power has produced the Subversion of cities, the desolation of countries, the Massacre of Nations, and filled the world with injustice and oppression," she warned. When he beheld his own country suffering from the effects of "Malignant passions," Abigail said that John Quincy should learn "to govern and controul yourself. Having once obtained this self government, you will find a foundation laid for happiness to yourself and usefullness to Mankind."[11]

Abigail stressed that self-control was the key to the pursuit of happiness. "Virtue alone is happiness below," she wrote, "and consists in cultivating and improveing every good inclination and in checking and subduing every propensity to Evil." Moreover, Abigail warned that self-control could be obtained only by rigorous daily self-accounting, "the knowledge and study of yourself." And in addition to his duties to himself, he also owed duties to society in general, and to God. "The only sure and permanent foundation of virtue is Religion," Abigail wrote sternly to her son. His present and future happiness depended on his "performance of certain duties which all tend to the happiness and welfare of

Society and are comprised in one short sentence expressive of universal Benevolence, 'Thou shalt Love thy Neighbour as thyself.'"[12]

John Adams was equally stern in admonishing his son to achieve self-mastery. Rather than religion, however, he thought that the best instructors were the classical moral philosophers he had read in his own youth. "I Should recommend to you Books of Morals, as the most constant Companions, of your Hours of Relaxation, through the whole Course of your Life," John Adams wrote to his son in May 1783.[13] In particular, Adams recommended the moral philosophies of Cicero and Seneca. The Adamses studied the works of Cicero together during their travels in France. And after John Quincy's defeat for reelection to the presidency in 1828, he spent more than a year rereading the complete works of Cicero in Latin every morning.

John Adams also recommended that his son read "with Care" the Enlightenment moral philosophy that he himself had read at Harvard, including works by Francis Hutcheson, a central influence on Jefferson's understanding of the pursuit of happiness. As a synthesis of all the moral writings, Adams recommended Jean Barbeyrac's *History of the Rise and Progress of the Science of Morality*. Emphasizing that the "Practical Science of Moral Actions" can be obtained by anyone, using his or her faculties of reason, Barbeyrac introduces his book by stressing that self-command is the key to happiness. "[E]very Man, who will be happy" must fulfill "the Duties, which tend to procure them that Happiness, which they so passionately seek after," Barbeyrac wrote. He noted that "[t]he *Stoicks*, who made Morality their principal Study," emphasized the importance of mastering the virtues that "entirely depend on yourself; Sincerity, Gravity, Humanity, Laboriousness and Industry, Contempt of Voluptuousness." By avoiding "Luxury, trifling Amusements, and vain Discourses," and bearing in mind that "all the Happiness of this Life" depends entirely on improving our own character, every individual has the capacity to develop a soul "judicious, free and great."[14]

If Abigail chastised her son for not writing frequently enough, John chastised him for wasting time. As the Revolutionary War was raging,

Adams urged his son to read Thucydides to learn the art of war and Demosthenes and Cicero to learn the disciplined use of time. In the Pythagorean spirit, he urged him to achieve excellence in sports as well as in his studies, noting that even ice skating could be an art form if it was practiced mindfully. His father emphasized a division of time between "a Taste for Literature and a Turn for Business," both of which, when "united in the same Person, never fails to make a great Man."[15] Adams urged the advantages of reading poetry as a form of high pleasure, an alternative to wasting his time in idle amusements. "You will never be alone, with a Poet in your Poket," Adams wrote. "You will never have an idle Hour."[16] Above all, Adams emphasized the importance of using his time wisely, to ensure that every moment of the day was devoted to self-improvement. "Make it a Rule, my dear Son, To loose no Time," Adams wrote in 1781. "There is not a moral Precept, of clearer Obligation, or of greater Import. Make it the grand Maxim of your Life, and it cannot fail to be happy, and usefull to the World."[17] Franklin and Jefferson said much the same.

The maxim "Lose no time" led John Quincy Adams to a lifelong sense that he was not living up to his potential, even as he appeared to the rest of the world to be surpassing expectations. Momentary lapses of focus and attention led to bouts of self-recrimination. In 1794, the year after he was upbraiding himself for laziness, Adams's essays defending American neutrality were circulated so widely that they caught the attention of President Washington, who appointed him minister to the Netherlands at the age of twenty-six. On his way to the Hague, he stopped in London to deliver papers to John Jay, who was negotiating an agreement that would become the Jay Treaty with Britain. "Just before we got to the London Bridge," he wrote in his diary on October 15, "we heard a rattling before us and immediately after a sound as of a trunk falling from the Carriage." Adams "instantly looked forward and saw that both our trunks were gone." He jumped from the carriage and, after he retrieved them from the side of the road, "our driver assured us that the trunks could not have fallen unless the straps had been cut away" by a thief.[18]

Reflecting on the near miss after arriving in his hotel, Adams chastised himself with melodramatic vehemence. If the trunk had been lost, Adams reflected, "How could I have informed the Secretary of State of the fate of his papers?" he wrote. The malicious and envious gossip, he feared, would have spread from one end of the United States to the other. Although Adams assured himself that "I had neglected no possible precaution" in securing the trunk, it was only luck that he had heard it fall, and he might have missed the sound if the trunk had fallen two minutes later. Despite going on to deliver the papers to Jay, Adams obsessively rehashed the incident for several pages, which was characteristic of his tendency to upbraid himself for any perceived failure of mindfulness and self-mastery.

Adams's Franklin-like focus on time management is reflected in the detailed daily schedules that he recorded in his diary at every stage of his career. "I rise at about 7," he wrote in 1803, after his appointment as a US senator by the Massachusetts legislature. He would write in his room until breakfast at nine, walk to the Capitol, sit in the Senate Chamber until about three, home for dinner at four, then "pass the Evening, idly," until bed at eleven.[19] Adams had become a loyal member of the Federalist Party, and had proved his party loyalty by writing a satirical ode in the style of Horace about Thomas Jefferson's controversial relationship with Sally Hemings, expressing hope that their children would display the talent of the Black poets Phillis Wheatley and Ignatius Sancho, the British abolitionist, writer, and former slave. Still, he resolved to put principle above politics and, in 1807, was the only Federalist in Congress to vote for President Jefferson's Embargo Act, which forbade American ships from trading abroad, to punish Britain and France for seizing American ships during the Napoleonic wars. At the same time, Adams chastised himself for not working on his lectures as the first Boylston Professor of Rhetoric and Oratory at Harvard, a post that he was juggling with his Senate duties.

· · ·

Adams's apostasy on the Embargo Act led him to resign from the Senate in 1808, but he continued to commute between Harvard and Washington, where his career as a Supreme Court advocate flourished. In 1809 he successfully argued the landmark Supreme Court case of *Fletcher v. Peck*, in which Chief Justice John Marshall struck down a state law for the first time, affirming the sanctity of contracts by invalidating Georgia's effort to abrogate the Yazoo Land Act of 1795. The same year, the newly inaugurated fourth president of the United States, James Madison, appointed Adams the first foreign minister to Russia, and he arrived in Saint Petersburg accompanied by his wife, Louisa Catherine, his sister-in-law and nephew, and his youngest son, Charles Francis. (Inspired by his time abroad, Charles Francis Adams went on to serve as President Lincoln's minister to Great Britain during the Civil War.)

At the urging of Abigail Adams, Madison then appointed Adams to the Supreme Court in 1811, and he was immediately confirmed by the Senate. Nevertheless, he declined the appointment, preferring to remain in Saint Petersburg. Despite these high honors, Adams continued to criticize himself for his perceived unproductiveness and lack of achievements. "I am forty-five years old," he wrote from Russia in 1812. "Two thirds of a long life are past, and I have done Nothing to distinguish it by usefulness to my Country, or to Mankind." Lamenting that "Passions, Indolence, weakness and infirmity" had "almost constantly paralyzed my efforts of good," he fruitlessly resolved "to cease forming fruitless Resolutions."[20]

Two years later, he continued to lament not only his lack of industry but also his lack of exercise. He rose between five and six o'clock, read five chapters of the Bible and wrote until breakfast at nine, had meetings until three, walked for an hour, dined at four, and then indulged in theater or a concert until bed at eleven. Adams worried that he was spending too much time at the theater. "The consequence is that I am growing uncomfortably corpulent, and that industry becomes irksome to me. May I be cautious not to fall into any habit of indolence or dissipation!"[21]

"Could I have chosen my own Genius and Condition," he reflected, "I should have made myself a great Poet," and he found himself writing poetry before sunrise on spiritual and classical subjects.[22] Morning Bible commentary also became a regular practice, and in 1811, while he was in Saint Petersburg, he began writing a remarkable series of letters about the Bible and its teachings to his oldest son, George Washington Adams, who had remained in Massachusetts with his brother John. Adams worried from the moment his first son was born that his expectations for the boy were too high. He wondered whether it was wise to give the "great and venerable name" of George Washington "to such a lottery-ticket as a new-born infant."[23] Nevertheless, in his letters to his son, Adams sternly urged him to seek the same perfection that Jesus urged on his disciples.

"[A]s a system of morality for regulating the conduct of men while on earth," Adams wrote in April 1813, the most "striking and extoardinary feature" of Christianity "is its tendency and exhortations to absolute perfection. The language of Christ to his disciples is explicit: 'Be ye therefore perfect, even as your father in heaven is perfect.'" Adams noted that, for Jesus, the way for men to achieve perfection on earth is to follow the commandment to "love their enemies." Mastering your anger and responding to injuries with love, Adams said, "is undoubtedly the greatest conquest which the spirit of man can achieve over its infirmities, and to him who can attain that elevation of virtue which it requires, all other victories over the evil passions must be comparatively easy."[24]

Adams acknowledged that the "principles of benevolence toward enemies and the forgiveness of injuries" could be found in the Old Testament and in "heathen writers" such as Socrates. But he said that the system of moral philosophy that most resembled that of Jesus was the Stoics, and the Stoic book that best taught how to achieve perfection through "self-subjugation" was the one that Jefferson said inspired his understanding of the pursuit of happiness: Cicero's *Tusculan Disputations.*[25]

"Among the Grecian systems of moral philosophy, that of the Stoics resembles the Christian doctrine in the particular of requiring the total subjugation of the passions," Adams wrote in May 1813. "You will find the question discussed with all the eloquence and ingenuity of Cicero, in the fourth of his Tusculan disputations, which I advise you to read and meditate upon."[26] (The fourth chapter of *Tusculan Disputations*, "On the Perturbations of the Mind," is the one that Jefferson cited as the best definition of the pursuit of happiness.) The same month, Adams reported to his father that he had been reading extensively in Cicero's moral philosophy: the *Academica*, *On the Nature of the Gods*, and *About the Ends of Good and Evil*, in addition to *Tusculan Disputations*. But while Adams had internalized the expectations of his own parents, George Washington Adams rebelled against his father's relentless exhortations to perfection, descending into alcoholism and depression.

In 1814 President Madison appointed Adams to head a commission that negotiated an end to the War of 1812 with Britain. Three years later, President James Monroe appointed him secretary of state, and Adams returned to the United States. He found the country beginning to fracture over the question of slavery. The Missouri Compromise of 1820 had admitted Missouri as a slave state and Maine as a free state. Adams insisted that Congress had the power to ban slavery, which, in his view, violated the principles of natural liberty and equality set out in the Declaration of Independence and the Bible. "The Declaration of Independence not only asserts the natural equality of all men, and their unalienable right to Liberty; but that the only *just* powers of government are derived from the consent of the governed," he wrote on March 3, 1820, a day after the Missouri Compromise passed. "A power for one part of the people to make slaves of the other can never be derived from consent, and is therefore not a just power."[27] Still, at this point, Adams refused to call himself an abolitionist, finding those who demanded the immediate elimination of slavery too extreme.

James Monroe was reelected in 1820, and Adams served for four more years as secretary of state. He then ran for president in 1824 and received eighty-four electoral votes, while Andrew Jackson received ninety-nine. William Crawford, the secretary of Treasury, received forty-one electoral votes, and Henry Clay, the speaker of the house, thirty-seven. Because no candidate received a majority, the election was thrown to the House of Representatives. At the beginning of January, Clay met with Adams and decided to support him, which clinched Adams's victory. Adams soon thereafter appointed Clay secretary of state, prompting charges of a "corrupt bargain," which Adams strenuously denied. On February 9, by a vote of thirteen out of the twenty-four state delegations, the House elected Adams the sixth president of the United States. "May the blessing of God rest upon the event of this day," he wrote in his diary, adding that he had written "a Letter of three lines to my father, asking for his blessing and prayers on the event of this day; the most important day of my life."[28]

In the White House, Adams continued to rise before sunrise for daily Bible study and poetry writing, followed by visitors until four o'clock, exercise from four to six, then dinner until seven, and signing papers or working on his diary from dark until eleven. Surprised not to have more control over his own schedule, Adams lamented, "There is much to correct, and reform, and the precept of Diligence is always timely."[29]

On June 13, during his afternoon exercises, Adams nearly drowned. He and his steward Antoine Guista had set off in a leaky boat to cross the Potomac for an afternoon swim when they capsized in the middle of the river. Adams had trouble swimming to the opposite shore, struggling in the water for nearly three hours as his puffy sleeves weighed him down. "Antoine, who was naked, reached it with little difficulty—I had much more, and while struggling for life, and gasping for breath had ample leisure to reflect upon my own discretion." Stripping down when he reached the shore, Adams sat "naked basking on the bank," waiting for Antoine to summon a carriage to bring him home. He finally returned to the White House around nine o'clock at night, "having been out nearly five hours." Always seeking to learn from his mistakes, Adams wrote, "This incident gave me a humiliating lesson, and solemn warning not to trifle with danger." In the future, he resolved, "I must strictly confine myself to the purposes of health, exercise, and salutary labour."[30]

By December, Adams had adjusted his schedule to exercising in the morning, rising between five and six, walking for four miles by moonlight, "returning home in time to see the Sun rise" from the East Room of the White House, and reading three chapters of the Bible until breakfast at nine.[31] During his morning walks before dawn, Adams wrote sonnets on spiritual themes. "This is my fathers birth day and the Sonnet here enclosed is the meditation of my Morning's walk," he wrote in November 1826, months after his father's death. The poem that followed is an inspiring meditation connecting his father's struggle for freedom during the Revolution with the struggle of the enslaved for freedom on his father's birthday.

> Who but shall learn that Freedom is the prize
> Man still is bound to rescue or maintain
> That Natures God commands the Slave to rise
> And on the oppressor's head to break his chain
> Roll, years of promise, rapidly roll round
> Till not a Slave shall on this earth be found.[32]

Adams was modest about his poem, noting, "If it were better poetry, I would have written it at full length" rather than in a shorthand that only he could read easily.[33] Nevertheless, he was more creatively fulfilled by his literary efforts than all of his impressive public service. "Literature has been the charm of my life, and could I have carved out my own fortunes, to Literature would my whole life have been devoted," he wrote in 1820. "The operations of my mind are slow; my imagination sluggish, and my powers of extemporaneous speaking very inefficient—But I have much capacity for and love of labour, habits, on the whole of industry and temperance, and a strong and almost innate passion for literary pursuits." In a revealing confession, Adams said, "The summit of my ambition would have been by some great work of literature to have done honour to my age and Country, and to have lived in the gratitude of future ages," but that "[t]his consummation of happiness has been denied me."[34] Adams's poetry was collected posthumously in a volume called *Poems of Religion and Society*, published in 1848.

In his inaugural address, Adams praised the Constitution for having largely "secured the freedom and happiness of this people." Since the treaty with Britain in 1814, "[t]en years of peace, at home and abroad" had "blended into harmony the most discordant elements of public opinion." Calling for the end of the "baneful weed of party strife," Adams exhorted citizens to discard "every remnant of rancor against each other . . . yielding to talents and virtue alone" rather than "party spirit." In particular, he pledged to continue President Monroe's policy of championing "internal improvements" and public works, noting that "the roads and aqueducts of Rome" were among "the imperishable glories of the ancient republics."[35] And in a message to Congress on December 5, he built on George Washington's vision and recommended the establishment of a national university, a Department of the Interior, a national naval academy and astronomical observatory, and a national network of roads and canals. Although Adams's critics mocked his proposal for observatories, which he called "lighthouses of the skies," most of his plans were eventually adopted.[36]

Adams's hope that Americans would set aside "party spirit" and unify under his administration was, he acknowledged after a year in office, unrealistic. He had been elected without majority support, "[w]ith perhaps two thirds of the whole people adverse to the actual result," and a year later, he had found "little change of the public opinions, or feelings."[37] Andrew Jackson had accepted the election results and greeted Adams cordially at his inauguration. But at the end of 1825, the Tennessee Legislature nominated Jackson to run for president again in 1828, and Jackson resigned from the US Senate to begin his permanent campaign, a move that Adams denounced as a dark conspiracy. In October 1827, however, he acknowledged to Henry Clay that the conspiracy would likely succeed because his opponents in Congress continued to promote the "infamous Slander" that he and Clay had struck a corrupt bargain to make Adams president. "General Jackson will therefore be elected,"

Adams wrote in his diary. "But it is impossible that his Administration should give satisfaction to the people of this Union. He is incompetent both by his ignorance, and by the fury of his Passions."[38]

Jackson was elected in November 1828, when he received 178 electoral votes to Adams's 83. Adams felt unappreciated by both the North and the South, and victimized by his Jacksonian opponents, whom he considered populist demagogues. "Posterity will scarcely believe it—but so it is—that this combination against me has been formed, and is now exulting in triumph over me, for the devotion of my life, and of all the faculties of my Soul, to the Union—and to the Improvement, Physical, Moral and Intellectual of my Country," he wrote after the election. "Passion, Prejudice, Envy and Jealousy will pass—The Cause of Union and of Improvement will remain; and I have duties to it and to my Country yet to discharge."[39]

Adams spent Inauguration Day, March 4, 1829, at his Washington home on F Street. Friends brought him a copy of Jackson's inaugural address, which he praised as "short, written with some elegance; and remarkable chiefly for a significant threat of Reform." He closed his diary entry with his customary prayer for diligence, not only for himself but also for his family. "From Indolence and despondency, and indiscretion may I specially be preserved."[40]

First, however, Adams had to deal with deepening depression, exacerbated by the mental health crisis of his eldest son, George Washington Adams. "My health has been languishing, without sickness," Adams noted in his diary in 1827. In addition to losing his appetite and experiencing stomach pains, he described an "uncontrollable dejection of spirits." His depression was so serious that he was experiencing "a sluggish carelessness of life, and imaginary wish that it were terminated."[41] While Adams had only "imaginary" thoughts of ending his life, his son was more determined. Elected to the Massachusetts House of Representatives in 1826, George had served only one year, continuing to drink compulsively. Before daylight on April 30, 1829, traveling from Boston to

Washington to join his father, George Washington Adams disappeared from the deck of the steamship *Benjamin Franklin*. From newspaper accounts, Adams understood that his son had died by suicide.

Adams poured out his agony to his diary, exacerbated by a sense of guilt for having burdened his son with his own impossible expectations. "Blessed God!" he wrote, "forgive the wanderings of my own mind under its excruciating torture!"[42] In the terrible days that followed, Adams reported that he and his wife were experiencing days of "deep and dreadful affliction," as "imaginations wild and unsustained by reason came over us both." As he walked around Harvard Square, "in the deepest anguish of my Soul," he "saw a rainbow suddenly spread before me," which struck him "as an admonition to trust in the goodness and mercy of God."[43] "Oh! My unhappy Son!" Adams wrote.[44] "There is a pressure upon my heart and upon my Spirits, inexpressible and which I never knew before.—As it subsides, it gives way to dejection and despondency, equally unknown to my feelings before."

Two weeks later, the body of his son washed up on the shore at City Island, New York. "All the prospects for the remnant of my life, in which I had delighted are broken up," Adams wrote, "and I have nothing left to rely on but the Mercy of God."[45] On December 31, 1829, at the close of a year in which he had lost both the presidency and his eldest son, Adams said that he could have endured the loss of the White House without complaint. "Its vanities I despised, and its flatteries never gave me a moment of enjoyment. But my beloved Son! Mysterious Heaven!" Adams prayed for the strength to practice the classical virtues in order to calm his turbulent mind. "Let me no longer yield to a desponding or distrustful Spirit—Grant me Fortitude—Patience—Perseverance; and active Energy—And let thy Will be done."[46]

In addition to prayer, Adams turned for consolation to Cicero. He had begun rereading his favorite Latin author to calm himself in the days after Jackson's inauguration. In the weeks before his son's death, he read Cicero's *Philippics*, and reminded himself that "[c]lassical learning is no useless lumber."[47] A year after his son's suicide, Adams was so fulfilled by his classical reading that he resolved to continue until the end of his days. "The practice which I have now adopted of allowing one hour every day to classical reading has been to me a source of so much enjoyment that I hope to persevere in it as long as life and health will permit," he wrote in May 1830. "One year will just carry me completely through Cicero."[48]

As he revisited Cicero, Adams was drawn, above all, to *Tusculan Disputations*. "It is, says Cicero," in the "1st Tusculan," "a tacit judgment of Nature herself, and the greatest argument in favour of the immortality of Souls, that all men take a deep interest in that which will happen after death," Adams wrote in August. Like Cicero, Adams was a defeated statesman, now retired to his farm to grieve the death of his child, and Adams reflected on the fact that his political and agricultural labors, too, might bear fruit only in future generations. "My leisure is now imposed upon me by the will of higher powers, to which I cheerfully submit, and I plant trees for the benefit of the next age, and of which my own eyes will never behold a berry," Adams wrote. He then translated a Latin phrase from *Tusculan Disputations* that he would continue to invoke for the rest of his life. "*Sero arbores quae alteri seculo prosint,*" Adams wrote. "He plants trees . . . for the benefit of another century."[49] Adams was so taken by Cicero's Latin phrase that in June 1833, when President Jackson was in Boston to inspect the troops, he proclaimed that *Alteri Seculo,* or "another century," would be his motto.[50] Adams designed a seal, with *Alteri Seculo* adorning an acorn and two oak leaves, and began using it to seal letters and to ornament his watch fob.[51] (Today "Alteri Seculo" is the motto of Adams House, an undergraduate dorm at Harvard, along with Adams's acorn and oak leaf seal.) "No period of life has ever yielded me so much quiet contentment," Adams wrote, contrasting his own "solitary tranquility" with the guns firing for Jackson. Although some of his "horticultural experiments" were beginning to "promise fruit," he was conscious that they hadn't yet borne any. "*Alteri Seculo* is the motto of all my plantations," Adams wrote, "but I am yet sensible and conscious that this life of pleasure is not a life of profit."[52]

That changed as Adams began to devote himself wholeheartedly to the cause of abolishing slavery. The publication of Thomas Jefferson's memoirs, which he read in 1830, prompted a series of reflections on Jefferson's moral hypocrisy. Lacking a belief in the afterlife, Adams speculated, all of Jefferson's "ideas of obligation or retribution were bounded by the present life," resulting in "insincerity and duplicity which were his besetting sins through life." (In fact, Jefferson's letters to Abigail and John Adams make clear that he did believe in an afterlife.) John Quincy noted that Jefferson had ended his memoirs before he became president and had said nothing about his correspondence with his longtime friend Colonel John Walker, after he'd tried to seduce Walker's wife, Elizabeth Moore Walker. In order to avoid a duel, President Jefferson had been forced to apologize in writing, in correspondence certified as authentic by Chief Justice John Marshall. In Adams's cool-eyed evaluation of his "double-dealing character," Jefferson "combined a rare mixture of infidel philosophy and Epicurean Morals—Of burning Ambition, and of Stoical self-controul—of deep duplicity and of generous sensibility." This double-dealing led Jefferson to treat his rivals—including Washington, Adams's father, and John Quincy Adams himself—with "perfidy, worthy of Tiberius Caesar, or Louis the 11th of France."[53]

Adams was especially struck by the rough draft of the Declaration of Independence, which Jefferson reproduced in his memoirs, and which contained the passage denouncing slavery that Congress struck out. "There is a very remarkable passage in page 39 and 40 of the Memoir, shewing that although Jefferson was not inclined in his last days to avow his perseverance in his opinions upon Negro-Slavery, he was willing to let them loose after his death—the motive for which appears to be to secure to himself posthumous fame as a prophet."[54] In Adams's view, Jefferson was a hypocrite for acknowledging that slavery was inconsistent with the natural law principles of the Declaration but refusing to lift a finger against slavery during his lifetime.

Adams, by contrast, resolved to fight slavery now. In November 1830 he became the first and only former president elected to Congress. A year later, he presented an antislavery petition from the citizens

of Pennsylvania calling for the abolition of slavery in the District of
Columbia—the first of a series of antislavery petitions he would introduce in Congress. In 1836, however, the House passed the "gag rule,"
providing that all petitions and resolutions relating to slavery should be
automatically tabled and not acted on. When a South Carolina representative proposed the gag rule, Adams rose to denounce it as a violation of the Constitution, and when he was prevented from speaking, he
exclaimed, "Am I gagged, am I gagged?"[55] Nevertheless, he persisted, and
in 1837, when Adams asked the Speaker of the House to consider a petition from the enslaved, Southern Congressmen demanded his censure.

In July of that year, Adams delivered a Fourth of July oration at
Newburyport, Massachusetts, arguing, "The inconsistency of the institution of domestic slavery with the principles of the Declaration of
Independence, was seen and lamented by all the southern patriots of
the Revolution," including, to his "dying day," Jefferson himself. Adams
quoted Jefferson's *Memoirs* for the prediction that the slaves would soon
have to be emancipated: "Nothing is more certainly written . . . in the
book of fate, than that these people are to be free."[56] And Adams added
his own belief that slavery and war were a violation of the natural right
to pursue happiness.

Based on his own close reading of the Bible, which he had studied
every morning for years, Adams predicted that the end of slavery and
war would fulfill a prophesy of Isaiah, who declared that "the Lord hath
anointed me . . . to proclaim liberty to the captives." Adams said that Isaiah's prophecy, in turn, was confirmed by the birth of Jesus, which the angels in the Gospel of Luke heralded by declaring: "Fear not: for, behold,
I bring you good tidings of great joy, which shall be *to all people*." Adams
italicized "*to all people*" to emphasize that the divine promise of liberty
applied to all people, Black and white alike.[57] In Adams's view, "the Declaration of Independence first organized the social compact on the foundation of the Redeemer's mission upon earth" and "laid the corner stone
of human government upon the first precepts of Christianity."[58]

In 1839 Adams introduced a constitutional amendment to end

slavery. And the following year, he agreed to defend before the Supreme Court forty enslaved Africans who had been captured on board the *Amistad*, a Spanish ship seized by the United States. The Africans had been charged with murder and piracy for killing the captain and seizing the ship, and the Spanish government was demanding their return. Adams initially tried to resist the invitation to represent the Africans, on the grounds that he hadn't argued before the court in thirty years. But being persuaded that it was "a case of life and death," he wrote, "I yielded." When he accepted the assignment, he steadied himself by praying for Ciceronian self-control to ensure the persuasiveness of his argument. "I implore the mercy of Almighty God, so to controul my temper, to enlighten my Soul and to give me utterance that I may prove myself in every respect equal to the task."[59]

In November 1840 Adams visited the enslaved Africans, who were imprisoned in New London, Connecticut, and described their efforts to learn English by reading the Bible. In December he "denied the right of the Spanish Minister to claim them as property"[60] and searched for legal authorities to "defeat and expose the abominable conspiracy" of President Martin Van Buren and the courts that had ruled against the captives. "How shall the facts be brought out? How shall it be possible to comment upon them with becoming temper—with calmness—with moderation—with firmness," he wrote. "Of all the dangers before me, that of losing my self possession is the most formidable."[61]

On January 16, 1841, Adams arrived at the old Senate chamber, where the Supreme Court sat, to argue the case. Because Justice Joseph Story was absent, however, Chief Justice Roger Brooke Taney postponed the argument for a month. Adams returned to the House, where he spent the next few weeks presenting petitions on behalf of Native Americans arguing against the enforcement of a fraudulent treaty. He also delivered a speech denouncing the Southern secessionist Henry Wise, who had won his congressional seat after killing his opponent in a duel. After his speech, he had a sleepless night, worrying that he had lost his self-composure in indicting Southern principles before the world. Adams was unsure what support he would receive for his antislavery crusade, inside or outside of Congress. Seven decades earlier, his father had chosen principle over popularity by successfully defending the Redcoats responsible for the Boston Massacre. Now John Quincy Adams was doing the same, taking on slavery at the risk of finding himself held in contempt, especially by other elites.

To prepare for his argument, Adams read Jefferson's *Notes on the State of Virginia* and Madison's speech at the Virginia ratifying convention. And on Wednesday, February 24, he spoke for four and a half hours before the Supreme Court, returning on March 1 to conclude with another four-hour appearance. "The structure of my argument," Adams wrote, "is perfectly simple and comprehensive" based on "the steady and undeviating pursuit of one fundimental principle, the ministration of *Justice*."[62] After his two days of argument, Adams walked across the Capitol to the House, where he resumed his congressional duties and waited for the court's decision. The following day, William Henry Harrison was inaugurated as the ninth president of the United States.

On March 9 Adams "waited on tenterhooks" for the court's decision and listened to Justice Story rule in favor of the African captives. Story "declares them to be free and directs the Circuit Court to order them to be discharged from the custody of the Marshal," Adams noted dispassionately.[63] He took steps to ensure that the captives would be freed within a few days. On March 29 Adams was struck by the "magnitude, the danger, the insurmountable burden of labour to be encountered in the undertaking to touch upon the Slave-trade," which he felt duty bound to oppose. As he prepared to turn seventy-four, "with a shaking hand, a darkening eye, a drowsy brain," Adams wondered what he could do "for the cause of God and Man? For the progress of human emancipation? For the suppression of the African Slave-trade?—Yet my conscience presses me on—let me but die upon the breach."[64]

John Quincy Adams's prayers were answered, and his final years were devoted to the fight against slavery. Around this time, in the early 1840s, he began calling himself an abolitionist. He was converted to the radical cause by South Carolina senator John C. Calhoun's attempts to annex Texas as a way of extending slavery. "I must fight the Devil with his own fire," Adams declared, earning him the respect of Frederick Douglass.[65] The World Antislavery Convention of 1843 in London adopted a resolution honoring "the moral heroism with which [Adams] has thrown himself into the breach."[66] And his opponent Henry Wise called him "the acutest, the astutest, the archest enemy of Southern slavery that ever existed."[67] Adams presented thousands of antislavery petitions to Congress, insisting that they rested on the Declaration of Independence. Finally, on December 3, 1844, Adams introduced a resolution to repeal the gag rule, and the House adopted it. That night, Adams wrote in his diary, "blessed ever blessed be the name of God!"[68]

On December 20, 1848, Adams voted against the ongoing war in Mexico with a defiant "No!" Rising to address the House, he suffered a stroke and collapsed at his desk. A colleague caught him, and he was carried to a sofa. "This is the end of earth," he murmured before he died on February 23, 1849. And then some heard him whisper, "I am content," while others heard, "I am composed."[69]

Either sentiment would have been a fitting epitaph, carefully chosen by a man who had spent his life preparing, like Cicero, for a calm and virtuous death. "I am content" encapsulated Cicero's ideal of the happy man as the one "at rest in his mind" who has achieved tranquility "through moderation and constancy," neither "dejected with fear" nor "inflamed with desire." Still, Adams was not content at any point in his long life, and as death approached, he continued to upbraid himself for not accomplishing more. If God had given him the talents of Cicero or Shakespeare, he wrote, he might "have banished War and Slavery from the face of the earth forever." (He always set for himself a high bar!) Instead, he lacked "the irresistible power of Genius, and the irrepressible energy of will" and had to "implore his forgiveness for all the errors and delinquencies of my life."[70] In addition, "I am content" were the penultimate words of Shylock in Shakespeare's *The Merchant of Venice*, making them an unlikely choice for Adams, who read Shakespeare closely and sometimes considered his language overwrought.[71]

It seems more likely that Adams had murmured, "I am composed," which embodied Cicero's ideal of happiness as something to be pursued by the man "in calm possession of himself." As Adams noted in his Boylston lectures, Cicero viewed "perfect and unalterable self command" as the touchstone of happiness. This was the self-command that Adams had achieved at the end of his virtuous and productive life, as he composed himself for happiness in the hereafter.

Adams's untiring crusade to end slavery inspired the next generation. In his most popular lecture, "Self-Made Men," Frederick Douglass singled out one American president for special praise: John Quincy Adams. Despite his privileged background, Douglass said, Adams was a model of the self-made man because of his industry, the virtue he worked hardest to cultivate. "'Toil and Trust!' was the motto of John Quincy Adams, and his Presidency of the Republic proved its wisdom as well as its truth," Douglass declared. "Great in his opportunities, great in his mental endowments and great in his relationships, he was still greater in persevering and indefatigable industry."[72] It would fall to Douglass and Abraham Lincoln to carry on the quest to make the ideals of the Declaration of Independence a reality.

Notes on Seneca's "On Anger"

America this morning burns with rage
Red sun at dawn ablaze at great divide
As victims protest wrong with hot rampage
Can righteous anger now be justified?

Anger to punish suffering desires
Injustice or felt injury's recompense
But in its furious haste and vengeful fires
It comes at wrathful punisher's expense

Injustice anywhere roils all our fate
We're bound in mutuality of light
Condemn all wrong with force but not with hate
Self-mastered calm will gird us for the fight

From Socrates to Dr. King, the way
Past hate is pure compassion, *agape*

Eleven

JUSTICE

Frederick Douglass and Abraham Lincoln's
Self-Reliance

I n his *Narrative of the Life of Frederick Douglass, an American Slave,*
Frederick Douglass describes the moment his master, Hugh Auld,
ordered his wife, Sophia, to stop teaching Douglass how to read. "If
you teach" a slave "how to read, there would be no keeping him," Hugh
exclaimed. Learning to read "would forever unfit him to be a slave" because he would become "unmanageable, and of no value to his master," as
well as "discontented and unhappy." The words "sank deep in my heart,"
Douglass recalled, and "[f]rom that moment, I understood the pathway
from slavery to freedom." In a flash of "revelation," Douglass realized
that slavery's evil consisted of attempts to shackle people's minds as well
as their bodies. Douglass was filled with "anguish" at the thought that he
might be a "slave for life." Not content to live only in the past and present, he longed to have a future. Auld's "argument ... against my learning
to read, only served to inspire me with a desire and determination to

THE PURSUIT OF HAPPINESS

learn," Douglass wrote, and he was "[s]eized with a determination to learn to read, at any cost." He continued lessons with his Irish playmates on the streets of Baltimore, paying his tuition fee to the other boys with bread. About the age of thirteen, around 1831, he saved up enough to buy, for fifty cents, a "very popular school book, viz: the *Columbian Orator*." The book changed his life. "Every opportunity I got, I used to read this book."[1]

The Columbian Orator was indeed "very popular." Published in twenty-three editions between 1797 and 1860, it sold about two hundred thousand copies and, along with the Bible, was among the only books in many nineteenth-century homesteads.[2] In addition to teaching principles of eloquence and oratory, *The Columbian Orator* offered nineteenth-century schoolchildren what Douglass called a "rich treasure" of primary texts, to be read aloud.[3] It included excerpts from the speeches and writings of many of the philosophers that inspired Franklin and Jefferson in their writings about the pursuit of happiness, including Cicero, Socrates, Milton, and *Cato's Letters*. It also included a selection from Benjamin Franklin's poetry, as well as a eulogy in Paris praising Franklin for his time management and industry and calling *Poor Richard's Almanack* a "catechism of happiness for all mankind."[4]

The Columbian Orator was compiled in Boston by Caleb Bingham, a Massachusetts school reformer with antislavery sympathies. Its antislavery message was so threatening to the slavocracy that, in 1850, the leading Southern newspaper included it on a blacklist of abolitionist books and effectively banned it.[5] Douglass was especially struck by "a short dialogue between a master and his slave" in which the "slave made a spirited defense of himself, and thereafter the whole argument, for and against slavery, was brought out."[6] Slavery is a form of "violence and injustice," the slave argued, which keeps men "in forced subjection, deprived of all exercise of their free will."[7] In other words, it didn't allow the enslaved to exercise their reason. In the dialogue, the slave makes arguments for his own emancipation, which convinces the slaveholder to free him. The argument "powerfully affected me," Douglass recalled, "and I could not help feeling that the day might come, when the well-directed answers made by the slave to the master, in this instance, would find their counterpart in myself."[8] Douglass was inspired by the dialogue to convince his country to end slavery, becoming the greatest abolitionist voice in American history.

The dialogue also helped Douglass cast aside any doubts that the Almighty, in some way, had willed his enslavement. *The Columbian Orator* "poured floods of light on the nature and character of slavery" and convinced Douglass that it was rooted in "the pride, the power and the avarice of man." Other primary texts in the book, such as Daniel O'Connell's speech on Catholic religious freedom in Ireland, fired Douglass's imagination with denunciations of oppression and vindications of the rights of man. As Douglass recalled, "the *Columbian Orator*, with its eloquent orations and spicy dialogues, denouncing oppression and slavery—telling of what had been dared, done and suffered by men, to obtain the inestimable boon of liberty" whirled through his mind and showed him that slavery violated "God's eternal justice."[9]

Douglass was not the only American of his generation whose life was changed by *The Columbian Orator*. Another was Abraham Lincoln. Their youthful encounters with classic texts convinced both Lincoln and Douglass that slavery was a violation of the natural right to pursue happiness. Like Douglass, Lincoln took from the book the idea that the right to pursue happiness means that all human beings should have an equal opportunity to improve their minds and educate themselves. And both Lincoln and Douglass viewed themselves as "self-made men," which they defined as those who have overcome obstacles and devoted their lives to building their character.

Lincoln first encountered *The Orator* at the age of twenty-two, in the winter of 1831–32, a year after Douglass bought the book on the streets of Baltimore.[10] With little formal schooling, Lincoln was also inspired by other popular "readers"—nineteenth-century anthologies of classical and Enlightenment rhetoric—including *Murray's English Reader*. "Mr. Lincoln told me in later years that *Murray's English Reader* was the best school-book ever put into the hands of an American youth," his law partner, William Herndon, recalled.[11] Like *The Columbian Orator* and *Poor Richard's Almanack, Murray's English Reader* sampled from the highlights of classical and Enlightenment moral philosophy, presenting them in easily digestible maxims that provide a guide for how to develop good character. All the selections were chosen, according to the preface, to inculcate "principles of piety and virtue." "Diligence, industry, and proper improvement of time are material duties of the young," chapter 1 begins. "In order to acquire a capacity for happiness, it must be our first study to rectify inward disorders." Many of the selections emphasize the importance of using reason to modulate our passions. "No person who has once yielded up the government of his mind, and given loose rein to his desires and passions, can tell how far they may carry him."[12] If Franklin, Washington, Madison, and Hamilton learned the importance of self-mastery and self-control from Cicero and Addison's *Spectator*, Lincoln and Douglass learned the same lessons from the Cicero and Addison excerpts in Bingham's and Murray's readers.

Douglass distilled the lessons of the ancient wisdom in his "Self-Made Men" speech, which he delivered for more than three decades after his historic escape from slavery in 1838. Written before the Civil War, the speech became Douglass's most frequently requested address during the Reconstruction era, as Douglass himself became its American prototype. Self-made men, Douglass said, were "men of work," and "honest labor faithfully, steadily and persistently pursued, is the best, if not the only, explanation of their success." Moreover, Douglass emphasized, the capacity for hard work was in everyone's grasp. "[A]llowing only ordinary ability and opportunity, we may explain success mainly by one word and that word is *Work! Work!! Work!!! Work!!!!*" Douglass exhorted.[13]

Channeling Benjamin Franklin, Douglass insisted that cultivating virtuous habits such as order and self-discipline was the best way to become healthy, wealthy, and wise. "Order, the first law of heaven, is itself a power," Douglass said. And he insisted, like Franklin, that virtuous habits were key to the pursuit of happiness. "We succeed, not alone by the laborious exertion of our faculties, be they small or great, but by the regular, thoughtful and systematic exercise of them." In Douglass's view, all people, no matter what their background, had the potential to avail themselves of this "marvellous power" of hard work, as long as they focused on expanding their minds through education. "The health and strength of the soul is of far more importance than is that of the body," Douglass declared. "[T]here can be no independence without a large share of self-dependence, and this virtue cannot be bestowed. It must be developed from within."[14]

In his "Self-Made Men" speech, Douglass distilled the principles that he first encountered in *The Columbian Orator* to make the case that the purpose of liberty is to allow all human beings to educate themselves. Quoting Abigail Adams's favorite poet, Alexander Pope ("the proper study of mankind is man"), Douglass says his subject is human nature and its potential for development—"what man, as a whole, is; what he has been; what he aspires to be, and what, by a wise and vigorous cultivation of his faculties, he may yet become." He embraces the central tenet of faculty psychology that the mind is its own place, responsible for its own happiness through virtuous self-control: "Nothing can bring to man so much of happiness or so much of misery as man himself," Douglass writes.[15]

Douglass defined "self-made men" as those who have overcome obstacles to "build up worthy character," those who are "indebted to themselves for themselves." Rejecting the traditional view of the established Church—that "liberty and slavery, happiness and misery, were all bestowed or inflicted upon individual men by a divine hand and for all-wise purposes"—Douglass insisted that we are responsible for our own happiness and success. "Faith, in the absence of work, seems to be worth little, if anything," he writes, in a crisp encapsulation of Franklin's creed. He also rebuked the "growing tendency" to seek happiness through "sport and pleasure." Douglass says that "real pleasure" can only be found in "useful work"—"in the house well built, in the farm well tilled, in the books well kept, in the page well written, in the thought well expressed, in all the improved conditions of life" all around us.[16]

• • •

In his speech, Douglass praised "the king of American self-made men": Abraham Lincoln.[17] And Lincoln himself embraced the label. After being born in poverty in a log cabin, Lincoln became an Illinois state legislator and US congressman. He lost the US Senate election in 1858 to the Democratic incumbent, Stephen Douglas, but went on to become the Republican nominee for president in 1860. That year, at the Republican state convention in Decatur, Illinois, a Democrat approached Lincoln. "They say you're a self-made man," he declared. "Well, yes," Lincoln is said to have replied, "what there is of me is self-made."[18]

The phrase "self-made man" had been coined by Lincoln's political hero, Henry Clay, in a speech to Congress in 1842. Defending the "American system," a Whig policy that combined federal tariffs to promote local industry with federal support for roads, canals, and a national bank, Clay contrasted the self-made entrepreneur with the aristocratic factory owner or slave owner, supported by hundreds of free or enslaved workers. "In Kentucky, almost every manufactory known to me is in the hands of enterprising, self-made men who have acquired whatever wealth they possess by patient and diligent labor," Clay declared.[19] In his 1852 eulogy on Clay's death, Lincoln praised him as a model of the self-made man, who proved that, in America, success depends not on external circumstances but on our own powers of lifelong learning. Clay's "lack of a more perfect early education," Lincoln said, "however it may be regretted generally, teaches that, in this country, one can scarcely be so poor, but that, if he *will*, he *can* acquire sufficient education to get through the world respectably." Lincoln praised Clay as moderate and deliberate; a statesman who used reason to calm sectional passions. "Whatever he did, he did for the whole country," Lincoln said. "In the construction of his measures, he ever carefully surveyed every part of the field and duly weighed every conflicting interest."[20]

Lincoln had also emphasized the importance of using reason to vanquish passion in his first major political speech, "The Perpetuation of Our Political Institutions," delivered for the Young Men's Lyceum of Springfield, Illinois, in January 1838. Running for reelection to the Springfield Legislature, Lincoln was alarmed by examples of mob violence throughout America. He singled out the lynching of "[a] mulatto man by the name of McIntosh" in Saint Louis and denounced mobs that "throw printing presses into rivers [and] shoot editors." (Here Lincoln was alluding to, without naming, Elijah Lovejoy, the abolitionist editor who had been shot by a mob in Alton, Illinois, the previous November after the warehouse containing his printing press was burned.) Lincoln said that the spread of "mob law" and the "mobocratic spirit" were destroying what the Founders considered the bulwark of self-government: namely, the "*attachment* of the People," or their belief in the government's legitimacy.

Using the word *mob* eight times, Lincoln invoked the specter of his Democratic political opponents Andrew Jackson (known as "King Mob") and Stephen Douglas. If the Founders had worried about Shays's Rebellion, where farmers mobbed the bankruptcy courts in western Massachusetts, Lincoln, too, worried about the "increasing disregard for law which pervades the country; the growing disposition to substitute the wild and furious passions, in lieu of the sober judgment of Courts." Also like the Founders, he worried about the rise of demagogues, like "an Alexander, a Caesar, or a Napoléon" (or a Jackson), "men of ambition and talents" who would "naturally seek the gratification of their ruling passion" by "pulling down" the Union, "whether at the expense of emancipating slaves or enslaving freemen." What was at stake, Lincoln said, was nothing less than "*the capability of a people to govern themselves.*" And the solution was to make "reverence" for the Declaration of Independence, the Constitution, and the rule of law a "*political religion.*"[21]

Like Cicero and Madison, Lincoln insightfully drew the connection between psychological self-government and political self-government. During the Revolution, passions such as "the jealousy, envy, and avarice incident to our nature" were "smothered and rendered inactive," while passions like "*hate*, and the powerful motive of *revenge*, instead of being turned against each other, were directed exclusively against the British nation." Now that personal memories of the Revolution had faded away, the self-sacrificing spirit that had sustained the "temple of liberty" was fading as well. Lincoln gathered his readings into a classical peroration. "Passion has helped us; but can do so no more," he concluded. "It will in future be our enemy. Reason—cold, calculating, unimpassioned reason—must furnish all the materials for our future support and defence."[22]

In addition to denouncing unchecked passions deployed for and against abolitionism, Lincoln was just as wary of zealotry on behalf of the cause of temperance itself. Lincoln himself drank little wine or liquor throughout his life. "I am entitled to little credit for not drinking," he told his law partner, William Herndon, "because I hate the stuff; it is unpleasant and always leaves me flabby and undone."[23] His temperance was part of his own lifelong quest for self-mastery, which he viewed as central to the pursuit of happiness. In 1842, in an address to the Springfield Temperance Society honoring Washington's 110th birthday, Lincoln made clear that, in his view, the Declaration of Independence proclaimed the right of all human beings to "govern themselves," in the sense of mastering their appetites and emotions.

"Of our political revolution of '76, we are all justly proud," Lincoln declared. "In it the world has found a solution of the long-mooted problem as to the capability of man to govern himself." For this reason, Lincoln looked forward to the day when the "Reign of Reason" would lead to the end of all forces that enslaved the mind, including both alcoholism and slavery. He anticipated the "Happy day" when "all appetites [would be] controlled, all poisons subdued, all matter subjected." Then, at last, there would be "neither a slave nor a drunkard on the earth," and the world would hail a Reign of Reason governed by "all-conquering *mind*," "the monarch of the world." Lincoln concluded with a melodramatic flourish. "Glorious consummation! Hail fall of Fury! Reign of Reason, all hail!"[24]

At the same time, Lincoln chastised the temperance zealots who addressed their fellow citizens "in the thundering tones of anathema and denunciation" rather than the cool voice of reason sweetened by "kind, unassuming persuasion." Lincoln summed up his moderate approach to politics and life. "It is an old and a true maxim that 'a drop of honey catches more flies than a gallon of gall,'" he said. "So with men. If you would win a man to your cause, *first* convince him that you are his sincere friend."[25]

From the beginning of his career, Lincoln insisted that slavery was immoral because it violated the natural rights of equal liberty and self-government articulated in the Declaration of Independence. In 1854, arguing in Peoria against the repeal of the Missouri Compromise, Lincoln quoted the Declaration at length, ending with the sentence that "to secure these rights governments are instituted among men, *deriving their just powers from the consent of the governed.*" The preamble to the Declaration showed, Lincoln said, "that, according to our ancient faith, the just powers of governments are derived from the consent of the governed," while "the relation of master and slave" was a "total violation of this principle." The only way to ensure "self-government" for all was to allow "*all* the governed an equal voice in the government." The "leading principle" of "American republicanism," Lincoln said, was that "no man is good enough to govern another man, *without that other's consent.*"[26] Like the texts in *The Columbian Orator*, Lincoln insisted slavery was immoral because it violated people's right and responsibility to govern themselves.

Two years later, in his speech to the first Illinois Republican Convention, Lincoln offered an even more extensive argument for why the principles of the Declaration of Independence forbade slavery. "Thomas Jefferson, a slaveholder, mindful of the moral element in slavery, solemnly declared that he trembled for his country when he remembered that God is just," Lincoln said. While "the corner-stone of the government, so to speak, was the declaration that '*all* men are created equal,' and all entitled to 'life, liberty, and the pursuit of happiness,'" Lincoln continued, the modern Democratic Party had inserted "the word *white* before *men*, making it read 'all white men are created equal.'" "Slavery is a violation of the eternal right," Lincoln told the Republican convention, and "*as sure as God reigns and school children read, that black foul lie can never be consecrated into God's hallowed truth.*"[27]

Lincoln criticized the Democratic Party for having abandoned the principles of Jefferson, insisting that he and the Republicans were Jefferson's heirs. "All honor to Jefferson," he declared in 1859, "the man who . . . had the coolness, forecast, and capacity to introduce into a mere revolutionary document an abstract truth, applicable to all men and all times."[28] Standing in front of Independence Hall in Philadelphia on Washington's birthday in February 1861, a month before assuming the presidency, he declared, "I have never had a feeling politically that did not spring from the sentiments embodied in the Declaration of Independence," which Lincoln defined as the "promise that in due time the weights should be lifted from the shoulders of all men." After raising a flag over Independence Hall, Lincoln exclaimed, in an eerie moment of prophecy, "I would rather be assassinated on this spot than surrender" the Declaration's principles.[29]

Lincoln always maintained that slavery violated the natural rights to self-government, equal liberty, and the pursuit of happiness. And after the *Dred Scott* decision in 1857, which held that the Founders believed that Black people "had no rights which the white man was bound to respect," Lincoln tore into Chief Justice Taney for his misreading of constitutional history.[30] According to Lincoln, the Founders intended the Declaration to set out an ideal—that "all men are created equal"—against which the Constitution should be judged. The Founders, he said, "meant to set up a standard maxim for free society . . . constantly spreading and deepening its influence, and augmenting the happiness and value of life to all people of all colors everywhere." Like Christ's injunction to "be perfect," Lincoln said, the Declaration's statement that "all men are created equal" was an ideal to be "constantly labored for" and approximated, "even though never perfectly attained."[31]

In 1852, around the same time that Lincoln was denouncing slavery in Peoria as a violation of the principles of the Declaration and the Constitution, Douglass delivered his "What to the Slave is the Fourth of July?" speech in Rochester, New York. Douglass called the Declaration of Independence "the RING-BOLT to the chain of your nation's destiny" and lamented that "the great principles of political freedom and of natural justice, embodied in that Declaration of Independence" were not extended to Black people. "The existence of slavery in this country brands your republicanism as a sham, your humanity as a base pretence, and your Christianity as a lie," Douglass declared. "It fetters your progress; it is the enemy of improvement, the deadly foe of education; it fosters pride; it breeds insolence; it promotes vice; it shelters crime; it is a curse to the earth that supports it."[32] Douglass emphasized again that slavery's evil consisted in the fact that it was the "enemy of improvement" and the "deadly foe of education," one that fostered vices such as "pride" and "insolence," rather than virtues like self-reliance and self-mastery.

At the same time, Douglass denied that the Constitution or its framers were proslavery. "I differ from those who charge this baseness on the framers of the Constitution of the United States. *It is a slander upon their memory*—at least, so I believe." Douglass agreed initially with the abolitionist William Lloyd Garrison, who had called the Constitution a "covenant with death" and an "agreement with Hell." But after reading the antislavery tracts of writers including Lysander Spooner, William Goodell, and Gerrit Smith, Douglass said he had changed his mind. "These gentlemen have, as I think, fully and clearly vindicated the Constitution from any design to support slavery for an hour," Douglass declared. "[I]nterpreted as it *ought* to be interpreted, the Constitution is a GLORIOUS LIBERTY DOCUMENT" in which "neither *slavery, slaveholding,* nor *slave* can anywhere be found."[33]

In 1840 James Madison's notes at the Constitutional Convention were published for the first time. They revealed that Madison had said explicitly that he "thought it wrong to admit in the Constitution the idea that there could be property in men," leaving room for the eventual restriction and elimination of slavery.[34] Reading Madison's notes changed Douglass's conception of himself as a man and a citizen. In a speech in Glasgow in 1860, Douglass reviewed the allegedly proslavery clauses of the Constitution and, citing Madison's notes, said, "I deny utterly that these provisions of the Constitution guarantee, or were intended to guarantee, in any shape or form, the right of property in man in the United States."[35] Lincoln, too, relied on Madison's notes to deny that the framers of the Constitution were proslavery. In an 1860 speech at the new Cooper Union for the Advancement of Science and Art, in New York City, Lincoln argued that "contemporaneous history proved that this mode of alluding to slaves" as persons, rather than property, "was employed on purpose to exclude from the Constitution the idea that there could be property in man."[36] The speech was widely credited for his election to the White House in November.

Like George Washington, Lincoln rarely displayed his temper in public. For both men, self-control was the most effective way of achieving their ultimate goal of preserving the Union. Lincoln practiced the habits of daily self-mastery throughout the Civil War, maintaining a cheerful appearance, and telling jokes despite the black periods of melancholy—he called it the "hypo"—that had seized him since his youth. Although the refusal of Union generals such as George McClellan to prosecute the war vigorously infuriated him, he restrained himself from issuing direct orders or rebukes because he knew they would undermine morale. During the bloody Battle of Antietam, a year and a half into the war, Lincoln warned McClellan of "overcautiousness." But the general continued to test Lincoln's patience by delaying for nineteen days before beginning to cross the Potomac. As McClellan dithered, the Confederate general, Jeb Stuart, led an embarrassing raid behind Union lines right before Election Day. Lincoln "well-nigh lost his temper over it," his aide John Nicolay reported, but the president restrained himself once again. Only when McClellan told him that he couldn't pursue Robert E. Lee, the commander of the Confederate army, after Antietam because his horses were "absolutely broken down from fatigue" did Lincoln finally snap. "Will you pardon me for asking," he replied, "what the horses of your army have done since the battle of Antietam that fatigue anything?"[37]

Lincoln was similarly restrained in dealing with the jockeying members of his cabinet, tolerating their sometimes direct challenges to his authority, always keeping in mind his long-term goal of restoring the Union. In 1862, as the Senate investigated Lincoln for failing to consult his cabinet, Lincoln bought time by telling amusing stories, forcing his warring secretary of state, William Seward, and his Treasury secretary, Salmon P. Chase, to deny publicly the discord they had been complaining about privately. After receiving letters of resignation from both men, he pocketed the letters and declined to accept them. But to emphasize the value of balancing opposing opinions, he compared himself to a farmer riding to market with his goods balanced across the horse, telling Senator Ira Harris of New York, "I can ride on now. I've got a pumpkin in each end of my bag!"[38]

Lincoln's moderation frustrated abolitionists, including Frederick Douglass. When Douglass met Lincoln for the first time, on August 10, 1863, he was unpersuaded by several pillars of Lincoln's policy. He had blasted Lincoln for stressing in his first inaugural that he had no "inclination" to interfere with slavery in the states where it existed, even though this was the official position of the Republican Party.[39] Douglass also ridiculed Lincoln's suggestion that Black people were the cause of the war. "No, Mr. President, it is not the innocent horse that makes the horse thief . . . but the cruel and brutal cupidity of those who wish to possess horses, or money and negroes by means of theft, robbery, and rebellion." He called Lincoln "a genuine representative of American prejudice" who lacked principles of "justice and humanity."[40]

Accompanied by Senator Samuel Pomeroy, an abolitionist from Kansas, Douglass was ushered into the executive office after giving the doorkeeper his card. He found Lincoln "taking it easy," as Douglass recounted it, with his feet "in different parts of the room." When Douglass proceeded to tell Lincoln who he was, the president "promptly, but kindly, stopped me, saying: 'I know who you are, Mr. Douglass; Mr. Seward has told me all about you. Sit down. I am glad to see you.'" Lincoln immediately brought up a speech in which Douglass had criticized his policies for not arming and liberating Black people as "tardy, hesitating, and vacillating." The president admitted that he took his time to make decisions but denied that he had vacillated, insisting that once he took a position, he never looked back.

Douglass praised him for having refused to abandon his antislavery policy, as well as for finally issuing a retaliatory order promising to shoot Confederates who killed or enslaved Black soldiers. He then asked Lincoln to guarantee equal pay and equal opportunity for promotion to Black soldiers, who were being openly discriminated against in the Union army. Lincoln replied that unequal pay was a "necessary concession" to "popular prejudice," but that Black soldiers would eventually receive equal pay. After the meeting, Douglass praised Lincoln's eloquence and lack of prejudice: "I was never in any way reminded of my humble origin or of my unpopular color," he recalled.[41] And for the rest of his life, he told the story of the meeting as a testament to the fact that Lincoln had received him at the White House with perfect cordiality and on equal terms.

It was also a testament to Lincoln's capacity for growth; his ability to learn from argument and experience. As the historian Eric Foner notes, "Had he died in 1862, it would be quite easy to argue today that Lincoln would never have issued a proclamation of emancipation, enrolled black soldiers in the Union army, or advocated allowing some black men to vote."[42] But Lincoln did all this before he was martyred on April 15, 1865, only six days after the South surrendered. The previous month, Douglass returned to Washington to hear Lincoln's second inaugural address. Congress had just passed the Thirteenth Amendment abolishing slavery in January, and Douglass had tea with the new chief justice, Samuel Chase, the day before the festivities. He listened to Lincoln describe the war as inscrutable divine punishment for the sin of 250 years of slavery in America. "The Almighty has His own purposes," Lincoln emphasized, and "the judgments of the Lord, are true and righteous altogether." And Douglass listened as Lincoln ended his second inaugural, as he had his first, by urging his fellow Americans to put aside their passions and restore the Union. "With malice toward none; with charity for all," Lincoln declared, "with firmness in the right, as God gives us to see the right, let us strive on to finish the work we are in."[43]

Douglass returned to the White House, where he was briefly blocked at the door. After presenting his card, however, he was once again ushered in to see the president. "Here comes my friend," Lincoln said when he saw Douglass approach in the crowded reception room. "I am glad to see you. I saw you in the crowd to-day, listening to my inaugural address." Declaring that "there is no man in the country whose opinion I value more than yours," Lincoln asked Douglass how he liked the speech. "Mr. Lincoln," Douglass replied, "that was a sacred effort."[44] Forty-one days later, Lincoln was assassinated at Ford's Theatre.

As the Civil War was drawing to a close, Frederick Douglass argued that the right to vote was the "keystone to the arch of human liberty" and the only secure foundation for all other rights.[45] "I am for the 'immediate, unconditional and universal' enfranchisement of the black man, in every State of the Union," he declared in 1865. "Without this, his liberty is a mockery. . . . He is at the mercy of the mob and has no means of protecting himself."[46] Despite the ratification of the Fifteenth Amendment in 1870, which guaranteed Black men the right to vote, the mob came. Although Black political participation surged for a brief, shining moment in the early 1870s, Reconstruction gave way to Southern "Redemption," as the Ku Klux Klan and racist state officials used violence, lynching, intimidation, poll taxes, and literacy tests to thwart the promise of the new constitutional amendments.

Applying the classical lessons he had learned from *The Columbian Orator*, Douglass denounced mob violence as the triumph of passion over reason—just as Lincoln had done before the war. "In its thirst for blood and its rage for vengeance, the mob has blindly, boldly and defiantly supplanted sheriffs, constables and police," Douglass declared in an 1894 speech, "The Lessons of the Hour." A "court of law," and not a "passionate and violent mob" should decide questions of guilt or innocence. As the Supreme Court turned a blind eye to the subversion of Reconstruction, Douglass reviewed the grim backlash. "The Supreme Court has surrendered," he continued. "State sovereignty is restored. It has destroyed the [1875] Civil Rights Bill, and converted the Republican Party into a party of money rather than a party of morals, a party of things rather than a party of humanity and justice." [47]

Douglass then applied the classical principles of faculty psychology to the phenomenon of racism itself, arguing that prejudice of any kind represented the triumph of passion over reason. "*Few evils are* less accessible to the force of reason, or more tenacious of life and power, than a long-standing prejudice," he declared in a magazine article on "The Color Line," in 1881. Douglass argued that unreasoning hatred, or the desire to feel superior to others, was not uniquely based on race or color but was found throughout human societies that failed to be governed by reason. "[T]his prejudice really has nothing whatever to do with race or color," and "it has its motive and mainspring in some other source"—namely, the desire to "dominate," Douglass said. It was the same feeling "that the Brahmin feels toward the lower caste, the same as the Norman felt toward the Saxon, the same as that cherished by the Turk against Christians, the same as Christians have felt toward the Jews." In Douglass's view, "The trouble is that most men, and especially mean men, want to have something under them." He concluded that only reason—or "enlightenment"—could conquer prejudice based on "ignorance, superstition, bigotry and vice." [48]

The solution to racial prejudice, in Douglass's view, was simply to allow African Americans to vote, as guaranteed by the Fifteenth Amendment. "They are not required to do much," he said of white people. "They are only required to undo the evil they have done, in order to solve this problem. In old times, when it was asked, 'How can we abolish slavery?' the answer was 'Quit stealing.' The same is the solution of the Race problem to-day. The whole thing can be done simply by no longer violating the amendment of the Constitution of the United States, and no longer evading the claims of justice." [49]

In his speeches after the war, Douglass demanded nothing more and nothing less than the freedom for African Americans to pursue happiness. As early as 1865, in the speech "What the Black Man

Wants," Douglass said in response to the rhetorical question "'What shall we do with the negro?' I have had but one answer from the beginning. Do nothing with us!" All he asked, Douglass said, was "give him a chance to stand on his own legs! Let him alone!"[50] In his "Self-Made Men" speech, Douglass used the same language. "I have been asked, 'How will this theory affect the negro?' and 'What shall be done in his case?' My general answer is 'Give the negro fair play and let him alone. If he lives, well. If he dies, equally well. If he cannot stand up, let him fall down.'"[51] For Douglass, the pursuit of happiness required equal opportunity for industrious work, so that all individuals could achieve their potential.

But Douglass believed the federal government had some role to play when it came to voting rights and education. Even if "the American people put a school house in every valley of the South and a church on every hill side and supply the one with teachers and the other with preachers, for a hundred years to come," he declared, "they would not then have given fair play to the negro."[52] He called for federal enforcement of voting rights laws, quoting "the great O'Connell," the Irish patriot he had first encountered in *The Columbian Orator*, who said that "the history of Ireland might be traced like a wounded man through a crowd by the blood." In Douglass's view, the same might be said of Black voters in the South. "They have marched to the ballot-box in face of gleaming weapons, wounds and death," he said in Louisville in 1883, the same year the Supreme Court struck down the Civil Rights Act of 1875. "They have been abandoned by the government and left to the laws of nature. So far as they are concerned, there is no Government or Constitution of the United States."[53]

In the end, Douglass believed that the solution to the violent passion of prejudice was the cool reason of education. In 1883 he called for a federal mandatory school attendance law and federal aid to schools in the states. "[W]e hold it to be the imperative duty of Congress . . . to enter vigorously upon the work of universal education," Douglass asserted. "The National Government, with its immense resources, can carry the benefits of a sound common-school education to the door of every poor man from Maine to Texas."[54] And months before his death in 1895, Douglass dedicated the Manassas Industrial School for Colored Youth, a private academy in Virginia founded by the formerly enslaved educator Jennie Dean to provide vocational training for Black youth in a Christian setting.

In the dedication ceremony, Douglass explicitly connected equal opportunity for education with the pursuit of happiness. "To deny education to any people is one of the greatest crimes against human nature," he maintained in a speech on "The Blessings of Liberty and Education." "It is to deny them the means of freedom and the rightful pursuit of happiness, and to defeat the very end of their being. They can neither honor themselves nor their Creator." Returning to the theme of intellectual freedom, which had launched his career as a free man, Douglass emphasized the indignity of prohibiting Black people from learning to read. By denying all people an equal opportunity for education, he reiterated, slavery inflicted wrongs even "deeper down and more terrible" than "the labors and the stripes"—namely, "mental and moral wrongs which enter into his claim for a slight measure of compensation." But how could the American people compensate the children of the enslaved "for the terrible wrong done to their fathers and mothers by their enslavement and enforced degradation"? Douglass called for equal access to education, without taking account of race or color. The Civil War was won, Douglass said, "not because the victim of slavery was a negro, mulatto, or an Afro-American," but because "Man saw that he had a right to liberty, to education, and to an equal chance with all other men in the common race of life and in the pursuit of happiness."[55]

By defining the pursuit of happiness as equal opportunity for education, Frederick Douglass called on America to fulfill the promise that had been imagined by Ben Franklin in his *Autobiography*, inscribed by Thomas Jefferson in the Declaration of Independence, thwarted by the compromises over slavery at the Constitutional Convention, resurrected by the abolitionist movement and by John Quincy Adams in Congress and Abraham Lincoln at Gettysburg, and finally inscribed in the Reconstruction amendments to the US Constitution. It would take another century for the civil rights movement and Dr. Martin Luther King Jr. on the Washington Mall to resurrect the promise once again and begin to make it a reality.

Notes on Xenophon's *Memorabilia* of Socrates

Each day I rise at dawn to greet the sun
To read and write with focus is the goal
Divine light shines within self-discipline
Nothing produces joy like self-control

Freedom's a noble state of mind to crave
No body's free when bodily pleasures rule
The man without self-mastery, passion's slave,
Grasps after fleeting impulse like a fool

So let me rise each day for golden hours
Give me the strength to browse less and read more
Let's cultivate constraining mental powers
In limits we the limitless explore

And now the morning birds are flying free
Self-mastered eagles of our liberty

Twelve

SILENCE

Pursuing Happiness Today

I n 1926 Justice Louis Brandeis was inspired by Thomas Jefferson to write the greatest free speech opinion of the twentieth century. The Supreme Court was preparing to decide a case called *Whitney v. California*, which involved Anita Whitney, a white woman, who had been criminally prosecuted for making a speech denouncing anti-lynching laws designed to protect the life and liberty of African Americans.

Over the summer of 1926, Brandeis, the first Jewish justice, read *The Life and Letters of Thomas Jefferson*, by Francis Hirst.[1] It contained Jefferson's original draft of the Virginia Bill for Establishing Religious Freedom as well as his first inaugural address. And in his concurring opinion in the *Whitney* case, in May 1927, Brandeis distilled Jefferson's core understanding of the pursuit of happiness, achieving a kind of constitutional poetry:

Those who won our independence believed that the final end of the State was to make men free to develop their faculties, and that, in its government, the deliberative forces should prevail over the arbitrary. They valued liberty both as an end, and as a means. They believed liberty to be the secret of happiness, and courage to be the secret of liberty. They believed that freedom to think as you will and to speak as you think are means indispensable to the discovery and spread of political truth; that, without free speech and assembly, discussion would be futile; that, with them, discussion affords ordinarily adequate protection against the dissemination of noxious doctrine; that the greatest menace to freedom is an inert people; that public discussion is a political duty, and that this should be a fundamental principle of the American government.[2]

Let's examine each of Brandeis's Jeffersonian sentences, one by one: "*Those who won our independence believed that the final end of the State was to make men free to develop their faculties, and that, in its government, the deliberative forces should prevail over the arbitrary.*" In other words, the revolutionaries of 1776, educated in classical principles of faculty psychology and moral philosophy, believed that the purpose of government is to make individuals "free to develop their faculties" of reason to ensure that reason prevails over passion in our pursuit of self-government.

"*They believed liberty to be the secret of happiness, and courage to be the secret of liberty.*" This is a quotation from Pericles's "Funeral Oration," which Brandeis took from one of his favorite books, Alfred Zimmern's *The Greek Commonwealth*. Brandeis read the book during the winter of 1913–14, and he said it pleased him more than any other book except Euripides's *Bacchae*.[3] He came to see Athens in the fifth century BC as the apotheosis of civilization, the time and place where citizens were freest to pursue happiness by devoting themselves to moral self-improvement. "For a whole wonderful half century, the richest and happiest period in the recorded history of any single community," Zimmern wrote, "Politics and Morality, the deepest and strongest forces of national and of individual life, had moved forward hand in hand towards a common ideal, the perfect citizen in the perfect state."[4]

Brandeis was especially struck by Zimmern's definition of the Greek conception of leisure: the time away from business when the citizens could be free to develop their faculties through lifelong education. "The Greek word for 'unemployment' is 'leisure,'" Brandeis wrote to his wife, Alice, in 1914, citing Zimmern. "[W]hat a happy land that." Brandeis developed a similarly strenuous Athenian conception of leisure as time away from work that should be devoted to reading and other forms of industrious self-improvement. "[L]eisure does not imply idleness," he wrote in a 1915 speech on "True Americanism." "It means ability to work not less but more, ability to work at something besides breadwinning, ability to work harder while working at breadwinning, and ability to work more years at breadwinning. Leisure, so defined, is an essential of successful democracy."[5] Leisure, in other words, as the Greeks defined it: namely, the time we devote every day to the pursuit of self-improvement, which is synonymous with the pursuit of happiness.

"They believed that freedom to think as you will and to speak as you think are means indispensable to the discovery and spread of political truth." Brandeis may have borrowed the phrase "think as you will and speak as you think" from a famous 1799 letter in which Jefferson defined intellectual freedom. "[T]o preserve the freedom of the human mind then & freedom of the press, every spirit should be ready to devote itself to martyrdom," Jefferson wrote, "for as long as we may think as we will, & speak as we think, the condition of man will proceed in improvement."[6] Jefferson, in turn, was borrowing from the Roman historian Tacitus, who began his *Histories* by celebrating the "Rare Happiness of our Times, that you may think as you will, and speak as you think." Tacitus's axiom appears on the title page of David Hume's *A Treatise of Human Nature* and was quoted in *Cato's Letters* and the *Theological Political Treatise* of the great seventeenth-century Jewish philosopher Baruch Spinoza.[7] Jefferson owned all four works.

Louis Brandeis's immersion in Thomas Jefferson's philosophy of happiness didn't end with *Whitney v. California.* Two months after *Whitney* came down, he read Jefferson's *Works* and traveled to Monticello in September "to pay homage . . . to Thomas Jefferson." He returned "with deepest conviction of T.J.'s greatness. He was a civilized man." Brandeis finished off his Jeffersonian year in December 1927 by reading Albert Jay Nock's biography, which celebrated Jefferson as "the great libertarian." Brandeis called the book "the worthiest account of our most civilized American and true Democrat."[8] (The fact that Brandeis stressed repeatedly that Jefferson was "civilized" without acknowledging that his civilized lifestyle was supported by enslaved labor represented a blind spot that Brandeis and Jefferson shared.)

Both Jefferson and Brandeis practiced a Pythagorean lifestyle, and the personal as well as philosophical affinities between the two men are striking. Both ate and drank in moderation, with Jefferson preferring wine over liquor and the more abstemious Brandeis sometimes enjoying a glass of Kentucky bourbon in his youth. Both remained fit into old age with vigorous physical exercise. Jefferson maintained his daily regime of horseback riding until his final years, and Brandeis reserved every August for horseback riding, hiking, and canoeing on Cape Cod. Both vigorously guarded and regimented their time. Jefferson maintained his rigorous daily reading and writing schedule from his school days until his death, and Brandeis, who also rose before dawn, sometimes required his clerks to slip drafts of legal opinions under his office door before sunrise. (He would silently retrieve the drafts without opening the door and then get down to work.)

In their personal economies, however, Jefferson and Brandeis diverged. Jefferson, an aestheticized shopaholic, never managed to balance his books and left the presidency $20,000 in debt; after his death, his daughters were turned out of Monticello, and most of his property was sold to pay the creditors. Brandeis, by contrast, was the model of Athenian frugality. His income as a lawyer was $100,000 a year—nearly $2.5 million in today's dollars—and yet he spent only a tenth of his income, living in austerely furnished apartments and eating small portions of simply cooked chicken. As a result, he saved his first million by the age of thirty, and, at his death in 1941, his estate totaled more than $3 million. Channeling the Stoic philosophers, Brandeis regarded money as a source of freedom that allowed him to care for the needs of his family while refusing to accept payment for his pro bono activities. In Brandeis's view, his surplus time and leisure should be invested on behalf of the public good.

Both Jefferson and Brandeis recognized the value of silence—that is, of thinking before you speak. Jefferson followed the advice he sent to his granddaughter: "when angry, count 10. before you speak; if very angry, 100." He showed drafts of sensitive letters to James Madison and sometimes decided not to send them. Brandeis, too, recognized the importance of choosing words carefully. He wrote many drafts of his judicial opinions, and, after what seemed like the final revision, asked his law clerk Paul Freund, "The opinion is now convincing, but what can we do . . . to make it more instructive?"[9] And both Brandeis and Jefferson devoted their hours of leisure to remarkably productive, steady, and disciplined reading, writing, and reflection.

Brandeis expressed his Athenian conception of the pursuit of happiness in a 1922 statement to the Federal Council of Churches that amounts to his creed: "[A]lways and everywhere the intellectual, moral and spiritual development of those concerned will remain an essential— and the main factor—in real betterment." Foreshadowing his conclusion in *Whitney* that the Founders saw liberty as both a means and an end, Brandeis continued, "This development of the individual is, thus, both a necessary means and the end sought. For our objective is the making of men and women who shall be free, self-respecting members of a democracy." Brandeis emphasized, like Jefferson, that personal self-government was necessary for political self-government because democracy is "a serious undertaking" that "substitutes self-restraint for external restraint." As Brandeis put it, democracy "demands continuous sacrifice by the individual and more exigent obedience to the moral law than any other form of government. . . . It is possible only where the process of perfecting the individual is pursued."[10]

For Brandeis, as for Franklin, the pursuit of happiness was a quest for self-improvement and moral perfection. It was a psychological and, ultimately, spiritual pursuit. In 1928, in *Olmstead v. United States*, the Supreme Court held that electronic wiretaps didn't violate the Fourth Amendment to the Constitution, which prohibits "unreasonable searches and seizures." In his dissenting opinion, Brandeis connected the right to pursue happiness with what he called "man's spiritual nature." "The makers of our Constitution undertook to secure conditions favorable to the pursuit of happiness," he wrote. "They recognized the significance of man's spiritual nature, of his feelings and of his intellect." Brandeis said the Founders understood that material well-being alone could not bring the happiness that came from spiritual freedom and fulfillment. "They knew that only a part of the pain, pleasure and satisfactions of life are to be found in material things. They sought to protect Americans in their beliefs, their thoughts, their emotions and their sensations," conferring "the right to be let alone—the most comprehensive of rights and the right most valued by civilized men."[11] For Brandeis, as for Jefferson, the government should leave us alone so that we can regulate our own beliefs, thoughts, emotions, and sensations in a quest for personal as well as political self-government.

Brandeis was not the only Supreme Court justice to connect the pursuit of happiness with the quest for the good life. In *The Slaughterhouse Cases*, after the Civil War, Justice Stephen Field quoted William Blackstone to support his conclusion that the Fourteenth Amendment protected the "inalienable right of every citizen to pursue his happiness." In the 1884 *Butchers' Union* case, Justice Joseph Bradley quoted *The Slaughterhouse Cases* and *Corfield v. Coryell*, an 1823 decision by Justice Bushrod Washington, to support his conclusion that "the liberty of pursuit—the right to follow any of the ordinary callings of life—is one of the privileges of a citizen of the United States" and "an inalienable right" recognized by the Declaration of Independence, which includes "the right to pursue and obtain happiness and safety."[12] In *Meyer v. Nebraska* in 1923, a unanimous Supreme Court, including Justice Brandeis, included the "orderly pursuit of happiness by free men" as a fundamental liberty protected by the Constitution, along with "the right of the individual to contract, to engage in any of the common occupations of life, to acquire useful knowledge, to marry, establish a home and bring up children, [and] to worship God according to the dictates of his own conscience."[13] More recently, the Supreme Court cited the *Meyer* opinion in recognizing that same-sex couples have a constitutional right to marry. "[M]arriage is 'one of the vital personal rights essential to the orderly pursuit of happiness by free men,'" the court held in *Obergefell v. Hodges* in 2015.[14]

The *Obergefell* decision was joined by Justice Ruth Bader Ginsburg who, like Louis Brandeis, embraced and exemplified the classical wisdom about pursuing happiness through emotional self-mastery. She would like to be remembered, she once said, as "[s]omeone who used whatever talent she had to do her work to the very best of her ability . . . to help repair tears in her society, to make things a little better through the use of whatever ability she has" by doing something "outside myself."[15] For Justice Ginsburg, as for the Founders, the pursuit of happiness was a quest to restrain our unproductive emotions in order to develop our talents to the fullest possible extent so that we can continue to serve others, learn, and grow. "Emotions like anger, remorse, and jealousy are not productive," Justice Ginsburg told me. "They will not accomplish anything, so you must keep them under control."[16] Justice Ginsburg learned this advice from her mother, Celia Ginsburg, a Jewish immigrant from Poland who was so absorbed by reading that once, while she was walking along the streets of the Lower East Side of Manhattan with her face buried in a book, she tripped and broke her nose. "My mother was very strong about my doing well in school and living up to my potential," Ginsburg told another interviewer. "Two things were important to her, and she repeated them endlessly. One was to 'be a lady,' and that meant conduct yourself civilly; don't let emotions like anger or envy get in your way. And the other was to be independent, which was an unusual message for mothers of that time to be giving their daughters."[17]

When I asked Justice Ginsburg how she was able to follow her mother's advice and keep her unproductive emotions in check, she replied, "Because I realize if I don't get past unproductive emotions, I'll just get bogged down and lose precious time from useful work." As a result of her determination to follow her mother's advice, Ginsburg was perhaps the most self-disciplined person I've ever met. She had a remarkable ability to focus entirely on the task at hand without being distracted by interruptions. She was a strict enforcer of deadlines, for herself and for others. She prided herself on turning in the first drafts of her opinions (she called them her homework assignments) more quickly than any other justice. A night owl, she governed her time with iron precision— always completely focused on the conversation at hand but also careful to reserve time every evening after dinner for reading and work until the early hours of the morning.

One of the most striking signs of Justice Ginsburg's self-discipline was her recognition of the power of silence. In one interview, I asked her about her unusual approach to conversation, noting that her friends and law clerks knew to wait during the long pauses between our questions and her answers, as she composed her thoughts. (After a long pause, she replied with a smile, "Well, I try to think before I speak."[18]) RBG said she learned the value of silence from her mother-in-law, who gave her the following advice about marriage on her wedding day: "Dear, in every good marriage, it helps sometimes to be a little deaf." And she applied the lesson about controlling your temper and weighing your words in fifty-six years of marriage and throughout her time on the Supreme Court. "If an unkind word is said," she told me, "you just tune out."[19]

In addition to her mother, Justice Ginsburg learned about the importance of mastering unproductive emotions from the books she devoured as a student in Brooklyn public schools in the 1940s. Around the age of eight, she began spending Friday afternoons at the local library and was drawn to tales from Greek mythology. She especially identified with Athena, goddess of reason and justice, who was known as "the industrious." At the age of thirteen, as a student at Brooklyn Elementary

Public School 238, Ginsburg wrote a moving essay about "four great documents" that she had read in school: the Ten Commandments, the Magna Carta, the English Bill of Rights of 1689, and the Declaration of Independence. She called them "great because of all the benefits to humanity which came about as a result of their fine ideals and principles." She connected these four documents to the recently passed Charter of the United Nations, which she said should inspire "we children of public school age" to "aid in the promotion of peace" and to "train ourselves and those about us to live together with one another as good neighbors."[20]

Like the Founders, in other words, Ruth Bader Ginsburg received an education that included primary texts from classical, Enlightenment, and American history. Some Founders—such as Adams, Madison, and Hamilton—had to read and master these texts in order to graduate from college. Other great Americans, including Douglass and Lincoln, educated themselves by reading texts that they found, previously compiled and condensed, in the popular readers and handbooks of their time. Closer to our time, Justices Brandeis and Ginsburg were exposed to the classics through American public schools. (My mother, who graduated from a New York City public high school in 1950, the same year as Justice Ginsburg, received a similar education.) And yet, by the time I graduated from high school three decades later, these texts had largely fallen out of the curriculum. Why?

One possible answer is that America's understanding of the pursuit of happiness in popular culture was transformed in the 1960s and 1970s from *being* good to *feeling* good; from *eudaimonia* (the pursuit of virtue) to *hedonia* (the pursuit of pleasure). This was a stark departure from the understanding of previous generations. Although the shift began much earlier, with the dawn of the Romantic era in the nineteenth century, *hedonia* wasn't fully embraced by pop culture until the second half of the twentieth century. The change from a popular culture that rejected pleasure seeking to one that celebrated it marked a shift in our understanding of happiness as something that requires delayed rather than immediate gratification.

The most perceptive nineteenth-century commentator on the pursuit of happiness in America, Alexis de Tocqueville, hoped that "the spirit of religion" in America would remind its citizens that "in democracies, as elsewhere, it is only through resisting the thousand trivial urges that the universal and anguished longing for happiness can be assuaged."[21] But Tocqueville was struck by the danger that Americans' incessant striving for wealth would degenerate into self-absorbed hedonism or anxious competition that could never bring lasting happiness. The "desire for equality becomes more insatiable as equality extends to all," Tocqueville observed, and "individualism" created an endless competition for material success, accounting "for that unusual melancholy often experienced by the inhabitants of democratic countries in the midst of plenty."[22]

In addition to the "spirit of religion," Tocqueville identified another, distinctively American idea that he hoped would persuade Americans to continue to avoid the pursuit of short-term pleasure and cultivate the self-mastery necessary for lifelong happiness. He called it "the doctrine of self-interest properly understood," and it was the doctrine of the ancient Stoics, channeled through Benjamin Franklin. In a succinct summation of the classical understanding of the pursuit of happiness, Tocqueville wrote: "Philosophers teaching this doctrine tell men that, to be happy in this life, they must keep close watch upon their passions and keep control over their excesses, that they cannot obtain a lasting happiness unless they renounce a thousand ephemeral pleasures, and that, finally, they must continually control themselves in order to promote their own interests." This doctrine by itself "could not make a man virtuous, but it does shape a host of law-abiding, sober, moderate, careful, and self-controlled citizens . . . through the imperceptible influence of habit."[23] For Tocqueville, as for Franklin, these habits of self-mastery, self-control, and delayed gratification would allow citizens to pursue their long-term interests rather than short-term pleasures.

But how could Americans be persuaded to pursue happiness through the habits of self-mastery, or "self-interest properly understood," as the orthodoxies of traditional religions began to be questioned by science in the nineteenth century? Tocqueville's answer was character education. Ralph Waldo Emerson, the most important neo-Stoic philosopher in America since Franklin, reached a similar conclusion, but he also urged every individual to find the resources to cultivate character within themselves. In his 1841 essay "Self-Reliance," which influenced Frederick Douglass and Lincoln, Emerson set out his vision of the self-mastered individual, following the dictates of conscience rather than those of the crowd, displaying the "character" that comes from "ancient virtue"—namely, "self-dependent" and "self-derived," moved by "the Spartan fife" rather than the "gong for dinner," by virtue rather than pleasure.[24]

Emerson further developed his concept of self-reliance in April 1861, the same month the Civil War began, when he gave a lecture in Boston that was published in the *Atlantic* magazine thirty years later. His topic was "[t]he American idea," which he defined as "Emancipation." By *emancipation*, he meant "freedom of intellection"—that is, emancipation of the mind, or the courage to follow the dictates of conscience rather than groupthink and the mob. He said that the spirit of self-mastery had come to Boston before the Revolution through the spirit of "Religion, the emancipator." This spirit was expressed in the free-thinking doctrines of the Puritans, who, despite their belief in predestination, insisted on reading Scripture themselves and making up their own minds about its meaning rather than accepting the authority of the Catholic Church.[25] In his own day, Emerson said, it was expressed by his fellow abolitionists such as William Lloyd Garrison, who opposed slavery as a violation of the spiritual equality promised by the Declaration of Independence.

Emerson said that Americans learned from the spirit of intellectual and spiritual self-reliance that man's "ruin is to live for pleasure and for show." We can only achieve happiness, he emphasized, not by hedonism, solipsism, or the accumulation of wealth, but by cultivating the habits of "piety . . . and the stern virtues that follow," including "courage, veracity, honesty, or chastity and generosity." Emerson recognized that the spirit of self-reliance united all the great wisdom traditions—from the

Bhagavad Gita (which he studied closely) to the Hebrew and Christian belief systems—although he located its roots in ancient Stoicism. In Emerson's time, however, traditional religion was beginning to be challenged by the Darwinian revolution. Charles Darwin's *On the Origin of Species* had been published in 1859, although it took longer to penetrate the public consciousness. But for Emerson, like the Stoics, living according to Reason and Nature was not a threat to religion; on the contrary, it was an affirmation of the Divine. Emerson said that all citizens of the world could find in the close observation of Nature a sense of mystic communion with what he called the "Over-soul" of the Universe.[26] Like the Stoics, from Cicero to Lucretius, he believed it is our duty to align our own, best selves with the natural laws of the universe, "[t]he spirit of the world, the great calm presence of the Creator."[27]

Emerson was inspiring but mystic, and, like all prophets, perhaps hard for elementary school students to understand. In the nineteenth century, therefore, the task of bringing the classical understanding of the pursuit of happiness to American students on a wide scale fell to textbook writers. A standard nineteenth-century law school textbook includes, in its section on moral philosophy, most of the books on Jefferson's reading list, including Cicero, Seneca, Xenophon, Locke, and Reid, as well as a prayer from Samuel Johnson and a Franklin-like list of practical virtues for daily living.[28] As for public school students, the most important influence on their nineteenth-century curriculum was Horace Mann. A Massachusetts abolitionist, school reformer, and associate of Emerson and John Quincy Adams, Mann became known as the founder of American public schools. "No one did more than he to establish in the minds of the American people the conception that education should be universal, non-sectarian, and free," the educational historian Ellwood Cubberley wrote in 1919, "and that its aim should be social efficiency, civic virtue, and character."[29] Mann argued that teachers should be trained in moral education and give students an opportunity to practice virtues like kindliness, self-discipline, and self-control in the classroom. In particular, Mann stressed the importance of daily reading about moral exemplars throughout history. Even fifteen minutes a day, he stressed, would inspire habits of self-mastery and good citizenship. "Let a child read and understand such stories as the friendship of Damon and Pythias, the integrity of Aristides, the fidelity of Regulus, the purity of Washington, the invincible perseverance of Franklin," he declared, "and he will think differently and act differently all the days of his remaining life."[30]

Mann's approach to character education persisted in American public schools from the mid-nineteenth to the mid-twentieth century. And for most of that period, the self-help textbook for self-made boys and girls across America was the McGuffey Reader, a primer that sold more than 120 million copies between 1837 and 1960. Like the *Columbian Orator*, which inspired Lincoln and Douglass, the McGuffey readers were full of Bible verses and hymns, although they became increasingly secularized. They began publication around the time Henry Clay coined the phrase "self-made man" and promised that students who practiced Ben Franklin's thirteen virtues, as well as more explicitly Christian ones, could be assured of following Franklin's path from rags to riches. They included homilies on industry ("[W]ork, work my boy, be not afraid; look labor boldly in the face; Take up the hammer or the spade, and blush not for your humble place") and the power of perseverance over inherited genius ("Thus plain, plodding people, who often shall find, Will leave hasty, confident people behind").[31]

The McGuffey Reader was the standard moral philosophy text for many generations of public school students; but it came to be seen, by the 1960s, as anachronistic and unconstitutional. In 1947 the Supreme Court held (correctly) that the state couldn't use taxpayer supported public schools to aid religious instruction without violating the First Amendment's Establishment Clause.[32] In 1962 the court banned nondenominational prayers in New York City public schools.[33] And in 1980 the court struck down a Kentucky law requiring the posting of the Ten Commandments in public school classrooms, on the grounds that it lacked a secular educational purpose.[34] Although the court, in all these cases, stressed that it was permissible to read religious texts as part of secular courses about history, ethics, and literature, many public schools responded by removing texts that mentioned God in any way. Partly as a result, the McGuffey Reader dropped out of the public school curriculum in the mid-twentieth century.[35]

As the silent generation of World War II gave way to the "me" generation of baby boomers, the hedonism of the 1960s gave way to the narcissism of the 1970s and the materialism of the 1980s. "You do you" became the new mantra, and everyone had an unalienable right to define their own bliss. In 1976, America's two hundredth birthday, the writer Tom Wolfe coined the phrase the Me Decade to describe the 1970s as a time when the hyper-individualism of hippie counterculture, rooted in sex, drugs, and rock and roll, broke out with a kind of religious ecstasy into a "Third Great Awakening." Two years later, in the best-selling *The Culture of Narcissism*, the sociologist Christopher Lasch agreed that the contemporary focus on self-gratification rather than self-improvement had transformed our understanding of the pursuit of happiness. "The culture of competitive individualism" that Tocqueville warned against had degenerated into "the extreme of a war of all against all, the pursuit of happiness to the dead end of a narcissistic preoccupation with the self."[36] Instead of encouraging us to regulate our emotions, popular culture encouraged us to let them all hang out.

Just as pop culture was rejecting the Stoics' ancient wisdom, however, new insights from social and behavioral psychology confirmed it. In 1990 the social psychologists John Mayer and Peter Salovey explored the skills necessary for "emotional intelligence," which they defined as "the subset of social intelligence that involves the ability to monitor one's own and others' feelings and emotions, to discriminate among them and to use this information to guide one's thinking and actions."[37] Emotional intelligence turned out to be another name for Aristotle's eudaimonia, or human flourishing through emotional self-regulation. The new term was popularized by the psychologist Daniel Goleman, whose 1995 best seller identified four components of emotional intelligence: "self-awareness, self-management, social awareness, and the ability to manage relationships." Key to the idea of emotional intelligence is the classical idea about the importance of balancing reason and emotion so that we can achieve a productive harmony. "[F]eelings are essential to thought, thought to feeling," Goleman writes, quoting the Renaissance humanist Erasmus. "But when passions surge the balance tips: it is the emotional mind that captures the upper hand, swamping the rational mind." For Goleman, as for the ancient philosophers, emotional intelligence includes "emotional self-regulation," or "the ability to deny impulse in the service of a goal."[38]

Psychologists have confirmed that skills of impulse control, which start to build from infancy, are, in fact, crucial to adult happiness. The Israeli psychologist Reuven Bar-On studied the relationship between emotional intelligence and self-actualization, or the fulfillment of human potential. He found that "emotional intelligence is highly associated with happiness," including "the quest for meaning in life."[39] "If, as Aristotle and the Humanistic psychologists claim, fulfillment and actualization are happiness, and if, as it appears, emotional intelligence is a refinement of Aristotle's concept of virtue," Samuel Franklin writes in *The Psychology of Happiness*, then new insights from social psychology confirm the ancient wisdom.[40] In other words, emotional self-regulation does, in fact, allow us to fulfill our potential, leading to long-term happiness.

At the same time that social psychologists were confirming Aristotle's insights about how emotional self-regulation leads to happiness, cognitive behavior psychologists were confirming Cicero's and Epictetus's insights about how tempering our thoughts can reduce anxiety and depression. Drawing on the ancient wisdom that reason could be used to calm the "perturbations of the mind," cognitive behavior therapists found that examining our thoughts can help us discard the "cognitive distortions" that contribute to depression and anxiety. "The philosophical origins of cognitive therapy can be traced back to Stoic philosophers, particularly Zeno of Citrium (fourth century BC), Chrysippus, Cicero, Seneca, Epictetus, and Marcus Aurelius," wrote Dr. Aaron Beck, the founder of cognitive therapy in 1979. "Like Stoicism, Eastern philosophies such as Taoism and Buddhism have emphasized that human emotions are based on ideas. Control of most intense feelings may be achieved by changing one's ideas."[41] Cognitive behavior therapy identifies a series of "cognitive distortions"—namely, unproductive thoughts, beliefs, and attitudes—that can lead to anxiety and depression. As summarized by Greg Lukianoff and Jonathan Haidt in *The Coddling of the American Mind*, the cognitive distortions include mind reading, fortune telling, catastrophizing, labeling, discounting positives, shoulds, blaming, unfair comparisons, and "emotional reasoning," where "you let your feelings guide your interpretation of reality."[42] And cognitive behavior therapy itself is a practical way of using reason to regulate emotions, which the Founders would call passion.

And then came social media. Soon after cognitive behavioral therapy resurrected the ancient wisdom about how to address anxiety and depression through reasoned self-reflection, Facebook, Twitter, and smartphones exploded on the scene. As Lukianoff and Haidt also note, after the iPhone was introduced in 2007, social media platforms began addicting Americans in large numbers, beginning in middle school. Facebook was founded in 2004, Twitter in 2006, Tumblr in 2007, Instagram in 2010, and Snapchat in 2011.[43] Between 2011 and 2016, rates of depression among adolescents began to rise, and the social psychologist Jean Twenge argues that the main cause of the teenage mental health crisis that began around 2011 is the spread of social media and smartphones. In her book *iGen*, Twenge found that two activities involving screens are highly correlated with depression and suicide: electronic devices (including smartphones, tablets, and computers) and watching TV. By contrast, time spent on five nonscreen activities have an inverse relationship with depression: sports, attending religious services, in-person social interactions, doing homework, and reading books and other print media.[44]

The Founders would not have been surprised that heavy use of social media increases anxiety and decreases happiness. Their neo-Stoic understanding of emotional intelligence emphasized the importance of deliberation and thinking before you speak; social media rewards immediate responses and tweeting before you think. The Founders counseled moderation in speech; social media rewards extremism. The Founders urged the need to think for yourself and form opinions without seeking the approval of the crowd; on social media, popular approval—in the form of likes, retweets, and shares—is the only currency. (Remember that John Adams wanted to make all offices hereditary after reading Adam Smith on the human ambition to be famous; the launch of Facebook might have led him to call off the Revolution.) The Founders insisted that happiness and good citizenship require that we moderate our unproductive emotions, such as anger and envy; social media encourages us to share those emotions as widely as possible.

But if our cell phones and screens represent the Founders' nightmare, they also offer a potential benefit. The most striking difference between the daily schedules of the Founders and our schedules today is how much time they spent reading books. It's inspiring to see the carefully regimented hourly reading schedules that Franklin and Jefferson, John and John Quincy Adams, Lincoln and Douglass set for themselves as young men, and how vigilantly they continued their voracious daily reading for their entire lives. (As John Adams told his son, you are never alone with a poet in your pocket.) Their challenge was access to books— think of how devastated Frederick Douglass was when his enslavers forbade him to learn to read, or how excited Adams was when he learned that ancient Hindu texts had survived the destruction of the library at Alexandria. As a young boy, Lincoln borrowed a copy of Parson Weems's *Life of George Washington* from a local farmer and then accidentally ruined it by leaving it out in the rain. When he returned the soaked book and explained what had happened, the farmer made him pull corn for two days in order to repay his debt.[45] In the Founders' time, books were scarce, and access to them precious.

Today, by contrast, the miracle of the Internet has given us access to all the surviving texts published since the dawn of time—on our cell phones and tablets, wherever we are, at every moment of the day, often free of charge. When I was young, I remember visiting the Library of

Congress in Washington, DC, with my mother for the first time. As I stood in the Great Hall of the magnificent Thomas Jefferson Building, I was filled with wonder at the thought that all the books in the world could be found in one place. Only a few decades later, for the first time in human history, we carry in our pockets all the wisdom of the ages, including the complete works of the ancient thinkers who inspired the Founders and actual copies of the books and editions that the Founders themselves read. All we need is the self-discipline to take the time to read them.

Here the Founders themselves are an inspiration. As their example shows, it helps to set aside dedicated time every day for deep reading rather than idle browsing and sharing. "I have given up newspapers in exchange for Tacitus and Thucydides, for Newton and Euclid," Jefferson wrote to Adams, "and I find myself much the happier." In their quest to become more perfect, the Founders fell short of many of their own ideals—except for lifelong learning, where youthful habits led most of them to keep up a disciplined daily reading schedule until the end of their lives.

In the hope that you may be inspired by the Founders' reading habits to read or listen to the books that shaped their pursuit of the good life, I've included the Founders' reading list in the appendix. There's a vast library of wisdom waiting to inspire us every day to learn and grow. Happy reading!

Acknowledgments

Rafe Sagalyn believed in this book at a time when others didn't and introduced me to Bob Bender, who believed in it as well. Bob is the Platonic ideal (and Pythagorean embodiment) of a wise editor, and working with him and his team at Simon & Schuster has been a dream come true. Jon Karp, the publisher of Simon & Schuster, was the editor for my first book nearly twenty-five years ago, and it's a privilege to come full circle.

At the National Constitution Center, my special assistant, Sam Desai, checked the footnotes, improved the text, talked through ideas about how to live, and with industry, order, temperance, and resolution, allowed both of us to meet our deadlines with calm focus. Thanks also to Tom Donnelly for a close reading of the manuscript and to all my wonderful NCC colleagues for working with me every day to inspire Americans of all ages to learn about history and the Constitution. Eric Slauter of the University of Chicago, Barry Strauss of Cornell University, and Caroline Winterer of Stanford University generously read the manuscript and offered invaluable suggestions for improvement.

As I was completing this book, my father, Sidney Rosen, MD, passed away at the age of ninety-five. Dad was one of the leading hypnotherapists of the twentieth century, a psychiatrist, sage, and best-selling author of *My Voice Will Go with You: The Teaching Tales of Milton H. Erickson*, written in collaboration with his legendary mentor. He gave me and thousands of others the gift of using hypnotic suggestions to tap into the power of the imagination, and he often quoted the sixteenth-century Swiss physician and philosopher Paracelsus: "Even as man imagines himself to be, such he is, and he is also that which he imagines."[1] Only after turning in the manuscript did I realize how closely Dad's teaching about hypnosis tracked the classical wisdom about the importance of using our faculties of reason and imagination to shape and guide our thoughts and emotions in order to achieve the calm self-mastery that defines happiness.

My sons, Hugo and Sebastian Rosen, are now completing high school. It's a joy to see them grow into such mature, balanced, self-disciplined, and self-directed young men. I'm so proud of both of them. And I'm so lucky to be on the path of spiritual learning and growth with my brilliant and beloved wife, Lauren Coyle Rosen. Together, every day, we pursue happiness and obtain it.

1. Cicero, *Tusculan Disputations* and *On Duties*

Grieving the death of his daughter Tulia, in 45 BC, the Roman statesman Cicero retired to his country villa in Tusculum, where he consoled himself with the study of philosophy. The result of his studies was *Tusculan Disputations*, a meditation on death, pain, grief, passion, and virtue and a classic text of the Stoic school. Franklin chose a quotation from it as the motto for his self-project and Jefferson, who read it for consolation after the death of his father, cited it as the source of his understanding of the pursuit of happiness. It was also a favorite of John Adams and John Quincy Adams, who adopted a quotation from the book as his personal motto.

One year after Tulia's death, Cicero wrote *On Duties*, a treatise on the good life, which also strongly influenced the Founders. The English philosopher John Locke said that anyone who read only two books— the Bible and *On Duties*—could attain a complete moral education in "the principles and precepts of virtue, for the conduct of his life."

2. Marcus Aurelius, *Meditations*

As the sixteenth Emperor of Rome, Marcus Aurelius faced wars on the frontier, a revolt within the Roman army, and the death of his wife in AD 175. To compose his emotions, he wrote about Stoicism in a private diary, which became known as the *Meditations*. It particularly influenced George Washington and John Quincy Adams, who told his father that Marcus "guards us most carefully against [life's] prosperities."

3. Seneca's *Essays*

Like Cicero and Marcus Aurelius, Seneca the Younger was a Roman statesman and Stoic. Exiled from Rome to Corsica in AD 41 after being accused (probably falsely) of an affair with the niece of the emperor Claudius, Seneca spent his time writing Stoic essays, letters, and dialogues. Later, he became an advisor to the emperor Nero who ordered him to commit suicide, which he did, stoically. As they experienced the shifting fortunes of politics and life, Founders including Franklin, Jefferson, and Adams turned to Seneca to maintain fortitude and tranquility. Washington read Seneca's essays on anger, courage, and retirement, and Abigail Adams cited Seneca to advocate for women's equality.

4. Epictetus's *Enchiridion*

Epictetus was another ancient Stoic philosopher, but unlike Cicero, Marcus, and Seneca, he was Greek and born into slavery. Disabled because of abuse he had endured from his master, Epictetus originated Stoicism's famous "dichotomy of control," which urges us to focus on what is in our control (our own thoughts and actions) rather than what is external to us (wealth, fame, and fortune). His *Enchiridion*, or *Handbook*, is a compilation of his precepts, and he influenced both John and Abigail Adams and their son John Quincy, who wrote that Epictetus "prepares us most effectually for the evils of life."

5. Plutarch's *Lives*

Plutarch, the most frequently cited classical author in the founding era, was a Roman biographer and essayist. His *Lives* are short biographies of eminent Greeks and Romans. Plutarch was especially interested in the character and motives of his subjects, and his *Lives* are filled with stories of virtue, honor, and heroism as well as vice, ambition, and defeat. Franklin and Jefferson found Plutarch's portrait of Cicero especially illuminating, while Hamilton and Madison focused on his biography of the Spartan lawgiver Lycurgus, which they both cited in *The Federalist Papers*. Hamilton also enjoyed Plutarch's account of Sparta's nude parades, and one of Plutarch's essays inspired Franklin to experiment with vegetarianism.

6. Xenophon's *Memorabilia of Socrates*

A Greek philosopher and (along with Plato) student of Socrates, Xenophon in his *Memorabilia* provides an account of Socrates's life and teachings. Franklin was especially influenced by the *Memorabilia*, and the book's vivid description of the myth of Hercules's choice between Vice and Virtue was one of Adams's favorites—though it also caused him to have at least one nightmare.

7. Hume's *Essays*

In his essays and treatises, English philosopher David Hume expounded on topics both personal and political, from economics to virtue to the nature of knowledge itself. He used the phrase "pursuit of happiness" twice. He was also one of the most-discussed philosophers of the Constitutional Convention and influenced Madison's discussion of factions in "Federalist No. 10."

8. Montesquieu's *The Spirit of the Laws*

The political treatise of the French judge and philosopher Charles Louis de Secondat, Baron de Montesquieu, *The Spirit of the Laws* was the single most-cited book of the founding era and convinced the Founders of the need for separation of powers to avoid tyranny and despotism. In "Federalist No. 47," Madison called him "the celebrated Montesquieu," paying homage to his influence on the Constitution's system of checks and balances. Hamilton read Montesquieu when he was a student at Columbia, and Adams once had a dream in which the figure of Virtue admonished him to read more Montesquieu.

9. Locke's *An Essay Concerning Human Understanding* and *Treatises on Government*

The most influential and frequently cited English philosopher for the founding generation, John Locke was famous for his theories about the social contract that individuals make when they form governments and about the mind as a blank slate, or *tabula rasa*. Along with Cicero, Aristotle, and Algernon Sidney, he was one of the four authors that Jefferson said most influenced the Declaration, and along with Francis Bacon and Isaac Newton, Locke was one of "the three greatest men that have ever lived, without any exception," in Jefferson's words. Among the other Founders who read him were Wilson, Hamilton, and Madison. His use of the phrase "the pursuit of happiness" occurs not in his *Two Treatises* but in *An Essay Concerning Human Understanding*.

10. Adam Smith's *The Theory of Moral Sentiments*

The Scottish philosopher Adam Smith eventually became world-renowned for his *Wealth of Nations*, which described the emerging system of capitalism, but to the Founders, Smith's first book, *The Theory of Moral Sentiments*, was equally important. In it, Smith described how passions influenced our actions. It was read by both the elder and younger Adams, among others.

Notes

One: Order. Twelve Virtues and the Pursuit of Happiness

1. Benjamin Franklin, *Autobiography*, in *The Works of Benjamin Franklin*, comp. and ed. John Bigelow (New York: G. P. Putnam's Sons, 1904), 1:188, 1999, Online Library of Liberty (referred to hereafter as OLL), https://oll.libertyfund.org/title/bigelow-the-works-of-benjamin-frank lin-vol-i-autobiography-letters-and-misc-writings-1725-1734.

2. Benjamin Franklin, "Articles of Belief and Acts of Religion," November 20, 1728, Founders Online, National Archives, https://founders.archives .gov/documents/Franklin/01-01-02-0032.

3. Franklin, *Autobiography*, 195. The lines are from Cicero, *Tusculan Disputations*, bk. 5, chap. 2.

4. Shai Afsai, "Benjamin Franklin's Influence on Mussar Thought and Practice: A Chronicle of Misapprehension," *Review of Rabbinic Judaism* 22, no. 2 (2019): 228–76, https://doi.org/10.1163/15700704-12341359.

5. Thomas Jefferson to Amos J. Cook, January 21, 1816, Founders Online, National Archives, https://founders.archives.gov/documents/Jefferson /03-09-02-0243. The lines are from Cicero, *Tusculan Disputations*, 4:17.

6. Ibid.

7. Thomas Jefferson to Cornelia J. Randolph, n.d., Thomas Jefferson Papers, Special Collections, University of Virginia Library, https://tjrs .monticello.org/letter/216?_ga=2.72362963.1546663750.1664389588 2075312804.1664389588.

8. Franklin, *Autobiography*, 189.

9. Declaration of Independence, July 4, 1776, America's Founding Documents, National Archives online, last modified January 31, 2023, https:// www.archives.gov/founding-docs/declaration-transcript.

10. Thomas Jefferson to Henry Lee, May 8, 1825, Founders Online, National Archives, https://founders.archives.gov/documents/Jefferson/98-01-02-5212.

11. Thomas Jefferson to John Minor, August 30, 1814, including Thomas Jefferson to Bernard Moore, [ca. 1773?], Founders Online, National Archives, https://founders.archives.gov/documents/Jefferson/03-07-02-0455.

12. For a ranked list of the most cited authors in the founding era, see Donald S. Lutz, "The Relative Influence of European Writers on Late Eighteenth-Century American Political Thought." *The American Political Science Review* 78, no. 1 (1984): 189–97.

13. For the most comprehensive study of how happiness was understood in the founding era, see Cari N. Conklin, *The Pursuit of Happiness in the Founding Era: An Intellectual History* (Columbia: University of Missouri Press, 2019).

14. See Pauline Maier, *American Scripture: Making the Declaration of Independence* (New York: Alfred A. Knopf, 1997), 134, Kindle edition ("For Jefferson and his contemporaries, happiness no doubt demanded safety or security.... The inherent right to pursue happiness probably also included 'the means of acquiring and possessing property,' but not the ownership of specific things since property can be sold and is therefore alienable.")

15. Adam Smith, *The Theory of Moral Sentiments* (London: Henry G. Bohn, 1853), 393, OLL, https://oll.libertyfund.org/title/smith-the-theory-of-moral-sentiments-and-on-the-origins-of-languages-stewart-ed.

16. Darrin M. McMahon, *Happiness: A History* (New York: Grove, 2006), 17.

17. *The Dhammapada*, 1:1, trans. Eknath Easwaran (Tomales, CA: Nilgiri Press, 2007).

18. Eknath Easwaran, *Gandhi the Man: How One Man Changed Himself to Change the World* (Tomales, CA: Nilgiri Press, 2011), 125.

19. I'm indebted to Barry Stuart Strauss of Cornell University for noting the modern scholarly consensus that Pythagoras's travels in the East are an invention of tradition later in antiquity and that, after 250 years of research, our modern understanding of classical Greece and Rome is often different than the Founders' understanding.

20. Aristotle, *The Nicomachean Ethics*, trans. W. D. Ross and J. O. Urmson, in *The Complete Works of Aristotle: The Revised Oxford Translation*, ed. Jonathan Barnes, Bollingen Series 71-2 (Princeton, NJ: Princeton University Press, 1984), 1.7, 1735, Kindle edition.

21. Jeanne Segal et al., "Improving Emotional Intelligence (EQ)," HelpGuide

.org, last modified August 31, 2022, https://www.helpguide.org/articles /mental-health/emotional-intelligence-eq.htm.

22. Plato, *Phaedrus*, trans. Benjamin Jowett, in *The Complete Works of Plato*, Ancient Classics Series (Hastings: Delphi Classics, 2015), Kindle edition.

23. Adam Smith, *Theory of Moral Sentiments*, 397.

24. Alexander Hamilton to James A. Bayard, April [16–21], 1802, Founders Online, National Archives, https://founders.archives.gov/documents /Hamilton/01-25-02-0321.

25. Abigail Adams to John Quincy Adams, March 20, 1780, Founders Online, National Archives, https://founders.archives.gov/documents /Adams/04-03-02-0240.

26. Ibid.

27. Jeffrey Rosen, *Conversations with RBG: Ruth Bader Ginsburg on Life, Love, Liberty, and Law* (New York: Henry Holt, 2019), 43.

28. Samuel Johnson, *A Dictionary of the English Language*, vol. 1 (London: United Kingdom: J. and P. Knapton, T. and T. Longman, C. Hitch and L. Hawes, A. Millar, and R. and J. Dodsley, 1755), https://www .google.com/books/edition/A_Dictionary_of_the_English_Language /cNrI9Y4bY_QC, https://catalog.loc.gov/vwebv/holdingsInfo?searchId =17316&recCount=25&recPointer=1&bibId=6819615.

29. John Locke, *An Essay Concerning Human Understanding*, in *The Works of John Locke* (London: Baldwin, 1824), 1:220–74, OLL, https://oll.liberty fund.org/title/locke-the-works-vol-1-an-essay-concerning-human-un derstanding-part-1.

30. Patrick Henry, "Give Me Liberty or Give Me Death," March 23, 1775, Yale Law School Avalon Project, accessed June 5, 2023, https://avalon .law.yale.edu/18th_century/patrick.asp.

31. Patrick Henry to Robert Pleasants, January 18, 1773, TeachingAmerican History.org, accessed June 5, 2023, https://teachingamericanhistory.org /document/patrick-henry-to-robert-pleasants/.

32. Leonard Bernstein, "Forever Beethoven," lecture presented at CBS Television Network Broadcast, January 28, 1968, Leonard Bernstein Office, https://leonardbernstein.com/lectures/television-scripts/young-peoples -concerts/forever-beethoven.

33. Cicero, *On the Republic*, trans. C. D. Yonge, in *The Complete Works of Cicero*, Ancient Classics Series (Hastings: Delphi Classics, 2014), 2:42, Kindle edition.

34. John Adams, *A Defence of the Constitutions of Government of the United*

States of America, vol. 1, in *The Works of John Adams*, vol. 4, ed. Charles Francis Adams (Boston: Charles C. Little and James Brown), 295, OLL, https://oll.libertyfund.org/title/adams-the-works-of-john-adams-vol-4.

35. Franklin, *Autobiography*, 59, 78, 91.
36. Benjamin Franklin, "Epitaph," 1728, Founders Online, National Archives, https://founders.archives.gov/documents/Franklin/01-01-02-0033.

Two: Temperance. Ben Franklin's Quest for Moral Perfection
1. Franklin, *Autobiography*, 199.
2. H. W. Brands, *The First American: The Life and Times of Benjamin Franklin* (New York: Doubleday, 2000), 564.
3. Ibid., 44.
4. Pierre Jean Georges Cabanis, "A Short Account of Benjamin Franklin, 1825," in *Franklin in His Own Time: A Biographical Chronicle of His Life, Drawn from Recollections, Interviews, and Memoirs by Family, Friends, and Associates*, ed. Kevin J. Hayes and Isabelle Bour (Iowa City: University of Iowa, 2011), 154–55. For Cabanis in the original French, see Pierre Jean Georges Cabanis, *Notice sur Benjamin Franklin*, in *Oeuvres Posthumes de Cabanis* (Paris: Bossange Brothers, 1825), 4:223, https://www.google.com/books/edition/Ouvres_Completes_Accompagnees_D_une_Noti/TQ9fAAAAcAAJ.
5. Franklin, *Autobiography*, 188–90.
6. Ibid., 201.
7. Ibid., 193.
8. Ibid., 191, 196.
9. Ibid., 197–98.
10. Ibid., 153.
11. Benjamin Franklin, "Standing Queries for the Junto," 1732, Founders Online, National Archives, https://founders.archives.gov/documents/Franklin/01-01-02-0088.
12. John Locke, "Rules of a Society," in *The Works of John Locke* (London: C. Baldwin, 1824), 9:312, OLL, https://oll.libertyfund.org/title/locke-the-works-of-john-locke-vol-9-letters-and-misc-works; Nick Bunker, *Young Benjamin Franklin: The Birth of Ingenuity* (New York: Alfred A. Knopf, 2018), 215, Kindle edition.
13. Franklin, *Autobiography*, 200–206.
14. Cabanis, "Short Account of Benjamin Franklin," 156.
15. Thomas Tryon, *Wisdom's Dictates, or Aphorisms & Rules, Physical, Moral*

and *Divine* (London: Tho. Salusbury, 1691), 4 ("Eat not to dullness, for that is a token of Gluttony, and a forerunner of difficulties.")

16. Cabanis, *Notice sur Benjamin Franklin*, 225.

17. Plutarch, *Moralia*, trans. Frank Cole Babbitt and William W. Goodwin, in *The Complete Works of Plutarch*, Ancient Classics Series (Hastings: Delphi Classics, 2013), 997, Kindle edition.

18. Cabanis, "Short Account of Benjamin Franklin," 156.

19. Franklin, *Autobiography*, 80.

20. Ibid., 191–92.

21. "A Letter from Father Abraham to His Beloved Son," August 1758, Founders Online, National Archives, https://founders.archives.gov/documents/Franklin/01-08-02-0032. For the attribution to Franklin, see Jack C. Barnes, "A Moral Epistle: A Probable Addition to the Franklin Canon," *New England Quarterly* 30, no. 1 (1957): 73–84, https://doi.org/10.2307/362730.

22. Thomas Stanley, *Pythagoras: His Life and Teachings, A Compendium of Classical Sources*, ed. James Wasserman and J. Daniel Gunther (Lake Worth, FL: Ibis, 2010), 1:2, Kindle edition. Published originally in 1687 as part of *The History of Philosophy*, Stanley's biography of Pythagoras translates and compiles various classical sources, including Iamblichus's *Life of Pythagoras*.

23. Ibid., 2:1.

24. John Dryden, "Of the Pythagorean Philosophy; From the Fifteenth Book of Ovid's Metamorphoses," in Dryden, *Complete Poetical Works*, Delphi Poets Series (Hastings, UK: Delphi Classics, 2013), lines 100–101, Kindle edition.

25. Iamblichus, *Life of Pythagoras*, trans. Thomas Taylor and Kenneth Sylvan Guthrie, in *The Complete Works of Iamblichus*, Ancients Classics Series (Hastings: Delphi Classics, 2021), chap. 31, Kindle edition.

26. Stanley, *Pythagoras*, 3:4.

27. Emphasis in original. M. Dacier, *The Life of Pythagoras*, in M. Dacier, *The Life of Pythagoras, with His Symbols and Golden Verses: Together with the Life of Hierocles, and His Commentaries upon the Verses* (London: J. Tonson, 1707), 21, https://www.google.com/books/edition/The_Life_of_Pythagoras/sIs3AAAAMAAJ.

28. Pythagoras, *Golden Verses*, trans. N. Rowe, in M. Dacier, *The Life of Pythagoras, with His Symbols and Golden Verses: Together with the Life of Hierocles, and His Commentaries upon the Verses* (London: J. Tonson, 1707), 155.

29. Abigail Adams to Charles Storer, April 28, 1783, Founders Online, National Archives, https://founders.archives.gov/documents/Adams/04-05-02-0077.

30. John Adams to Rufus King, June 14, 1786, Founders Online, National Archives, https://founders.archives.gov/documents/Adams/06-18-02-0179.

31. Pythagoras, *Golden Verses*, i.

32. Benjamin Franklin, "Proposals and Queries to Be Asked the Junto," 1732, Founders Online, National Archives, https://founders.archives.gov/documents/Franklin/01-01-02-0089.

33. Cabanis, "Short Account of Benjamin Franklin," 157–59.

34. Xenophon, *Memorabilia*, trans. E. C. Marchant, in *The Complete Works of Xenophon*, Ancient Classics Series (Hastings: Delphi Classics, 2013), 1.2.1, Kindle edition.

35. Ibid., 1.5.4.

36. Franklin, *Autobiography*, 208.

37. Jonathan Shipley to Benjamin Franklin, September 22, 1782, Founders Online, National Archives, https://founders.archives.gov/documents/Franklin/01-38-02-0105.

38. Franklin, *Autobiography*, 202–3.

39. Cabanis, "A Short Account of Benjamin Franklin," 157.

40. Franklin, *Autobiography*, 51.

41. Joseph Addison, *Spectator* No. 10, March 12, 1711, in *The Complete Works of Joseph Addison*, Series Eight (Delphi Classics, 2017), Kindle edition.

42. Alexander Pope, *Spectator* No. 408, June 18, 1712, in *The Complete Works of Joseph Addison*.

43. Richard Steele, *Spectator* No. 6, March 7, 1711, in *The Complete Works of Joseph Addison*.

44. Joseph Addison, *Spectator* No. 624, November 24, 1714, in *The Complete Works of Joseph Addison*.

45. Benjamin Franklin, "Poor Richard Improved," 1749, Founders Online, National Archives, https://founders.archives.gov/documents/Franklin/01-03-02-0143.

46. Thomas Fuller, *Introductio ad Prudentiam: Or, Directions, Counsels, and Cautions, Tending to Prudent Management of Affairs in Common Life* (London: W. Innys, 1731), xiii, 217, https://www.google.com/books/edition/Introductio_Ad_Prudentiam/Wgmk5czFrOkC.

47. Benjamin Franklin, *Poor Richard*, 1735, Founders Online, National Archives, https://founders.archives.gov/documents/Franklin/01-02-02-0001.

48. Fuller, *Introductio ad Prudentiam*, 116.

49. Franklin, *Autobiography*, 195.

50. Cabanis, "A Short Account of Benjamin Franklin," 158.

51. Margot Minardi, "The Boston Inoculation Controversy of 1721–1722: An Incident in the History of Race," *William and Mary Quarterly* 61, no. 1 (2004): 47, https:/3491675://doi.org/10.2307/.

52. Bunker, *Young Benjamin Franklin*, 115–16.

53. Benjamin Franklin to Samuel Mather, July 7, 1773, Founders Online, National Archives, https://founders.archives.gov/documents/Franklin /01-20-02-0156.

54. Cabanis, "A Short Account of Benjamin Franklin," 157.

55. Ibid.

56. William Wollaston, *The Religion of Nature Delineated* (London: J. Beecroft, 1759), 53, Kindle edition.

57. Benjamin Franklin, "A Dissertation on Liberty and Necessity," 1725, Founders Online, National Archives, https://founders.archives.gov/docu ments/Franklin/01-01-02-0028.

58. Samuel Johnson, *Autobiography*, in *Samuel Johnson, President of King's College: His Career and Writings*, ed. Herbert Schneider and Carol Schneider, *Autobiography and Letters* (New York: Columbia University Press, 1929), 1:26.

59. Franklin, *Autobiography*, 91.

60. Cabanis, "A Short Account of Benjamin Franklin," 157–58.

61. Benjamin Franklin, "Articles of Belief and Acts of Religion," November 20, 1728, Founders Online, National Archives, https://founders .archives.gov/documents/Franklin/01-01-02-0032.

62. Franklin, *Autobiography*, 204–5.

63. Benjamin Franklin, "Doctrine to Be Preached," 1731, Founders Online, National Archives, https://founders.archives.gov/documents/Franklin /01-01-02-0068.

64. Samuel Johnson, *Autobiography*, 143.

65. Benjamin Franklin, "Proposals Relating to the Education of Youth in Pennsylvania," [October 1749], Founders Online, National Archives, https://founders.archives.gov/documents/Franklin/01-03-02-0166.

66. John Adams, February 1756, in *The Diary of John Adams*, Founders Online, National Archives, https://founders.archives.gov/documents/Adams/01 -01-02-0002-0002.

67. John Tillotson, "Sermon 96: The Wisdom of Religion," in *The Works of the Most Reverend Dr. John Tillotson* (Edinburgh: G. Hamilton & J. Balfour,

W. Sands, J. Trail, W. Miller, and J. Brown, 1748), 5:134, https://www.google.com/books/edition/The_Works_of_the_Most_Reverend_Dr_John_T/C5B7nPhmmqsC.

68. Jacob M. Blosser, "John Tillotson's Latitudinarian Legacy: Orthodoxy, Heterodoxy, and the Pursuit of Happiness," *Anglican and Episcopal History* 80, no. 2 (2011): 142–73, http://www.jstor.org/stable/42612630.

69. John Tillotson, "Sermon 132: Of the Happiness of Good Men, in the Future State," in *The Works of the Most Reverend Dr. John Tillotson* (London: Ralph Barker, 1712), 2:199, https://www.google.com/books/edition/The_Works_of_the_Most_Reverend_Dr_John_T/IwMiAQAAMAAJ.

70. Samuel Johnson, *Autobiography*, 7.

71. Samuel Johnson, *Elementa Philosophica* (Philadelphia: B. Franklin and D. Hall, 1752), in *Samuel Johnson, President of King's College: His Career and Writings*, ed. Herbert Schneider and Carol Schneider (New York: Columbia University Press, 1929), II:358.

72. Ibid., 420, 450, 452.

73. Benjamin Franklin to Samuel Johnson, August 9, 1750, Founders Online, National Archives, https://founders.archives.gov/documents/Franklin/01-04-02-0008.

74. Benjamin Franklin, "Idea of the English School," [January 7, 1751], Founders Online, National Archives, https://founders.archives.gov/documents/Franklin/01-04-02-0030.

75. Neil C. Olsen, *Pursuing Happiness: The Organizational Culture of the Continental Congress* (Milford, CT: Nonagram, 2013), 386, Kindle edition.

76. Ibid., 299.

77. Samuel Johnson, *Elementa Philosophica*, 2:364.

78. Ibid., 372.

79. Ibid., 427.

80. Ibid., 420, 450, 452.

81. Ibid., 478.

82. Ibid., 490, 498–500.

83. Alexander Pope, *Essay on Man*, in *The Complete Poetical Works of Alexander Pope*, ed. Henry W. Boynton (Boston: Houghton, Mifflin, 1903), 143, OLL, https://oll.libertyfund.org/title/boynton-the-complete-poetical-works-of-alexander-pope.

84. Benjamin Franklin, *Reflections on Courtship and Marriage* (Philadelphia: Benjamin Franklin, 1746), 8, https://quod.lib.umich.edu/e/evans/N04639.0001.001; Alexander Pope, *Moral Essays*, in *Complete Poetical Works of Alexander Pope*, 167.

85. Samuel Johnson, *Raphael, or the Genius of the English America,* in *Samuel Johnson, President of King's College: His Career and Writings,* 2:523.

86. Ibid., 535.

87. B. Franklin and Maurice J. Quinlan, "Dr. Franklin Meets Dr. Johnson," *Pennsylvania Magazine of History and Biography* 73, no. 1 (1949): 34–44, http://www.jstor.org/stable/20088056.

88. Benjamin Franklin to John Waring, December 17, 1763, Founders Online, *National Archives,* https://founders.archives.gov/documents/Frank lin/01-10-02-0214.

89. Benjamin Franklin, "An Address to the Public from the Pennsylvania Society for Promoting the Abolition of Slavery," in *The Works of Benjamin Franklin,* 12:158–59.

90. Benjamin Franklin to John Adams, February 9, 1790, Founders Online, National Archives, https://founders.archives.gov/documents/Adams/06 -20-02-0149.

91. Benjamin Franklin, "Last Will and Testament," April 28, 1757, Founders Online, National Archives, https://founders.archives.gov/documents /Franklin/01-07-02-0085.

92. Max Farrand, ed., *The Records of the Federal Convention of 1787* (New Haven, CT: Yale University Press, 1911), 2:641–42, OLL, https://oll .libertyfund.org/title/farrand-the-records-of-the-federal-convention-of -1787-vol-2.

93. Ibid., 643.

94. Thomas Jefferson to James Madison, July 29, 1789, Founders Online, National Archives, https://founders.archives.gov/documents/Jefferson /01-15-02-0307.

95. John Adams to James Warren, April 13, 1783, Founders Online, National Archives, https://founders.archives.gov/documents/Adams/06-14-02 -0253.

96. John Adams to Mercy Otis Warren, August 3, 1807, Founders Online, National Archives, https://founders.archives.gov/documents/Adams/99 -02-02-5201.

97. Ibid.

Three: Humility. John and Abigail Adams's Self-Accounting

1. John Adams, December 1758, in *Diary of John Adams,* https://founders .archives.gov/documents/Adams/01-01-02-0003-0003.

2. Ibid.

3. Ibid.

4. David McCullough, *John Adams* (New York: Simon & Schuster, 2001), 36, Kindle edition.

5. John Adams, June 1756, in *Diary of John Adams,* https://founders.ar chives.gov/documents/Adams/01-01-02-0002-0006.

6. Joseph J. Ellis, *American Sphinx: The Character of Thomas Jefferson* (New York: Vintage, 1996), 237, Kindle edition.

7. John Adams, May 1756, in *Diary of John Adams,* https://founders.ar chives.gov/documents/Adams/01-01-02-0002-0005.

8. John Adams, July 1756, in *Diary of John Adams,* https://founders.archives .gov/documents/Adams/01-01-02-0002-0007.

9. John Adams, February 1756, in *Diary of John Adams.*

10. Cicero, *On Duties,* trans. Walter Miller, in *The Complete Works of Cicero,* Ancient Classics Series (Hastings: Delphi Classics, 2014), 1.26, Kindle edition.

11. John Adams, November 1760, in *Diary of John Adams,* Founders Online, National Archives, https://founders.archives.gov/documents/Adams/01 -01-02-0005-0007.

12. John Adams, July 1756, in *Diary of John Adams.*

13. John Adams, May 1756, in *Diary of John Adams.*

14. John Adams, April 1759, in *Diary of John Adams,* Founders Online, National Archives, https://founders.archives.gov/documents/Adams/01-01 -02-0004-0004.

15. John Adams to Thomas Jefferson, January 20, 1820, Founders Online, National Archives, https://founders.archives.gov/documents/Adams/99 -02-02-7297.

16. James Harris, *Concerning Happiness, a Dialogue,* in *The Works of James Harris,* ed. Earl of Malmesbury (London: Luke Hansard, 1801), 101, 111, 165, https://www.google.com/books/edition/The_Works_of_James _Harris_Esq/IHIgAQAAMAAJ.

17. Xenophon, *Memorabilia,* II.1.33.

18. John Adams, January 1759, in *Diary of John Adams,* Founders Online, National Archives, https://founders.archives.gov/documents/Adams/01 -01-02-0004-0001.

19. John Adams to Abigail Adams, August 14, 1776, Founders Online, National Archives, https://founders.archives.gov/documents/Adams/04-02 -02-0059.

20. Ibid.

21. Franklin, *Reflections on Courtship and Marriage,* 11, 34, 35.

22. John Adams, January 1759, in *Diary of John Adams.*

23. John Adams, Spring 1759, in *Diary of John Adams*, Founders Online, National Archives, https://founders.archives.gov/documents/Adams/01-01-02-0004-0005-0001.

24. John Adams, Summer 1759, in *Diary of John Adams*, Founders Online, National Archives, https://founders.archives.gov/documents/Adams/01-01-02-0004-0007-0001.

25. John Adams, December 1772, in *Diary of John Adams*, Founders Online, National Archives, https://founders.archives.gov/documents/Adams/01-02-02-0002-0008.

26. John Adams, Summer 1759, in *Diary of John Adams*.

27. Declaration of Independence.

28. Samuel Johnson, *Dictionary of the English Language*, vol. 1.

29. Alexander Hamilton, "Federalist No. 67," March 11, 1788, Founders Online, National Archives, https://founders.archives.gov/documents/Hamilton/01-04-02-0217. See also Albert Furtwangler, "Strategies of Candor in the 'Federalist,'" *Early American Literature* 14, no. 1 (1979): 91–109, http://www.jstor.org/stable/25070913.

30. Joseph Addison, *The Spectator* No. 449, Tuesday, August 5, 1712.

31. Joseph Addison, *The Spectator* No. 285, January 26, 1712.

32. John Adams, Summer 1759, in *Diary of John Adams*.

33. John Adams to John Quincy Adams, February 19, 1790, Founders Online, National Archives, https://founders.archives.gov/documents/Adams/04-09-02-0010.

34. Adam Smith, *Theory of Moral Sentiments*, 221–22.

35. Abigail Smith to John Adams, April 16, 1764, Founders Online, National Archives, https://founders.archives.gov/documents/Adams/04-01-02-0026.

36. Gordon S. Wood, *Friends Divided: John Adams and Thomas Jefferson* (New York: Penguin, 2017), 52.

37. Abigail Adams to Elizabeth Smith Shaw Peabody, February 12, 1796, Founders Online, National Archives, https://founders.archives.gov/documents/Adams/04-11-02-0087.

38. Abigail Adams to John Adams, August 14, 1776, Founders Online, National Archives, https://founders.archives.gov/documents/Adams/04-02-02-0058.

39. John Adams to Abigail Smith, April 20, 1763, Founders Online, National Archives, https://founders.archives.gov/documents/Adams/04-01-02-0006.

40. Elizabeth Carter, introduction to *All the Works of Epictetus*, trans. Elizabeth

Carter (London: S. Richardson, 1758), xxviii, https://www.google.com /books/edition/All_the_Works_of_Epictetus/Re9WAAAAcAAJ.

41. Epictetus, *The Enchiridion*, trans. W. A. Oldfather, in *The Complete Works of Epictetus*, Ancient Classics Series (Hastings: Delphi Classics, 2018), chap. 1, Kindle edition.

42. Ibid., chap. 14.

43. Ibid., chap. 8.

44. Abigail Smith to John Adams, August 11, 1763, Founders Online, National Archives, https://founders.archives.gov/documents/Adams/04-01 -02-0007.

45. Seneca, *The Moral Epistles*, CIV.

46. Ibid.

47. Ibid., 5.

48. Samuel Richardson, *Pamela; Or, Virtue Rewarded*, in *The Complete Works of Samuel Richardson*, Series Five (Delphi Classics, 2014), "Introduction to This Second Edition," Kindle edition.

49. Ibid., Vol. 5, Letter 10.

50. Abigail Adams to Lucy Cranch, August 27, 1785, Founders Online, National Archives, https://founders.archives.gov/documents/Adams/04-06 -02-0097.

51. Epictetus, *Discourses*, trans. W. A. Oldfather, in *The Complete Works of Epictetus*, Ancient Classics Series (Delphi Classics, 2018), Book III, Chapter X, Kindle edition.

52. Abigail Smith to John Adams, April 30, 1764, Founders Online, National Archives, https://founders.archives.gov/documents/Adams/04-01-02 -0032.

53. John Adams to Abigail Smith, May 7, 1764, Founders Online, National Archives, https://founders.archives.gov/documents/Adams/04-01-02 -0035.

54. Abigail Smith to John Adams, May 9, 1764, Founders Online, National Archives, https://founders.archives.gov/documents/Adams/04-01-02-0037.

55. John Adams, Summer 1759, in *Diary of John Adams*.

56. John Adams to Abigail Smith, September 30, 1764, Founders Online, National Archives, https://founders.archives.gov/documents/Adams/04 -01-02-0038.

57. Ibid.

58. Abigail Smith to John Adams, October 4, 1764, Founders Online, National Archives, https://founders.archives.gov/documents/Adams/04-01 -02-0039.

59. John Adams, October 1758, in *Diary of John Adams*, Founders Online, National Archives, https://founders.archives.gov/documents/Adams/01 -01-02-0003-0001.

60. John Adams to William Tudor Sr., March 29, 1817, Founders Online, National Archives, https://founders.archives.gov/documents/Adams/99 -02-02-6735.

61. James Otis, "Speech Against Writs of Assistance," February 24, 1761, *Teaching American History*, https://teachingamericanhistory.org/docu ment/speech-against-writs-of-assistance/.

62. John Adams to Tudor Sr., March 29, 1817.

63. James Otis, *The Rights of the British Colonies Asserted and Proved* (Boston: Edes and Gill, 1764), in *Collected Political Writings of James Otis*, ed. Richard Samuelson (Indianapolis: Liberty Fund, 2015), 140, OLL, https://oll .libertyfund.org/title/collected-political-writings.

64. Ibid., 120.

65. Rosemarie Zagarri, *A Woman's Dilemma: Mercy Otis Warren and the American Revolution* (Malden, MA: Wiley, 2015), 13, Kindle edition.

66. Ibid., 52.

67. Quoted in Nancy Rubin Stuart, *The Muse of the Revolution: The Secret Pen of Mercy Otis Warren and the Founding of a Nation* (Boston: Beacon, 2008), 40, Kindle edition.

68. Mercy Otis Warren, *History of the Rise, Progress and Termination of the American Revolution*, ed. Lester H. Cohen (Indianapolis: Liberty Fund, 1989), 1:49–50, OLL, https://oll.libertyfund.org/title/cohen-history -of-the-rise-progress-and-termination-of-the-american-revolution -vol-1.

69. John Adams, February 1770, in *Diary of John Adams*, Founders Online, National Archives, https://founders.archives.gov/documents/Adams/01 -01-02-0014-0002; quoted in Stuart, *Muse of the Revolution*, 41.

70. Mercy Otis Warren, "A Thought on the Inestimable Blessing of Reason," in Edmund M. Hayes, "The Private Poems of Mercy Otis Warren," *New England Quarterly* 54, no. 2 (1981): 214, https://doi.org/10.2307/364970.

71. Mercy Otis Warren to John Adams, October 11, 1773, Founders Online, National Archives, https://founders.archives.gov/documents/Adams/06 -01-02-0106.

72. John Adams to James Warren, December 22, 1773, Founders Online, National Archives, https://founders.archives.gov/documents/Adams/06-02 -02-0002.

73. Mercy Otis Warren to Abigail Adams, February 27, 1774, Founders

Online, National Archives, https://founders.archives.gov/documents/Adams/04-01-02-0072-0001.

74. Mercy Otis Warren, "Enclosure: Poem on the Boston Tea Party," February 27, 1774, Founders Online, National Archives, https://founders.archives.gov/documents/Adams/04-01-02-0072-0002.

75. Mercy Otis Warren to Hannah Fayerwether Tolman Winthrop, 1774, in *Mercy Otis Warren: Selected Letters*, ed. Jeffrey H. Richards and Sharon M. Harris (Athens: University of Georgia Press, 2009), 28.

76. Bernard Mandeville, *The Fable of the Bees* (Oxford: Clarendon Press, 1924), 1:37, OLL, https://oll.libertyfund.org/title/kaye-the-fable-of-the-bees-or-private-vices-publick-benefits-vol-1.

77. Mercy Otis Warren to John Adams, January 30, 1775, Founders Online, National Archives, https://founders.archives.gov/documents/Adams/06-02-02-0074.

78. John Adams to Mercy Otis Warren, March 15, 1775, Founders Online, National Archives, https://founders.archives.gov/documents/Adams/06-02-02-0081.

79. John Adams, January 1759, in *Diary of John Adams*.

80. John Adams, "Note Regarding Genesis of Thoughts on Government," July 21, 1811, Founders Online, National Archives, https://founders.archives.gov/documents/Adams/99-02-02-5661.

81. "A Proclamation by the General Court," January 19, 1776, Founders Online, National Archives, https://founders.archives.gov/documents/Adams/06-03-02-0195-0005.

82. John Adams, "Thoughts on Government," April 1776, Founders Online, National Archives, https://founders.archives.gov/documents/Adams/06-04-02-0026-0004.

83. Ibid.

84. Francis Hutcheson, *An Inquiry into the Original of Our Ideas of Beauty and Virtue*, in *The Collected Works and Correspondence of Francis Hutcheson*, ed. Wolfgang Leidhold (Indianapolis: Liberty Fund, 2008), 125, OLL, https://oll.libertyfund.org/title/leidhold-an-inquiry-into-the-original-of-our-ideas-of-beauty-and-virtue-1726-2004.

85. Jean-Jacques Burlamaqui, *The Principles of Natural and Politic Law*, trans. Thomas Nugent, ed. Petter Korkman (Indianapolis: Liberty Fund, 2006), 346, OLL, https://oll.libertyfund.org/title/korkman-the-principles-of-natural-and-politic-law.

86. John Adams, 1758, in *Diary of John Adams*, Founders Online, National

Archives, https://founders.archives.gov/documents/Adams/01-03-02-00 16-0006.

87. Burlamaqui, *Principles of Natural and Politic Law*, 89, 288, 301.

88. John Adams, Tuesday, October 1, 1776, in *Diary of John Adams*, Founders Online, National Archives, https://founders.archives.gov/documents /Adams/01-03-02-0016-0203.

89. Edward Wortley Montagu, *Reflections on the Rise and Fall of the Ancient Republicks*, ed. David Womersley (Indianapolis: Liberty Fund, 2015), 8, OLL, https://oll.libertyfund.org/title/reflections-on-the-rise-and-fall-of -the-ancient-republicks.

90. Adams, "Thoughts on Government."

91. Ibid.

92. Quoted in Wood, *Friends Divided*, 112.

93. John Adams to Thomas Jefferson, November 13, 1815, Founders Online, National Archives, https://founders.archives.gov/documents/Adams/99 -02-02-6539.

94. John Adams, "Thoughts on Government."

95. Ibid.

96. Ibid.

97. Abigail Adams to Mercy Otis Warren, July 16, 1773, Founders Online, National Archives, https://founders.archives.gov/documents/Adams/04 -01-02-0063.

98. Mercy Otis Warren to Abigail Adams, July 25, 1773, Founders Online, National Archives, https://founders.archives.gov/documents/Adams/04 -01-02-0064.

99. Seneca the Younger, "To Marcia, On Consolation," in *The Complete Works of Seneca the Younger*, trans. Aubrey Stewart, Ancient Classics Series (Hastings: Delphi Classics, 2014), xvi, Kindle edition.

100. Abigail Adams to John Adams, March 31, 1776, Founders Online, National Archives, https://founders.archives.gov/documents/Adams/04-01 -02-0241.

101. John Adams to Abigail Adams, April 14, 1776, Founders Online, National Archives, https://founders.archives.gov/documents/Adams/04-01 -02-0248.

102. Abigail Adams to Mercy Otis Warren, April 27, 1776, Founders Online, National Archives, https://founders.archives.gov/documents/Adams/04 -01-02-0257.

103. Abigail Adams to John Adams, August 14, 1776, Founders Online,

National Archives, https://founders.archives.gov/documents/Adams/04 -02-02-0058.

104. John Adams to Abigail Adams, August 25, 1776, Founders Online, National Archives, https://founders.archives.gov/documents/Adams/04-02 -02-0068.

105. John Adams to Mercy Otis Warren, January 8, 1776, Founders Online, National Archives, https://founders.archives.gov/documents/Adams/06 -03-02-0202.

106. Mercy Otis Warren to John Adams, March 10, 1776, Founders Online, National Archives, https://founders.archives.gov/documents/Adams/06 -04-02-0019.

107. John Adams, *A Defence of the Constitutions of Government of the United States of America*, 392.

108. John Adams, *Discourses on Davila*, in *The Works of John Adams*, 6:245–46.

109. Adam Smith, *Theory of Moral Sentiments*, 73.

110. Wood, *Friends Divided*, 250.

111. John Adams, *Discourses on Davila*, in Zoltán Haraszti, "The 32nd Discourse on Davila," *William and Mary Quarterly* 11, no. 1 (1954): 90, https://doi.org/10.2307/1923151.

112. John Adams to Mercy Otis Warren, August 19, 1807, Founders Online, National Archives, https://founders.archives.gov/documents/Adams/99 -02-02-5208.

113. Mercy Otis Warren, *History of the Rise, Progress, and Termination of the American Revolution*, ed. Lester H. Cohen (Indianapolis: Liberty Fund, 1989), 2:675–76, 678, OLL, https://oll.libertyfund.org/title/warren-his tory-of-the-rise-progress-and-termination-of-the-american-revolution -vol-2.

114. Ibid., 677, 692.

115. Mercy Otis Warren, *History of the Rise, Progress, and Termination of the American Revolution*, 1:xliv.

116. John Adams to Mercy Otis Warren, July 11, 1807, Founders Online, National Archives, https://founders.archives.gov/documents/Adams/99-02 -02-5193.

117. Ibid.

118. Mercy Otis Warren to John Adams, July 16, 1807, Founders Online, National Archives, https://founders.archives.gov/documents/Adams/99-02 -02-5194.

119. John Adams to Mercy Otis Warren, July 20, 1807, Founders Online,

National Archives, https://founders.archives.gov/documents/Adams/99 -02-02-5195.

120. Ibid., July 27, 1807, Founders Online, National Archives, https://found ers.archives.gov/documents/Adams/99-02-02-5196.

121. Ibid., August 19, 1807, Founders Online, National Archives, https:// founders.archives.gov/documents/Adams/99-02-02-5208.

122. Ibid., July 20, 1807, Founders Online, National Archives, https://found ers.archives.gov/documents/Adams/99-02-02-5195.

123. Mercy Otis Warren to John Adams, July 28, 1807, Founders Online, National Archives, https://founders.archives.gov/documents/Adams/99 -02-02-5198; ibid., August 7, 1807, Founders Online, National Archives, https://founders.archives.gov/documents/Adams/99-02-02-5202.

124. Ibid., August 27, 1807, Founders Online, National Archives, https:// founders.archives.gov/documents/Adams/99-02-02-5210.

125. Ibid., July 10, 1814, Founders Online, National Archives, https://found ers.archives.gov/documents/Adams/99-02-02-6316.

126. John Adams to Mercy Otis Warren, July 15, 1814, Founders Online, National Archives, https://founders.archives.gov/documents/Adams/99-02 -02-6319.

127. Ibid., August 17, 1814, Founders Online, National Archives, https:// founders.archives.gov/documents/Adams/99-02-02-6326.

Four: Industry. Thomas Jefferson's Reading List

1. *Jefferson's Literary Commonplace Book*, ed. Douglas L. Wilson (Princeton, NJ: Princeton University Press, 1989), 61, Kindle edition. Jefferson copied the passages in the original Greek and Latin. Following Wilson, I use the translation from the Loeb Classical Library editions.

2. Cicero, *Letters to Atticus*, trans. Evelyn S. Shuckburgh in *The Complete Works of Cicero*, book 12, letter 14.

3. Thomas Jefferson, *Autobiography*, in *The Complete Works of Thomas Jefferson*, Series Ten (Delphi Classics, 2019).

4. Quoted in Francis W. Hirst, *The Life and Letters of Thomas Jefferson* (New York: Macmillan, 1926), 15, https://www.google.com/books/edition /Life_and_Letters_of_Thomas_Jefferson/JUB2AAAAMAAJ.

5. Henry C. Merwin, *Thomas Jefferson* (Cambridge, MA: Riverside, 1901), 4, https://www.google.com/books/edition/Thomas_Jefferson/CoZJAAA AIAAJ.

6. "Sayings of Thomas Jefferson," in *Complete Works of Thomas Jefferson*.

7. Thomas Jefferson to William Roscoe, December 27, 1820, Founders On-line, National Archives, https://founders.archives.gov/documents/Jefferson/03-16-02-0404.

8. Jeffrey Rosen, *The Supreme Court: The Personalities and Rivalries That Defined America* (New York: Henry Holt, 2006), 32; Ellis, *American Sphinx*, 22, 159.

9. Thomas Jefferson to Martha Jefferson, May 5, 1787, Founders Online, National Archives, https://founders.archives.gov/documents/Jefferson/01-11-02-0327.

10. Ibid., May 21, 1787, Founders Online, National Archives, https://founders.archives.gov/documents/Jefferson/01-11-02-0350.

11. Thomas Jefferson to Peter Carr, August 19, 1785, Founders Online, National Archives, https://founders.archives.gov/documents/Jefferson/01-08-02-0319.

12. Ibid., December 11, 1783, Founders Online, National Archives, https://founders.archives.gov/documents/Jefferson/01-06-02-0302.

13. Thomas Jefferson to Cornelia J. Randolph, undated, The Thomas Jefferson Papers, Special Collections, University of Virginia Library, https://www.monticello.org/research-education/thomas-jefferson-encyclopedia/canons-conduct/#fn-1.

14. Thomas Jefferson to Minor, August 30, 1814, including Jefferson to Moore, [ca. 1773?].

15. Ibid.

16. Douglas L. Wilson, introduction to *Jefferson's Literary Commonplace Book*.

17. Plutarch, "Cicero," in Plutarch, *Plutarch's Lives: The Lives of the Noble Grecians and Romans*, trans. John Dryden, ed. Arthur Hugh Clough (New York: Modern Library, 1992), Kindle edition.

18. *Jefferson's Literary Commonplace Book*, 56.

19. Ibid., 59.

20. Cicero, *Tusculan Disputations*, 2:4.

21. Ibid., 2:13.

22. Ibid., 3:1.

23. Cicero, *Tusculan Disputations*, 3:4–5.

24. *Jefferson's Literary Commonplace Book*, 60.

25. Cicero, *Tusculan Disputations*, 4:5.

26. Ibid., 4:3.

27. Donald S. Lutz, "The Relative Influence of European Writers on Late Eighteenth-Century American Political Thought," *American Political Science Review* 78, no. 1 (1984): 194, https://doi.org/10.2307/1961257.

28. David Fott, "Preface to Translation of Montesquieu's 'Discourse on Cicero,'" *Political Theory* 30, no. 5 (2002): 728–32, http://www.jstor.org/stable/3072500.

29. John Locke, *Some Thoughts Concerning Education*, in *The Works of John Locke* (London: C. Baldwin, 1824), 8:176, OLL, https://oll.libertyfund.org/title/locke-the-works-vol-8-some-thoughts-concerning-education-posthumous-works-familiar-letters.

30. Ibid., 27.

31. Thomas Jefferson, *Autobiography*.

32. "Wythe's Library," *Wythepedia*, Wolf Law Library, http://lawlibrary.wm.edu/wythepedia/index.php/Wythe's_Library.

33. Thomas Jefferson to John Trumbull, February 15, 1789, Founders Online, National Archives, https://founders.archives.gov/documents/Jefferson/01-14-02-0321.

34. Thomas Jefferson to James Madison, August 30, 1823, Founders Online, National Archives, https://founders.archives.gov/documents/Jefferson/98-01-02-3728.

35. Declaration of Independence; John Locke, *Two Treatises of Government*, in *The Works of John Locke* (London: C. Baldwin, 1824), 4:472, OLL, https://oll.libertyfund.org/title/locke-the-works-of-john-locke-vol-4-economic-writings-and-two-treatises-of-government.

36. John Locke, *An Essay Concerning Human Understanding*, in *The Works of John Locke* (London: Baldwin, 1824), 1:419, OLL, https://oll.libertyfund.org/title/locke-the-works-vol-1-an-essay-concerning-human-understanding-part-1.

37. Ibid., 77.

38. Ibid., 224.

39. Ibid., 251–52.

40. Ibid., 237–38.

41. Ibid., 243.

42. Ibid., 254.

43. Hutcheson, *An Inquiry*, 125.

44. Sophia Rosenfeld, *Common Sense: A Political History* (Cambridge: Oxford University Press, 2021), 22–23.

45. Francis Hutcheson, *A Short Introduction to Moral Philosophy*, ed. Luigi Turco (Indianapolis: Liberty Fund, 2007), 3–4, 66, OLL, https://oll.libertyfund.org/title/hutcheson-philosophiae-moralis-institutio-compendiaria-1747-2007.

46. Ibid., 25.

47. Ibid., 28–29, 38.

48. Hutcheson, *An Inquiry*, 104, 186.

49. Hutcheson, *Short Introduction to Moral Philosophy*, bk. 2, chap. 4, 139.

50. Thomas Jefferson, "A Bill for Establishing Religious Freedom," June 18, 1779, Founders Online, National Archives, https://founders.archives .gov/documents/Jefferson/01-02-02-0132-0004-0082.

51. Ibid.

52. James Madison, "Memorial and Remonstrance Against Religious Assessments," ca. June 20, 1785, Founders Online, National Archives, https:// founders.archives.gov/documents/Madison/01-08-02-0163.

53. David Hume, *A Treatise of Human Nature*, ed. L. A. Selby-Bigge (Oxford: Clarendon, 1896), 415, OLL, https://oll.libertyfund.org/title/bigge-a -treatise-of-human-nature.

54. John Adams to Thomas Boylston Adams, February 2, 1803, Founders Online, National Archives, https://founders.archives.gov/documents /Adams/99-03-02-1143.

55. Ibid., February 1803, Founders Online, National Archives, https://found ers.archives.gov/documents/Adams/99-03-02-1149.

56. Henry Home, Lord Kames, *Essays on the Principles of Morality and Natural Religion*, ed. Mary Catherine Moran (Indianapolis: Liberty Fund, 2005), 42, OLL, https://oll.libertyfund.org/title/moran-essays-on-the -principles-of-morality-and-natural-religion.

57. Ibid.

58. Ibid., 234.

59. Thomas Jefferson to Peter Carr, with Enclosure, August 10, 1787.

60. Ibid.

61. Thomas Jefferson to Robert Skipwith, with a List of Books for a Private Library, August 3, 1771; Thomas Jefferson to Minor, August 30, 1814, including Jefferson to Moore, [ca. 1773?].

62. Laurence Sterne, "Inquiry After Happiness," in *The Complete Works of Laurence Sterne*, Series Three (Delphi Classics, 2013), Kindle edition.

63. Garry Wills, "The Aesthete," *New York Review of Books* 11, no. 14 (1963): https://www.nybooks.com/articles/1993/08/12/the-aesthete/.

64. Thomas Jefferson to James Madison, September 6, 1789, Founders Online, National Archives, https://founders.archives.gov/documents/Jeffer son/01-15-02-0375-0003.

Five: Frugality. James Wilson and George Mason's Debts

1. James Wilson, "An Address to the Inhabitants of the Colonies," 1776, in *Collected Works of James Wilson*, ed. Kermit L. Hall and Mark David Hall (Indianapolis: Liberty Fund, 2007), 1:53, OLL, https://oll.libertyfund .org/title/hall-collected-works-of-james-wilson-vol-1.

2. Benjamin Franklin to Lord Kames, January 3, 1760, Founders Online, National Archives, https://founders.archives.gov/documents/Franklin /01-09-02-0002.

3. Walter Isaacson, *Benjamin Franklin: An American Life* (New York: Simon & Schuster, 2003), 195–96; see also Thomas D. Eliot, "The Relations Between Adam Smith and Benjamin Franklin Before 1776," *Political Science Quarterly* 39, no. 1 (1924): 67–96, https://doi.org/10.2307/2142684.

4. Charles Page Smith, *James Wilson: Founding Father, 1742–1798* (Chapel Hill: University of North Carolina Press, 1956), 22.

5. Charles Wilson (The Visitant), "No. 1," *Pennsylvania Chronicle* 2, no. 1 (January 1768): 1.

6. Wilson (The Visitant), "No. 13," *Pennsylvania Chronicle* 2, no. 13 (April 1768): 97.

7. Wilson (The Visitant), "No. 3," *Pennsylvania Chronicle* 2, no. 3 (February 1768): 17.

8. Wilson (The Visitant), "No. 1," 1.

9. Wilson (The Visitant), "No. 3," 17.

10. *Man doth not resign his Liberty unless in Consideration of a greater Good.* Sid. On Gov. Ch. 1. Sec. 2. ¶ 5.

11. Bur.

12. *No people can give away the Freedom of themselves and their Posterity: such a Donation ought to be esteemed of no greater Validity than the gift of a Child or of a Madman. People can no more part with their legal Liberties, than Kings can alienate their Crowns.* Molesworth in his Preface to his Acco' of Denmark.

13. Bur. 2.50.32.

14. *The Right of Sovereignty is that of commanding finally—but in order to procure real Felicity; for if the End is not observed, Sovereignty ceases to be a legitimate Authority.* Bur. 32.

15. James Wilson, *Considerations on the Legislative Authority of the British Parliament*, manuscript, Quill Project at Pembroke College, https://www .quillproject.net/resources/resource_collections/19.

16. Algernon Sidney, *Discourses Concerning Government*, ed. Thomas G. West (Indianapolis: Liberty Fund, 1996), 8, OLL, https://oll.libertyfund.org /title/sidney-discourses-concerning-government.

17. Ibid., 51.
18. Burlamaqui, *Principles of Natural and Politic Law*, 297.
19. Locke, *Two Treatises of Government*, 345.
20. Ibid., 340–41.
21. Sir William Blackstone, *Commentaries on the Laws of England* (Philadelphia: J. B. Lippincott, 1893), 1:40–42, OLL, https://oll.libertyfund.org/title/sharswood-commentaries-on-the-laws-of-england-in-four-books-vol-1.
22. Locke, *Two Treatises of Government*, 432.
23. Burlamaqui, *Principles of Natural and Politic Law*, 385.
24. Blackstone, *Commentaries on the Laws of England*, 46n1.
25. Burlamaqui, *Principles of Natural and Politic Law*, 151.
26. John K. Alexander, "The Fort Wilson Incident of 1779: A Case Study of the Revolutionary Crowd," *William and Mary Quarterly* 31, no. 4 (1974): 589–612. https://doi.org/10.2307/1921605; C. Page Smith, "The Attack on Fort Wilson," *Pennsylvania Magazine of History and Biography* 78, no. 2 (1954): 177–88. http://www.jstor.org/stable/20088567.
27. Smith, *James Wilson*, 292–93.
28. James Wilson, "Oration Delivered on the Fourth of July 1788," in *Collected Works of James Wilson*, 290–93.
29. James Wilson to George Washington, April 21, 1789, Founders Online, National Archives, https://founders.archives.gov/documents/Washington/05-02-02-0098.
30. Smith, *James Wilson*, 160.
31. James Wilson, "On the Improvement and Settlement of Lands in the United States," in *Collected Works of James Wilson*, 379, 384.
32. Smith, *James Wilson*, 351.
33. Quoted in Michael H. Taylor, *James Wilson: The Anxious Founder* (New York: Lexington Books, 2021), 197.
34. John Quincy Adams to Thomas Boylston Adams, June 23, 1793, Founders Online, National Archives, https://founders.archives.gov/documents/Adams/04-09-02-0251.
35. Smith, *James Wilson*, 367.
36. Quoted in Bruce H. Mann, *Republic of Debtors: Bankruptcy in the Age of American Independence* (Cambridge, MA: Harvard University Press, 2002), 202.
37. Smith, *James Wilson*, 384.
38. James Wilson to Joseph Thomas, May 12, 1798, in *The Documentary*

History of the Supreme Court of the United States, 1789–1800, ed. Maeva Marcus (New York: Columbia University Press, 1990), 3:266.

39. Jeff Broadwater, *George Mason: Forgotten Founder* (Chapel Hill: University of North Carolina Press, 2006), 1, Kindle edition.

40. B. Brown, "The Library of George Mason of Gunston Hall" (unpublished manuscript, pdf).

41. George Mason, "The Virginia Declaration of Rights—First Draft," George Mason's Gunston Hall online, accessed June 5, 2023, https://gun stonhall.org/learn/george-mason/virginia-declaration-of-rights/virginia -declaration-of-rights-first-draft/.

42. Thomas Jefferson, "Jefferson's 'Original Rough Draught' of the Declaration of Independence, June 11–July 4, 1776," Founders Online, National Archives, https://founders.archives.gov/documents/Jef ferson/01-01-02-0176-0004.

43. Thomas Jefferson to Augustus Elias Brevoort Woodward, April 3, 1825, Founders Online, National Archives, https://founders.archives.gov/docu ments/Jefferson/98-01-02-5105.

44. "The Virginia Declaration of Rights—Ratified Version," *Gunston Hall*, https://gunstonhall.org/learn/george-mason/virginia-declaration-of -rights/the-virginia-declaration-of-rights-ratified-version/.

45. John Trenchard, "No. 59," in John Trenchard and Thomas Gordon, *Cato's Letters: Or, Essays on Liberty, Civil and Religious, and Other Important Subjects*, vol. 2 (Indianapolis: Liberty Fund, 2019), Kindle edition, OLL, https://oll.libertyfund.org/title/gordon-cato-s-letters-or-essays-on-lib erty-civil-and-religious-and-other-important-subjects.

46. Thomas Gordon, "No. 48," in Trenchard and Gordon, *Cato's Letters*, vol. 2.

47. Thomas Gordon, "No. 25," in Trenchard and Gordon, *Cato's Letters*, vol. 1.

48. Thomas Gordon, "No. 11," in Trenchard and Gordon, *Cato's Letters*, vol. 1.

49. Thomas Gordon, "No. 6," in Trenchard and Gordon, *Cato's Letters*, vol. 1.

50. Sidney, *Discourses Concerning Government*, 83.

51. Thomas Gordon, "No. 16," in Trenchard and Gordon, *Cato's Letters*, vol. 1.

52. "The Virginia Declaration of Rights—Ratified Version."

53. Broadwater, *George Mason*, 245.

Six: Sincerity. Phillis Wheatley and the Enslavers' Avarice

1. Thomas Hutchinson et al., "To the Publick," in Phillis Wheatley, *Complete Writings*, ed. Vincent Carretta (New York: Penguin, 2001), 8.

2. John Wheatley, "Letter Sent by the Author's Master to the Publick," in Wheatley, *Complete Writings*, 8.

3. Henry Louis Gates Jr., *The Trials of Phillis Wheatley: America's First Black Poet and Her Encounters with the Founding Fathers* (New York: Basic Books, 2003), 29.

4. David Waldstreicher, *The Odyssey of Phillis Wheatley: A Poet's Journey Through American Slavery and Independence* (New York: Farrar, Straus and Giroux, 2023), 201.

5. Hutchinson et al., "To the Publick," in Wheatley, *Complete Writings*, 8.

6. Phillis Wheatley, "On Virtue," in Wheatley, *Complete Writings*, 11.

7. Phillis Wheatley, "Thoughts on the Works of Providence," in Wheatley, *Complete Writings*, 28.

8. Phillis Wheatley, "To Maecanas," in Wheatley, *Complete Writings*, 10n2.

9. Phillis Wheatley, "To the Right Honourable William Earl of Dartmouth," in Wheatley, *Complete Writings*, 40.

10. Gates Jr., *Trials of Phillis Wheatley*, 33.

11. Benjamin Franklin to Jonathan Williams Sr., July 7, 1773, Founders Online, National Archives, https://founders.archives.gov/documents/Franklin/01-20-02-0158.

12. Carretta, introduction, xxvi–xxvii.

13. Phillis Wheatley, "To His Excellency General Washington," in Wheatley, *Complete Writings*, 88–90.

14. George Washington to Phillis Wheatley, February 28, 1776, Founders Online, National Archives, https://founders.archives.gov/documents/Washington/03-03-02-0281.

15. George Washington to Lieutenant Colonel Joseph Reed, February 10, 1776, Founders Online, National Archives, https://founders.archives.gov/documents/Washington/03-03-02-0209.

16. Phillis Wheatley, "On the Death of General Wooster," in Wheatley, *Complete Writings*, 93.

17. Thomas Jefferson, *Notes on Virginia*, in *The Works of Thomas Jefferson*, ed. Paul Leicester Ford (New York: G. P. Putnam's Sons, 1904), 4:49, 51–52, OLL, https://oll.libertyfund.org/title/jefferson-the-works-vol-4-notes-on-virginia-ii-correspondence-1782-1786.

18. Ibid., 52–53.

19. Ibid., 54–56.

20. Ibid., 57–59.

21. See, generally, Annette Gordon-Reed, *The Hemingses of Monticello: An American Family* (New York: W. W. Norton, 2008).

22. Thomas Jefferson, *Notes on Virginia*, 48–49.

23. Ibid., 82–83.

24. Ibid., 83–84.

25. Paul Finkelman, *Slavery and the Founders: Race and Liberty in the Age of Jefferson*, 3rd ed. (New York: Routledge, 2014), 218.

26. Hirst, *Life and Letters of Thomas Jefferson*, 32.

27. Richard Price, *Observations on the Importance of the American Revolution* (London: T. Cadell, 1785), 83, OLL, https://oll.libertyfund.org/title/ricard-observations-on-the-importance-of-the-american-revolution.

28. Thomas Jefferson to Richard Price, August 7, 1785, Founders Online, National Archives, https://founders.archives.gov/documents/Jefferson/01-08-02-0280.

29. Thomas Jefferson, *Notes on Virginia*, 58.

30. Ellis, *American Sphinx*, 363.

31. Broadwater, *George Mason*, 14.

32. George Mason to George Washington, December 23, 1765, Founders Online, National Archives, https://founders.archives.gov/documents/Washington/02-07-02-0270.

33. "The Declaratory Act," *The Avalon Project*, https://avalon.law.yale.edu/18th_century/declaratory_act_1766.asp.

34. "Fairfax County Resolves, July 18, 1774," Founders Online, National Archives, https://founders.archives.gov/documents/Washington/02-10-02-0080.

35. "Resolutions and Association of the Virginia Convention of 1774," [August 1–6, 1774], Founders Online, National Archives, https://founders.archives.gov/documents/Jefferson/01-01-02-0091.

36. Thomas Jefferson, "'Original Rough Draught' of the Declaration of Independence."

37. Farrand, *Records of the Federal Convention of 1787*, 2:370.

38. Ibid., 587–88.

39. Thomas Jefferson to George Mason, May 26, 1788, Founders Online, National Archives, https://founders.archives.gov/documents/Jefferson/01-13-02-0117.

40. James Wilson, *Lectures on Law*, in *Collected Works of James Wilson*, ed. Kermit L. Hall and Mark David Hall, 2:1077, OLL, https://oll.libertyfund.org/title/garrison-collected-works-of-james-wilson-vol-2.

41. James Wilson, "Remarks of James Wilson in the Pennsylvania Convention to Ratify the Constitution of the United States, 1787," in *Collected Works of James Wilson*, 1:241.

42. Finkelman, *Slavery at the Founding*, 12.

43. Farrand, *Records of the Federal Convention of 1787*, 1:587, OLL, https://
    oll.libertyfund.org/title/farrand-the-records-of-the-federal-convention
    -of-1787-vol-1.
44. Ibid., 2:221–22.

Seven: Resolution. George Washington's Self-Command

1. George Washington to Officers of the Army, March 15, 1783, Founders Online, National Archives, https://founders.archives.gov/documents
   /Washington/99-01-02-10840.
2. Major J. A. Wright to Major John Webb, March 16, 1783, quoted in
   The Writings of George Washington, ed. Worthington Chauncey Ford (New
   York: G. P. Putnam's Sons, 1891), 10:178n1, OLL: https://oll.libertyfund
   .org/title/ford-the-writings-of-george-washington-vol-x-1782-1785.
3. Joseph Addison, *Cato: A Tragedy*, in Joseph Addison, *Cato: A Tragedy and
   Selected Essays*, ed. Christine Dunn Henderson and Mark E. Yellin (Indianapolis: Liberty Fund, 2004), 8, OLL, https://oll.libertyfund.org/title
   /henderson-cato-a-tragedy-and-selected-essays.
4. George Washington to Officers of the Army, March 15, 1783.
5. *The Life and Journals of Major Samuel Shaw*, ed. Josiah Quincy (Boston: WM. Crosby and H. P. Nichols, 1847), 104–5, https://www
   .google.com/books/edition/The_Journals_of_Major_Samuel_Shaw
   /V3VCAAAAIAAJ.
6. George Washington to Bryan Fairfax, January 20, 1799, Founders Online,
   National Archives, https://founders.archives.gov/documents/Washington
   /06-03-02-0229.
7. Thomas Jefferson to Walter Jones, January 2, 1814, Founders Online,
   National Archives, https://founders.archives.gov/documents/Jefferson
   /03-07-02-0052.
8. John Adams to Benjamin Rush, November 11, 1807, Founders Online,
   National Archives, https://founders.archives.gov/documents/Adams/99
   -02-02-5216.
9. Ibid.
10. Kevin J. Hayes, *George Washington: A Life in Books* (New York: Oxford
    University Press, 2017), 8.
11. Ron Chernow, *Washington: A Life* (New York: Penguin, 2010), 11.
12. George Washington to Mary Ball Washington, February 15, 1787,
    Founders Online, National Archives, https://founders.archives.gov/docu
    ments/Washington/04-05-02-0030.

13. Seneca, *A Happy Life*, trans. Sir Roger L'Estrange, in *Seneca's Morals*, trans. Sir Roger L'Estrange (London: Sherwood, Neely and Jones, 1818), 89, https://www.google.com/books/edition/Seneca_s_Morals_by_Way_of _Abstract/gd0AAAAAYAAJ.

14. Ibid., 89–90.

15. Seneca, "Of True Courage," trans. Sir Roger L'Estrange, in *Seneca's Morals*, 417.

16. Chernow, *Washington*, 59.

17. Alexander Hamilton to Elias Boudinot, [July 5, 1778], Founders Online, National Archives, https://founders.archives.gov/documents/Ham ilton/01-01-02-0499; quoted in Chernow, *Washington*, 343.

18. Thomas Jefferson to George Washington, April 16, 1784, Founders Online, National Archives, https://founders.archives.gov/documents/Jeffer son/01-07-02-0102.

19. François-Jean de Beauvoir, Marquis de Chastellux, to George Washington, August 23, 1783, Founders Online, National Archives, https:// founders.archives.gov/documents/Washington/99-01-02-11733.

20. George Washington to Chastellux, February 1, 1784, Founders Online, National Archives, https://founders.archives.gov/documents/Washing ton/04-01-02-0062.

21. Seneca, "The Blessings of a Virtuous Retirement," trans. Sir Roger L'Estrange, in *Seneca's Morals*, 369.

22. Seneca, "A Good Man Can Never Be Miserable, Nor a Wicked Man Happy," trans. Sir Roger L'Estrange, in *Seneca's Morals*, 132.

23. Seneca, "On Saving Time," trans. Richard M. Gummere, in Seneca, *Ad Lucilium Epistulae Morales*, trans. Richard M. Gummere (London: William Heinemann, 1917), 1:3–5, https://www.google.com/books/edition /Ad_Lucilium_Epistulae_Morales/H3w6AQAAMAAJ.

24. George Washington, [August 1768], Founders Online, National Archives, https://founders.archives.gov/documents/Washington/01-02-02 -0003-0022; George Washington, [February 1771], Founders Online, National Archives, https://founders.archives.gov/documents/Washing ton/01-03-02-0001-0003.

25. Chernow, *Washington*, 119–20.

26. M. L. Weems, *The Life of George Washington* (Philadelphia: Joseph Allen, 1837), 208, https://www.google.com/books/edition/The_Life_of_George _Washington_with_Curio/6tc56rgYE1YC.

27. Ibid., 205.

28. Seneca, "Of Anger," trans. Sir Roger L'Estrange, in *Seneca's Morals*, 260, 306, 309.

29. Quoted in Chernow, *Washington*, 275.

30. Quoted in ibid., 342.

31. Charles C. Tansill, "The Treaty-Making Powers of the Senate," *American Journal of International Law* 18, no. 3 (1924): 463–65, https://doi .org/10.2307/2188358.

32. James Madison, "Notes on Debates," February 20, 1783, Founders Online, National Archives, https://founders.archives.gov/documents/Madi son/01-06-02-0083.

33. Kevin J. Hayes, *George Washington*, 12.

34. 597 U.S. ___ (2022)

35. Matthew Hale, *Contemplations Moral and Divine* (London: D. Brown, J. Walthoe, J. Sprint, M. Wotton, G. Conyers, and D. Midwinter, 1711), 375–76, https://www.google.com/books/edition/Contemplations_Moral _and_Divine/vpRah_XrD90C.

36. Kevin J. Hayes, *George Washington*, 121.

37. "True Happiness," in *Gentleman's Magazine*, February 1734, 102, https://www.google.com/books/edition/The_Gentleman_s_Magazine _Or_Monthly_Inte/I1c3AAAAYAAJ.

38. Moncure D. Conway, Julius F. Sachse, and Joseph Meredith Toner, "George Washington's Rules of Civility," in *The Complete Works of George Washington* (Prague, Czech Republic: Madison & Adams Press, 2017), 949, Kindle edition.

39. Charles Moore, ed., *George Washington's Rules of Civility and Decent Behavior in Company and Conversation* (Boston: Riverside Press, 1926), 27, 32, 47, 55, https://www.google.com/books/edition/George_Washington_s _Rules_of_Civility_an/3rZEAAAAIAAJ.

40. Ibid., 51, 52, 56, 64.

41. Thomas Aquinas, *On Law, Morality, and Politics*, trans. Richard J. Regan, ed. William P. Baumgarth and Richard J. Regan, 2nd ed. (Indianapolis: Hackett, 2002), 3–4.

42. Moore, *George Washington's Rules of Civility*, 65.

43. George Washington to the Hebrew Congregation in Newport, Rhode Island, August 18, 1790, Founders Online, National Archives, https:// founders.archives.gov/documents/Washington/05-06-02-0135.

44. George Washington, "List of Books at Mount Vernon," 1764, Founders Online, National Archives, https://founders.archives.gov/documents /Washington/02-07-02-0216.

45. Thomas Gordon, "No. 39," in Trenchard and Gordon, *Cato's Letters*, vol. 2.
46. George Washington to Patrick Henry, March 28, 1778, Founders Online, National Archives, https://founders.archives.gov/documents/Washington /03-14-02-0310.
47. George Washington, "Farewell Address to the Army," November 2, 1783, Founders Online, National Archives, https://founders.archives.gov/documents/Washington/99-01-02-12012.
48. George Washington to The States, June 8, 1783, Founders Online, National Archives, https://founders.archives.gov/documents/Washington /99-01-02-11404.
49. Ibid.
50. George Washington to George Mason, April 5, 1769, Founders Online, National Archives, https://founders.archives.gov/documents/Washington/02-08-02-0132.
51. George Washington to Bryan Fairfax, July 20, 1774, Founders Online, National Archives, https://founders.archives.gov/documents/Washington/02-10-02-0081.
52. George Washington to George Mason, March 27, 1779, Founders Online, National Archives, https://founders.archives.gov/documents/Washington/03-19-02-0609.
53. George Washington to John Augustine Washington, May 12, 1779, Founders Online, National Archives, https://founders.archives.gov/documents/Washington/03-20-02-0402.
54. George Washington to Henry Laurens, November 5, 1779, Founders Online, National Archives, https://founders.archives.gov/documents /Washington/03-23-02-0152.
55. George Washington to John Jay, May 18, 1786, Founders Online, National Archives, https://founders.archives.gov/documents/Washington /04-04-02-0063.
56. George Washington to James Madison, November 5, 1786, Founders Online, National Archives, https://founders.archives.gov/documents /Washington/04-04-02-0299.
57. Farrand, *Records of the Federal Convention of 1787*, 1:3–4.
58. George Washington, "First Inaugural Address: Final Version," April 30, 1789, Founders Online, National Archives, https://founders.archives.gov/documents/Washington/05-02-02-0130-0003.
59. George Washington to the Pennsylvania Legislature, September 12, 1789, Founders Online, National Archives, https://founders.archives.gov/documents/Washington/05-04-02-0014.

60. George Washington to Lafayette, July 28, 1791, Founders Online, National Archives, https://founders.archives.gov/documents/Washington/05-08-02-0260.

61. George Washington to Bushrod Washington, November 9, 1787, Founders Online, National Archives, https://founders.archives.gov/documents/Washington/04-05-02-0388.

62. Alexander Hamilton, "Concerning the Public Conduct and Character of John Adams, Esq., President of the United States," [October 24, 1800], Founders Online, National Archives, https://founders.archives.gov/documents/Hamilton/01-25-02-0110-0002.

63. Thomas Jefferson to Jones, January 2, 1814, Founders Online, National Archives, https://founders.archives.gov/documents/Jefferson/03-07-02-0052.

64. James Madison to George Washington, June 20, 1792, Founders Online, National Archives, https://founders.archives.gov/documents/Madison/01-14-02-0294.

65. Thomas Jefferson, "Notes of Cabinet Meeting on Edmond Charles Genet," August 2, 1793, Founders Online, National Archives, https://founders.archives.gov/documents/Jefferson/01-26-02-0545.

66. George Washington, "Enclosure: GW's Draft for a Farewell Address," May 1796, Founders Online, National Archives, https://founders.archives.gov/documents/Washington/05-20-02-0108-0002.

67. George Washington, "Farewell Address," September 19, 1796, Founders Online, National Archives, https://founders.archives.gov/documents/Washington/05-20-02-0440-0002.

68. Ibid.

69. George Washington, "Last Will and Testament," July 9, 1799, Founders Online, National Archives, https://founders.archives.gov/documents/Washington/06-04-02-0404-0001.

70. Ibid.

71. George Washington to the US Senate and House of Representatives, December 7, 1796, Founders Online, National Archives, https://founders.archives.gov/documents/Washington/05-21-02-0142.

72. George Washington, "Last Will and Testament."

73. Albert Jay Nock, *Jefferson* (Harcourt Brace Jovanovich, 1926), 313.

74. George Washington to the US Senate and House, December 7, 1796, https://founders.archives.gov/documents/Washington/05-21-02-0142.

75. George Washington to Patrick Henry, January 15, 1799, Founders Online,

National Archives, https://founders.archives.gov/documents/Washing ton/06-03-02-0225.

76. George Washington to Bushrod Washington, May 5, 1799, Founders Online, National Archives, https://founders.archives.gov/documents /Washington/06-04-02-0037.

Eight: Moderation. James Madison and Alexander Hamilton's Constitution

1. James Madison, "Notes on Ancient and Modern Confederacies," [April–June?] 1786, Founders Online, National Archives, https://founders.ar chives.gov/documents/Madison/01-09-02-0001.

2. James Madison, "Federalist No. 55," [February 13], 1788, Founders Online, National Archives, https://founders.archives.gov/documents/Madi son/01-10-02-0292.

3. James Madison, "Federalist No. 10," [November 22], 1787, Founders Online, National Archives, https://founders.archives.gov/documents/Madi son/01-10-02-0178.

4. Ibid.

5. Jeffrey Rosen, "America Is Living James Madison's Nightmare," *Atlantic*, October 2018, https://www.theatlantic.com/magazine/archive/2018/10 /james-madison-mob-rule/568351/.

6. Daniel W. Howe, "The Political Psychology of the *Federalist*," *William and Mary Quarterly* 44, no. 3 (1987): 490–91, https://doi.org/10 .2307/1939767.

7. Daniel Walker Howe, *Making the American Self: Jonathan Edwards to Abraham Lincoln* (Oxford: Oxford University Press, 2009), 87–88.

8. Alexander Hamilton, "Federalist No. 78," [May 28], 1788, Founders Online, National Archives, https://founders.archives.gov/documents/Ham ilton/01-04-02-0241.

9. Howe, *Making the American Self*, p. 91.

10. James Madison, "Federalist No. 62," [February 27], 1788, Founders Online, National Archives, https://founders.archives.gov/documents/Madi son/01-10-02-0309.

11. Alexander Hamilton, "Federalist No. 71," [March 18, 1788], Founders Online, National Archives, https://founders.archives.gov/documents /Hamilton/01-04-02-0222.

12. Alexander Hamilton, "Rules for Philip Hamilton," [1800], Founders Online, National Archives, https://founders.archives.gov/documents/Ham ilton/01-25-02-0152.

13. E. P. Panagopoulos, "Hamilton's Notes in His Pay Book of the New York State Artillery Company," *American Historical Review* 62, no. 2 (1957): 317, https://doi.org/10.2307/1845185.

14. Ron Chernow, *Alexander Hamilton* (New York: Penguin, 2004), 52.

15. Alexander Hamilton, "Pay Book of the State Company of Artillery," [1777], Founders Online, National Archives, https://founders.archives .gov/documents/Hamilton/01-01-02-0350.

16. Ibid.

17. Plutarch, *Lycurgus*, trans. John Dryden and A. H. Clough, in vol. 1, A. H. Clough, *Plutarch's Lives: The Translation Called Dryden's* (Boston: Little, Brown, 1859), 102, 125, https://www.google.com/books/edition /Plutarch_s_Lives/0SQtAAAAYAAJ.

18. James Madison, "Commonplace Book," 1759–1772, Founders Online, National Archives, https://founders.archives.gov/documents/Madison /01-01-02-0002.

19. Howe, "Political Psychology of the *Federalist*," 489.

20. John Witherspoon, *The Dominion of Providence over the Passions of Men*, in *Political Sermons of the Founding Era, 1730–1805*, 2nd ed., ed. Ellis Sandoz (Indianapolis: Liberty Fund, 1998), 1:549, 557, OLL, https://oll .libertyfund.org/title/sandoz-political-sermons-of-the-american-found ing-era-vol-1-1730-1788--5.

21. Dennis F. Thompson, "Bibliography: The Education of a Founding Father. The Reading List for John Witherspoon's Course in Political Theory, as Taken by James Madison," *Political Theory* 4, no. 4 (1976): 523–29, http:// www.jstor.org/stable/191140.

22. Forrest McDonald, *Novus Ordo Seclorum: The Intellectual Origins of the Constitution* (Lawrence: University Press of Kansas, 1985), 188.

23. David Hume, "The Stoic," in David Hume, *Essays: Moral, Political, and Literary*, ed. Eugene F. Miller (Indianapolis: Liberty Fund, 1987), 148, OLL, https://oll.libertyfund.org/title/hume-essays-moral-political-liter ary-lf-ed.

24. David Hume, "The Sceptic," in Hume, *Essays: Moral, Political, and Literary*, 176.

25. Ibid., 167–68.

26. Douglass Adair, " 'That Politics May Be Reduced to a Science': David Hume, James Madison, and the Tenth Federalist," *Huntington Library Quarterly* 20, no. 4 (1957): 343–60, https://doi.org/10.2307/3816276.

27. David Hume, "Idea of a Perfect Commonwealth," in Hume, *Essays: Moral, Political, and Literary*, 523.

28. Madison, "Federalist No. 55," https://founders.archives.gov/documents /Madison/01-10-02-0292.

29. David Hume, "Idea of a Perfect Commonwealth," 527–28.

30. Madison, "Federalist No. 10," https://founders.archives.gov/documents /Madison/01-10-02-0178.

31. Ibid.

32. James Madison, "Federalist No. 63," [March 1], 1788, Founders Online, National Archives, https://founders.archives.gov/documents/Madison /01-10-02-0312.

33. James Madison, "Federalist No. 49," [February 2], 1788, Founders Online, National Archives, https://founders.archives.gov/documents/Madi son/01-10-02-0270.

34. Madison, "Federalist No. 10," https://founders.archives.gov/documents /Madison/01-10-02-0178.

35. James Madison, "Federalist No. 51," [February 6], 1788, Founders Online, National Archives, https://founders.archives.gov/documents/Madi son/01-10-02-0279.

36. Alexander Hamilton, "Philo Camillus No. I," [July 27, 1795], Founders Online, National Archives, https://founders.archives.gov/documents /Hamilton/01-18-02-0313.

37. Hume, *Treatise of Human Nature*, 415, 418.

38. Madison, "Federalist No. 51," https://founders.archives.gov/documents /Madison/01-10-02-0279.

39. Alexander Hamilton, "Federalist No. 72," [March 19, 1788], Founders Online, National Archives, https://founders.archives.gov/documents /Hamilton/01-04-02-0223.

40. Alexander Hamilton, "Federalist No. 1," [October 27, 1787], Founders Online, National Archives, https://founders.archives.gov/documents /Hamilton/01-04-02-0152.

41. Maynard Smith, "Reason, Passion and Political Freedom in the *Federalist*," *Journal of Politics* 22, no. 3 (August 1960): 530, https://doi.org /10.2307/2126895.

42. Alexander Hamilton, "Federalist No. 84," [May 28, 1788], Founders Online, National Archives, https://founders.archives.gov/documents/Ham ilton/01-04-02-0247.

43. Alexander Hamilton, "Federalist No. 57," [February 19, 1788], Founders Online, National Archives, https://founders.archives.gov/documents /Hamilton/01-04-02-0206.

44. Adam Smith, *An Inquiry into the Nature and Causes of the Wealth of Nations*,

ed. Edwin Cannan (London: Methuen & Co., 1904), 1:421, OLL, https://oll.libertyfund.org/title/smith-an-inquiry-into-the-nature-and -causes-of-the-wealth-of-nations-cannan-ed-vol-1.

45. Hamilton, "Federalist No. 72," https://founders.archives.gov/documents /Hamilton/01-04-02-0223.

46. Alexander Hamilton, "Notes," [June 18, 1787], Founders Online, National Archives, https://founders.archives.gov/documents/Hamilton/01 -04-02-0098-0002.

47. Ibid.

48. Alexander Hamilton to Rufus King, January 5, 1800, Founders Online, National Archives, https://founders.archives.gov/documents/Hamilton /01-24-02-0127.

49. Alexander Hamilton to Edward Carrington, May 26, 1792, Founders Online, National Archives, https://founders.archives.gov/documents /Hamilton/01-11-02-0349.

50. Alexander Hamilton to Theodore Sedgwick, May 10, 1800, Founders Online, National Archives, https://founders.archives.gov/documents /Hamilton/01-24-02-0387.

51. Hamilton, "Concerning the Public Conduct and Character of John Adams."

52. Alexander Hamilton to James A. Bayard, August 6, 1800, Founders Online, National Archives, https://founders.archives.gov/documents/Ham ilton/01-25-02-0040.

53. Alexander Hamilton to Harrison Gray Otis, [December 23, 1800], Founders Online, National Archives, https://founders.archives.gov/docu ments/Hamilton/01-25-02-0140.

54. Alexander Hamilton to James A. Bayard, December 27, 1800, Founders Online, National Archives, https://founders.archives.gov/documents /Hamilton/01-25-02-0146.

55. William Kent, *Memoirs and Letters of James Kent* (Boston: Little, Brown, 1898), 327–28, https://www.google.com/books/edition/Memoirs_and _Letters_of_James_Kent/9uMEAAAAYAAJ.

56. Hamilton to Bayard, April [16–21], 1802, Founders Online, National Archives, https://founders.archives.gov/documents/Hamilton /01-25-02-0321.

57. Chernow, *Alexander Hamilton*, 659.

58. Alexander Hamilton to Elizabeth Hamilton, March [16–17], 1803, Founders Online, National Archives, https://founders.archives.gov/docu ments/Hamilton/01-26-02-0001-0071.

59. Ibid., [July 10, 1804], Founders Online, National Archives, https://found ers.archives.gov/documents/Hamilton/01-26-02-0001-0262; Chernow, *Washington*, 681, 706.

60. Ibid., [July 4, 1804], Founders Online, National Archives, https://found ers.archives.gov/documents/Hamilton/01-26-02-0001-0248.

61. James Madison to Thomas Jefferson, [March 13], 1791, Founders On-line, National Archives, https://founders.archives.gov/documents/Madi son/01-13-02-0306.

62. Colleen A. Sheehan, *The Mind of James Madison: The Legacy of Classical Republicanism* (Cambridge: Cambridge University Press, 2015), 127.

63. M. De Condorcet, *Outlines of an Historical View of the Progress of the Human Mind* (Philadelphia: Lang and Ustick, 1796), 146, 149, OLL, https://oll.libertyfund.org/title/condorcet-outlines-of-an-historical -view-of-the-progress-of-the-human-mind.

64. Ibid., 148, 150.

65. James Madison, "Notes for the *National Gazette* Essays," [ca. Decem-ber 19, 1791–March 3, 1792]," Founders Online, National Archives, https://founders.archives.gov/documents/Madison/01-14-02-0144.

66. Ibid.

67. James Madison, "For the *National Gazette*," [ca. December 19], 1791, Founders Online, National Archives, https://founders.archives.gov/docu ments/Madison/01-14-02-0145.

68. Madison, "Notes for the *National Gazette* Essays."

69. Madison, "For the *National Gazette*."

70. James Madison to Unknown, March 1836, Founders Online, Na-tional Archives, https://founders.archives.gov/documents/Madison/99 -02-02-3240.

71. Ibid.

72. Colleen A. Sheehan, *James Madison and the Spirit of Republican Self-Government* (Cambridge: Cambridge University Press, 2009), 40.

Nine: Tranquility. Adams and Jefferson's Reconciliation

1. Thomas Jefferson, "First Inaugural Address," March 4, 1801, Founders Online, National Archives, https://founders.archives.gov/documents/Jef ferson/01-33-02-0116-0004.

2. Ibid.

3. Thomas Jefferson to Abigail Adams, June 13, 1804, Founders Online, National Archives, https://founders.archives.gov/documents/Jefferson /01-43-02-0472.

4. Ibid., September 11, 1804, Founders Online, National Archives, https://founders.archives.gov/documents/Jefferson/01-44-02-0341.

5. Thomas Jefferson to Benjamin Rush, December 5, 1811, Founders Online, National Archives, https://founders.archives.gov/documents/Jeffer son/03-04-02-0248.

6. Benjamin Rush to John Adams, December 16, 1811, Founders Online, National Archives, https://founders.archives.gov/documents/Adams/99 -02-02-5725.

7. John Adams to Thomas Jefferson, January 1, 1812, Founders Online, National Archives, https://founders.archives.gov/documents/Adams/99-02 -02-5735.

8. Thomas Jefferson to John Adams, January 23, 1812, Founders Online, National Archives, https://founders.archives.gov/documents/Jefferson /03-04-02-0339.

9. Ibid., January 21, 1812, Founders Online, National Archives, https://founders.archives.gov/documents/Jefferson/03-04-02-0334.

10. John Adams to Thomas Jefferson, February 3, 1812, Founders Online, National Archives, https://founders.archives.gov/documents/Adams/99- 02-02-5749.

11. Ibid., June 28, 1812, Founders Online, National Archives, https://found ers.archives.gov/documents/Adams/99-02-02-5816.

12. Ibid., August 9, 1813, Founders Online, National Archives, https://founders.archives.gov/documents/Adams/99-02-02-6124.

13. Akihito Matsumoto, "Happiness and Religion: Joseph Priestley's 'Theological Utilitarianism,'" *Kyoto Economic Review* 79, no. 2 (167) (2010): 58, http://www.jstor.org/stable/43213392.

14. Jeremy Bentham, "Elogia—Locke, Priestley, Beccaria, Johnson," in *The Works of Jeremy Bentham*, ed. John Bowring (Edinburgh: William Tait, 1843), 10:142, https://oll.libertyfund.org/title/bentham-the-works-of -jeremy-bentham-vol-10-memoirs-part-i-and-correspondence.

15. Thomas Jefferson to John Adams, August 22, 1813, Founders Online, National Archives, https://founders.archives.gov/documents/Jefferson /03-06-02-0351.

16. Thomas Jefferson, "Doctrines of Jesus Compared with Others," April 21, 1803, Founders Online, National Archives, https://founders.archives .gov/documents/Jefferson/01-40-02-0178-0002.

17. Ibid.

18. Thomas Jefferson, "Doctrines of Jesus."

19. John Adams to Thomas Jefferson, September 22, 1813, Founders Online,

National Archives, https://founders.archives.gov/documents/Adams/99
-02-02-6159.

20. Ibid., September 1813, Founders Online, National Archives, https://
founders.archives.gov/documents/Adams/99-02-02-6170.

21. Ibid.

22. Ibid., December 25, 1813, Founders Online, National Archives, https://
founders.archives.gov/documents/Adams/99-02-02-6217.

23. Ibid.

24. Mark 12:29–31 (King James Version).

25. John Adams to Thomas Jefferson, December 25, 1813.

26. Ibid., June 28, 1812.

27. Ibid., December 3, 1813, Founders Online, National Archives, https://
founders.archives.gov/documents/Adams/99-02-02-6209.

28. Thomas Jefferson to John Adams, October 14, 1816, Founders Online,
National Archives, https://founders.archives.gov/documents/Jefferson
/03-10-02-0332.

29. John Adams to Thomas Jefferson, December 12, 1816, Founders Online,
National Archives, https://founders.archives.gov/documents/Adams/99
-02-02-6670.

30. John Adams to Thomas Jefferson, February 1814 to March 3, 1814,
Founders Online, National Archives, https://founders.archives.gov/docu
ments/Adams/99-02-02-6258.

31. John Adams's copy of Joseph Priestley, *A Comparison of the Institutions of Moses
with Those of the Hindoos and Other Ancient Nations* (Northumberland, UK:
A. Kennedy, 1799), 23, https://archive.org/details/comparisonofinst00prie/.

32. John Adams to Thomas Jefferson, February 1814 to March 3, 1814.

33. Priestley, *Comparison of the Institutions of Moses*, 156.

34. Charles Wilkins, *Bhagvat-Geeta* (London: Nourse, 1785), 41, 45, 58.

35. Ibid., 56, 63–65.

36. John Adams to Thomas Jefferson, December 25, 1813, Founders Online, National Archives, https://founders.archives.gov/documents/Jeffer
son/03-07-02-0040.

37. Ibid., March 2, 1816, Founders Online, National Archives, https://found
ers.archives.gov/documents/Adams/99-02-02-6585.

38. Thomas Jefferson to John Adams, April 8, 1816, Founders Online, National Archives, https://founders.archives.gov/documents/Jefferson/03
-09-02-0446.

39. Ibid., June 27, 1813, Founders Online, National Archives, https://found
ers.archives.gov/documents/Jefferson/03-06-02-0206.

40. Thomas Jefferson to William Short, October 31, 1819, Founders Online, National Archives, https://founders.archives.gov/documents/Jefferson/03-15-02-0141-0001.

41. Thomas Jefferson, "Enclosure: Syllabus of the Doctrines of Epicurus," [before October 31, 1819], Founders Online, National Archives, https://founders.archives.gov/documents/Jefferson/03-15-02-0141-0002.

42. Ibid.

43. Thomas Jefferson to Short, October 31, 1819, https://founders.archives .gov/documents/Jefferson/03-15-02-0141-0001.

44. Thomas Jefferson to John Adams, April 8, 1816, Founders Online, National Archives, https://founders.archives.gov/documents/Jefferson/03 -09-02-0446.

45. John Adams to Thomas Jefferson, May 6, 1816, Founders Online, National Archives, https://founders.archives.gov/documents/Jefferson/03 -10-02-0006.

46. Ibid.

47. Antoine Nicolas de Condorcet, *Sketch for a Historical Picture of the Progress of the Human Mind*, trans. June Barraclough (New York: Noonday, 1955), 179.

48. Ibid., 4–5.

49. John Adams to Thomas Jefferson, July 16, 1814, Founders Online, National Archives, https://founders.archives.gov/documents/Adams/99-02 -02-6321.

50. Ibid., November 13, 1815, Founders Online, National Archives, https:// founders.archives.gov/documents/Adams/99-02-02-6539.

51. Ibid., February 2, 1816, Founders Online, National Archives, https:// founders.archives.gov/documents/Adams/99-02-02-6575.

52. Thomas Jefferson to John Adams, December 10, 1819, Founders Online, National Archives, https://founders.archives.gov/documents/Jefferson/03-15-02-0240.

53. John Adams to Thomas Jefferson, December 21, 1819, Founders Online, National Archives, https://founders.archives.gov/documents/Adams/99 -02-02-7287.

54. Ibid.

55. Thomas Jefferson to John Holmes, April 22, 1820, Founders Online, National Archives, https://founders.archives.gov/documents/Jefferson /03-15-02-0518.

56. Ibid.

57. Dennis C. Rasmussen, *Fears of a Setting Sun: The Disillusionment of America's Founders* (Princeton, NJ: Princeton University Press, 2021), 4.
58. Thomas Jefferson to Isaac Story, December 5, 1801, Founders Online, National Archives, https://founders.archives.gov/documents/Jefferson /01-36-02-0025.
59. Thomas Jefferson to John Adams, November 13, 1818, Founders Online, National Archives, https://founders.archives.gov/documents/Jefferson/03-13-02-0353.
60. Ibid., June 27, 1822, Founders Online, National Archives, https://founders.archives.gov/documents/Jefferson/98-01-02-2907.
61. Ibid., August 15, 1820, Founders Online, National Archives, https://founders.archives.gov/documents/Jefferson/03-16-02-0152.
62. Ibid., February 15, 1825, Founders Online, National Archives, https://founders.archives.gov/documents/Jefferson/98-01-02-4962.
63. Ibid.
64. John Adams to Thomas Jefferson, January 14, 1826, Founders Online, National Archives, https://founders.archives.gov/documents/Adams/99-02-02-8010.

Ten: Cleanliness. John Quincy Adams's Composure
1. John Quincy Adams, *Lectures on Rhetoric and Oratory* (Cambridge, MA: Hilliard and Metcalf, 1810), 1:367–78, https://www.google.com/books/edition/Lectures_on_Rhetoric_and_Oratory/WRGqbsLHBO4C.
2. Ibid., 364–65.
3. John Quincy Adams to John Adams, May 30, 1811, Founders Online, National Archives, https://founders.archives.gov/documents/Adams/99-03-02-1975.
4. John Quincy Adams to George Washington Adams, November 28, 1827, in John Quincy Adams, *Diaries*, ed. David Waldstreicher (New York: Library of America, 2017), 2:7.
5. John Quincy Adams, *Diaries*, ed. David Waldstreicher, vol. 1 (New York: Library of America, 2017), 740.
6. November 25, 1793, in John Quincy Adams, *Diaries*, 1:60.
7. May 16, 1792, in John Quincy Adams, *Diaries*, 1:56.
8. Ibid., 56–58.
9. Abigail Adams to John Quincy Adams, January 19, 1780, Founders Online, National Archives, https://founders.archives.gov/documents/Adams/04-03-02-0207.

10. Ibid., March 20, 1780, Founders Online, National Archives, https://founders.archives.gov/documents/Adams/04-03-02-0240.
11. Ibid.
12. Ibid.
13. John Adams to John Quincy Adams, May 19, 1783, Founders Online, National Archives, https://founders.archives.gov/documents/Adams/04-05-02-0088.
14. Jean Barbeyrac, *An Historical and Critical Account of the Science of Morality, and the Progress It Has Made in the World*, trans. George Carew, in Samuel von Pufendorf, *Of the Law of Nature and Nations*, trans. Basil Kennett (London: 1729), 1–2, https://www.google.com/books/edition/Of_the_Law_of_Nature_and_Nations/7MchAQAAMAAJ.
15. John Adams to John Quincy Adams, March 16, 1777, Founders Online, National Archives, https://founders.archives.gov/documents/Adams/04-02-02-0130.
16. Ibid., May 14, 1781, Founders Online, National Archives, https://founders.archives.gov/documents/Adams/04-04-02-0078.
17. Ibid., December 14, 1781, Founders Online, National Archives, https://founders.archives.gov/documents/Adams/04-04-02-0176.
18. October 15, 1794, in John Quincy Adams, *Diaries*, 1:70.
19. October 31, 1803, in John Quincy Adams, *Diaries*, 1:131.
20. July 11, 1812, in John Quincy Adams, *Diaries*, 1:298.
21. November 30, 1814, in John Quincy Adams, *Diaries*, 1:401.
22. October 16, 1816, in John Quincy Adams, *Diaries*, 1:494.
23. John Quincy Adams, *Diaries*, 1:746.
24. John Quincy Adams to George Washington Adams, April 4, 1813, Founders Online, National Archives, https://founders.archives.gov/documents/Adams/99-03-02-2270.
25. Ibid., "Letter VII," in *Letters of John Quincy Adams to His Son, on the Bible and Its Teachings* (Auburn, NY: James M. Alden, 1850), 94, 99.
26. Ibid.
27. March 3, 1820, in John Quincy Adams, *Diaries*, 1:662.
28. February 9, 1825, in John Quincy Adams, *Diaries*, 2:120, 122.
29. April 30, 1825, in John Quincy Adams, *Diaries*, 2:131.
30. June 13, 1825, in John Quincy Adams, *Diaries*, 2:140–41.
31. December 31, 1825, in John Quincy Adams, *Diaries*, 2:157.
32. October 30, 1826, in John Quincy Adams, *Diaries*, 2:179–80.
33. Ibid.
34. December 25, 1820, in John Quincy Adams, *Diaries*, 1:710–11.

35. John Quincy Adams, "Inaugural Address," March 4, 1825, *The Avalon Project*, https://avalon.law.yale.edu/19th_century/qadams.asp.
36. John Quincy Adams, "First Annual Message," December 6, 1825, The Miller Center, https://millercenter.org/the-presidency/presidential-speeches/december-6-1825-first-annual-message.
37. December 31, 1825, in John Quincy Adams, *Diaries*, 2:157.
38. December 17, 1827, in John Quincy Adams, *Diaries*, 2:204.
39. February 28, 1829, in John Quincy Adams, *Diaries*, 2:242.
40. March 4, 1829, in John Quincy Adams, *Diaries*, 2:247–48.
41. July 1827, in Adams, *Diaries*, John Quincy Adams Digital Diary, https://www.masshist.org/publications/jqadiaries/index.php/document/jqadiaries-v37-1827-07-xx-p236.
42. May 3, 1829, in John Quincy Adams, *Diaries*, 2:260.
43. May 4, 1829, in John Quincy Adams, *Diaries*, 2:260–61.
44. May 5, 1829, in John Quincy Adams, *Diaries*, 2:261.
45. May 7, 1829, in John Quincy Adams, *Diaries*, 2:262.
46. December 31, 1829, in John Quincy Adams, *Diaries*, 2:270.
47. April 1, 1829, in John Quincy Adams, *Diaries*, 2:254.
48. May 14, 1830, in John Quincy Adams, *Diaries*, 2:285.
49. August 14, 1830, in John Quincy Adams, *Diaries*, 2:290–91.
50. June 22, 1833, in John Quincy Adams, *Diaries*, 2:382.
51. Rhonda Barlow, "'He Plants Trees for the Benefit of Later Generations': John Quincy Adams's Motto," *The Beehive* (blog), Massachusetts Historical Society online, last modified May 8, 2019, https://www.masshist.org/beehiveblog/2017/06/he-plants-trees-for-the-benefit-of-later-generations-john-quincy-adamss-motto/.
52. June 22, 1833, in John Quincy Adams, *Diaries*, 2:382.
53. January 11, 1831, in John Quincy Adams, *Diaries*, 2:300–303.
54. January 17, 1831, in John Quincy Adams, *Diaries*, 2:307.
55. Paul C. Nagel, *John Quincy Adams: A Public Life, A Private Life* (New York: Alfred A. Knopf, 1997), chap. 14, Kindle edition.
56. John Quincy Adams, *An Oration Delivered Before the Inhabitants of the Town of Newburyport, At Their Request, on the Sixty-First Anniversary of the Declaration of Independence, July 4th, 1837* (Newburyport, MA: Charles Whipple, 1837), 50, https://www.google.com/books/edition/An_Oration_Delivered_Before_the_Inhabita/nll2AAAAMAAJ.
57. Ibid., 55–56, quoting Isaiah 61:1, Luke 2:10 (King James Version).
58. John Quincy Adams, *Oration Delivered Before the Inhabitants of the Town of Newburyport*, 5–6.

59. October 27, 1840, in John Quincy Adams, *Diaries*, 2:593.

60. December 11, 1840, in John Quincy Adams, *Diaries*, 2:600.

61. December 12, 1840, in John Quincy Adams, *Diaries*, 2:601.

62. February 24, 1841, in John Quincy Adams, *Diaries*, 2:613.

63. March 9, 1841, in John Quincy Adams, *Diaries*, 2:615.

64. March 29, 1841, in John Quincy Adams, *Diaries*, 2:618.

65. John Minor Botts, *The Great Rebellion: Its Secret History, Rise, Progress, and Disastrous Failure* (New York: Harper & Brothers, 1866), 96, https://www.google.com/books/edition/The_Great_Rebellion/Vy4OAAAAIAAJ; John Stauffer, *Giants: The Parallel Lives of Frederick Douglass and Abraham Lincoln* (Twelve, 2008), 166.

66. J. F. Johnson, *Proceedings of the General Anti-Slavery Convention* (London: John Snow, 1843), 308.

67. Quoted in Nagel, *John Quincy Adams*, 386.

68. December 3, 1844, in vol. 2, Adams, *Diaries*, 738.

69. Nagel, *John Quincy Adams*, 414.

70. October 31, 1846, in vol. 2, Adams, *Diaries*, 761.

71. William Shakespeare, *The Merchant of Venice*, ed. A. R. Braunmuller (New York: Penguin, 2017), 4:1.392.

72. Frederick Douglass, "Self-Made Men: An Address," March 1893, in Frederick Douglass, *Speeches & Writings*, ed. David Blight (New York: Library of America, 2022), 888.

Eleven: Justice. Frederick Douglass and Abraham Lincoln's Self-Reliance

1. Frederick Douglass, *Narrative of the Life of Frederick Douglass, An American Slave* (Boston: Anti-Slavery Office, 1845), 33–34, 39, https://www.google.com/books/edition/Narrative_of_the_Life_of_Frederick_Dou gl/ds08RYrDBPIC; Frederick Douglass, *My Bondage and My Freedom* (New York: Miller, Orton & Mulligan, 1855), 161, 157, 272, https://www.google.com/books/edition/My_Bondage_and_My_Freedom/rKk JAAAAIAAJ.

2. David W. Blight, "The Peculiar Dialogue Between Caleb Bingham and Frederick Douglass," in Caleb Bingham, *The Columbian Orator*, ed. David Blight (New York: New York University Press, 1998), xvii.

3. Douglass, *Bondage and Freedom*, 157.

4. Bingham, *The Columbian Orator*, 56.

5. Stauffer, *Giants*, 63.

6. Douglass, *Bondage and Freedom*, 157.

7. Bingham, *The Columbian Orator*, 211.

8. Douglass, *Bondage and Freedom*, 158.

9. Ibid., 159, 275.

10. Blight, "The Peculiar Dialogue," xviii.

11. William H. Herndon and Jesse W. Weik, *Abraham Lincoln: The True Story of a Great Life* (New York: D. Appleton, 1900), 1:34, https://www.google.com/books/edition/Abraham_Lincoln/-hGcH1GDMvsC.

12. Jeremiah Goodrich, *Murray's English Reader* (Albany, NY: S. Shaw, 1829), 2, 25–26, https://www.google.com/books/edition/Murray_s_English_Reader_Or_Pieces_in_Pro/lWYQAQAAIAAJ.

13. Douglass, "Self-Made Men," 877, 883.

14. Ibid., 878, 883, 885.

15. Ibid., 865–66.

16. Ibid., 869–70, 875–76, 887–88.

17. Ibid., 889.

18. Ward H. Lamon, *The Life of Abraham Lincoln: From His Birth to His Inauguration as President* (Boston: James R. Osgood, 1872), 446, https://www.google.com/books/edition/The_Life_of_Abraham_Lincoln/-qfVEWN0OEsC.

19. Henry Clay, "The American System," February 2, 3, and 6, 1832, in *Classic Speeches, 1830–1993*, comp. Robert C. Byrd and ed. Wendy Wolff, vol. 3, *The Senate, 1789–1989* (Washington, DC: US Government Printing Office, 1994), 100, https://www.senate.gov/artandhistory/history/common/generic/Classic_Speeches.htm.

20. Abraham Lincoln, "Eulogy on Henry Clay," in *The Collected Works of Abraham Lincoln*, ed. Roy P. Basler (New Brunswick, NJ: Rutgers University Press, 1953), 2:124, 126, https://quod.lib.umich.edu/l/lincoln/lincoln2/1:193?rgn=div1;singlegenre=All;sort=occur;subview=detail;type=simple;view=fulltext.

21. Abraham Lincoln, "Address Before the Young Men's Lyceum of Springfield, Illinois," January 27, 1838, in *Collected Works of Abraham Lincoln*, 1:109–11, 112–14, https://quod.lib.umich.edu/l/lincoln/lincoln1/1:130?rgn=div1;singlegenre=All;sort=occur;subview=detail;type=simple;view=fulltext.

22. Ibid., 1:114–15.

23. William H. Townsend, "Lincoln and Liquor," *Atlantic*, February 1934, https://www.theatlantic.com/magazine/archive/1934/02/lincoln-and-liquor/651563/.

24. Abraham Lincoln, "Temperance Address," in *Collected Works of Abraham Lincoln*, 1: 278–79.

25. Ibid., 1:273.

26. Abraham Lincoln, "Speech at Peoria, Illinois," October 16, 1854, in *Collected Works of Abraham Lincoln*, 2:266, https://quod.lib.umich.edu/l/lincoln/lincoln2/1:282?rgn=div1;singlegenre=All;sort=occur;subview=detail;type=simple;view=fulltext.

27. Abraham Lincoln, "Speech Delivered Before the First Republican State Convention of Illinois," May 29, 1856, Northern Illinois University, 253–54, 267, https://digital.lib.niu.edu/islandora/object/niu-lincoln%3A38321.

28. Abraham Lincoln, "To Henry L. Pierce and Others," in *Collected Works of Abraham Lincoln*, 3:376, https://quod.lib.umich.edu/l/lincoln/lincoln3/1:98?rgn=div1;singlegenre=All;sort=occur;subview=detail;type=simple;view=fulltext.

29. Abraham Lincoln, "Speech in Independence Hall, Philadelphia, Pennsylvania," February 22, 1861, in *Collected Works of Abraham Lincoln*, 4:240, https://quod.lib.umich.edu/l/lincoln/lincoln4/1:376?rgn=div1;singlegenre=All;sort=occur;subview=detail;type=simple;view=fulltext.

30. *Dred Scott v. Sandford*, 60 U.S. 393 (1857).

31. Abraham Lincoln, "Speech at Springfield, Illinois," June 26, 1857, in *Collected Works of Abraham Lincoln*, 2:406, https://quod.lib.umich.edu/l/lincoln/lincoln2/1:438?rgn=div1;singlegenre=All;sort=occur;subview=detail;type=simple;view=fulltext.

32. Frederick Douglass, "What to the Slave Is the Fourth of July?: An Address," July 5, 1852, in Douglass, *Speeches & Writings*, 223, 227, 244.

33. Ibid., 245–46.

34. Farrand, *Records of the Federal Convention of 1787*, 2:417; Sean Wilentz, *No Property in Man: Slavery and Antislavery at the Nation's Founding* (Cambridge, MA: Harvard University Press, 2018), xii.

35. Frederick Douglass, "The American Constitution and the Slave: An Address," March 26, 1860, in Douglass, *Speeches & Writings*, 428.

36. Abraham Lincoln, "Address at Cooper Institute, New York City," February 27, 1860, in *Collected Works of Abraham Lincoln*, 3:545, https://quod.lib.umich.edu/l/lincoln/lincoln3/1:199?rgn=div1;singlegenre=All;sort=occur;subview=detail;type=simple;view=fulltext.

37. David Herbert Donald, *Lincoln* (New York: Simon & Schuster, 1995), 388–89.

38. Ibid., 404–5.

39. Abraham Lincoln, "First Inaugural Address," in *Collected Works of Abraham*

Lincoln, 4:263; Frederick Douglass, "The Inaugural Address," in Douglass, *Speeches & Writings*, 473–75.

40. Frederick Douglass, "The President and His Speeches," in Douglass, *Speeches & Writings*, 593–94.

41. Stauffer, *Giants*, 19–20; Frederick Douglass, *The Life and Times of Frederick Douglass, from 1817 to 1882* (London: Christian Age Office, 1882), 321.

42. Eric Foner, *The Fiery Trial: Abraham Lincoln and American Slavery* (New York: W. W. Norton, 2010), 335.

43. Abraham Lincoln, "Second Inaugural Address," in vol. 8, *Collected Works of Abraham Lincoln*, ed. Roy P. Basler (New Brunswick: Rutgers University Press, 1953), 333, https://quod.lib.umich.edu/l/lincoln/lincoln8/1:711?rgn=div1;singlegenre=All;sort=occur;subview=detail;type=simple;view=fulltext.

44. Douglass, *Life and Times*, 320–21.

45. Quoted in David W. Blight, *Frederick Douglass: Prophet of Freedom* (New York: Simon & Schuster, 2018), 442.

46. Frederick Douglass, "What the Black Man Wants: An Address," January 26, 1865, in Douglass, *Speeches & Writings*, 690.

47. Frederick Douglass, "Lessons of the Hour: An Address," January 9, 1894, in Douglass, *Speeches & Writings*, 904, 913.

48. Frederick Douglass, "The Color Line," *North American Review*, June 1881, in Douglass, *Speeches & Writings*, 810, 814, 818–19, 821.

49. Douglass, "Lessons of the Hour," 937–38.

50. Douglass, "What the Black Man Wants," 698.

51. Douglass, "Self-Made Men," 878.

52. Ibid., 879.

53. Frederick Douglass, "Address of Hon. Fred. Douglass, Delivered before the National Convention of Colored Men, at Louisville, Kentucky," September 24, 1883, Colored Conventions Project, https://omeka.coloredconventions.org/items/show/554.

54. Ibid.

55. Frederick Douglass, "Blessings of Liberty and Education," September 3, 1984, *Teaching American History*, https://teachingamericanhistory.org/document/blessings-of-liberty-and-education/.

Twelve: Silence. Pursuing Happiness Today

1. Jeffrey Rosen, *Louis D. Brandeis: American Prophet* (New Haven, CT: Yale University Press, 2016), 9.

2. *Whitney v. California*, 274 U.S. 357 (1927).

3. Rosen, *Louis D. Brandeis*, 152–53.

4. Alfred Zimmern, *The Greek Commonwealth: Politics & Economics in Fifth-Century Athens*, 4th ed. (Oxford: Clarendon Press, 1924), 432, https://www.google.com/books/edition/The_Greek_Commonwealth/qDcbAAAAYAAJ.

5. Quoted in Rosen, *Louis D. Brandeis*, 123–24.

6. Thomas Jefferson to William G. Munford, June 18, 1799, Founders Online, National Archives, https://founders.archives.gov/documents/Jefferson/01-31-02-0112.

7. David Hume, *A Letter from a Gentleman to His Friend in Edinburgh*, in *The Complete Works of David Hume*, Series Seven (Delphi Classics, 2016), Kindle edition; Hume, *Treatise of Human Nature*, 1; Thomas Gordon, "No. 62," in vol. 2, John Trenchard and Thomas Gordon, *Cato's Letters*; Baruch Spinoza, *A Theologico-Political Treatise*, trans. R. H. M. Elwes, in vol. 1, *The Chief Works of Benedict de Spinoza* (London: George Bell and Sons, 1891), OLL, https://oll.libertyfund.org/title/elwes-the-chief-works-of-benedict-de-spinoza-vol-1.

8. Rosen, *Louis D. Brandeis*, 9–10.

9. Ibid., 8.

10. Ibid., 25–26.

11. *Olmstead v. United States*, 277 U.S. 438 (1928).

12. *The Slaughterhouse Cases*, 83 U.S. 36 (1872); *Butchers' Union Co. v. Crescent City Co.*, 111 U.S. 746, 764 (1884) (Bradley, J., concurring).

13. *Meyer v. Nebraska*, 262 U.S. 390 (1923).

14. *Obergefell v. Hodges*, 576 U.S. ___ (2015).

15. Irin Carmon, "Exclusive Justice Ruth Bader Ginsburg interview: Full transcript," *MSNBC*, February 17, 2015, https://www.msnbc.com/msnbc/exclusive-justice-ruth-bader-ginsburg-interview-full-transcript-msna531191.

16. Rosen, *Conversations with RBG*, 43.

17. Ruth Bader Ginsburg, Mary Hartnett, and Wendy W. Williams, *My Own Words* (New York: Simon & Schuster, 2016), 5.

18. Rosen, *Conversations with RBG*, 99.

19. Ibid., 42–43.

20. Ginsburg, Hartnett, and Williams, *My Own Words*, 10–11.

21. Alexis de Tocqueville, *Democracy in America*, trans. Gerald E. Bevan (New York: Penguin, 2003), 55, 637, Kindle edition.

22. Ibid., 587, 625.

23. Ibid., 611–13.
24. Ralph Waldo Emerson, "Self-Reliance," in *The Works of Ralph Waldo Emerson*, Fireside Edition (Boston: 1909), 2:60–61, OLL, https://oll .libertyfund.org/title/emerson-the-works-of-ralph-waldo-emerson-vol -2-essays-first-series.
25. Ralph Waldo Emerson, "Boston," *The Atlantic*, January 1892, https:// www.theatlantic.com/magazine/archive/1892/01/boston/539493/.
26. Ralph Waldo Emerson, "The Over-Soul," in *Works of Ralph Waldo Emerson*, vol. 2.
27. Ralph Waldo Emerson, "The Poet," in *Works of Ralph Waldo Emerson*, 3:82, OLL, https://oll.libertyfund.org/title/emerson-the-works-of-ralph -waldo-emerson-vol-3-essays-second-series.
28. David Hoffman. *A Course of Legal Study: Addressed to Students and the Profession Generally* (Baltimore: Joseph Neal, 1836).
29. Ellwood V. Cubberly, *The History of Education: Educational Practice and Progress Considered as a Phase of the Development and Spread of Western Civilization* (Boston: Houghton Mifflin, 1920), 690, https://www.google .com/books/edition/The_History_of_Education/Rq8VAAAAIAAJ.
30. Horace Mann, "Lecture VI: On District School Libraries," in Horace Mann, *Lectures on Education* (Boston: WM. B. Fowle and N. Capen, 1845), 280, https://www.google.com/books/edition/Lectures_on_Edu cation/WfMSAAAAIAAJ.
31. Irvin G. Wyllie, *The Self-Made Man in America: The Myth of Rags to Riches* (New Brunswick, NJ: Rutgers University Press, 1954), 36, 42.
32. *Everson v. Board of Education*, 330 U.S. 1 (1947).
33. *Engel v. Vitale*, 370 U.S. 421 (1962).
34. *Stone v. Graham*, 449 U.S. 39 (1980).
35. Jess McHugh, "The Man Who Taught Millions of Americans to Read Before Being Forgotten," *Washington Post* online, May 23, 2021, https:// www.washingtonpost.com/history/2021/05/23/william-holmes-mc guffey-readers-schools/.
36. Christopher Lasch, *The Culture of Narcissism: American Life in an Age of Diminishing Expectations* (New York: W. W. Norton, 1991), xv.
37. Peter Salovey and John D. Mayer, "Emotional Intelligence," *Imagination, Cognition and Personality* 9, no. 3 (March 1990): 189, https://doi .org/10.2190/DUGG-P24E-52WK-6CDG.
38. Daniel Goleman, *Emotional Intelligence: Why It Can Matter More Than IQ* (New York: Bantam Books, 2005), xv, 9, 83.
39. Reuven Bar-On, "Emotional Intelligence: An Integral Part of Positive

Psychology," *South African Journal of Psychology* 40, no. 1 (2010): 58, https://doi.org/10.1177/008124631004000106.

40. Samuel Franklin, *The Psychology of Happiness: A Good Human Life* (Cambridge: Cambridge University Press, 2010), 126.

41. Aaron T. Beck, et al., *Cognitive Therapy of Depression* (New York: Guilford Press, 1979), 8.

42. Greg Lukianoff and Jonathan Haidt, *The Coddling of the American Mind: How Good Intentions and Bad Ideas Are Setting Up a Generation for Failure* (New York: Penguin Books, 2018), 38.

43. Ibid., 147.

44. Ibid., 152–53; Jean M. Twenge, *iGen: Why Today's Super-Connected Kids Are Growing Up Less Rebellious, More Tolerant, Less Happy—and Completely Unprepared for Adulthood* (New York: Atria, 2017), 82.

45. Doris Kearns Goodwin, *Team of Rivals: The Political Genius of Abraham Lincoln* (New York: Simon & Schuster, 2005), 52.

Acknowledgments

1. Sidney Rosen, M.D., *Understanding Ericksonian Hypnotherapy: Selected Writings of Sidney Rosen*, ed. Victor Kiarsis (New York: Routledge, 2020), 26.

Index